THE STATE AND ECONOMIC LIFE
EDITORS: Mel Watkins, University of Toronto; Leo Panitch, Carleton University

6 JAMES STRUTHERS
No Fault of Their Own: Unemployment and the Canadian Welfare State, 1914–1941

This book examines one of the most significant developments in the creation of the Canadian welfare state, the transition from local poor relief and private charity to national unemployment insurance as our principal means of caring for the jobless. Focusing primarily upon the post-war unemployment crisis of 1920–5 and the Great Depression, the study traces the evolution of federal unemployment policy from the creation of the Employment Service of Canada in 1918 to the development of relief works, the dole, camps for single men, and unemployment insurance. Canadian unemployment policy in this period, the author argues, was a battleground for the conflicting interests of organized labour, farmers, businessmen, the municipal, provincial, and federal governments, social workers, and the unemployed themselves. At issue were two closely related questions. Who was responsible for unemployment and the unemployed? How could those out of a job through no fault of their own be provided with decent minimum living standards without undermining their incentive to seek work?

The book provides a thorough and detailed examination of how the Bennett and King governments and the emerging social work profession dealt with the problem of unemployment during the Great Depression. Although Ottawa insisted that the care of the jobless was primarily a local and provincial matter, the fiscal breakdown of Canadian federalism produced by this stance, the impact of Keynesian ideas as reflected in two federal government commissions, and the outbreak of war in 1939 forced the abandonment of this policy and the creation of national unemployment insurance and an employment service system in 1940. Nevertheless, benefit levels under the new scheme were graded to wage rates, not family need, and those most liable to joblessness were excluded from coverage. National unemployment insurance, as it emerged from the Great Depression, was designed to reinforce the work ethic, not to provide the jobless with an adequate and defensible minimum standard of living.

JAMES STRUTHERS is a member of the Canadian Studies Programme at Trent University.

THE STATE AND ECONOMIC LIFE

Editors: Mel Watkins, University of Toronto; Leo Panitch, Carleton University

This series, begun in 1978, includes original studies in the general area of Canadian political economy and economic history, with particular emphasis on the part played by the government in shaping the economy. Collections of shorter studies, as well as theoretical or internationally comparative works, may also be included.

JAMES STRUTHERS

No Fault of Their Own: Unemployment and the Canadian Welfare State

1914-1941

UNIVERSITY OF TORONTO PRESS
Toronto Buffalo London

© University of Toronto Press 1983
Toronto Buffalo London
Printed in Canada

ISBN 0-8020-2480-7 (cloth)
ISBN 0-8020-6502-3 (paper)

Canadian Cataloguing in Publication Data

Struthers, James, 1950–
No fault of their own
Includes index.
ISBN 0-8020-2480-7 (bound). – ISBN 0-8020-6502-3 (pbk.)
1. Insurance, Unemployment – Canada – History – 20th
century. 2. Unemployment – Canada – History – 20th
century. 3. Canada – Economic policy – History –
20th century. 4. Canada – Social policy – History –
20th century. 5. Public welfare – Canada – History –
20th century. I. Title.
HD7096.C3S77   368.4'4'00971   C83-094155-X

Cover illustration: The Single Men's Association parading to Bathurst Street United
Church, Toronto, in the 1930s. PAC, C-29397

Contents

TO BETSY

Preface

In 1940 Canada became one of the last western industrial nations to create a national system of unemployment insurance, ending a twenty-eight-year period during which local poor relief and private charity provided the only means of coping with three of the worst industrial depressions of the twentieth century. This change has quite rightly been viewed as a landmark in the development of the Canadian welfare state. Together with old-age pensions, workmen's compensation, and medicare, unemployment insurance now constitutes part of a crucial network of state social-insurance schemes designed to protect the individual from the most pervasive risks to income in a market economy.

Unlike these other measures of social security, however, unemployment insurance remains uniquely controversial. While there is widespread support today (at least in principle) for generous treatment of the old, the injured, and the sick, no such consensus surrounds our treatment of the unemployed. The reasons are not hard to find. Welfare programs for these other groups deal with people who are clearly the victims of problems beyond their control. One cannot help being sick or accidentally hurt; one can do nothing to prevent old age. These physical realities of life all must face; consequently, their victims command ready sympathy.

Not so with the unemployed. There is nothing intrinsically wrong with the able-bodied man out of work 'through no fault of his own.' As the well-worn phrase implies, the cause of his dependency lies within society, not himself. In practice, the issue is never clear-cut. While market economies do produce periods when jobs are scarce, there is never a point at which jobs are non-existent. Even in 1933, the nadir of the Great Depression, there was work to be found for some.

The result is a dilemma that has plagued attempts to care for the unemployed since at least the British Poor Law reforms of 1834. Granted that trade cycles make it impossible to provide work for all, how can the jobless be afforded security during periods of depression without destroying their incentive to seek work? How can the unskilled be kept working at poorly paid, repetitive tasks if those out of a job are treated well? In short, at what point do the needs of the market outweigh the need of the individual?

Between 1914 and 1941, under the impact of three major depressions and two world wars, Canadians first came to grips with this issue. In the transition from poor relief to unemployment insurance, the nature of the federal system was reformed and the role of the national government in economic life vastly expanded. This book is a study of that change.

Many people have helped to make this book possible. Through his teaching, Michael Bliss sparked my interest in the social history of Canada. As supervisor of the doctoral thesis from which this study sprang, he was a continual source of ideas, editorial advice, and much-needed encouragement. I am greatly in his debt. In Ottawa, Blair Neatby aided my understanding of the Bennett and King administrations through conversation and generous access to his own research. John Smart and Glenn Wright of the Public Archives of Canada skilfully guided me through the records of the era.

Both Veronica Strong-Boag and Peter Neary have shown a constant interest in the development of my work; the former, especially, has provided important perspectives on social work in the interwar years. I owe a particular debt of gratitude to Desmond Glynn, who contributed insights from his own research and read large portions of the manuscript. His friendship, wit, and good sense have proved invaluable.

In accomplishing the transition from thesis to book, I owe special thanks to Alan Wilson of Trent University and to the Neathern Trust for their aid and encouragement; to R.I.K. Davidson and the anonymous readers at the University of Toronto Press and especially to Rosemary Shipton, who did a superb job editing the manuscript. I should also like to thank the Canada Council for doctoral fellowships which supported my research. The book has been published with the help of a grant from the Social Science Federation of Canada using funds provided by the Social Sciences and Humanities Research Council of Canada, and a grant from the Publications Fund of the University of Toronto Press.

My deepest debt is to Betsy Struthers. Her companionship, advice, and constant support over the years have contributed enormously to the completion of this book in ways I can only inadequately acknowledge.

NO FAULT OF THEIR OWN

Introduction

Unemployment, as John Garraty points out, is a 'disease of capitalism.' It is the obverse side of wage labour. '[O]nly those who work for wages or a salary, who are at liberty to quit their jobs yet who may also be deprived of them by someone else, can become unemployed.'[1] In Canada, as in other capitalist societies throughout the world, unemployment emerged as a major political issue in the late nineteenth and early twentieth centuries as progressively more people made the transition from self-employment in agriculture to wage employment in industry. In Canada, as elsewhere, a series of trade cycles of escalating intensity, culminating in the Great Depression of the 1930s, transformed unemployment into the single greatest challenge to the legitimacy of capitalism as an economic system.

The way in which Canadians responded to this challenge, however, was profoundly shaped by the nature of their economy and work force, the structure of their federal system, and assumptions about poverty and the meaning of work which they inherited from Britain, the United States, and their own experience as an agricultural society in the New World.

Of first importance was the fact that, well before Canada industrialized, her harsh winter climate had forced Canadians to acknowledge that they lived in an 'eight months' country' which could not provide steady work on a year-round basis. With the onset of winter, shipping, farming, and construction activity annually ground to a halt, stranding thousands of landless labourers in towns and villages throughout the country with nothing to depend upon but their summer earnings and the whims of intermittent charity. As a result, seasonal unemployment constituted the most important source of poverty in colonial British North America. Nor did the problem disappear with the onset of industrialization. Our first reasonably accurate unemployment statistics, which date from the 1920s, show the number of jobless doubling and tripling between August and December of each year.[2] Even today 'a seasonally adjusted' unemployment rate and winter works programs provide Canadians with a grim annual reminder of the effect of climate upon their livelihood.

Canadian workers were vulnerable to seasonal unemployment because of the economy's heavy dependence on staple exports. In 1911 39.5 per cent of the Canadian labourforce worked in primary industries (agriculture, fishing, trapping, mining, and forestry) and another 5 per cent in construction. Thirty years later these proportions had shrunk to only 30.5 and 4.7 per cent, respectively.[3] In short, much of the work provided by Canada's economy before World War II was out-of-doors and thus particularly sensitive to climate.

Canadian workers in staple industries had to place a premium upon occupational pluralism. In February a labourer might find himself 'a lumber worker in Iroquois Falls, Ontario; in June a railroad navvy along the National Transcontinental; in August a harvester in Grenfell, Sakatchewan; in November a coal miner in Fernie, British Columbia.'[4] The time lost between such frequent job changes over long distances cut deeply into whatever savings a man might accumulate even in a good year.

Regular employment for the labourer was unusual. The labour market for primary sector workers was dominated by an immigration policy shaped to suit the needs of Canada's agricultural and resource industry employers. As a result, there was a constant tendency towards over-supply in order to keep wages down and to ensure that enough men were available for the peak demands of summer and late autumn. Chronic unemployment and an inevitable drift to the cities in winter became the fate of Canada's bunkhouse men. In 1930–1 58 per cent of all male unskilled workers were unemployed for more than six months of the year. Even during the eight preceding years of the 'roaring' twenties, unemployment in Canada averaged almost 11 per cent; 30 per cent of all workers lost some time each year and the average spell of joblessness lasted eighteen weeks.[5]

Since much of the work provided by Canada's primary sector was unskilled, Canadian workers were doubly vulnerable to unemployment. They were easily replaceable, and their low wages provided scant resources upon which to subsist when out of work. In 1931 hired farm workers comprised 15 per cent of the Canadian labourforce compared to only 7 per cent in the United States and 4 per cent in Great Britain. Skilled workers, in contrast, made up 15 per cent of the American and 21 per cent of the British labourforce, but only 12 per cent in Canada. Although the movement away from agriculture was the most important occupational shift in Canada between the wars (until World War II farming was still the largest single employer in the country), for most of those involved this was a move from one form of unskilled labour to another, usually into the service, transportation, and construction industries which, if anything, were even more vulnerable to unemployment. In the 1930s unskilled workers constituted 40 per cent of the nation's labourforce, making them by far the largest occupational class in Canada.[6]

In order to keep wages low for the unskilled, immigrants were recruited to do much of the work. During the 1920s railway navvies, loggers, and harvesters could earn from $3.00 to $5.00 a day but with deductions for board, clothing, transportation, and lodging, their take-home pay was usually half that. The 1931 census, although admittedly taken during a bad year, showed that the average annual earnings of an unskilled male worker were less than $500, or below $10 a week, at a time when $1040 was considered the minimum yearly income needed to provide a family with the 'barest essentials.' Edmund Bradwin, in his study of frontier resource workers, concluded that it was 'an impossibility for even one man in five, working by the day, to make a fair monthly wage.'[7]

Finally, the resource industries themselves were particularly vulnerable to unemployment. Since they were export-oriented, they were especially sensitive to price changes in world markets or to tariff changes by importing nations over which Canadians could exercise little control. For the country as a whole before World War II, dependence on staple exports created a 'small and open economy, a marginal area responding to the exogenous impact of the international economy.'[8] Canadians enjoyed a high national income but were constantly vulnerable to depressions imported from abroad. In the years 1913–15, 1920–3, and 1929–33 the collapse of export markets and the rapid spread of joblessness were particularly violent and swift, provoking the emergence of unemployment as a national political issue.

Staples also helped to create an economy that was more regional than national. Until the development of the Canadian West as a major wheat-producing region between 1896 and 1930, few economic links existed to bind the diverse regions of Canada together. Trade was more often with an external metropolis than with another Canadian province. As a result, the economic fortunes of Canada's regions, particularly where secondary manufacturing was weak, could and did vary widely, depending on the health of their export staples. Unemployment rates east of the Ottawa River have traditionally been double those of Ontario and the West, and wage levels between the regions have varied widely as well. Until the 1920s, labour markets in Canada flowed more frequently along a north-south than an east-west axis, with the United States providing a major focal point for the talented and the jobless.[9]

To the extent that a 'national' labour market did exist, it revolved around western wheat which, in the words of the Rowell–Sirois report, 'transformed the static and isolated regions into an integrated and expanding national economy.'[10] Between 1890 and 1930 the massive labour requirements of settling the West, building two new transcontinental railways, and providing a migrant farm labour supply drew the federal government, the transportation companies, and more than 300 private employment agencies into the recruitment and placement of more than a million farmers and hundreds of thousands of railway navvies and agricultural labourers. By the 1920s Ottawa and the railways were shipping out 30,000 to 50,000 harvest excursionists each fall from eastern Canada to bring in the western wheat crop.[11]

Combined with the tremendous national manpower requirements of World War I, this rapid development of an east–west wheat economy provided the major impetus for the emergence of unemployment as a national responsibility during the interwar years. Nevertheless, Canada still remained a country characterized by wide variations in regional standards of living, population flows, and the incidence of joblessness. Developing a consensus on either the causes or treatment of unemployment under these circumstances remained exceedingly difficult.

As in other market societies during the nineteenth and twentieth centuries, Canadian attitudes towards the unemployed were overwhelmingly conditioned by the cultural imperatives of enforcing a work ethic. During the nineteenth century this tendency became particularly pronounced owing to a key assumption of classical political economy; namely, 'the existence of some wage rate at which ... full employment was feasible.' Unemployed workers, it was widely believed, could 'remedy their situation at any time; all they had to do was accept lower wage rates.' From this assumption flowed two others. First, apart from temporary seasonal idleness for which the worker was expected to save, prolonged involuntary unemployment among the able-bodied was impossible. A healthy unemployed man was presumed to be idle deliberately. Second, to provide such a man with relief would not only deter him from seeking work but would encourage others already working to join him in idleness.[12] Armed with these assumptions, British politicians and economists in the early nineteenth century had a ready explanation for the growth of able-bodied poverty in their midst. The sixteenth-century Elizabethan poor laws which guaranteed the indigent outdoor relief in the parish of their birth were seen as a massive subsidy for idleness.

To reform them, the British government through its 1834 Poor Law Report decided to surround the treatment of the unemployed with a new principle, that of 'less eligibility.' As the report argued, the 'first and most essential' characteristic of all relief to the able-bodied was to ensure that their 'situation on the whole shall not be made really or apparently so eligible as the situation of the independent labourer of the lowest class.' Otherwise, these workers would be 'under the strongest inducements to quit the less eligible class of labourers and enter the more eligible class of paupers.' The 'condition of those ... maintained by the public' had therefore to be kept below 'the condition of those who are maintained by their own exertions.'[13] In short, the first goal of unemployment policy was not to relieve the need of the indigent but to preserve the motivation of those who worked, particularly of those in the worst jobs a society had to offer.

The Poor Law Report did concede that some poverty, such as that arising from sickness, injury, or old age, was legitimate. For that reason, society had to have some means of distinguishing between the 'deserving' and the 'undeserving' poor. The method it hit upon was the 'workhouse test.' If the conditions surrounding relief were made sufficiently degrading, only those genuinely bereft of all resources would be tempted to seek it. The Poor Law Report recommended that 'outdoor' relief, paid to the indigent in his home, should be abolished and replaced by relief dispensed only inside central workhouses, modelled along the lines of penitentiaries, where work could be compelled in exchange for subsistence. By so stigmatizing the unemployed through forced labour, confinement, and separation of families, relief could be made 'less eligible' than the worst-paid unskilled work. Other workers would be motivated to seek labour at any price by the horrible fate of those who did not.[14]

'Less eligibility' was quickly transferred to Canada and remained virtually unchallenged as the key assumption underpinning the Canadian approach to poverty and unemployment until the beginning of World War I. Even though it was generally recognized that thousands were put out of work each winter by seasonal factors, this did not soften attitudes towards the destitute. Why could the labourer not save over the summer months so that he and his family might exist independently during the winter? Instilling the 'habit of economy' in the poor became the principal response of the middle class to poverty and unemployment.[15]

Savings banks, temperance societies, public education, and Christian evangelism were instrumental in this campaign. Relief was always a last resource. Some provinces, such as New Brunswick and Nova Scotia, had enacted poor laws in the late eighteenth century which acknowledged the principle of local public responsibility for the indigent. In most Canadian towns and cities, however, this function was discharged by private charities usually organized on a religious basis. The goal of such assistance, whether public or private, was to promote individual self-reliance by keeping relief discretional, minimal, and degrading. As the Toronto *Globe* put it during the 1877 depression, 'we do not advocate a system which could leave them to starve, but we do say that if they are ever to be taught economical and saving habits, they must understand that the public have no idea of making them entirely comfortable in the midst of their improvidence and dissipation. If they wish to secure that they must work for it and save and plan. Such comfort is not to be had by loafing around the tavern door, or fleeing to charity at every pinch.'[16]

Despite rapid industrialization during the remainder of the century and convincing evidence by its end that unemployment was a new problem of alarming dimensions beyond the control of the worker,[17] these attitudes surrounding the provision of relief did not change. In 1912 Winnipeg's Associated Charities could still maintain that most applications for aid were caused by 'thriftlessness, mismanagement, unemployment due to incompetence, intemperance, immorality, desertion of the family and domestic quarrels.' They concluded that to give help to these cases was more likely to 'induce pauperism than to reduce poverty.' At Toronto's House of Industry, men seeking relief in 1915 were still required to 'break up a crate of rocks weighing 650 pounds.'[18]

This indifference to the plight of the unemployed reflected Canada's preoccupation with the land. Almost alone among modern industrial nations Canada was still developing an agricultural frontier at a time when other countries were thoroughly urbanized, had developed strong class-conscious labour and socialist movements, and were beginning to devise new methods of dealing with unemployment.

The agrarian orientation of Canada's economy affected the response to joblessness in several ways. As long as Canada was scouring Europe each year for hundreds of thousands of immigrants to fill the vast tracts of vacant land in the West and North, there seemed little excuse for any Canadian to complain that he could not find work. Periodically, it was true, jobs might become scarce in this or that trade but there was always a need for more manpower on the land. If a man's luck gave out in carpentry, could he not make a go of farming or at least work for his room and board on a homestead during the winter?

Growing fears of rural depopulation also added strength to this 'back-to-the-land' sentiment. The same economic forces that produced the emergence of unemployment as a serious urban problem were also held responsible for the drift from the countryside and for the alarming growth of metropolitan values and institutions over rural life. It was easy for many Canadians who viewed the rapid growth of cities with unease to make a simple cause and effect equation between the problems of urban 'congestion' on the one hand and 'abnormal' unemployment on the other. The proper balance between city and country had gone out of line. 'Bright city lights' and the prospect of 'easy' work had lured too many Canadians from their true vocation on the land. The unemployed were considered to be morally weak and unwilling to do the work that had to be done if the country was to grow and develop. The fact that so many of the jobless were immigrants who had been brought to Canada specifically for agricultural settlement was an added reason for this general lack of sympathy for the unemployed.

Finally, 'back to the land' remained a popular panacea for unemployment because it nicely served the class interests of farm and resource-industry employers. In the first place, it provided a convenient excuse for doing little to help those without work. Costly experiments such as Britain's unemployment insurance scheme introduced in 1911, which taxed industry for some of the social costs of joblessness, could be dismissed out of hand as unsuited to Canada's 'agrarian' nature. 'Why "bonus" idle men to remain in the city when there was work to be done on the frontier?' farm and industry spokesmen asked.

Second, 'back to the land' provided an excellent rationale for maintaining a constant 'reserve army' of the unemployed so that the supply of labour could be kept cheap and available. Why cut back on immigration needed to settle the West simply because there was 'temporary' surplus of factory hands? By so insisting on the fiction of separate markets for agricultural and industrial labour, Canadian businessmen could counter persistent working-class demands for the restriction of immigration during periods of depression.

Finally, 'back to the land' as a solution to unemployment ensured that this 'reserve army' would be willing to work under conditions and for rates of pay that were unattractive by any standards. At bottom, it was the ideology of 'less eligibility' applied to a Canadian setting. If the urban unemployed could expect only the stigma, humiliation, and paltry resources of nineteenth-century poor relief, they would have no more eligible option than the prospect of bunkhouse life or farm work for room and board and a few dollars a month. In this sense, 'back to the land' was an approach to unemployment that conformed to the nature of work offered by the economy before World War II. As long as western settlement and the growth of wheat exports kept agrarian values and agrarian spokesmen politically powerful in Canada, this approach prevailed. Farmers were both the largest employers of unskilled labour and the most class-conscious protest group in the years between the wars. Ultimately, what they had to say on unemployment differed little from what other Canadian entrepreneurs had to say. In an era in which alternative perspectives from organized labour or socialist parties were weak, this unity ensured that 'back to the land' would dominate discussions of unemployment.

Behind the issue of what should be done with the unemployed was the question of who should do it. At the heart of the controversy was the federal system. The British North America Act, not surprisingly, made no mention of unemployment. However, according to poor-law tradition, the care of the destitute was a local responsibility. In a broader sense, the provinces, with their jurisdiction over the 'property and civil rights' of their citizens, were generally held responsible for the merging fields of health and social welfare, conditions of employment, and the debts of their municipalities.

After 1914 a variety of factors converged to draw Ottawa into the fray. First there was the mounting cost of relief itself. As cyclical depressions increasingly took their toll, the task of caring for jobless men began to overwhelm the fiscal resources of private charities and local governments.[19] Since only Ottawa had an unrestricted legal capacity to raise revenue, both local and provincial officials looked to that government as a logical place for help.

The federal government's responsibility for recruiting immigrants gave it a steadily growing influence over the nation's labour supply as the century progressed. Organized labour was quick to hold Ottawa responsible when, as in 1913 or 1929, immigration totals reached a peak precisely when the economy was diving into depression. Local governments that were pressed to the limit caring for their own unemployed citizens expected Ottawa to assume financial responsibility for immigrants brought into the country who could not find work. There was also the legacy of the Great War. To save the empire and make the world safe for democracy, the national government took 600,000 men out of the nation's labour market between 1914 and 1918. It had a moral obligation to provide them with work or adequate relief when the war ended.

New measures for dealing with unemployment in other countries, such as state labour exchanges and unemployment insurance, also seemed to fall logically under the scope of the national government. Since they were twentieth-century innovations, their constitutional jurisdiction in Canada was uncertain. However, from an administrative and financial perspective, federal responsibility seemed essential given the national mobility of the labourforce, the expected cost of the schemes, and the desire for uniformity in social legislation. The fact that both measures were administered nationally in Britain was an additional argument.

Ottawa's pre-eminent ability to create jobs was the final factor linking it to unemployment. Poor relief may have been a local responsibility, but no constitutional obstacles prevented the federal government from spending money to put people to work. For those who saw public employment as the most effective remedy for mass joblessness, the superior fiscal strength of the federal government and its ability to spend money anywhere in the country made it the logical authority to be held responsible for unemployment. Here the barriers to action were ideological, not legal.

Since the adoption of the National Policy of tariff protectionism in 1879, Ottawa had at least tacitly accepted some obligation for providing work. The Conservative party under Sir John A. Macdonald had sold the National Policy to the country in part as a job-creating measure that would bring Canada out of depression and prevent the drift of unemployed workers to the United States.[20] From that time onward, Canadian politicians had never ceased to link the tariff to unemployment and in the process they linked Ottawa to the issue.

Despite the cogency of these arguments, federal prime ministers from Sir Robert Borden in 1914 to Mackenzie King in 1938 clung to the poor-law heritage by insisting that the care of the unemployed was primarily a provincial and local matter. The constitution provided the excuse but not the reason for their inaction. Indeed, the price of their intransigence was the near collapse of Canadian federalism itself.

National responsibility for the jobless carried with it the far more dangerous implication of providing the unemployed with a national minimum wage. Ultimately, it was the threat posed by this claim to the market distribution of income which played the largest role in keeping Ottawa away from the jobless. By 1940, when a national system of unemployment insurance finally became law, there was a host of reasons compelling the federal government to abandon poor relief as the principal means of supporting those out of work. Providing a national minimum standard of living was not one of them.

1
Prelude to depression: unemployment and Canadian politics, 1914–30

Canadians did not discover unemployment in the Great Depression. It was not 'only then that the precarious nature of industrial society became glaringly apparent.'[1] Instead, two severe economic slumps struck this country well before the onset of the 'dirty thirties,' one in 1913–15 and the other between 1920 and 1925. It was the impact of these depressions, combined with the war they surrounded, which produced the emergence of unemployment as a national political issue. During these years Canadians first came to grips with the question of who was responsible for joblessness and debated the efficacy of public works, state labour exchanges, and unemployment insurance as methods of coping with modern industrial depressions. They also began to demand that the care of the unemployed become a national, not a local obligation. By 1921 the dominion government had created a national network of employment offices, provided the first federal funds for unemployment relief, and produced a draft unemployment insurance scheme, making Canada during the early post-war years the North American pioneer in unemployment research and relief. Four years later, however, all these initiatives lay in tatters. Canada entered the greatest economic crisis in its history unprepared not through what was unknown but through what had been forgotten and abandoned.

In 1914 Canadians found themselves embroiled in a severe depression and a world war. This deeply unsettling combination of events began to change established ways of viewing both the unemployed and the responsibilities of the state.

The economic crisis hit first. By the spring of 1913 it was clear that the tremendous boom which had fuelled the settling of the prairies, the opening of the Canadian Shield, and the industrial expansion of central Canada was over. Foreign investors, alarmed at the rapid over-expansion of Canada's economic infrastructure as well as by events in Europe, were no longer willing to finance the frenetic pace of the nation's development. Once pricked, the balloon of credit collapsed. Never before had the economy reached such peaks of activity as between 1896 and 1912. Consequently, never before had the country so far to fall. By autumn, eastern manufacturers as well as western railroads were laying off tens of thousands of men. To make matters worse, debt-stricken farmers flocked into prairie cities in search of work while immigration brought in over 400,000 new arrivals. In January 1914 opposition leader Wilfrid Laurier charged that more than 100,000 men across Canada were without employment, while Toronto and Montreal each reported estimates of over 15,000 unemployed within their limits. Across Ontario, one government report claimed the number of jobs in manufacturing was down 14 per cent.[2]

In actual fact, no one really knew how many were without work since no government had any way of keeping statistics on unemployment. What was clear was the severity of this crisis, which had quickly overwhelmed the capacity of both private charities and local poor-relief programs to care for those in need. As Toronto mayor Horatio Hocken said, '[W]e have tried to deal with [unemployment] ... but after we spend all the money we have to spend, after we find all the work that it is possible to find, we feel absolutely helpless in dealing with the problem as we find it today: it is too large for the city of Toronto, it is too large for any city. It has to be taken hold of in a more comprehensive way than any municipality can do.'[3]

Hocken was not alone in these sentiments. During that same winter both the *Toronto Daily Star* and the *Globe* denounced Canada's 'superficial' and 'haphazard' methods of relieving unemployment and called upon the federal and provincial governments to follow the example set by Great Britain in 1911 by introducing a system of state labour exchanges and unemployment insurance. In the Ontario legislature, Liberal opposition leader Newton Rowell, fresh from a recent visit examining the social legislation of the 'New Liberalism' in England, echoed the same cry. In Ottawa, Canada's first Social Service Congress issued a call for a federal royal commission on unemployment.[4] Coming at the crest of the social gospel movement, the 1913–14 unemployment crisis, although serious, appeared to many middle-class Canadians as yet one more social problem that could be solved by scientific social reform. As the *Star* argued:

The question ... ought to be dealt with in ... such a manner that acute and widespread distress through unemployment will be impossible. This can be done. We know that, because it has been done. Great Britain does provide, by law, insurance against the evils due to unemployment ... [T]he difficulties are ten times more difficult there than here ... Great Britain is an old, a small, and a congested country, while Canada is a young country, vast in area, resources and opportunity and sparsely populated. It was a daring thing for Lloyd

George to face the dragon of unemployment in England. But we, with our greater resources and our smaller population, can handle the problem easily, if we only exercise a little foresight. We can choke the dragon in its infancy.[5]

Despite this optimism and charges from organized labour that Ottawa's immigration policy was to blame for the crisis, federal officials refused to take any responsibility for unemployment. The country was passing through a 'very trying period,' finance minister Thomas White conceded, but there was 'nothing exceptional or peculiar about the .. situation.' In the meantime, apart from cutting off immigration into British Columbia ports and asking the railways to keep on as many men as possible, Robert Borden's government declined to take any special action to deal with the depression, a position duplicated by the country's nine provincial governments, despite the fact that severe unemployment continued into the spring and summer months.[6]

The outbreak of war in August 1914 jolted both levels of government out of their complacency by changing the nature of the job crisis. Foreign capital dried up along with important foreign markets, and credit tightened even further. An already serious unemployment problem, federal labour minister Thomas Crothers pointed out in October, threatened to become even worse 'owing to the war in Europe.'[7] Ottawa, moreover, was responsible for the war effort in a way it had never been for trade cycles.

The result was a flurry of government activity on unemployment once war was declared. During a special session of Parliament in August, the Borden government established the Canadian Patriotic Fund, a privately-financed and administered national charity, to insure that destitute families of enlisted men would enjoy a 'reasonable standard of comfort' during their absence.[8] Since thousands of unemployed men joined the army simply to earn a living, the fund filled a real need. Over the course of the war it would spend almost $40 million caring for an average of 60,000 families each month.[9]

At the same time, Borden ordered his labour and public works ministers to obtain 'exact and correct information as to unemployment' and to 'mak[e] provision for any necessary future action by the Government.' In September Bryce Stewart, a young Queen's University graduate in economics, was hired by the Labour Department as a researcher to devise a national system of employment offices. The department also suggested the creation of a National Industrial Fund, modelled along the lines of the Patriotic Fund, to care for the jobless. By providing more uniform methods of relief, such a scheme would 'reduce the movements of the unemployed towards the larger centres of population and ... prevent the whole burden falling on those municipalities which take steps to deal with the problem.'[10]

In October, Crothers wrote to the premiers urging their co-operation in this plan.

Because of the war, he pointed out, heavy unemployment was expected over the winter and it was best to make 'an organized effort ... to avert such an undesireable condition,' an effort similar to what was being done in Great Britain. Since Crothers made no offer of financial help, however, the provinces replied that they were 'able to deal adequately with their own unemployment problem.'[11] Nevertheless, both his letter and the idea of a national fund revealed the distance Ottawa had travelled on unemployment in a short time. In January, finance minister White had been willing to let 'history repeat itself.' By October Crothers was pleading for an 'organized effort' to avert the crisis. Along with all other economic matters, the war quickly expanded the government's responsibility for unemployment.

Confirmation of this point came in December when the Ontario government appointed a royal commission to 'examine ... the permanent causes of recurring unemployment ... and to recommend measures to mitigate or abolish the evil.' Although this initiative was a response to opposition leader Rowell's threat to appoint his own commission, it none the less signified the arrival of unemployment as an important new political issue. However, the commission's report, issued two years later, was an ambiguous document. The commission conceded that 'personal causes of unemployment' had received a 'disproportionate amount of attention.' Business cycles were a 'characteristic feature of modern industry' to which young countries like Canada were particularly prone and their effects could be mitigated if not abolished through 'efficient organization of the labour market.' To this end the commission recommended the creation of a provincial Department of Labour, a network of state labour exchanges, 'planning' of public works and immigration policy to coincide with swings in the business cycle, vocational guidance in the school system, and modest state assistance for unemployment benefit schemes administered by trade unions.[12] While these recommendations were moderately progressive, the report harkened back to the workhouse by calling for 'industrial centres' and 'industrial farms,' modelled along the lines of penitentiaries, to extract labour from vagrants and unskilled seasonal workers who, the report acknowledged, were often 'unwillingly out of employment.' These men must be required to work 'in exchange for security against ... destitution' if they were to be 'prevented from drifting, with gradually weakening resistance, into the ranks of the unemployable.' Echoing the widespread fears of rural depopulation, the report also argued that more extensive state assistance for land settlement in northern Ontario would go 'some distance towards abolishing unemployment in Canada.'[13] This jumbling together of nineteenth- and twentieth-century ideas perhaps accurately reflected the confusion in the country as a whole over what to do about unemployment.

However, by the time the report was published in 1916, the problem had all but disappeared under the stimulus of wartime production and massive recruitment. The commission's recommendations were, as the *Financial Post* predicted, 'put away and forgotten.' In response to the war-induced labour shortage, the Ontario government did establish a modest provincial employment service supervized by a Bureau of Labour. Otherwise, the Hearst administration ignored its own commission's report.[14]

While war temporarily eased the unemployment crisis, it also heightened expectations and anxieties over what would happen when hostilities ended, war industries shut down, and the soldiers returned home to look for work. By 1918 the federal government regulated prices, taxed incomes, and prohibited drinking, striking, and loafing. It also controlled an army of 600,000 men. Could a state which had assumed so much authority over the nation's workers during the war disavow all responsibility for their fate during peace? Had so much been sacrificed only for a return to the conditions of 1914? 'People are not ... in a normal condition,' Newton Rowell (now Privy Council president in the Union government) warned Sir Robert Borden on the eve of the armistice. 'There is less respect for law and authority than we probably have ever had in the country. If ... Canada faces acute conditions of unemployment without any adequate programme to meet the situation, no-one can foresee just what might happen.'[15]

It was an accurate prediction. The early post-war years produced just such a crisis of working-class unrest, and 'unemployment ... and the fear of unemployment' were at the heart of it according to a royal commission appointed to investigate the problem. 'Five years ago I ... stood in Vancouver streets and existed on five cents a day,' one returned soldier testified, 'but tomorrow, if I had to come to the same thing there would be nothing doing because my foot would be through the first window I came to and I would take out my goods. That is the spirit of labour today.' Another argued that post-war Canadian workers were no longer willing to be treated like 'a piece of merchandise ... their chances of life ... consisting in the possibility of someone coming along tomorrow to buy them for a day.' Instead, they wanted 'security, particularly to earn bread and food and clothing and shelter' for themselves and their families.[16] It was just this search for security and the unrest it fuelled which dragged a reluctant government into a wider responsibility for the unemployed.

Ottawa's first problem was the threat of jobless returned men. Federal officials estimated that demobilization was sure to produce unemployment, perhaps throwing as many as 250,000 people out of work in 1918 alone. Since Ottawa had recruited the manpower in the first place, it would be held responsible for the problem regardless of the poor-law tradition that the unemployed were a municipal obligation. Moreover, the jobless veterans were apt to be more dangerous than their pre-war counterparts. During the past four years they had been trained to kill and no one was quite certain how they would respond to finding themselves without work. For this reason alone, a Labour Department official warned 'the unemployment of 10,000 men is much more serious than the unemployment of 25,000 men five or six years ago.'[17]

To deal with this problem the Union government developed two new programs. The first was the Soldier Settlement scheme which provided land and financial assistance to veterans willing to take up farming. Although it was the most expensive reconstruction initiative, Soldier Settlement actually embodied the least departure from previous federal policies. Ottawa traditionally had played a prominent role in the settling of the West; therefore, placing returned soldiers on the land was not really breaking into a new field of activity. The implications of the scheme were more significant as they represented the first indication that the government viewed the land as its principal solution to unemployment.[18]

The Employment Service of Canada, created by the Employment Offices Co-ordination Act of 1918, was a more innovative experiment. The ESC was a national network of labour exchanges jointly financed and administered by the federal and provincial governments. Through it Ottawa established a crucial link with the nation's labour markets as well as its first tangible responsibility for finding jobs.

The immediate origin of the ESC was the acute manpower shortage in the spring of 1918, particularly the scarcity of farm labourers which placed the planting of that year's wheat crop in jeopardy. The Employment Service emerged out of this crisis as a compromise solution to the more radical agrarian demand for the conscription of labour to work on the farms. However, with the war's sudden end in November, demobilization quickly became the ESC's principal responsibility.

Before the war, employment offices were a provincial matter but only Ontario and Quebec had moved into this field and then in a very limited way. Nevertheless, the Employment Offices Co-ordination Act, which became law on 18 May 1918, recognized provincial primacy in this area. The purpose of the bill was to 'aid and encourage the organization and co-ordination of employment offices and promote uniformity of methods among them,' not to create directly a nationally administered labour exchange network. The provinces retained complete authority over the establishment and operation of employment offices but the federal government supervised the entire system through a national headquarters in Ottawa and four regional clearing-houses.[19]

Like much of the Union government's subsequent legislation in housing, technical eduction, health, and highways, the ESC was financed through a system of conditional grants. Ottawa provided a permanent subsidy of $150,000 a year for the operation of the service and, in addition, promised 'during the period of reconstruction' to match the amount spent by any province on the system in order to promote its rapid development. Faced with this offer of 50 per cent federal funding for a service which they would otherwise have to develop on their own, all of the provinces outside of the Maritimes quickly agreed to participate in the scheme. By December the ESC was in operation.[20]

In one sense Ottawa was simply following the example of its neighbour to the south. In 1918 the United States government also established a federal employment service to help demobilize its army and ease the transition to a peace-time economy. But there was one crucial difference. The US Employment Service was a temporary agency whose authority expired in 1920. Its purpose was strictly to deal with the immediate post-war demobilization problem. The ESC, in contrast, was given permanent federal funding. On one level this was sheer political expediency. A permanent grant was the only way of enticing the provinces into the scheme and this in itself was a key goal of the legislation. As the ESC's director later pointed out, 'The Dominion authorities were not willing to accept full responsibility for the placement of returned soldiers, and indeed, felt they had achieved something of a victory when they placed upon the provinces a large part of the problem of unemployment incident to demobilization, properly a dominion duty.'[21]

Apart from this political motivation, there were signs that some federal officials saw the ESC as a necessary response not simply to demobilization but to the consequences of an industrial society as well. Even before the war, as John English has pointed out, Robert Borden had favoured a modest expansion in the role of the state in order to cope with the problems of a more complex and increasingly polarized society. Although opposed to welfare-state legislation such as unemployment or health insurance and old-age pensions, he believed strongly in enhancing the bureaucratic efficiency of government through civil service reform and more direct state regulation of the economy.[22]

Newton Rowell, Borden's Liberal lieutenant in the coalition Union government, was an even more passionate supporter of social reform. A devout Methodist, Rowell had been a key figure in the crusade for prohibition during his tenure as leader of the opposition Liberal party in Ontario. Yet his interest in reform went beyond the elimination of alcohol. Drawing his inspiration from the 'New Liberalism' of British politicians such as Henry Asquith, David Lloyd George, and Winston Churchill, Rowell had campaigned in 1914 for a comprehensive system of state social-insurance schemes to protect workers against the ravages of joblessness, sickness, and old age. When he entered the Union government in 1917, he brought his reform predilections with him and he soon emerged as the leading spokesman within the cabinet for a far-ranging post-war reconstruction settlement to appease industrial unrest. Included in his suggestions for reform were state social insurance, subsidized low-cost housing, an eight-hour working day, worker participation in management, and higher taxes on wealth. Rowell initially hoped to see Ottawa's reconstruction plans co-ordinated by the creation of a new federal department of social welfare that would oversee not only health care but housing and unemployment policy as well.[23]

With these broader goals close to the heart of at least one Union government cabinet minister, it is not surprising that the federal order-in-council which gave the Employment Service its final form also authorized its director to 'study and report on unemployment and ways and means of lessening unemployment.' It also created a broadly representative advisory council to oversee the service and report to the federal government on ways of 'preventing unemployment.'[24] In short, the creation of a permanent Employment Service was the most tangible evidence of a new federal commitment to tackling unemployment as an industrial, not merely as a reconstruction, problem.

Its first director certainly thought so. As noted previously, Bryce Stewart had been investigating labour exchanges for the Department of Labour since 1914. As the most knowledgeable authority on the subject in Canada, he was the logical choice to design and run the new system. In fact, Stewart had already established his reform credentials in the pre-war social-gospel movement as the author of a massive social survey of Port Arthur, Ontario. It was one of the first of its kind in Canada and was prepared under the auspices of the Presbyterian and Methodist churches of that city in 1913.

Born in Lyn, Ontario, in 1883, Stewart grew up in Brockville and later attended Queen's University where he received a Master's degree in economics in 1911. A believer in the essential compatibility of Christianity and socialism,[25] Stewart was also a devoted follower of William Beveridge, England's pioneer researcher into unemployment and the architect of that country's fledgling system of state labour exchanges and unemployment insurance. Like Beveridge, Stewart was convinced that unemployment was essentially a technical problem, the result of disorganization in the labour market, which could be eliminated through state intervention. To this end no institution was more crucial than an efficiently administered system of government labour exchanges. Stewart began his work as the first director of the Employment Service of Canada with a broad conception of its potential. To him, the ESC was 'only the first step in dealing with unemployment,' part of a 'co-ordinated attack' that would have to include 'vocational guidance and technical education, regulation of private employment agencies, regularization of industry, systematic distribution of public employment, unemployment insurance,' and a 'well thought out immigration policy' to prevent labour from 'being dumped on the market faster than it can be absorbed.' Above all, Stewart believed that 'too much stress cannot be laid on the importance of acquiring more and more information.'[26]

In keeping with his ambitions for the ESC, Stewart worked quickly to expand the service between 1919 and 1921. When it came into existence in December 1918 there were only twelve government employment offices in the entire country, nine in Ontario and three in Quebec. By March 1919 the ESC had mushroomed to sixty-six offices in response to the pressures of rapid demobilization. By June the number had grown to eighty-eight. During its first full year of operation the ESC made almost 400,000 job placements, mostly among unskilled seasonal labourers. Moreover, in one significant achievement it supplied the entire demand for harvest labour that autumn from within the country, thus avoiding the traditional importation of agricultural labourers from the United States and abroad.[27]

Stewart did not confine his activities to the mere placement of labour. Along with fellow Queen's graduate W.C. Clark, he developed North America's first national statistical survey of employment trends which was published biweekly in a newsletter sent free to employers and provincial governments. The value of such a measure was threefold. It allowed the ESC to follow the trend of seasonal fluctuations in Canada, enabling it to 'transfer workers from industries in seasonal decline to those in seasonal expansion.' By the same token, it provided the government with valuable information on 'which areas should get government contracts and where immigration should be directed.' Finally, it supplied data that were essential for estimating the cost of unemployment insurance. As University of Toronto economist Gilbert Jackson pointed out in 1920, the country as yet could 'scarcely claim to possess the data from which a calculation of the risks of unemployment could be made.'[28] Stewart also sponsored research into the feasibility of public employment as a remedy for trade depressions; established separate divisions of the ESC to handle the special employment problems of women, juveniles, professionals, and businessmen; inspected provincial employment offices; instituted a course in employment office management at the University of Toronto; and ensured that the ESC governing council met regularly to provide a continuing forum for discussion on unemployment.[29]

The service's ultimate success in tackling the problem would depend on the degree of influence it was able to exert on the nation's labour market. This in turn was contingent on provincial co-operation. Although the dominion supplied half of the ESC's costs, it only staffed the national headquarters in Ottawa and four regional clearing-houses. The provinces controlled the local offices, the actual core of the service. Here there were problems. Although provincial governments rapidly developed their labour exchange networks once Ottawa offered to pay half the cost, they did not hire competent personnel to staff them. 'Recommendation of the local member of the Dominion House of Commons or of the provincial legislative assembly was the decisive factor' in getting a job with the service at the provincial level, Stewart wrote, and 'the low salaries general throughout the provincial services ... made it difficult ... to secure well-qualified staffs.'[30]

At the same time, Ontario, Quebec, and British Columbia refused to antagonize their resource industries by abolishing private employment agencies as they had agreed to do in 1918. Too many of these organizations preyed on the chronic underemployment of the nation's bunkhouse men in order to sign them to poorly paid and often fraudulent employment contracts.[31] By refusing to eliminate these agencies, the three provincial governments condemned the ESC to a minor role in the employment market for unskilled railway, mining, and logging workers and crippled any potential attack it might have made on seasonal unemployment.

Finally, neither the provinces nor the federal government were willing to provide the ESC with the advertising budget it needed to publicize its activities. The ultimate success of the service in penetrating the labour market hinged on the quality of the jobs and workers it was able to offer. This, in turn, rested on making its facilities attractive and well-known both to high-wage employers and to skilled workers. Traditionally, the stigma of relief surrounded public employment offices. If the service were to succeed, this must be broken down and employers must be convinced that the workers recommended by the ESC had more qualifications than poverty for a job. For that reason the ESC advisory council's first annual meeting recommended an extensive 'preliminary advertising campaign to place before the public the fact that there is a national system of employment offices.'

This proposal was rejected. The Labour Department replied that 'an aggressive advertising campaign would be too heavy a drain upon the budget of the Employment Service.' A paltry $5100 was the total amount spent by both Ottawa and the provinces in publicizing the ESC during its first and most crucial year. The service soon fell victim to the self-fulfilling stereotype that it was 'exclusively for common labour.'[32]

Despite these setbacks, the ESC's prospects in 1920 did look bright. There were, after all, eighty-eight government employment offices where before there had only been twelve. More important, the crucial first step had been taken. There was now a government body with a permanent interest in unemployment; this surely meant a solution was in sight. As economist W.C. Clark, Stewart's most important adviser in designing the ESC, pointed out to a conference of employment officials, 'Ten years ago practically nothing had been done anywhere in the world to solve the unemployment problem ... To-day the problem is being grappled with as never before in the world's history. And it will be solved, no matter what agencies it is necessary to call into action. Call it a quickened social conscience or call it simply enlightened selfishness, the world is coming to regard as intolerable the concept of workmen as simply parts of a machine which are to be laid on the shelf when the machine is not working.'[33]

More than the ESC lay behind Clark's optimism. At the same time that the labour-exchange network was being established, Ottawa also appeared to be moving the country towards a national system of unemployment insurance. Once more the motivating factor was social unrest.

In 1919 working-class militancy in the form of union membership and strike activity reached a peak in Canada that would not be equalled again until 1943. Concurrently, unemployment insurance achieved unprecedented popularity. At the first International Labour Conference in Washington, Canadian government officials endorsed a draft recommendation favouring state-administered unemployment insurance. Back in Ottawa the National Industrial Conference, a joint meeting of business and labour representatives, recommended that the federal government conduct an investigation into its feasibility. The federal Liberal party, not to be outdone, committed itself to enacting such legislation as soon as Canada's financial position made it 'practicable.'[34]

Within the Union government, Newton Rowell, who had favoured such a scheme even before the war, pressed for 'consideration' of the question. The Royal Commission on Industrial Relations, which Borden had appointed in the spring to investigate the causes of social unrest, came out flatly in favour of immediate action. Unemployment insurance, its report concluded, 'would remove the spectre of fear which now haunts the wage earner and make him a more contented and better citizen.'[35]

Other factors besides unrest contributed to the popularity of the idea. The British scheme created in 1911 had built up a large surplus of funds during the full employment produced by the war and appeared to be a successful experiment. It also provided a valuable cushion in that country to ease the transition from a wartime to a peacetime economy. In 1920 its benefits were extended to include almost all of the British labourforce. If Canada's previous experience with workmen's compensation legislation were any guide, unemployment insurance seemed capable of preventing, not merely relieving joblessness. Since both the employer and the employee had to contribute to the fund, the Social Service Council of Canada argued, 'economy, even greed itself is on the side of careful prevention.' It was 'both a scientific and Christian' form of social service.[36]

Finally, compared to the workhouse, unemployment insurance appeared as a positive, innovative approach to the problem of dependency in that it avoided the traditional stigma of charity by strictly relating benefits to past contributions. Since the worker had 'earned' the money he received from the unemployment insurance fund, he could hardly be accused of being 'pauperized' or 'demoralized' by it. For the same reason, men could accept these payments without loss of self-respect. As the *Globe* pointed out, this was a crucial difference: 'Spasmodic handing out of doles to the unemployed, such as we see to-day in cities all over the Dominion will aggravate rather than allay social unrest. If the men who are forced by circumstances to accept these doles were in a position to draw unemployment insurance to which they had made a substantial contribution while at work, the entire industrial atmosphere would be changed.'[37] No other piece of social legislation seemed so capable of both appeasing working-class discontent and fulfilling the promise of a better world for which the war had supposedly been fought.

In response to these pressures, the Borden government promised that it would conduct a thorough investigation into unemployment insurance. That autumn the Department of Labour was at work on the subject. By 1920 it had produced the rough draft of a scheme modelled closely on the British legislation of 1911. Limited to 500,000 workers in manufacturing (judged the most stable from an employment perspective), it involved contributions from workers, employers, the provinces, and the federal government. It would cost the state $4 million a year, the department estimated, if unemployment did not rise above 6 per cent. For a maximum period of ten weeks' unemployment each worker would receive a $10.00 benefit, provided he had made at least six weekly contributions of 25¢.[38]

The speed with which this draft scheme was produced reflected the department's enthusiasm for unemployment insurance. Its merits did not have to be debated on theoretical grounds, one internal memo argued, 'for the experience of many countries and communities has demonstrated its practability.' In one form or another it was in use in thirteen European nations and, although a form of compulsory saving, it was still 'not as objectionable as the suffering which arises from ... unemployment.' Moreover, the statistics such a scheme would furnish could form the basis for 'public policies dealing with the problem.'

Assistant deputy minister of labour Gerald Brown agreed with this analysis. Sent to England the following year to study that country's newly expanded scheme, Brown sent back an encouraging report. 'The general view of the Government officials, labour leaders and employees with whom I discussed the subject was that insurance against unemployment ... is sound in principle,' he wrote to his superiors. Bryce Stewart added his support as well. 'Unemployment insurance goes hand in hand with labour exchanges,' he argued, and there would be little progress in preventing unemployment 'until we have placed it ... on the basis of dollars and cents.'[39] By 1921 Department of Labour officials unanimously agreed that a national unemployment insurance system for Canada was practical, feasible, and necessary.

But was it constitutional? Ottawa already had conceded that the provinces had primary jurisdiction over employment offices and that the municipalities were responsible by tradition for poor relief. On what grounds, then, could the dominion enact a national system of unemployment insurance?

Within the Justice Department, opinion varied. At first its officials maintained that the international character of the 1919 Washington conference recommendation placed unemployment insurance within federal jurisdiction under Section 132 of the BNA Act. When the Labour Department warned that such a sweeping interpretation of Ottawa's treaty-making powers and obligations would 'meet with very strong opposition in Parliament,' Justice officials changed their minds. Still basking in the glow of Ottawa's wartime authority, they simply argued that the dominion's residual authority to enact laws for the 'peace, order and good government' of Canada was sufficient to justify legislation on unemployment insurance.[40] The only barrier to action was political, not legal.

And the barrier was considerable. By 1920 the Union government was well down the road towards political disintegration and, unlike Great Britain in 1911, it lacked the presence of either a Winston Churchill or forty Labour MPs to goad it into action. The previous summer Thomas Crerar, minister of agriculture and key western spokesman in the cabinet, had resigned in protest against the government's failure to reduce the tariff. By 1920 he was joined in Parliament by ten other MPs who had formed the new National Progressive party. That July Sir Robert Borden, exhausted after nine years in office, resigned. His successor was Arthur Meighen, a lawyer from Portage la Prairie and solicitor-general within the Union government. Young, ambitious, and gifted with an incisive mind and scathing oratorical ability, Meighen had stood at the centre of nearly every domestic controversy surrounding the Union government over the past three years. Author of the Military Service Act, he also shepherded the Railway Nationalization Bill through the House of Commons and, along with Gideon Robertson, played a key role in co-ordinating the federal government's aggressive response to the Winnipeg General Strike.

Meighen's choice as Borden's successor signalled the end of the Unionist experiment. His high-tariff views alienated any chance of support from former western Canadian Liberals within the party. Equally important, Meighen was no friend of social reform. He had opposed even such limited measures as civil service reform and women's suffrage during the war. When Meighen became prime minister, Newton Rowell resigned from the cabinet, convinced that his plans for a reconstructed post-war Canada would find little sympathy within a Union government that was rapidly re-emerging as the old Conservative party in all but name.[41]

Even if Meighen *had* been personally in favour of unemployment insurance, which he was not, the political obstacles standing in the way of its passage by his government were formidable regardless of Canada's commitment to the International Labour Organization. Organized labour in this country, in contrast to the United States, did endorse unemployment insurance but in the aftermath of the Winnipeg General Strike its influence was waning.[42]

Far more important was the hostility of business and agrarian spokesmen towards the idea. The Canadian Manufacturers' Association argued that since unemployment insurance did not exist south of the border, to create such a scheme in Canada would make competition with the US 'impossible.' Moreover, as a general rule, the manufacturers claimed, the 'surest way to create unemployment is to bonus it.' Within Parliament agricultural spokesmen agreed. The country already provided 'opportunity enough for labour to those who are willing to work,' Crerar, leader of the new National Progressive party, claimed. Unemployment insurance might be needed 'some time in the future,' but at present a 'programme of rigid economy in every department of the public service' was far more urgent.[43]

With Rowell now gone from the cabinet there was no one in the Union administration to counter these views. Labour minister Gideon Robertson, as a former trade unionist, might have been expected to champion unemployment insurance. Instead he insisted that neither the British nor the European schemes had produced 'satisfactory results,' despite numerous reports from his own department to the contrary. Prime Minister Meighen simply told Parliament that there was not enough information available to form a policy and that he was determined to 'make no commitments that I do not absolutely know I can carry out.' He promised only that his government would continue investigations.[44]

Behind Meighen's caution lay the reality of economic collapse. Starting in the fall of 1920 the Canadian economy began a steep slide into depression. By February 1921 almost a quarter of a million men, or 12 per cent of the labourforce, were unemployed and the onset of spring brought scant relief. By June 212,000 workers, or 10.5 per cent of the labourforce, were still without work. It was the beginning of a severe post-war slump whose effects would linger on into 1925. Ironically, as even the Social Service Council of Canada finally conceded in 1921, 'hard times such as the present, when the need of Unemployment Insurance is the greatest, do not allow the starting of such a scheme immediately.'[45]

Yet something had to be done for the unemployed even if no one was sure what that should be. Although Union government officials had long expected such an economic collapse, few preparations for dealing with it had actually been made. The ESC could only find jobs, not create them, and the Soldier Settlement plan was not much use to the thousands of returned men who chose to try their luck in the nation's cities. A year after the armistice, however, the federal government had set a crucial precedent. Realizing it would be difficult for many returned soldiers to find jobs in the midst of winter, Borden decided that his government would pay the total cost of supporting unemployed veterans over that winter of 1919–20.

Since the government itself possessed no machinery to investigate the claims for unemployment assistance, it turned to the Patriotic Fund for help. Although many of its business executives were 'not even in accord with the principle of unemployment pay,' the fund reluctantly agreed to help deal with the problem. Over that winter it spent $6 million out of a special federal grant to care for returned men who could not find work.[46]

When spring came the program was terminated, with the expectation that Ottawa had discharged all its responsibilities for the care of unemployed veterans during the demobilization period. No record was kept of how many returned men actually found work; therefore, federal officials had no idea six months later how many were still unemployed. Thousands, they knew, had headed for Montreal, Toronto, Winnipeg, and Vancouver to spend their accumulated war pay. Borden himself guessed that most were still 'awaiting the cessation of payment of War Service Gratuities before seeking employment.'[47] When these ran out, he supposed, the economy would still be buoyant and they would find work.

It did not happen that way. The depression struck exactly when most veterans had exhausted their war pay. The result for the Union government was an acute dilemma. Should there be yet another special federal appropriation for the care of unemployed returned men? If there was, would Ottawa ever rid itself of responsibility for their fate?

As far as the municipalities were concerned the answer to the latter question was no. During November and December, as unemployment mounted, telegrams poured into Ottawa from the nation's largest cities warning of dangerous levels of unrest among returned men. The federal government had paid their fares to any destination in Canada, the mayors complained; therefore, jobless veterans were Ottawa's responsibility since most of the men were not legally residents of the cities they were in. Moreover, municipal finances were already strained to the breaking point. 'We can care for our own permanent citizens,' Vancouver's mayor complained, 'but the floating class is causing us great concern.'[48]

It was just the argument that Meighen feared. Even before the war the municipalities had urged that unemployment was a problem of such national dimensions that it justified federal assistance to their relief efforts. At that time Ottawa had used the poor-law tradition to resist such pleas but 'now that there are among the unemployed and always will ... be a proportion of returned soldiers, it gives the local authorities a chance to load the whole thing on the Dominion,' Meighen complained to a political confidant.[49]

For that very reason he wanted at all costs to 'avoid ... the resumption of direct distribution of money from the Government' to jobless veterans during the upcoming winter. 'In previous ... depressions,' labour minister Robertson pointed out, 'appeals for aid were always made to the local authority first,' and if Ottawa did not want to assume a costly new responsibility it was crucial that 'Municipal and Provincial authorities ... not be permitted to continue as in war time, to pass every local question on to the Federal Government to find a solution.' The key was to convince the public that there was 'no longer any recognized distinction between the physically fit returned man and other unemployed workmen.'[50]

To this end Meighen and Robertson hit upon a clever strategy. On 14 December came a precedent-breaking announcement from Ottawa. In a public letter to Ontario's labour minister, Walter Rollo, Robertson spelled out the dominion's new unemployment policy. Unlike the previous winter there would be no special nationally administered emergency fund for the relief of jobless returned men. Instead, Ottawa would pay one-third of the cost of all municipal direct relief regardless of whether the provinces contributed or not. It was the first time any North American national government had acknowledged a responsibility for the relief of the unemployed. This action, the letter stated, was justified not because there were veterans among the unemployed but because the depression itself was related to the 'extraordinary circumstance' of the war. There would always be unemployed veterans and cyclical depressions. There would be only one war-related unemployment crisis. When it passed, so too would Ottawa's responsibility for direct relief which, as the government took pains to point out, was 'dealt with wholly locally' in 'normal times.'[51] Unlike the ESC, federal involvement with this aspect of the unemployment problem was intended to be strictly a once-in-a-lifetime affair.

However, this last-minute resort to the dole was not a popular move. Essentially it was designed to minimize Ottawa's responsibility, not to deal realistically with the unemployment crisis. The $500,000 Meighen set aside for the dominion's share of direct relief was a mere pittance compared to the $6 million it had spent the previous winter for the support of unemployed veterans. The delay of the announcement until mid-December, the provision of money through a governor general's warrant, the absence of prior consultation with the provinces and the cities, and the resort to direct relief rather than public works were all striking indications of ad hoc policy-making. 'Unemployment ... spread so quickly that there [was] little time for preparation,' Robertson argued,[52] but this was a poor defence. The depression, although delayed, was none the less expected; yet when it came the federal government was caught without any plans. Its hasty contribution to municipal relief thus pleased no one but fuelled a growing demand for a national conference on unemployment.

All could agree that too many men were out of work, that this was somehow related to the war, and that the dole was the wrong approach to the problem. Beyond this there was little consensus on the causes and possible remedies for the crisis. At the heart of the controversy was a basic disagreement between workers and employers over who was responsible for unemployment.

Business organizations such as the CMA argued that the present depression was the abnormal result of a 'large influx of labor to the cities who previous to the war followed agriculture for a livelihood.' Such people had been 'attracted to the city by the hope of finding easier work at higher pay and enjoying the excitement of city life.' Now, along with most returned men, they 'preferred to remain in the Cities than go back to farm work.'[53]

Not surprisingly, within Parliament representatives from Canada's rural ridings agreed. Men might be out of work, they argued, but the country was not. 'In our section,' one noted, ' ... a great many of these people could find work on the farms – not perhaps at five or six dollars a day but at a reasonable pay.' Another complained that farmers for years had been 'trying to get along with only about one-quarter of the labour needed'; yet in the cities there were 'great numbers of idle men.'

Donald Sutherland, MP for Oxford South, put their case most succinctly. During the war when wages were high there was a 'great influx of people from all parts of the country into the large industrial centres.' Now, although the war was over and the jobs gone, these people clung obstinately to the cities. If thousands were out of work, it was their own fault: ' ... there was never a time in the history of Canada when labour was so necessary as it is at the present ... True, it may be impossible for some people to get employment in the trades and industries in which they had been previously engaged, but if they are out of employment to-day it is largely because they will not do the work which is to be done and which must be done before we shall be able to get back to a normal state.' The only solution to the unemployment crisis, farmers and businessmen agreed, was a 'back-to-the-land' policy which would provide work for the jobless and allow farmers to 'get labour more cheaply.'[54]

From the working-class perspective, telling the unemployed to go back to the land was ridiculous. As the Toronto Great War Veterans' Association said, the returned man had not been separated from his family for four years only so he could 'take employment mucking in the bush, far from his own fire-side.' The sacrifices of the war were justified only if they ushered in a new age in which labour, as the Versailles peace treaty maintained, was not an 'article of commerce.' 'Workingmen have no property rights in their jobs,' labour witnesses told the Royal Commission on Industrial Relations. '[L]abour is a commodity to be sold or to be bought like PE Island potatoes or Newfoundland fish.' Employment, they argued, should be put on a basis 'where [men] would be absolutely sure that just so long as they wanted to do useful service and give their very best to society, they would have the right to work and receive remunerative wages.' As a result, organizations like the Trades and Labour Congress of Canada argued that the cost of unemployment should be made a 'first charge upon industry' through a state-administered scheme of unemployment insurance financed solely by business. Since industry demanded a reserve army of unemployed workers, it should be 'called upon to pay for [their] support.'[55]

Given such basic disagreement over the ethics of the labour market and the meaning of work, there seemed little chance that the national conference on unemployment demanded by the CMA, the TLC, the Social Service Council of Canada, and two provincial governments would reach any consensus. Such failure would reflect on the federal government. Realizing this conflict, the Union government decided to do nothing in the hope that delay might 'cause some of the workingmen's complaints to be diverted from the federal arena to where they belong.'[56]

Shifting responsibility to the provinces became the dying administration's last desperate unemployment policy. Ottawa's contributions to direct relief were terminated in the spring of 1921 in the hope that summer would bring an end to depression. Conditions did improve but not enough to obviate the possibility of severe social unrest. In fact, unemployment was so serious that Borden warned Meighen that it threatened to 'break into violence at some points within the next six or eight months.' Robertson agreed. There was a 'fear in the public mind, where there is possibility of trouble, that if it comes it will be serious.' The military commander in Vancouver was already urging 'preparation for emergencies.' The whole crisis was bound to have a 'serious effect on the political situation.'[57]

This was the election which would have to be held before the end of the year. The time could hardly have been less suitable. That autumn there were over 214,000 men out of work and unemployment had again climbed to over 10 per cent.[58] The government could delay calling conferences, but if it wanted to avoid riots and win the election there would at least have to be some announcement of what it proposed to do about the crisis over the coming winter. On 7 October the government stated that it would resume paying one-third the cost of municipal direct relief and would in addition pay one-third of any excess cost incurred by municipalities which undertook winter public works as unemployment relief.

At the same time, the Union government put forward a new concentric circle theory on the care of the jobless. Unemployment relief, the order-in-council announced, was 'primarily a municipal responsibility,' but, 'in the second instance,' it was the 'responsibility of the Province.' Federal contributions for the first time would be contingent on provincial participation on an equal basis. If relief costs could no longer be kept within urban boundaries, Ottawa's new strategy was to shift the burden to provincial coffers. Federal aid would last only 'until the emergency period is past.'[59]

When the Union government went to the polls in December 1921 it had taken initiatives on unemployment that were unprecedented in North American history. Unlike the United States, it had established a permanent national employment service, provided national funds for unemployment relief, and committed Canada, in principle, to a draft ILO recommendation favouring unemployment insurance. It would be wrong, however, to exaggerate the extent to which that government recognized unemployment as a new and permanent national responsibility. Each of its initiatives was a specific response to what it perceived as temporary, war-related problems and obligations, in much the same way as a federal Department of Health was created to cope with the emergency of the 1918 influenza epidemic.[60] The ESC was guaranteed 50 per cent funding only 'during the period of reconstruction'; Ottawa's contributions to relief were designed to shed its existing burden of supporting jobless veterans; and its 'investigations' into unemployment insurance were not more than a sop to post-war labour unrest.

Canadian workers and veterans endured far more sacrifices during the war than their American counterparts. Following the example of Great Britain, they expected much more from their government in return. As Newton Rowell pointed out in 1918, they were not in a 'normal condition' and, for a time, to appease them, Ottawa had to assume 'abnormal' responsibilities. The motivation was fear of the unemployed, not a commitment to ending unemployment. As a result, the obligations were seen as temporary, not permanent. When the unrest which fuelled them faded, so too would Ottawa's sense of responsibility for the jobless.

In December, Arthur Meighen suffered a crushing defeat at the polls. But the election produced more than a change in government. During the early post-war years the Union administration had viewed the industrial unrest as '*the* problem which the Nations of the world must face in the immediate future.' Its unemployment initiatives between 1918 and 1921 were at least an attempt to respond to this urban crisis. However, despite the fact that 15 per cent of the labourforce was unemployed when the campaign was in progress,[61] the 1921 election produced an agrarian, not a working-class political upheaval. The Liberals, under their new leader William Lyon Mackenzie King, won the largest number of seats, but the balance of power belonged to sixty-five Progressive MPs who represented the disenchanted votes of Canadian farmers.

It was an ironic outcome. King's successful campaign for the Liberal leadership in 1919 had been based in no small part on his appeal to the urban working-class and social-reform vote. With the exception of Newton Rowell, no Liberal politician in Canada had more impressive reform credentials. Grandson of the rebel William Lyon Mackenzie, King over the past two decades had harnessed his immense political ambition to a highly sophisticated grasp of the sources of labour unrest in order to carve out a distinctive political career as Canada's leading industrial statesman.

Lured away from a possible academic career at Harvard by the Laurier government in 1900, King succeeded over the next eight years in building the federal Department of Labour around his initial position as editor of the *Labour Gazette*. In 1902, at the age of twenty-eight, he became Canada's first deputy minister of labour and six years later, after running successfully in the 1908 election, he became minister of labour in the Laurier government until its defeat in 1911. During this period King created the framework for Canada's labour-relations system through the Industrial Disputes Investigation Act of 1907 and played a key role as conciliator in a number of crucial strikes.[62] After 1911, until his successful bid for the Liberal party leadership, he worked as industrial relations consultant for the Rockefeller empire in the United States. He capped off this portion of his career in 1918 with the publication of *Industry and Humanity*, a pious and awkwardly written book on social reform which nevertheless contained a number of acute insights into the sources of labour conflict under industrial capitalism.

In the book, King recognized that 'nothing is so dangerous to the standard of life or so destructive of minimum conditions of healthy existence as widespread ... unemployment.' For this reason, he endorsed unemployment insurance as the state's acknowledgment 'that an isolated human being, not less than a machine must be cared for when idle.'[63] Thanks in part to King's efforts, unemployment insurance became part of the platform adopted by the Liberal party at its 1919 national convention.

By the time of the 1921 election, however, political realities in Canada had changed. Within the party itself, support for social reform was waning. The left wing of the party, represented by Ontario Liberals such as Newton Rowell and *Toronto Daily Star* editor Joseph Atkinson, had been discredited by their support of conscription and disavowal of Laurier during the war. King was heavily beholden to the conservative Quebec caucus for support and here social legislation found little sympathy. Even in Ontario, where the election would be decided, King was under strong pressure to reassure businessmen that a Liberal victory would not mean low tariffs or expensive welfare measures.[64] Countervailing pressure from labour was weak, given the total disarray of the union movement following the disastrous Winnipeg General Strike and steadily mounting unemployment.

But it was the dramatic breakthrough of the Progressive party in rural Canada that sealed the fate of unemployment insurance in the post-war era. With the election over, King lost no time concluding that an 'alliance with the rural elements' would have to be the 'solid foundation of the Liberal party through the years to come.'[65] It was a crucial decision that would shape the course of Liberal unemployment policy for the remainder of the decade.

The Progressives had little sympathy for the Union government's expensive urban legislation. Costly new programs in public health, housing, technical education, labour exchanges, and relief offered few benefits to farmers and promised only to increase their taxes. They would also aggravate the crisis of rural depopulation by making cities more attractive. Ottawa's priorities had to be reversed. As Robert Forke, one of the Progressive leaders, put it, 'when you have the countryside a good place to live in and have helped to make rural homes happy and prosperous ... you will have gone a long way toward solving your industrial problems.' The government's first duty was to develop Canada's natural resources and 'nothing can be done in this direction by herding people into large cities.' The leader of the party, T.A. Crerar, agreed. '[R]igid economy' in government, he quickly made it known, would be one strict condition attached to his party's political support. In response, federal finance minister W.S. Fielding promised a 'great slashing' in public expenditures.[66] It did not bode well for the unemployed.

Canadian farmers, particularly in the West, were caught in a vicious cost-price squeeze by 1922. Record high prices for wheat and other agricultural commodities during the war had prompted them recklessly to expand their productive capacity and in the process they contracted a heavy burden of debt. Yet by 1922 agricultural prices had plummeted and wheat was selling at 50 per cent less than it had in 1917. Farm incomes shrank drastically. Fixed interest charges had to be met somehow and prices could not be raised. Only wage costs were left to make up the difference. As a result, farmers along with other Canadian employers were determined to expand the farm labour supply in order to bring agricultural wages back into line with reduced prices. A return to the 'open door' immigration policy of the pre-war era was one way of accomplishing this aim. Cutting off support to the urban unemployed was another. Both became explicit goals of the Progressive party and both were soon adopted by Mackenzie King.

At first, however, King had little choice but to continue the Union government's relief policy. When he took office in late December, the post-war depression was still acute. By the beginning of February 1922 employment had dropped a full 25 per cent from 1920 levels and over 263,000 men were out of work. They could not be left without support in the midst of winter; therefore, King decided to continue the federal contribution towards unemployment relief. A new order-in-council issued in January provided slightly more generous terms for federal assistance to municipal relief efforts until the end of March. It also reiterated Meighen's position. Relief was 'fundamentally a municipal and provincial responsibility,' PC 191 stated. Only the 'abnormal economic and industrial conditions' created by the war provided a justification for federal assistance.[67]

As soon as the order-in-council expired in the spring, King began to back away from relief. '[T]he obligation of looking after men who are unemployed,' he told the House in April, ' ... [is] primarily a matter for individuals in the first instance, between municipalities and the people living within their bounds in the second instance, next, between the provinces and the citizens of the respective provinces.' Unemployment only became a federal problem when 'both the municipalities and the provinces have found it impossible to cope with a situation that is completely beyond their control.' Even the last winter's crisis did not fit this new definition. No request for federal assistance had been received from any province east of Ontario, King pointed out, which raised doubts as to whether there had truly been a 'national obligation' to provide relief.[68]

When the summer arrived and the thousands of surplus labourers departed for the United States, the economic crisis relaxed. King lost no time in cutting all of Ottawa's ties with unemployment relief. In September, the government announced that it was at last calling the long-awaited national conference on unemployment. Its purpose, however, was to dismantle, not to extend Ottawa's responsibility for the jobless.

It was an exclusive gathering. Only the provinces were invited to send delegates. There were no representatives from business, labour, or farm organizations, nor were any municipal spokesmen asked to attend even though the cities paid the major cost of unemployment relief. From the start, King made it plain that Ottawa was changing the direction of its policy. The time had come to reverse the 'centralizing tendency' which had developed since the war, he told the provincial delegates, and to return to the old-fashioned doctrine of self-reliance 'instead of looking to the State for aid in every emergency ... [The] whole problem should be brought home as nearly as possible to the individual.' It was quite a change from the man who, six years earlier, had predicted that 'government ... will more and more be expected to find a means of adequately meeting the new order of social relations which a changing condition of society begets.'[69]

It was just the argument western municipal leaders feared. Suspecting that their failure to be invited to the conference was a prelude to a federal pull-out from relief, a delegation of western mayors crashed the proceedings to plead their case. It was all very well to debate the matter academically, Edmonton's mayor told the gathering, but when you had 'two or three hundred men camp on your doorstep crying out for relief ... that is where you have to face the problem.' A Vancouver alderman agreed. '[U]nder normal conditions the relief of the sick and the destitute, the aged and infirm, is a municipal matter ... but ... it was never designed that they should take care of such an abnormal situation as exists today. We have not the powers, we have not the possibilities to do it ... We find ourselves hampered in the ways in which we can raise money.'[70]

Although the mayors were asked to leave, the issue they had raised could not so easily be dismissed. What *was* the difference between unemployment 'as distinct from want,' a Nova Scotian official asked. 'Most of the older provinces at least have laws with respect to the poor ... and generally municipalities are charged with looking after [them] ... Now the question is, how far are we going in ... abrogating these laws by the assistance ... rendered in the matter of unemployment?'[71]

This was indeed the crux of the entire issue. Was unemployment relief a new problem or merely an extension of the traditional local obligation to care for the poor? If it was the former, then perhaps the mayors were right in arguing that it did not fit within their traditional responsibility for poor relief. In the end, the conference side-stepped this dangerous implication by accepting the distinction offered by Ontario premier E.C. Drury. '[W]e have to deal not with unemployment,' he argued, 'but the unemployed' – people he defined as 'reduced to a condition of dependence' because they could not find work. A man who made more than $2000 a year would not be 'unemployed' even if out of a job because he was not poor.[72] By posing the issue in these terms, the federal and provincial delegates were able to hand the whole problem of jobless men back to the municipalities with a clear conscience.

Tracing the cause of the depression back to rural depopulation made this task easier. 'Not one provincial representative here today,' federal minister H.S. Beland stated, 'has failed to state that the cities have an almost irresistible attraction for the people in the rural districts, and that really is one of the general causes of unemployment all over the world.' People who could have stayed on the land were moving to the city because 'life there, apparently, was easier, more attractive, more full of enjoyment than the country.' By making relief so available, Ottawa and the provinces only aggravated this tendency. 'The very fact that we have been forced to put up one-third of the cost, the Dominion Government and the municipality putting up the other two-thirds, has brought men into our cities from the country looking for relief, rather than working for board wages or a little better on the farm,' complained the representative from Saskatchewan.[73] By linking unemployment to rural depopulation, the conference not only expressed a widespread uneasiness over urbanization but also indirectly pinned the blame for their plight on the unemployed themselves. If the jobless crisis was either caused or aggravated by too many people flocking to the cities, surely the solution was not to provide them with relief so they could remain where there was no work. Ottawa's post-war unemployment policy had only offered a 'lure of money from the Federal government' and had given the cities a chance to 'shelve responsibility which for 50 years has been theirs.' Beland summed up the consensus of the meeting: 'If unemployment was to be permanent from now on for the next 10 years, I would say let us sit down here and work for years until we have found the remedy.' But since everyone agreed that the current problem was 'of a temporary nature,' it was only necessary to find a 'temporary relief.'[74] That could best be provided, the delegates concluded, by cutting off all further federal and provincial support for the dole.

Despite vigorous protest from the larger cities, King held firm to this policy throughout the winter of 1922–3. He also placed the responsibility for relief squarely on provincial shoulders. Before the war, he told a group of veterans who were demanding a resumption of federal aid, it had never been proper to approach Ottawa for unemployment relief and 'it looked now as though the Provinces were beginning to get away from their obligations.' The period of national emergency was over, he informed the House that spring, and 'the time has come when it is necessary to draw the line.' Dealing with matters of employment was clearly a provincial responsibility; therefore, 'action regarding unemployment would also seem to fall within the same category.' The federal government was shouldering the full burden of war debt. Let the provinces 'find the means of dealing with those matters that come within their particular jurisdiction.' From the prime minister's remarks, one MP observed, one could conclude 'that the federal government has finished with the question of unemployment.' King did not contradict him.[75]

However, he soon discovered that there were other ways besides the war of linking Ottawa to unemployment. In response to pressure from businessmen and farmers, his administration also announced that spring that the government would be reopening the door to agricultural immigrants. On the same day that King was justifying Ottawa's withdrawal from relief, William Irvine, a United Farmer MP from Alberta, asked, '[W]ill the present government now promise to assume responsibility for all such unemployed?'[76] He had placed his finger on a crucial weakness in the government's argument. If Ottawa had no constitutional obligation to spend money on relief which it claimed was within provincial jurisdiction, could the provinces not complain with equal justice about having to pay for mistakes in immigration policy, an area under federal control?

It was a prophetic insight. Immigration did replace the war as the key argument linking Ottawa to unemployment for the remainder of the decade. Control over immigration policy gave the federal government a vital role in regulating the nation's labour supply, in much the same way as its control over the army had made Ottawa responsible for the fate of demobilized men. Consequently, if there was a surplus of labour, was not the federal government at least in part to blame? Put differently, why should cities be forced to pay the full cost of unemployment relief when they had no say in determining how many might need it?

It was the height of irresponsibility, municipal spokesmen charged, for the federal government to withdraw completely from the dole at the same time it was expanding its immigration policy. When the brief recovery petered out in the fall of 1924 and unemployment once more climbed over 10 per cent, these criticisms reached a peak. To appease them and to counter criticism that the government lacked an unemployment policy, King's labour minister, James Murdock, convened yet another conference on unemployment. This time the municipalities were invited, along with representatives from business and organized labour. It took little time for the gathering to reach a deadlock over immigration. Because Ottawa had withdrawn its support from unemployment relief, TLC president Tom Moore pointed out, municipalities were now restricting their own relief payments to those who had lived within city boundaries for at least a year. At the same time, the federal government continued to import thousands of immigrants who could not possibly fulfil such a requirement. 'Who is going to look after them?' Moore asked. Winnipeg's mayor made the same point. Thousands were admitted annually for the western harvest and when it was over 'they are simply thrown to one side and no one cares what becomes of them afterwards.' His Calgary colleague added that the cities could not assume responsibility for these people because 'we have not the taxing power.'

This was not only a western viewpoint. Transients constituted 40 per cent of Toronto's relief load between December and March. One of its aldermen observed, 'The Federal Government should not try to "get out from under." Their responsibility is with the transient; there is no question of it. The municipality has a duty to take care of its residents and taxpayers.' What was needed, these municipal spokesmen concluded, was a 'national policy for Canadian employment.' As a first step, the delegates passed resolutions calling for stricter regulation of immigration until there was a 'reasonable demand for labour'; a reduction of the municipal share of relief costs to 50 per cent, the balance to be picked up by the provinces and federal government; and the immediate initiation of all contemplated provincial and federal public works.[77]

Ottawa's response to these proposals was so intransigent that it made the calling of the conference in the first place appear ludicrous. Finance minister James Robb told the delegates that while they were discussing possible unemployment remedies, western farmers lacked enough men to bring in the harvest. 'That is the reason for unemployment. There are too many people flocking to the cities ... There is work for them on the farms if they want to work.' Labour minister Murdock, for his part, simply shifted the burden to provinces. The cities were now claiming their responsibility ended with their own citizens and that all others were 'wards of the Federal Government.' Moreover, they 'no longer ask assistance as of grace, but as a matter of constitutional right.' This was ridiculous. The BNA Act clearly placed 'responsibility for the relief of poverty, no matter from whatever cause it arises ... upon the provinces' and it did 'not make any exception regarding any class of persons.' In any event, most of the unemployed were men who could 'not get away from the pool room, the movies and the big bright lights ... [and] go out into the open spaces as some of us immigrants in days gone by had to do.' Ottawa had already promised to find farm work for any jobless immigrant. 'What more is asked for?' he wanted to know. Progressive MPs agreed. Providing unemployment relief was exactly the opposite of what was needed. 'We want to make the conditions more difficult in the cities; we want to make them less attractive ... otherwise we cannot hope to hold our people on the farms.'[78]

Provincial governments proved equally adept at this game of passing the buck. Ontario's premier Howard Ferguson gave advice to Toronto's city council in 1925 that was typical of the political squeeze-play in which Canadian cities and the unemployed were trapped. Unemployment was a joint dominion-municipal responsibility, Ferguson argued. The federal government controlled immigration and the cities profited from the labour of their workers during good times and thus had an obligation to look after them during depressions. 'Where the Province has any direct responsibility,' he ingenuously observed, 'I confess I am at a loss to understand.'[79]

The end result of these cynical tactics on the part of Ottawa and the provinces was increased suffering for the unemployed. Although over 200,000 were without work throughout most of the winter of 1924–5, the financially beleaguered municipalities were unable to provide jobs and had to restrict direct relief to married men with families. All others, Winnipeg's mayor advised, 'should be on the lookout for winter jobs' and those working for farmers were 'strongly advised to remain with them during the winter.'[80] The following winter Winnipeg went one step further, slashing its relief rolls by 80 per cent largely through restricting support only to married men with two or more dependents who had been in Canada at least five years and could prove one year's continuous residence in the city. 'I am getting tired of being besieged by men who say they are unable to obtain work and who are on the verge of starvation,' one alderman complained. 'The thing is getting on my nerves, having to meet the unemployed day by day,' another added. Despite these hardening attitudes, the jobless crisis remained acute. A Manitoba government report on seasonal unemployment later estimated that even in the boom year 1927, a 'conservative deduction' from available statistics demonstrated that '25% to 30% of those gainfully employed in [the province] could not find employment at their regular occupations during the winter months.'[81] Denied urban relief and unable to find winter work, thousands of unemployed single men had no choice but to take to the road, launching a phenomenon that would become frighteningly familiar during the 1930s: an endless trek of jobless transients across the country searching for work or a meal and a place to sleep during the winter months.

The Employment Service of Canada also fell victim to King's attempt to disengage his government entirely from unemployment. Although he continually insisted that Ottawa's support of the ESC constituted its most important 'contribution towards the only really satisfactory solution to the problem of unemployment,' King in fact had little use for the agency. It was funded by a conditional grant, a device he detested in principle because it allowed Ottawa to be 'blamed for taxing people for monies that go to provinces over which [we] cannot be expected to exercise ... supervision.'[82]

As part of its general drive for economy and a balanced budget, the Liberal cabinet decided to terminate all of the Union government's conditional grant programs when their governing statutes expired. Although the federal government was committed to a permanent annual subsidy of $150,000 for the ESC, a supplementary grant of $100,000 a year had been required to keep Ottawa's share of the funding at 50 per cent. Between 1923 and 1924, pointing to the 'general clamour for economy in the country,' labour minister James Murdock eliminated this additional support and the dominion's share of the ESC's costs fell to 34 per cent.[83]

The agency was doubly vulnerable to these cuts because agrarian employers, who were its most important patrons, had come to the conclusion that the ESC did 'not function for the material benefit of the farming community.'[84] At issue was the attempt of its director, Bryce Stewart, to attack Canada's chronic problem of seasonal unemployment by closely regulating the supply of farm labour.

In the years immediately after the war when immigration had slowed to a mere trickle, the ESC had emerged as a key supplier of farm labour. Stewart wanted to extend this control throughout the remainder of the decade by taking over the re-cruitment of harvest excursions from the two national railways and also by keeping the inflow of agricultural immigrants to a minimum. With the supply of farm labourers closely subjected to the scientific control of his agency, Stewart was convinced that there would be 'fewer unemployed farm hands in the cities of the West during the winter and with the spreading of harvest employment over a smaller number of workers, those that are unemployed will have larger earnings as a measure of unemployment insurance.'[85]

Not surprisingly, Canadian farmers did not share this view. Before the war the old immigration branch of the Interior Department had always supplied them with a plentiful number of farm hands at low cost. This new ESC, one Progressive MP complained, seemed 'more interested in getting higher wages for the men they want to put out than they are in getting labour for the farmer at a price possible for him to pay.' To him and to other farmers, this was proof that 'labour unions ... control the labour bureaus.'[86]

Here was the conflict in a nutshell. Whose interests was a state labour exchange to serve – those of the employer or of the unemployed? As it turned out, the good intentions of the ESC were no match for the political power of sixty-five Progressive MPs and the economic power of the railways. Throughout 1924 both groups demanded that the immigration branch of the Interior Department once more be allowed to resume its farm placement activities. Their wishes were granted. A year later the two transcontinental railways were given a *carte blanche* by the King administration to recruit agricultural immigrants from Europe and to establish their own employment services to place them. Instead of one organization placing farm workers there were now four. In disgust, Murdock claimed that the government might as well take the Employment Offices Co-ordination Act off the statute books.[87] All hopes of easing seasonal unemployment came to an end.

With few friends among the farmers, the ESC became easy prey for the 'great slashing' in government expenditures which the Progressives demanded as the price of their support. In addition to the elimination of the $100,000 supplementary grant, Ottawa's administrative expenditures on its own branch of the ESC were reduced from $116,565 to $45,625 over the same two-year period. As a result, the number of federal employees working for it dropped from fifty-four to twenty.[88]

The effect of this sudden cut-back was devastating. Unemployment research was abandoned and Stewart's pioneering statistical work was transferred to the Dominion Bureau of Statistics, which had little interest in unemployment. The bulletin *Employment* was discontinued. Two regional clearing-houses were closed. Federal inspection of provincial offices was terminated along with the annual conferences of ESC officials held to familiarize the mostly untrained staff with employment work. Provincial standards, already low, dropped to the point where many local offices were little more than engines of patronage. The juvenile, women's, professional, and businessmen divisions of the service were dismantled, condemning it to the placement of only the most unskilled casual labour and to a minor role in the nation's labour market. Stewart, his 'hunch as to what the politicians in and out of Parliament would do to it' confirmed by the cuts, resigned as director in 1922 and left for the greener opportunities in the United States. Canada lost the services of one of North America's leading experts on unemployment. Seventeen years later, in 1939, he would return as deputy minister of labour to supervise the creation of a new National Employment Service and Unemployment Insurance Commission.[89]

In the long run, the most serious effect of Ottawa's unilateral cut-back in ESC funding was to poison the entire atmosphere of dominion-provincial co-operation on unemployment. The leadership provided by the ESC's advisory council, with its broadly representative members, was lost since provincial governments refused to listen to 'a body that operates under a federal government charter and is re-imbursed by the federal government to instruct the provincial governments how they shall spend their money.' More important, with the federal share of the ESC's costs frozen at a permanent grant of $150,000, the provinces soon realized that Ottawa was 'either anxious ... to have the Employment Offices discontinued or ... they desire to have the provinces carry the entire cost of maintenance by gradually reducing [their] contribution until this has been accomplished.'[90] Provincial governments consequently froze their own expenditures on the service at 1924 levels to prevent the federal share from dropping below one-third. This effectively killed any hope of future expansion of the ESC. Ottawa had placed political expediency above the need for leadership on the unemployment question. Why should the provinces take up the slack?

After 1924 the ESC was little more than a patronage-ridden clearing-house for casual help. Embittered service officials complained about the 'policy of parsimony' which had 'crippled' their organization and railed against politicians who lacked a 'true vision' of its importance.[91] The label fit Mackenzie King. His callous destruction of the agency Stewart worked so hard to establish was convincing proof that, despite the pious overtones of *Industry and Humanity*, he was indifferent to the plight of the unemployed. With the eclipse of the ESC, Ottawa lacked any effective link to the nation's labour market. The legacy of this blindness would come to haunt King in the next decade.

In the light of these cut-backs to the ESC and the withdrawal from unemployment relief, King's refusal to deal with his party's 1919 platform pledge to implement unemployment insurance is understandable. King, of course, always cited the constitution as his reason for not acting and recently some historians have echoed this view.[92] By 1928 the Justice Department had changed its mind and argued that the contributory provisions of unemployment insurance placed it within provincial jurisdiction over 'property and civil rights.'[93] But the BNA Act was more a shield from responsibility than a barrier to action for King. Having taken great trouble to extract his government from its post-war responsibilities for labour exchanges and relief, he was hardly willing to plunge Ottawa back into the fray by pushing for a national system of unemployment insurance.

This was clear to James Murdock. The problem was political, not constitutional, the labour minister reminded the prime minister in 1924. '[T]he Dominion Parliament has power to enact a national system of unemployment insurance should it desire to do so,' but it would be politically unwise to act since 'acceptance of Federal responsibility with regard to unemployment insurance would seem to be somewhat inconsistent with the Federal view that the Federal authorities should accept no responsibility in normal times with regard to unemployment relief.'[94] Two years earlier at the 1922 unemployment conference, Murdock had helped to bury the ILO's unemployment insurance recommendation by assuring the provincial delegates that it was 'entirely all right' with Ottawa if they did not want action on the ILO labour conventions. 'If the provinces say "no" to the draft conventions or if they permit the draft conventions to just go without further recognition or action, there will not be any pressure or any effort made particularly by the Dominion Government ... If this conference says "Nothing doing" why that would simplify the matter so far as these drafts are concerned.'[95]

Behind Murdock's reluctance to act lay not only political expediency but also the degeneration of Britain's unemployment insurance scheme into what most commentators viewed as nothing more than a cash dole. Heavy unemployment combined with strong political pressure by labour following the war forced the British government into extending insurance benefits to most of the unemployed well past any point justified by past contributions or actuarial principles. By the late 1920s, unemployment insurance had become such a heavy drain on the British treasury that many feared national bankruptcy was imminent.[96]

These problems in Britain killed any hopes of similar legislation becoming law in Canada. Businessmen gleefully pointed out that unemployment insurance had 'conspicuously failed' in the mother country and 'hung like a millstone around Great Britain's neck preventing her ... from competing with other nations.' The Americans had enacted no such plan, the CMA argued, and in matters of social legislation it was clear that 'Canada cannot lead such powerful competitors as the United States.'[97]

Politicians tended to agree. The heavy cost of unemployment insurance in Britain, Murdock warned King in 1924, demonstrated its 'futility as a remedy for the unemployment evil' and proved that it would not command much support in Parliament. To provide such a measure in Canada, finance minister J.A. Robb argued a year later, would simply attract those 'spoiled by doles in the Old Country.' Ontario's deputy minister of labour put his finger on perhaps the most important source of opposition to the idea. With unemployment insurance in place in the cities, he said, workers would be 'unwilling ... to engage in the kind of work offered by the essential industries of this Province, namely farming, mining, lumbering, building and constructing,' most of which existed outside of the urbanized south.[98]

In any event, King's own views on the subject made action unlikely. '[T]he whole business of State aid to unemployment,' he confessed to his diary in 1929, 'is a mistake except as insurance to which all parties contribute and then as a prov'l obligation.' Since provincial fingers had been badly burnt by their experience with the ESC, they would hardly be expected to muster the enthusiasm for any new federal suggestions that they take on the additional expense of unemployment insurance, especially when its costs could not be calculated. Research in unemployment statistics, begun by Stewart and Clark in 1919, had been terminated with the cut-backs to the ESC in 1923. Consequently, in 1928 the ESC's new director, R.A. Rigg, would 'not even hazard a guess' when asked by a parliamentary inquiry what Canada's unemployment rate had been for the past five years. As University of Toronto economist Gilbert Jackson complained, 'No country ... has better materials for the study of [unemployment] than we have, but little has been done here.'[99] This too would be part of King's legacy to the Depression.

Rapid economic growth and high employment during the last half of the 1920s made unemployment fade from the public mind. King was able to continue to saddle the provinces and municipalities with the most expensive social costs of urbanization while claiming a record of budget surpluses, reduced taxation, and lower public debt for his own administration. It was a formula sure to produce victory when his government went to the polls in 1930.

Instead, depression struck Canada over the winter of 1929–30. King's past rigidity on unemployment now turned into a disastrous political liability. Although by February 323,000 men were jobless and unemployment stood at 12½ per cent, King refused to take the crisis seriously. It was only a 'temporary seasonal slackness.' Provincial and municipal pleas for federal aid were nothing more than a Tory plot to reduce Ottawa's carefully accumulated budget surplus before the election. As far as 'giving moneys out of the federal treasury to any Tory government in this country for these alleged unemployment purposes,' King told the House on 3 April, 'I would not give them a five-cent piece.'[100]

That evening he faced the enormity of his blunder. From a reading of the speech King noted in his diary, 'it would seem I was indifferent to the conditions of the unemployed.' Instead of pursuing this accurate insight, he consoled himself with the thought that his position would 'appeal to the people when limited to unemployment, as most persons get nothing therefrom.' He had moved a long way from the politician who in 1919 had at least realized that 'the fear of unemployment ... lies at the root of most of the minor fears which labor entertains.'[101]

The decade of the 1920s ended as it began, with federal unemployment policy once again a controversial political issue. Most of the lines the controversy would follow in the Depression were already evident during the preceding ten years of supposed prosperity. Municipalities which had railed against the heavy burden of unemployment relief during the twenties would go bankrupt during the thirties and would drag some provincial governments along with them. A federal policy which led cities to abandon responsibility for unemployed single men would become the direct precursor of the Depression relief camps. An annoying lack of accurate unemployment statistics in the 1920s would become a crippling burden for those investigating unemployment insurance during the Depression. A patronage-ridden Employment Service would deprive Ottawa of an effective link to the local labour market and local relief efforts in the next decade. Finally, King's politically expedient use of the constitution as a barrier shielding Ottawa from the unemployment issue would make the task of seeking a constitutional amendment for unemployment insurance exceedingly difficult.

Whatever its long-term consequences, however, King's policy of abandoning responsibility for unemployment during the 1920s was, in the short run at least, a wise move politically. As the agrarian revolt of 1921 showed only too clearly, much of the nation was still profoundly disturbed over the transition to an urban society. Consistently throughout the early post-war years the 'abnormality' of severe unemployment was equated with the 'abnormal' conditions of city life itself. By linking unemployment to urbanization in this way, opponents of unemployment insurance or federal relief could blame the victims of depression for their plight. Their lack of work was the result of a personal decision either to migrate to or remain in a city, not the fault of any intrinsic flaws in the economy itself. The solution to the crisis of joblessness, then, was to encourage them to go back to the land, not to remain in the cities where there was nothing to do.

Behind this thinking lay the old poor-law doctrine of 'less eligibility.' Throughout the 1920s federal and provincial government policies were directed towards continued settlement of the West and the development of northern resources. As a result, neither level of government could long concede the right of the post-war unemployed to remain in the cities when work, albeit at little better than room-and-board wages, beckoned on the frontier. Farmers in particular were still Canada's largest employers of unskilled labour. By electing sixty-five Progressive MPs to Parliament in 1921, they ensured that federal unemployment policy would conform to their economic interests which, as one Progressive put it, was to 'get labour more cheaply.' As a result, 'back to the land' and not 'work and maintenance' became the dominant motif of Canadian social policy during the 1920s. This did not worry Mackenzie King. For more dedicated liberal reformers, such as Bryce Stewart, the frustration produced by the lost opportunity of the early post-war years was acute. 'If we wait long enough,' he prophesied during the 1921 depression,

the bread lines and out-of-work doles will cease, unemployment will be gone, men and women will rise out of dull inaction and find joy again in the work of head and hands. The present time will be referred to as the 'hard times of 1920–21' an unfortunate experience to be forgotten if possible. Men will pursue their usual ways and in 1925, or 26 or 27 or some other year, the dark ogre of unemployment will again thrust his long arm into the factories and mines and shops and offices, tear the workers from their tasks, bank the fires, hang out the 'No Help Wanted' signs and shut the doors against them. We shall then have the satisfaction of knowing that the divine right of unpreparedness has been upheld.[102]

2
'Work and Wages': Bennett and the Depression, 1930–2

The 1930 contest between King and the Conservative party's new leader, R.B. Bennett, was the first modern federal election in which the issue of unemployment proved decisive. Although the 1921 election had been fought during a depression, the startling success of the agrarian-based Progressive party overshadowed all other aspects of that contest. As noted previously, 1921 represented an agrarian, not a working-class political upheaval. But after 1924 Mackenzie King, through continual persuasion, lower tariffs, and clever exploitation of divisions within the Progressive ranks, gradually absorbed the bulk of that party's supporters and MPs back within the fold of Canadian Liberalism. By 1928 all that remained of the Progressives as an independent force in federal politics were eleven United Farmer of Alberta MPs who, together with labour spokesmen J.S. Woodsworth and A.A. Heaps, formed the left-leaning 'Ginger Group' in Parliament. Throughout the 1920s, moreover the urbanization of Canada continued apace. By 1931 54 per cent of the nation's population lived and worked in towns and cities, and urban issues such as old-age pensions and mothers' allowances had become increasingly important in Canadian politics. When the country plunged once more into depression, it is not surprising that unemployment quickly emerged to dominate all other issues in the campaign.

The Liberals and Conservatives adopted strikingly different attitudes to unemployment. Throughout most of the campaign King attempted to ignore the issue by concentrating instead on his party's record of budget surpluses and reduced taxation. Conditions were not 'unduly alarming or critical' in Canada at the present time, the prime minister informed a Brandon, Manitoba, audience on 1 July 1930. In fact, there was 'less relative unemployment in Canada than in any other country in the world' and most of that was confined to the western provinces as a result of a poor wheat crop. Bennett was trying merely to 'exploit the present situation for political advantage.' Moreover, he had forgotten that the primary obligation for relieving unemployment was a municipal and provincial responsibility. 'Only when the situation has gone beyond the resources of municipal and provincial authorities,' King said, did the federal government have any responsibility to act. So far no provincial government had reached this sorry state; consequently, there was no need for federal action.[1] Some of King's advisers – in particular his minister of labour, a former trade unionist, Peter Heenan – warned him against such a complacent attitude. Unemployment was 'figuring quite largely' in the campaign in industrial centres and Heenan urged King to make a 'further Federal initiative,' such as proposing a conference on unemployment insurance, as one means of combating this alarming trend. His suggestion was rebuffed. There was 'little … to be gained by bringing up [the] subject at all in [the] present campaign,' King replied to him. Heenan would be 'wiser to leave [the] matter alone.' Convinced that his administration had pursued sound economic policies, King refused to take the current depression seriously. Although he recognized that Bennett was 'seeking to make unemployment the issue,' King comforted himself with the thought that 'the men who are working are not going to worry particularly over some of those who are not.' On what was fast becoming the most important political issue in urban Canada, King, for all his previous sophistication on labour questions, was astoundingly naïve.[2]

Bennett, it seemed, was not. He had won the Conservative party leadership in 1927 at the age of fifty-seven in the year following Arthur Meighen's disastrous electoral defeat. The product of a devoutly Methodist New Brunswick family of modest means, Bennett had gained his first political experience making speeches as a youth on behalf of temperance. For the rest of his life his personality remained strongly shaped by the stern moral imperatives of his Methodist upbringing, particularly its emphasis on duty, service, and self-reliance.[3]

As a young man, Bennett taught school in order to earn the money he needed to attend Dalhousie Law School. After a few years of practising law in Chatham, New Brunswick, he moved to Calgary in 1897 to join the prestigious Conservative firm of Sir James Lougheed. Soon he became one of Canada's leading corporation lawyers and counted the CPR among his clients. It was in Calgary that he began his political career. He served intermittently as a member of the territorial assembly and provincial legislature between 1898 and 1911 and represented Calgary in the House of Commons between 1911 and 1917. Leaving politics in that year, Bennett returned briefly in 1921 as Meighen's minister of justice. Defeated in the election, he stayed out of politics until 1926 when he re-emerged as minister of finance in Meighen's second short-lived administration. After the election that year he was the Conservative party's only remaining western Canadian MP.[4]

By 1927 Bennett was a millionaire thanks to judicious investment opportunities provided by his old New Brunswick friend Max Aitken (Lord Beaverbrook) and a large inheritance from his widowed sister. With his fortune made, Bennett decided to dedicate the rest of his life to public service by running for the Conservative party leadership.

To this position Bennett brought great wealth (he spent $600,000 of his own fortune on the 1930 election), impressive western Canadian and business support, and tremendous enthusiasm.[5] Like King he was a bachelor who, once in office, concentrated his total energies on political affairs. Unlike King, however, his personality was not suited to political leadership. Arrogant and domineering, Bennett's immense confidence in his own abilities was at one and the same time his greatest strength and weakness. It gave him a penchant for decisive action but it also made him insensitive to criticism or advice and totally inept at the arts of conciliation.

In the context of the 1930 election, however, Bennett's earnest conviction and sense of mission proved to be a tremendous political asset. With 13 per cent of the labourforce unemployed during what were usually the busiest months of the year, he was willing at least to recognize that something was wrong with the economy. He appeared willing to do something about it by promising direct federal action to provide both jobs and relief for the unemployed. On 13 June in Calgary he declared that unemployment 'has now ceased to be local and provincial and has become national in its importance' and he promised a 'definite plan for permanent relief' to give work rather than doles to the unemployed. The same day, speaking in Edmonton, Bennett pledged that he would provide 'employment for all who can and will work.' Two weeks later in Montreal he reiterated that unemployment was a national problem and charged that 'the first duty of the Canadian government is to provide work for Canadians.' In Moncton on 10 July he made his famous promise: 'The Conservative party is going to find work for all who are willing to work, or perish in the attempt ... Mr. King promises consideration of the problem of unemployment. I promise to end unemployment. Which plan do you like best?'[6] An electorate deeply uneasy over growing unemployment naturally preferred this more positive approach to King's total denial of responsibility for the problem. Bennett was swept into office with a resounding mandate.

But a mandate for what? Taken at face value, Bennett's promise to 'abolish the dole' and provide 'work and wages' for the jobless appeared as a bold new extension of the national government's responsibility for unemployment. This was certainly Peter Heenan's conclusion. In an election post-mortem King's defeated labour minister noted: 'up to ... the last Session of Parliament, employment and unemployment was not considered a Federal affair ... [A]s a result of recent events this has all changed, that is to say, the Conservatives contended that the question of unemployment was a Federal affair ... [T]he people of Canada had given Mr. Bennett a mandate to look after employment and unemployment, and no matter what the written word of the Constitution may be, the Canadian people have now placed this matter in the lap of the federal Government.'[7]

There is no evidence that Bennett felt this way. Tariff protectionism had been the traditional Conservative response to depression since 1878. Bennett's extravagant election promises simply represented his inflated confidence in this time-worn remedy and his own abilities, but not an expanded conception of Ottawa's economic responsibilities. This became quite clear when Parliament assembled at a special session in September.

Bennett presented two unemployment packages to the newly elected House. The first, and in his view the more important, was a stiff across-the-board hike in the tariff. This was the policy that would 'end unemployment,' he said. It was also the only direct acion taken by his government at the special session. However, even the Tory leader conceded that at best the tariff hike could only provide 25,000 new jobs during his first year of office. Yet by his labour minister's own estimate over 200,000 were out of work and that number was expected to grow before the onset of winter.[8] To deal with this temporary unemployment crisis Bennett introduced an unemployment relief act that provided $20 million – ten times more than Ottawa had spent on relief during the 1920s – to provide work for the jobless.

Although the amount itself was unprecedented, the significance of the 1930 Relief Act lay in its preamble. Unemployment, the act insisted, was still 'primarily a provincial and municipal responsibility,' something Bennett had not taken pains to mention during the campaign. The bulk of the $20 million grant, the prime minister told the House, would be spent in the traditional fashion as part of a federal contribution to relief works or direct relief initiated and administered by the local governments. His government was not assuming any 'new constitutional obligations.'[9] Despite his sweeping election promises, Bennett's actual unemployment policy merely duplicated that of the Union administration of 1920–1 in acknowledging only an indirect responsibility for the unemployed.

There were three reasons for this traditional approach. First, Bennett had not merely promised to create more jobs. He had pledged to find 'employment for all who can and will work.' With over 200,000 jobless, this was an expensive proposition. By forcing the municipalities to provide 50 per cent and the provinces 25 per cent of the cost of relief projects, Bennett could buy over three times as many jobs for his $20 million than if he had put it into exclusively federal public works.

Second, even if Bennett had wanted to administer aid to the unemployed directly, his government lacked any mechanism to do it. The provinces and municipalities, he averred, 'had ... the machinery to investigate each of these various relief claims,' whereas Ottawa did not. By relying on the personnel of existing local relief agencies and provincial old-age pension and mothers' allowance commissions, Bennett could 'utilize the provincial authorities' staff and knowledge.'[10]

Finally, despite his extravagant campaign rhetoric, the Tory leader was convinced that the present depression was a passing, mostly seasonal phenomenon. As a result, he timed his first Relief Act to expire on 31 March 1931. With the stimulus to industry provided by his tariff policy, Bennett was confident that unemployment would drop to its normal level of 5 or 6 per cent with the coming of spring. The 1930 Relief Act was designed to deal with an accentuated seasonal unemployment problem, not with a cyclical depression. By assuming that both unemployment and his relief program would end in the spring, Bennett felt under no obligation to develop more permanent policies for aiding the jobless. Rather than create a new and perhaps expensive federal bureaucracy, he was content to rely on local ones. The unemployment relief branch of the federal Department of Labour remained strictly an 'accounting office.' It neither inspected nor audited provincial and municipal relief projects. The $16 million slated for public works was divided among the provinces in October on the basis of population, not need.[11]

Inside the provinces the same pattern prevailed. Apart from a preference for married over single men, relief jobs were rotated arbitrarily among the unemployed regardless of family size or means. Moreover, since municipalities administered and paid for 50 per cent of the projects, the amount of work provided depended not on the needs of the unemployed but on the size of the municipal debt and the strength of labour on the city council. In Windsor, Ontario, where labour was strong, an unemployed married man averaged $157.00 for forty days work. His Toronto counterpart received only eleven days work for $53.00. Since lack of work, not complete destitution, was the only qualification for a relief job, the $16 million did not reach those who needed it most. Ontario's provincial average of $86.00 for three weeks' work was nowhere near enough to keep a family with no other resources off direct relief. Widespread complaints of political discrimination were further testimony to the arbitrary distribution of the grant.[12]

Since Ottawa and most provincial governments provided no funds for administration, municipalities had no incentive to hire competent personnel or to develop efficient structures for dispensing relief. As a result, direct relief under Bennett's 1930 Relief Act was distributed by a ramshackle collection of private charities and hastily organized emergency relief committees. In Winnipeg, one of the few Canadian cities to possess a public welfare department, overworked staff members reported that they were 'unable to give what they considered adequate relief' owing to political interference from a city council anxious to keep property taxes down. In Toronto, five private family charities struggled to develop a working arrangement with the city's two public relief agencies, the Division of Social Welfare and the House of Industry. The results were not always successful. Since the House of Industry insisted on making its own investigations, very often 'two agencies [would be] working on the same family at the same time.' As one harassed social worker concluded, the whole relief set-up was 'most bewildering' and potentially 'volcanic.'

In Quebec and the Maritimes the situation was worse. Montreal had 'no outdoor relief department, no Mothers' Allowances, nor Old Age Pensions.' All social aid was channelled through the city's four private religious charities. Within two years that city would possess a dubious claim of distinction: more of its population (30 per cent) would be on relief than in any other Canadian city and they would be receiving less *per capita* (84¢) than their counterparts elsewhere.[13]

In New Brunswick and Nova Scotia public relief remained governed by Dickensian nineteenth-century principles. Destitute families in Saint John, a survey of that city's social welfare structure revealed, had to 'apply [for relief] to the [poor law] Commissioner of the ward in which they live ... If there is indication that relief will be needed over a long period of time, the procedure is to place the whole family regardless of the welfare of the children, in the Municipal Home, where aged, infirm, feeble-minded and idiots are housed.' In Halifax the situation was hardly more humane. That city also lacked a civic welfare department, and public relief to the poor in their homes was forbidden by statute. Instead, children under the age of sixteen were separated from their parents and 'placed elsewhere' before the latter were incarcerated in the municipal poor house.[14]

Personnnel needed to distribute relief were rounded up wherever they could be found. There were only 400–500 trained social workers in all of Canada throughout the Depression and most of these worked in the country's private charities.[15] In any event, their skills were relatively costly to local governments who were receiving no extra funds to help defray the added administrative expenses of dispensing public relief on a mass scale. Municipal and provincial governments consequently made do with what they had. Dorothy King, head of Montreal's School of Social Work, described the situation best: 'In the administration of unemployment aid in ... Northern Alberta, the Royal Canadian Mounted Police are the agents; in other provinces, Provincial and City Police, Public Health Nurses and officers of the Children's Aid Society have been pressed into investigation services. "White collared" and other unemployed have been used freely, the general supervision being usually assigned to officers of the municipal and provincial government, whose previous experience has been in other fields.'[16]

For Canada's few trained social workers, the immediate impact of the 1930 unemployment crisis was devastating as caseloads doubled and there was no increase in staff. 'One meets some Workers of whom one thinks – "How old she looks! I never before thought of her as being old," ' noted Ethel Parker of Toronto's Neighbourhood Workers' Association in September. It was small wonder 'many of us have grown a bit brittle and required "handling" as to our tempers. Can you see your cherished standards, one by one, go by the board; can your sympathies be torn day after day by tragedies of which most of the rest of the city remain unheeding; can you stand day after day in the position of being the only person to whom these families have to turn and yet be absolutely unable to relieve their anxiety and suffering?'[17]

As final proof of the ad hoc nature of the unemployment relief program, Ottawa did not require a registration of those who benefitted from it. There was no way of knowing how many *separate* families and individuals were included in the 326,900 who received jobs or the 581,000 who received direct relief under its terms.[18]

In short, because he opted for indirect administration of this relief grant with only nominal federal controls, Bennett had no way of ensuring that the money was fairly and wisely spent. He placed himself in the dangerous position of responsibility for the mistakes and incompetence of the local governments. During the election campaign and the special session of Parliament, his government took the initiative in meeting the Depression. He, not the provincial leaders, promised 'work and wages' for the unemployed. When unprecedented unemployment during the winter of 1930–1 made the pledge impossible to fulfil, Bennett received the blame. One angry Tory supporter summed up the frustration undoubtedly felt by many when Bennett's promise of employment failed to materialize:

I haven't done any work since June 28 1930; I have a wife and three girls aged 13 yrs, 11 yrs and 9 yrs ... I've been going and regoing to the City to get work: all I get is We will see what can be done: Our rent is back from Nov. Dec. 1930 and this month God only knows where are [sic] going to get it from: I have asked & asked the City to help, and they say its been turned down for some reason, the reason they won't tell: Today I whent [sic] to get $3 to keep us for a week and Mr. Valcourt of the city Office said I couldn't get it because someone said we had a radio ... Then he says he don't have to give us help if he don't want to: I ask you Sir, 'who was this money given to and what for?' is it for a man to crawl on his hands and knees to get a loaf for his family? I ask you Sir how do you think we live on $3 a week and cant get that because some people make up a lie: What sort of a country have we: I dont want help: I want work; I'll do anything to keep my family.[19]

On 31 March 1931 the Relief Act expired with $2 million still unspent and almost 15 per cent of the labourforce unemployed. Two months later 17 per cent were out of work and there was still no prospect of federal aid for emergency jobs or direct relief. Most provincial governments followed the federal lead by cutting off their assistance as well. Forced to carry the full weight of the staggering relief burden, the municipalities had no choice but to get tough with non-residents. As one social worker said, 'Any humane treatment of these men ... make[s] it impossible to eliminate the number.' Those who could not prove twelve months' continuous residence before applying for assistance were cut off.[20]

Transient single men were the principal victims of this new policy. Most worked in seasonal industries such as railway construction, agriculture, or pulp and paper manufacturing which took them out of the cities from six to eight months every year. A large number were recent immigrants or fresh off the farm. For one reason or another few could satisfy the residence requirements of any city. But in the spring of 1931 there was nowhere for these men to go. Because they worked in the most exposed industries of Canada's 'open' economy, they bore the full brunt of the Depression. Bush work, for example, which normally drew 10,000 men out of Winnipeg during the winter, provided only 800 jobs. To make matters worse, early April brought reports from the West that 'farmers would not be hiring men this season because of the general depression in the agricultural field.'[21] An anomolous situation quickly developed. The men most affected by unemployment and with the least personal resources were denied any access to relief. Their plight was effectively portrayed to Bennett by one of their number:

Please tell me why it is a single man always gets a refusal when he looks for a job. A married man gets work & if he does not get work, he gets relief ... Last year I was out of work three months. I received work with a local farm. I was told in the fall I could have the job for the winter; I was then a stable man. Now I am slacked off on account of no snow this winter. Now I am wandering the streets like a beggar with no future ahead. There are lots of single men ... who would rather walk the streets & starve than work on a farm ... Myself I work wherever I can get work ... There are plenty of young men like myself, who are in the same plight. I say again, whats to be done for us single men? Do we have to starve? Or do we have to go round with our faces full of shame, to beg at the doors of the well to do citizen ... Did you ever feel the pangs of hunger? My idea is we shall all starve. I suppose you will say I cant help it, or I cant make things better. You have the power to make things better or worse. When you entered as Premier you promised a lot of things, you was going to do for the country. I am waiting patiently to see the results.[22]

Others were not so patient. From Edmonton in early June came reports of a 'tense' situation. Single men cut off from relief in that city had 'assumed a somewhat threatening attitude' and violence was only averted 'by restoring a minimum of food relief to the extent of a bowl of porridge twice a day and the temporary stationing of a portion of the Calgary Strathcona Horse here.'[23] British

Columbia's premier, S.F. Tolmie, sent Ottawa an identical warning: '[Q]uite a number of men will be released from the logging camps, some 2000 I think, about the end of this month. Those who know the young logger fear that these fellows accustomed to dangerous work in the woods and possessing many adventurous spirits among them will not stand for much hardship in the city and if relief is not provided for them, will promptly help themselves ... [T]he unemployment situation is becoming daily much more acute and with communistic agitation it is a much more serious question than when it was discussed some time ago ... The Reds in Vancouver are already talking about a revolution.'[24]

Menaced by this growing unrest and imminent civic bankruptcy, western boards of trade, social workers, and city councils pressured Ottawa to take some action to get the men out of the cities. At first their pleas met stubborn disbelief. Bennett denied that there was any agricultural crisis at all; his labour minister, Gideon Robertson, refused to believe that the summer season was not 'opening up.' Reports of unemployment, he felt, were 'substantially exaggerated.' By mid-May, however, even Robertson conceded that the 'spring exodus of labour to the rural and lumbering districts ... is not occurring as in more normal years.'[25] Finally in June, as if he had to see the crisis to believe in it, Robertson departed for the West.

The tall elderly senator was now serving his second term as minister of labour, a position he held during the last years of the Union government between 1918 and 1921. Then he had achieved notoriety for his ruthless intervention in the Winnipeg General Strike. A deeply conservative man, Robertson, although a trade unionist himself, had viewed the strike as an attempted revolution which justified the arrest of its leaders and the use of the RCMP to prevent demonstrations.[26]

After visiting all four western provinces during the last three weeks of June 1931, Robertson learned from municipal representatives that another serious crisis was brewing in the West. The numbers of unemployed single men had reached an explosive stage and prairie cities were denying them relief on the grounds that transients were a federal responsibility. Winnipeg's delegation stated the case clearly:

The very mobility of the transient worker has made it impossible for him to establish residence any place in Canada. He is essentially a national problem, working in every province, spending his money in every city. He is the man who has made possible the development of Canada's natural resources of water power, pulp and paper, mine and railways, farm and factory. He is not the responsibility of any one municipality, and no one municipality dare commence any relief of his distress ... If we were to attempt to feed these men at this time, without similar provision being made in all other parts of Canada, our City would be overwhelmed by the Migration of hungry men from East and West who would flock here for food.[27]

By this logic these men, as well as any immigrants with fewer than five years' residence, were Ottawa's exclusive responsibility. Saskatoon's relief committee recommended that 'camps should be established by the Federal Government in sections of the country where work of a reasonably useful nature can be done' and a 'nominal amount' paid to the men.[28] The main priority was to get them out of the cities.

Robertson liked the idea. Although he did not agree that transients were a federal responsibility, he did believe that they posed a double threat. On the one hand, because 'so large a proportion of them are of alien origin and communistic sympathies,' they represented a serious menace to public order in all western cities. On the other, their very mobility proved the existence of a national labour market and thus undermined Ottawa's argument that the care of the unemployed was primarily a municipal problem.

To meet these dangers, Robertson recommended that Ottawa's first priority should be the 'removal of thousands of transients from urban centres' to relief camps constructed along the proposed route of the Trans-Canada Highway. Here, single men would be 'put to work promptly under supervision equivalent to semi-military control.' Those who refused to go would 'forfeit their right to State assistance.' In this way, relief camps would play two roles. By getting the men out of the cities, they would reduce the dangers of communist-inspired social unrest. Freed thus of their transient burden, municipalities could reasonably be expected to 'care for their own remaining residents.'[29] Robertson was convinced this was all the help municipalities would need. A good harvest, he told Bennett, might eliminate the need for any other federal assistance; therefore, he advised against making any plans for a new relief act until August, when 'crop results' would provide 'more accurate knowledge' of what the winter's requirements would be.

On the trip back to Ottawa, Robertson's complacency was shattered by his confrontation with the drought-stricken Palliser's Triangle. 'Having known the West quite intimately for twenty-five years,' he wrote to the prime minister, '... one could never believe the desolation existing in southern Saskatchewan did he not see it himself ... The drought had become so serious that strong winds blowing the surface soil in thick clouds across the country has entirely covered up what little grass remained with its roots alive, and the whole country for more than one hundred miles in extent across southern Saskatchewan is a barren drifting desert, with no vegetation in sight at all, and water supply is almost wholly exhausted except as found in certain water holes and drawn long distances by the farmer. This scene of desolation beggars description.'[30] Robertson had gambled on the harvest and lost.

As a result a new Unemployment Relief Act, designed to deal with the crisis in the West, was rushed into Parliament on Dominion Day. Its urgent task was to provide food and fuel for the drought-stricken residents of southern Saskatchewan.

Since neither the local municipalities nor the province had the resources for this assistance, Bennett agreed to finance the burden provided the aid was distributed through an independent relief commission established by the provincial government. In this way his constitutional position that relief was still a local matter could be preserved, despite the total financial incapacity of the governments in question.

The second goal of the act followed Robertson's advice on getting the transient men out of the cities. Here, too, Bennett resisted the argument that these men were an exclusive federal responsibility. Rather than establish its own relief camps, his government provided financial assistance to provincial road-building programs designed to draw single men away from urban centres. To make sure they would go, he used indirect coercion. As he explained to Parliament, 'where there is work there will be pay, and ... if an individual is capable of work and will not work, there will be no benefits.' Law enforcement was a provincial responsibility, he reminded the House, and his government possessed no direct means of dealing with 'those who, offered work, will not take it but demand that they be maintained.' However, his 1931 Relief Act did give the provinces some help by providing fines of up to $1000 and prison terms of up to three years for anyone disobeying orders or regulations under its terms. In this way, any communist opposition to the removal of single men from the cities would be effectively crushed.[31]

The 1931 Relief Act, like its predecessor, stipulated that municipalities and provinces were primarily responsible for the care of the remaining unemployed, a responsibility Bennett hoped could be met through federal aid to local relief projects similar to that of the previous year. Alternative suggestions from both the leader of the opposition, Mackenzie King, and from within his own party that he appoint a non-partisan national relief board composed of 'experts ... who understand social, industrial and economic conditions' to administer federal relief funds were dismissed by the prime minister as being unconstitutional.[32] In actual fact, Bennett's opposition to the idea was more pragmatic than legal. Since both he and his cabinet ministers were still convinced that the present crisis would end in a year 'with a bit of luck,' it appeared both easier and cheaper in the short run to give the money needed for relief directly to the provinces and municipalities rather than try to create some sort of new ad hoc federal structure.[33]

Bennett did make one important concession to the demands for national action. In a remarkably comprehensive speech to the House in April, he promised a long-term plan to create a national system of unemployment insurance so that the government would possess the necessary machinery to deal with unemployment on a permanent basis. It was a long-range promise that cost nothing and deflected attention away from the failure of his more celebrated 1930 vow to provide work for all who wanted it. In any case, true to his Methodist upbringing, he still remained convinced that 'following close upon the condition of to-day will come an era of true prosperity, fore-ordained.'[34] Unemployment insurance could wait until then.

In the meantime, his 1931 Relief Act was set to expire on 1 March 1932. Once more the Tory leader gambled that spring would bring an end to his government's increasingly costly connection with unemployment aid. Unlike the previous year, however, Bennett refused to specify in advance how much money his government planned to spend. Despite opposition criticism that he was 'inviting the dole,' the prime minister defended this move as an economy measure. By naming a definite sum in 1930 he believed he had only encouraged a 'contest among the provinces to get ... their share.' Now these governments would have to prepare their programs on the basis of what they really needed rather than what they felt they deserved. In contrast to 1930, Bennett no longer claimed that he had 'more faith ... [than King] ... in the governments who will administer this money.'[35]

The winter of 1931–2 turned this scepticism into utter paranoia. Bennett's 'fore-ordained prosperity' proved to be so much whistling in the dark. The country entered the nadir of the Depression. From 16 per cent at the end of August, the unemployment rate rose almost vertically to 25 per cent by the end of February, the date when the Relief Act was due to expire. It continued to rise, almost unchecked, until March 1933 when it reached the incredible level of 30 per cent.[36] Against this economic collapse Bennett's ad hoc relief policy was reduced to a shambles as provincial governments, particularly in the West, proved incapable of financing the cost of unemployment relief programs which relied primarily on public works. The plight of one unemployed man that winter was typical. 'Since February I have had 3 days of City Relief work as a laborer,' he wrote Bennett in June,

2 days relief work as a laborer on the addition to the local Parliament Buildings earning in Cash $21.60 and also some relief work for the local Poppy Fund which took care of rent and gas bills etc. to the extent of $70.00 which they paid direct. We haven't a cent, are dependent on the City for our food (which *does not* provide proper nourishment for a young family) are 4 months behind with our rent and are apparently up against a blank wall ... Were I alone, I should take my medicine without a whimper, but what of my kiddies? ... Is this what we fought for? that the man who will gladly sink education, experience, pride and everything he values to work in any menial capacity at any return which will provide the necessities of life for his family, food shelter and clothing, cannot, despite super-human efforts, find even that consolation. What kind of a chance are my children to get?[37]

Transients provided the symbolic battleground for the crisis. By September 1931 so many unemployed single men were flowing into British Columbia that Vancouver's chief of police requested Ottawa to establish 'internment camps' at the BC-Alberta border in which to place those removed from the trains. The four western provinces called on Ottawa to assume at least 75 per cent of the cost of transient relief. Bennett rejected both demands. '[T]here is no action we can take to prevent the movement of people from one province to another,' he replied to a Vancouver property-owner's group – words which would later come back to haunt him. Nor could Ottawa take over direct responsibility for transients without violating the 'constitutional rights of the provinces.'[38]

On 4 September, one day after receiving these provincial demands, Bennett did make an important concesssion. In the four western provinces only, his government would pay half the cost of approved municipal relief projects and lend the provincial governments what they needed to make up the difference. If he wanted to preserve his doctrine of provincial responsibility for unemployment, Bennett had little choice for, as his labour minister pointed out, the prairie provinces were 'financially helpless, except with federal aid.'[39]

Bennett was now in a curious position. As BC's finance minister quickly noticed, whether or not the provinces provided adequate relief was solely 'contingent upon the facilities of financing.'[40] In the West, at least, provincial responsibility for the unemployed was now a fiction. As the western governments' last remaining creditor, Ottawa *de facto* if not *de jure* determined the extent to which their unemployed received assistance. Yet the federal government still exercised only nominal control over the way in which the money it provided was spent. This quickly proved to be an untenable and highly embarrassing position.

British Columbia reached almost a fever-pitch of excitement over the transient menace. In response to this anxiety, the Conservative administration of Dr S.F. Tolmie embarked on a massive relief-camp scheme to remove these men along with other unemployed from the cities to remote areas of the province. Confident after 4 September of federal financial backing, his government constructed 237 camps with a capacity to care for 18,340 men. Tolmie announced that he was now 'acting as [Ottawa's] agents on behalf of the municipalities to take care of large numbers of unemployed citizens, transients, single men, etc.' Horrified, Bennett reminded Tolmie that unemployment was a provincial responsibility and that he was 'in no sense acting as agents of [the] Federal Government on behalf of [the] Municipalities or otherwise.'[41]

The warning came too late. Thinking he had access to extensive federal credit, Tolmie spent money on relief camps at a reckless pace. Soon they held 14,912 single men who were paid a subsistence wage of $2.00 a day less 85¢ board and lodging for a six-day work week. This proved expensive enough but, to compound the problem, Tolmie's minister of public works, R.W. Bruhn, indulged in such an orgy of patronage in building the camps that by November the province had spent almost its total federal allotment for provincial and municipal relief works for the entire year. Consequently, relief work ended on 1 December and the $2.00 daily wage was replaced by direct relief of $7.50 a month pending the arrival of fresh funds from Ottawa.[42]

These were not to come. On 21 September Britain abandoned the gold standard and Bennett determined on a policy of the 'most rigid economy.' As he explained to one MP, '[W]e must now talk in thousands where we previously spoke in millions or we will be bankrupt.' He asked Robertson to keep a careful check of BC's expenditures and in October formed a six-member cabinet committee to scrutinize each provincial and municipal relief-work request. He warned the provinces that Ottawa's financial situation had been 'greatly complicated' by Britain's departure from the gold standard 'necessitating [a] complete rearrangement of plans for [the] future.'[43] In effect, loans to finance relief works would have to be curtailed severely. It was not a propitious moment for Tolmie's government to run out of funds.

Throughout December Tolmie's finance and public works ministers pleaded with Bennett for help. They needed at least $500,000 to $600,000 a month to keep the camps going on a relief-work basis as well as a loan of $1 million to pay for municipal relief-work accounts which were shortly coming due. 'Possibly there was a little too much speed shown' in removing the men to the camps, the finance minister admitted, but the government was 'alarmed at the Communistic tendencies' developing in the cities. In any event, 'it was almost impossible to keep these men out of the camps. Everybody demanded a job.'[44]

Bennett was not impressed, especially as his own federal Department of Labour representative in the province warned that Tolmie's government was trying to 'lay the whole blame on the Federal Government' for their failure to provide work.[45] He refused to provide any more money. As a result, the situation in BC became increasingly chaotic. Fifteen thousand single men who had been promised work at $2.00 a day now found themselves collecting direct relief in isolated parts of the province. At the same time, the cities had no money for the relief work programs promised to their married men. Ottawa refused to pay a cent towards the cost of relieving single men who drifted back into the cities from the camps.

Although Tolmie's administration came in for severe criticism, a good deal of provincial anger was directed at Ottawa. The Union of Municipalities of British Columbia claimed that the onus was on Bennett to 'have [the] work relief program as originally presented and agreed to by Senator Robertson put into force.' Angered, Bennett accused the province's finance minister of cheating the municipalities out of their share of federal money. His own government was helpless. 'We have no contact with municipalities and can only look to [the] provinces to discharge their obligations,' he said. The provincial government had already been paid in full and would not receive another cent from Ottawa.[46]

An angry body of unemployed single men left the camps in February to protest their plight in the provincial capital. While passing through Vancouver they staged a hunger march marked by violent confrontations with the police. At almost the same time, the legislature began an inquiry into charges of corruption in the expenditure of provincial relief funds.[47] In British Columbia, Bennett's relief-work program degenerated into violent protests because of incompetent and corrupt provincial administration unchecked by federal supervision. The fact that both governments were Conservative made it even more embarrassing.

Unfortunately, Bennett's problems with relief were not confined to BC. In fact, throughout the winter of 1931–2 only the Conservative governments in Ontario and Nova Scotia and Alberta's UFA government escaped major controversy with Ottawa over relief administration. Next to BC, the worst problem occurred in Quebec. Throughout August, the Liberal government of L.A. Taschereau was engaged in a bitter struggle to secure re-election against a Conservative opposition invigorated by the leadership of Camillien Houde. Taschereau pulled out all the stops in using relief works as a means of buying votes. He won the election but the next month complaints from defeated Tory candidates poured into Ottawa. Known Conservatives had been refused jobs on relief works; municipalities with Tory leanings were starved of funds; three weeks before the election a massive roads program employing 40,000 men had been started and the men threatened with dismissal if they did not vote Liberal; and so on. To continue providing federal funds to the Taschereau government would be 'political suicide,' the Quebec Conservatives claimed. On 15 September Bennett's Quebec caucus of federal MPs demanded that Ottawa assume control of all federal relief money spent in Quebec.[48]

To a certain extent, of course, these charges represented sour grapes – an attempt to pass the blame of defeat on to the federal party. However, the volume of complaints, the fact that they were supported by federal MPs, and the passage of Taschereau's notorious Dillon Act which retroactively precluded the possibility of contesting the election results all suggest that the Liberals in fact had misused relief funds for partisan purposes. Bennett believed this was so but as long as he clung to his doctrine of provincial responsibility for unemployment, there was nothing he could do. 'We cannot humiliate Quebec by treating her differently from the other provinces,' he replied to those suggesting his government should take over administration of relief in that province. Similar problems cropped up in other provinces. Bennett bluntly warned the New Brunswick government to stop political discrimination in its relief works and in Manitoba his interior minister charged that the Liberal-Progressive government of John Bracken was making 'political use ... of the unemployment relief funds.'[49]

Plagued by partisanship, patronage, and incompetent provincial administration, Bennett's 1931 relief program also failed to provide work. In this crucial respect it did not even measure up to its predecessor let alone Bennett's 25 August promise that 'there will be work for all who desire it.' In Ontario, for example, earnings per man over the eight months from September to April averaged $68.00 for a total of fourteen days' work. Corresponding figures for the previous year were $86.00 for twenty-one days' work.[50] What was the problem?

In the first place, unemployment was 6 to 8 per cent higher; consequently, there were more unemployed looking for work. In addition, on 21 September Great Britain went off the gold standard. Since the value of the Canadian dollar was tied to British sterling, the initial effect of this decision was to depreciate it in terms of American currency, thus raising the cost of paying back debts to US creditors. The American money market was a major source of capital for many Canadian cities which had gone heavily into debt during the 1920s in order to finance the ballooning demand for municipal services in a period of rapid population growth. The devalued Canadian currency enormously complicated their efforts to finance the 50 per cent municipal share of unemployment relief.[51]

After three winters of depression, municipal tax collections had fallen drastically, in some cases 40 per cent below normal. Ontario cities had far less money in 1932 to provide jobs for a much greater number of unemployed. In the West, provincial as well as municipal governments faced identical problems with an even greater number of unemployed, a much higher debt, and the sole resource of Ottawa to raise money. Although the four western provinces received $22,431,923 in loans from the federal government, only $4,294,733 of this was for relief works.[52] This was not enough aid to make relief works a feasible policy.

Nor was it close to what they expected to receive. Although Bennett refused to specify a figure in the 1931 act, privately he discussed a $50,000,000 relief work program for that winter. After Britain went off the gold standard, however, this plan was scrapped and the federal government, seriously alarmed at what it perceived to be a major threat to the nation's credit, provided only $28,238,480 – twice as much as the previous year but only half what was originally intended.[53] As a result, the expensive programs initiated by the provinces, especially in the West, were forced to close early in the winter through lack of funds.

Manitoba, Saskatchewan, and British Columbia, the three provinces most dependent on federal financial aid, all blamed Ottawa for their inability to provide work. Had Bennett allowed the Relief Act to expire on 1 March 1932 as planned, the others would have joined in. As one Ontario Tory MP warned, if road work in that province stopped at the end of February, the provincial government would put 'all the blame on us, so if it stops, we will be the target for those thrown out of work.'[54] And this was from a supposedly friendly Conservative administration.

By the time the parliamentary session opened in February 1932 the facile confidence which marked the previous two sessions had evaporated. The government, thoroughly bewildered by Britain's departure from the gold standard, by the failure of its relief and tariff recovery programs, and by the ever-increasing number of unemployed, had no new legislation to offer. Faced with a staggering $160 million deficit and stung by business criticism that his relief work program was now 'holding back normal business development' by endangering the nation's credit, Bennett summed up his sole remaining policy in two words: 'rigid economy.'[55] His first priority from February onwards was to achieve a balanced budget for the new fiscal year through higher taxes and reduced expenditures, especially on relief.

In fact, all signs pointed towards a total abandonment of relief works for a policy of direct relief. Instead of introducing a new Relief Act when the 1931 statute expired, Bennett brought down legislation to extend its term for two more months so that existing relief projects could be carried on until the beginning of spring. Only fears of arousing the wrath of provincial governments and the unemployed prevented him from following his original inclination to close down all relief work at the end of February. Nonetheless, this 'phasing out' process, as the opposition was quick to note, hinted at a major shift in policy along lines urged by some businessmen towards cutting public works expenditure to an 'irreducible minimum' and confining unemployment assistance to direct relief alone.[56]

The Liberals had little to offer in the way of alternatives. King indulged himself in a righteous attack on the blank cheque provisions of Bennett's Relief Act but this constitutional crusade did not represent a different unemployment policy. In this area, King could only repeat his previous recommendation that Bennett appoint an unemployment relief commission of outside experts whose task would be not merely to supervise the expenditure of federal relief money but to find solutions to unemployment. Such a commission would offer Bennett's administration a chance to 'get ... away from partisanship' and to 'throw off ... some of the burdens that are dragging them down.' Faced with a growing split in his own party over how to deal with the Depression, King may well have appreciated the advantages of entrusting this thorny problem to a commission of 'experts' for a few years.[57]

This sense of aimlessness within the House fuelled a growing demand throughout the country that the federal government either introduce new policies for dealing with unemployment or turn the problem over to some commission or organization which could. The two areas in which new federal initiatives were most frequently demanded were unemployment insurance and relief administration. Of the two, unemployment insurance was the more popular. Although it had been pressed upon successive federal governments by organized labour without effect since 1922, the nation's municipalities now added their almost unanimous support to some form of insurance scheme.[58] Pressed to the limits of bankruptcy, municipal governments, backed by an indignant body of middle-class taxpayers, grasped at unemployment insurance as one possible means of lightening the staggering burden of unemployment relief on an ever-shrinking property-tax base. Since the 'dole' was a pervasive and demoralizing reality in all urban communities, previous fears that unemployment insurance would lead to a welfare state now seemed rather pointless.

Pressure was also mounting from the unemployed themselves. Between February and April of 1931 the Workers' Unity League – the industrial arm of the Communist party of Canada during the 1930s – organized a massive campaign for non-contributory unemployment insurance. In effect, this was a national relief minimum to be financed through a levy on appropriations for armaments and stiff taxes on all incomes over $5000 a year. On 23 February 1931 a national day of protest against unemployment was held in cities across Canada. Two months later, on 15 April, Bennett was presented with a monster petition containing 94,169 signatures. It demanded that national non-contributory unemployment insurance be put into effect.[59]

The prime minister, not surprisingly, denounced the idea as sheer confiscation and promised it would never be enacted during his administration. Nevertheless, the following week he did rise in the House of Commons to promise that 'at the earliest possible moment consistent with obtaining information that is essential to make any measure of social insurance worth while' his government would submit unemployment insurance legislation. This information would be contained in the June 1931 census which, for the first time, measured the actual volume and character of unemployment. When these data were processed, Bennett promised, his government would know 'the extent of the obligation we must incur' and could then introduce an actuarially sound scheme of unemployment insurance.[60]

Bennett's April 1931 pledge was of crucial importance in two respects. In the first place, it committed his government to action before seeking a new mandate. Secondly, it made the timing of this action contingent on bureaucratic preparation, not dominion-provincial agreement. Like King, Bennett conceded that any federal scheme of unemployment insurance required provincial assent. Unlike the Liberal leader, however, he did not consider this to be a difficult obstacle. There was 'no reason to doubt that ... some satisfactory solution of this problem can be found,' he assured the House. The main problem, he insisted, was 'the amount of actuarial work which must be done.'[61]

When Parliament met in February 1932, over eight months had elapsed since the taking of the census. With his relief-work policy a failure, many expected that Bennett would announce at least some progress on an unemployment insurance scheme. They were wrong. Bennett received the first report on the census from the Dominion Bureau of Statistics in about February 1932. It was hardly encouraging. On 1 June 1931 approximately 471,000 wage earners, or 18.6 per cent of the labourforce, had been unemployed. Now, the DBS informed him, a 'conservative estimate of the unemployed ... would lie between 600,000 and 700,000.' A few weeks were still needed before a final breakdown of the unemployment data could be completed and the 'possible scope of unemployment insurance in Canada' predicted. Even then, however, 'careful study' would still be required before deciding 'the extent to which it is feasible or desirable.' Moreover, if it were decided to proceed with unemployment insurance, the DBS recommended that any first scheme should be 'experimental' and limited only to those industries where 'continuous employment statistics are available.'[62]

The cautious tone of this report reflected the private doubts of DBS director R.H. Coats as to whether 'any unemployment insurance fund ... could possibly avoid bankruptcy' given the 'continuing decline in prices.' Pessimism from this source only fuelled similar fears in Bennett. Since he worried that railway and relief deficits were already pushing the country towards national bankruptcy, he was unwilling to sanction any new scheme which even if soundly administered would cost the state 'millions of dollars.' In an attempt to stall for time, Bennett resorted to King's arguments from the previous decade by asserting that any federal measure would require 'some constitutional adjustment' and that now was not the proper time to 'call a [dominion-provincial] conference of this character.'[63]

At this point organized labour, the municipalities, and the unemployed provided the major pressure for unemployment insurance. Pressure for reform in relief administration came from a different source. For the past two years Bennett had proceeded on the assumption that unemployment was a temporary emergency; consequently, he had no great interest in fostering the development of a sophisticated bureaucracy for relieving it. He was content to rely on whatever ad hoc structures the municipalities were able to put together. After three years of depression this system was breaking down everywhere and complaints of political discrimination, corruption, incompetence, and cruelty in the distribution of relief were endemic.

'In many larger communities,' a federal government report stated in the fall of 1932, 'there is little doubt of the interplay of municipal politics in the selection of relief staff, in the letting of fuel, grocery, and clothing contracts, in the fixing of relief schedules and procedures, and in the actual granting of relief and work. In the smaller communities, the direct administration of relief to the individual has rested almost entirely with the Councillor for his ward ... In many municipalities, a rough guess was hazarded as to the amount of unemployment relief that should be sought; this was then apportioned in equal amounts to each Councillor who handled its distribution in his ward.'[64] Since the unemployment crisis was widely regarded as temporary, the report went on, relief 'administration was handed to any official or "heeler" who might be "handy."' Staff was recruited from 'the streets or works branches, the police force and the ranks of the unemployed themselves.' As a result, widespread abuse of the unemployed was inevitable:

the overbearing ignorance, abrupt roughness, discourtesy and general lack of consideration with which the unemployed are received in only too many relief offices; the dark, dingy, ramshackle quarters in old firehalls, basements ... etc. into which men and women must crowd and wait, often in long queues, standing against walls, herded indiscriminately; the routine mass treatment accorded the weary, unending, often 'haggard' lines can only darken despair already deep and desolate; can only wear down pride and self-respect already endangered; can only lead to bitter, brooding resentment and determination to 'beat the system' that allows such things. All these are the very concomitants [of unemployment] that rapidly develop pauperism and revolution among those forced to submit to them.'[65]

By the spring of 1932 both Canadian social workers and businessmen were calling for an end to this haphazard approach to the administration of relief. Social workers wanted change because their endurance was strained to the limit by the sheer magnitude of the problem. One Toronto worker reported that January:

[I]n 1930 we thought ... that we were pressed to the uttermost and that we could not possibly drive the staff any harder. Never in our experience have we faced anything to equal this winter. The staff is working literally day and night to deal with the situation ... The District Offices are interviewing anywhere from 50–90 clients daily. The toll on the physical and nervous energy of one's workers, who day in and day out are interviewing 20–30 clients each is appalling ... Month by month the pressure has been heavier and there is no indication of any change. Just how we can go on facing it I do not know.[66]

Although worn out by the crisis, social workers also sensed in it a great opportunity. At the onset of the Depression they possessed little influence in Canadian society, having only organized themselves into a profession in 1926. Now, suddenly, their services were in demand everywhere by governments with no expertise in social welfare. The impending switch in policy from public works to direct relief promised to increase their importance. Their field was 'opening up amazingly throughout the length and breadth of Canada,' as one noted, and they were determined to use this chance to increase their professional status and influence. Relief administration presented that opportunity. The country could not continue 'from month to month unless a very definite long range policy is worked out,' the director of the Canadian Council of Child and Family Welfare realized early in 1932. 'There must be a national policy and as far as the voluntary group is concerned I suppose we should submit it.'[67]

The initiative was seized by a Toronto coalition of businessmen, social workers, and academics who, in the summer of 1931, organized the Unemployment Research Committee of Ontario to 'perform the neglected function of fact-finding and scientific analysis of the facts regarding unemployment in Canada.'[68] That this first sustained attempt at research into unemployment since Ontario's 1916 royal commission emerged from the private sector was itself a commentary on the lack of government leadership at both the federal and provincial levels. It also reflected the fears of businessmen on the committee that without 'some thorough-going piece of research carried on by competent persons' the government might be pressured into a hasty duplication of Britain's unemployment insurance scheme which had driven that country to the verge of bankruptcy.[69]

The committee's first act was to commission Dr Harry Cassidy, a University of Toronto professor, to undertake a survey of relief administration in Ontario since the onset of the Depression. Cassidy was one of the first of a new breed in Canada: the academically trained social policy expert. A tall, handsome man of great energy and mildly leftist political convictions, Cassidy was one of the founding members of the League for Social Reconstruction, an organization that played a crucial role in shaping the thought of the Co-operative Commonwealth Federation after 1932. Born in Vancouver in 1900, he studied at the University of British Columbia before heading south to receive a PH D in economics from the Robert Brookings Graduate School of Economics and Government in Washington, DC. He was then only twenty-six. After teaching at the university level in the United States for two years, he decided to return to Canada in 1929 in order, as he said, to 'play some part in the social engineering that is essential to the development ... of a worthwhile culture.' In that year he became a lecturer at the University of Toronto's School of Social Work.[70]

Cassidy began his project in July and extended his research to cover the operation of the 1931 Relief Act through the winter of 1931–2. Altogether he surveyed the relief practices of Ontario's twelve largest municipalities. Until the publication of the National Employment Commission's final report in 1938, his work represented the only published study of direct relief. It was a devastating indictment of Bennett's unemployment policy.

In brief, Cassidy argued that by holding the municipalities primarily responsible for the care of the jobless, the provincial and federal governments had created a veritable patchwork quilt of aid practices which nowhere provided adequate assistance to the unemployed. Relief-work projects were hastily organized, poorly financed, and, in too many cases, simply wasted the taxpayer's money. Since jobs often rotated arbitrarily, they missed those whose need was greatest and, in any case, there were too few of them. By the winter of 1932 almost as much was being spent on direct relief as on public works in assisting the unemployed.[71]

Standards in this area were equally abysmal. Depending on where they lived, an

Ontario family of five members received from $3.50 to $8.50 per week in direct relief food vouchers. In two-thirds of the cities studied relief officers themselves admitted that these food allowances were inadequate to maintain health. Most municipalities made no attempt to determine what a minimum food budget should be and in no city did Cassidy discover a budget which came even close to existing nutritional guidelines. Toronto's $6.32 weekly food allowance, a subsequent federal study showed, was 'among the more adequate provided by Canadian cities'; yet even it fell 22 per cent below the Ontario Medical Association's recommended minimum adequate diet for a family of five and 52.5 per cent below the nutritional standard set by the League of Nations to prevent deficiency disease.[72]

Neither the province nor the dominion, as noted previously, provided any assistance towards the cost of relief administration; consequently, trained social workers were involved in relief distribution in only four of the cities Cassidy studied. Residence and eligibility requirements varied from town to town (from three months in East York where the unemployed were well organized to twelve months within the City of Toronto itself). Few provided facilities for relieving single men and none aided single women. Consequently, 'existing social policy,' not unemployment, had caused the great increase in transiency as the unmarried jobless had no alternative but to take to the road.[73]

Cassidy held Ottawa's ad hoc unemployment policy directly to blame. By assuming that the Depression was an emergency 'likely to be of brief duration,' Bennett's government had ensured that there was no co-ordination of public and private relief machinery, no national or provincial relief organizations, nor 'even an "intelligence service" which would measure the extent of the problem and offer advice as to what should be done.' As Cassidy wryly noted, '[A]n "emergency" which has already been upon us for the better part of three years cannot be treated as an emergency forever.' The time had come for a 'drastic revision' in federal and provincial policy.[74] Ottawa and the provinces had to end the 'haggling' over which administration was responsible for relief. Well-planned public projects should replace relief works as a means of providing jobs to the unemployed. Direct relief should be accepted for the present as the major means of assisting those out of work but 'standards ... throughout the province with respect to scale of allowances, eligibility rules, residence rules and methods of administration ... [should be] ... uniform,' particularly to ensure that 'food allowances [were] brought up to the minimum requisite for the maintenance of health.' In addition, Cassidy wanted to see the provision of rental and clothing allowances, more recreational and educational facilities, and the use of social service projects to allow the unemployed to 'work ... out relief.' These recommendations might require a 'large increase in relief expenditures,' he conceded, but to skimp in this area now would only lead to the eventual 'deterioration in the quality of our working-class population' and 'huge social service expenditures later on.' 'The most important thing,' he concluded, '[was] the assumption of leadership by the Dominion, or Province, or both.'[75]

Cassidy's study was potentially quite valuable. It represented the only serious analysis of an unemployment relief policy which, it was generally agreed, had failed disastrously in the past two years and which was in the process of being abandoned by the government. Cassidy indicated the reasons for its failure and suggested sensible and workable alternative policies which, if they had been implemented, would have saved both the federal government and the unemployed much grief over the next few years. His analysis and recommendations received support and financial backing from prominent businessmen, which suggests his report was politically acceptable. No less a Conservative party stalwart than W.F. Nickle forwarded an outline of Cassidy's study to Bennett in mid-March 1932, at the very time when the prime minister was searching desperately for a new relief policy. Nickle thought the document was extremely important and might 'if considered and used as a guide, save this country a great deal of money.' He wanted Bennett to have it printed at government expense and sent to provincial and municipal governments as well as to all the other organizations interested in relief problems. A month later, Nickle arranged to have the study sent to Bennett in manuscript form. Because it represented the results of a non-partisan investigation, he pointed out, it would be of 'great value to you by way of giving a lead in public opinion.'[76] Although Bennett promised to read it, it is doubtful whether he did. Nor did he agree to have the study printed and distributed at government expense. By the spring of 1932 the Tory leader was hardly enthusiastic about any suggestions for a 'large increase in relief expenditures.' Instead, in early April, he convened the first dominion-provincial conference on relief since he assumed office in order to achieve exactly the opposite result.

It was no secret that the purpose of this dominion-provincial conference was to ratify a switch in policy from relief work to direct relief – an inevitable result once Britain's departure from the gold standard made the preservation of the nation's credit the major task of the Bennett government. No record was kept of the proceedings. W.A. Gordon, the new minister of labour, informed the House on 28 April that the 'premiers ... were unanimous ... that the provinces ... were financially unable for any length of time to carry on the program of public works projected or to carry on the scheme formulated since the last session of parliament.'[77]

Such unanimity was hardly surprising given Ottawa's refusal to continue to finance the western provinces' share of relief works. Whatever their personal views, the western premiers realized that switching to direct relief was Bennett's minimum price for keeping them solvent. Nor were their eastern counterparts anxious to become wards of the federal government by continuing to increase their debt through public works. One possible solution was a rearrangement of taxing powers, but the circumstances were not conducive to compromise. As Bennett noted, the provinces were 'not in a position to readjust their whole field of taxation and we certainly are not in a position to contemplate the changes that some of them would like us to make.' Another suggestion saw the dominion taking over control completely of direct relief. Gordon ruled this out as 'utterly impossible' because 'the provinces are the only ones who are in touch with their own people and have the machinery set up to distribute the relief that these funds will provide.'[78] So the irony was complete: having won office by promising to 'abolish the dole,' Bennett was forced now to rely on it as the sole remaining unemployment policy of his administration.

The irony did not sit well with the prime minister. With some justification he lashed out at his Liberal critics for 'nagging, nagging, nagging' without proposing constructive alternative policies. Their only suggestion was unemployment insurance and 'what would unemployment insurance mean at this time with unemployment as it is? It would mean the state would pay the insurance, for no one would have the money to pay the premiums.' With less right, however, Bennett attempted to absolve himself from responsibility for resorting to the dole by blaming the provinces. Unemployment relief was their 'duty,' not the dominion's, he argued, and '[they] themselves ... determine how that help shall be given.'[79]

This, of course, was utter nonsense. Since his first Relief Act in 1930, Bennett had determined the relief policies of the provinces by stipulating the circumstances under which dominion aid would be available. The 1932 act was no different. The switch to direct relief, although supported by all provincial premiers, was Bennett's own policy dictated by his determination to preserve the nation's credit 'at whatever sacrifice.'[80] Since most of this sacrifice would come from the unemployed, it made political, if not administrative sense to have other governments responsible for implementing the dole even if, as in the case of the western provinces, most of the money came from Ottawa in the form of loans and subsidies. In this way, responsibility for a certainly harsher policy could be dispersed away from the government which initiated it.

There were, however, two modifications in the 1932 act which indicated a new direction in Bennett's thought. The first was an extension of a policy inaugurated the previous year in which the dominion contributed 50 per cent of the cost of farm placement plans initiated by the Manitoba and Saskatchewan governments. Under these schemes the governments paid $5.00 a month to each single man placed on a farm during the winter months and another $5.00 to the farmer each month for his room and board ($10.00 a month in Saskatchewan). The plan was mildly successful, creating work for 1602 men in Manitoba and 7937 men in Saskatchewan. Under the new legislation this plan was extended to include the two other western provinces as well and the federal government assumed the total cost of the $5.00 monthly wage. Eventually, 10,456 men found work under this expanded scheme during the life of the 1932 act.[81]

More significant was the relief settlement plan negotiated between the provinces and the dominion government during May. Its genesis lay in the offer of the Department of Immigration and Colonization and the railways to recruit settlers from among the unemployed to replace agricultural immigrants who had stopped entering the country with the onset of the Depression. During 1930 and 1931 7406 families moved from the cities and settled the land under the auspices of these agencies. Only families with sufficient capital to begin farming were selected and no financial assistance was provided by the railways or by the government. By the spring of 1932 the department had 'exhausted that class of people'; yet, provincial governments and social workers reported large numbers of people with previous agricultural experience and no capital on relief who would be willing to take up farming once more if given a chance.[82]

W.A. Gordon, who now held both the Immigration and Colonization as well as the Labour portfolio after Robertson's death from overwork early in 1932, wanted to give them this chance. A middle-aged lawyer from Haileybury, Ontario, Gordon was a political novice who was elected for the first time in 1930.[83] He was a political disaster as labour minister. He had no ties whatsoever with the labour movement and absolutely no qualifications for administering the highly sensitive Labour portfolio with its mushrooming responsibilities for unemployment relief. Bennett's decision to combine the departments responsible for agricultural settlement and aid to the unemployed under one minister can only be explained by his growing belief that placing the jobless on the land provided one of the most viable remedies to the unemployment crisis.

The previous spring, Gordon had urged some form of relief settlement scheme on the cabinet with no effect. Bennett was sceptical of the results achieved under the old Soldier Settlement scheme and was wary of involving his government with what he considered to be a costly failure. Gordon, however, insisted that he was not interested in 'any wide scheme of state-aided settlement looking to the relief of unemployment' but only wanted one 'strictly limited to carefully selected families.'[84]

When the relief-work policy was discredited by early winter, Gordon received permission to prepare a feasible plan. He appointed a committee within his own department to work out a scheme and by the end of March 1932 they submitted a proposal. It recommended advancing $600 to carefully selected families on relief who possessed previous agricultural experience and placing them on Canada's 32,700 abandoned farms. The first $200 would be an outright grant to provide for subsistence during the first year. The remaining $400 was a loan at 6 per cent interest for a five-year period beginning after the second year and which was to pay for livestock, equipment, building, or clearing costs. The municipalities, the provinces, and the federal government would split this expense in the usual three-way fashion with the first two governments responsible for the selection of suitable families. They would also be responsible for ensuring that such families were kept off direct relief for at least two years.

The key to the plan's success, the committee argued, lay in regarding it 'primarily as a relief measure and not as a colonization scheme.' The $600 figure itself was derived from the estimated cost of maintaining a family on direct relief in a city for two years and not from any calculation of the amount needed to farm successfully. Moreover, the plan aimed at subsistence, not commercial farming. The object was to 'get ... people back on the land ... where they can ... keep themselves. The question of selling ... their surplus produce will have to come later on,' Gordon noted. Unlike colonization, the success of this plan would be measured by the extent to which it relieved urban relief rolls, not the extent to which successful farms were established, although the committee hoped 'a proportion of permanent settlement will ensue.' Even Gordon confessed that, given present conditions, he was 'at a loss to know whether to-day a man should be on a farm or in a city. [N]o matter where [he] may be ... he is in a very bad way.'[85]

Seen in this light, the relief settlement scheme which was negotiated with all nine provinces in May 1932 was more a confession of despair than a bold new departure in relief policy. Only in contrast to the miserable conditions of urban relief did it offer any hope to the unemployed. On this level, even a socialist such as J.S. Woodsworth could endorse it. Its appeal to the provinces and municipalities was chiefly financial. It could not cost them any more than they were already spending on relief and, consequently, might lighten their load. No one, however, suggested that it offered even a partial solution to unemployment. The most relief settlement promised was a chance of 'helping people to help themselves.'[86] Like the rest of Bennett's policies it was a stop-gap, not a remedy.

By the spring of 1932 Bennett, with the rest of the country, seemed to have struck rock bottom. He had promised to 'abolish the dole.' Now it was his sole relief policy. He had promised to 'end unemployment.' Now it stood at 25 per cent. He had claimed that unemployment was a 'national problem.' Now he maintained that it was a provincial responsibility. He had argued that governments must be held responsible for unemployment. Now he conceded that 'conditions are ... operating in this country ... which we are not able to control.'[87] Although the country had escaped bankruptcy, his administration, it seemed, had not. With the exception of unemployment insurance which he was afraid to pursue because of the country's financial condition, Bennett had no alternatives to offer. He was at the mercy of events.

In large part, Bennett's plight was unavoidable. The previous Liberal administration had left him virtually no legacy on which to build constructive unemployment policies. Indeed, its only contribution had been to terminate most of the Union government's programs connecting Ottawa to unemployment. Furthermore, Bennett assumed with everyone else that he was dealing with a temporary phenomenon and had governed his policies accordingly. He could not foresee that over one-quarter of the labourforce would soon be unemployed. He could not anticipate that his ad hoc relief-work program would quickly be overwhelmed. Finally, he was not responsible for the fact that, when he took office, the nation's social welfare structure owed more to the nineteenth than to the twentieth century.

None the less, the future success of his administration depended on how he responded to these unforeseen developments. The nation looked to Ottawa for leadership in 1930. Two years later its gaze was even more anxious. No one now assumed that unemployment was a temporary problem. There was no longer any excuse for tolerating a ramshackle relief structure or ad hoc federal policies. If for no other reason, growing municipal and provincial insolvency discredited the doctrine that unemployment was not constitutionally a federal responsibility. Ottawa paid for most relief costs in the West regardless of who administered the programs. Under these circumstances, there was little reason for the unemployed to continue to tolerate gross discrimination in the conditions and standards of relief distribution. 'The stubborn facts of the situation,' Harry Cassidy observed, 'will force both the Dominion and the provinces to assume even more responsibility for unemployment in the future than they have in the past, whatever constitutional arguments they may be able to muster in favour of standing aloof.'[88] Bennett's only choice after this spring of 1932 was to exploit or resist this trend of events.

3
The abyss of relief:
Bennett and the Depression, 1932–3

The abandonment of relief work for direct relief was a shattering blow both for Bennett and for the unemployed. Politically it represented the antithesis of everything Bennett had stood for in the 1930 election campaign. Psychologically its impact was even more devastating. Although irregular and inadequate, relief work provided the unemployed with a means of preserving pride and self-respect. The wages were low but not humiliating and useful labour was performed in return. By working on such projects, men could still feel they 'earned' their living; as one MP noted, 'many men who would never ask for direct relief will, without any feelings of humiliation, take a quota of relief work.'[1] Relief work offered the only escape from the stigma of being on the 'dole.' Now only direct relief remained and, as one administrator recalled, it 'was a disgrace. Men would say that never in the history of their family – and they'd usually mention something about the British Empire Loyalists, or coming West with the first CPR trains – never had they had to go on relief. These were men whose families back at the house were without food ... These men, a few told me they had to walk around the block eight or a dozen times before they had the nerve to come in and apply for relief ... I've seen tears in men's eyes, as though they were signing away their manhood, their right to be a husband and sit at the head of the table and carve the roast. It was a very emotional time, that first time when a man came in and went up to the counter.'[2]

The system for distributing direct relief deliberately fostered such humiliation. Until 1932 the majority of recipients were unskilled, casual labourers, many of them immigrants, who had few personal resources and slight hold on their jobs. For both reasons, they were always the first victims of any depression and the first to apply for relief. City governments across the country shared a common fear of 'demoralizing' these labourers by a too generous relief policy. In consequence, relief payments were kept below normal wages for the unskilled, indeed even below what was needed to maintain health and decency, while the distribution system stressed the degradation of accepting the dole.

It did this in a variety of ways. To qualify for relief, families had to submit to humiliating means tests in order to prove that they were absolutely bereft of resources and that their relatives were unable to provide support. In most municipalities driver's permits, licence plates, and liquor permits were confiscated. Bank deposits, insurance policies, and even possession of a telephone or radio could be grounds for disqualification.[3] A.P. Kappele, Hamilton's public welfare commissioner, outlined how the process worked in his city:

On the first visit to the home a history is taken of the case, and a complete survey is made of the home and the quantity of furniture, clothing, supplies, etc. is noted. This information is forwarded to the office and is filed with the family record. The visitor then leaves the orders for supplies to cover a two-week period and makes a notation on the daily report sheet of what was given. This daily report form is very complete and calls for considerable detail, there being eighteen questions that must be answered each visit ... These daily reports are carefully checked each day by the supervisor and are then turned over to three ledger keepers. Each family has a ledger sheet ... This ledger sheet gives the name, age and occupation of each member of the family and records the date and value of everything supplied ... When a member of the family asks for any article, reference to the ledger sheet shows the date of the last time it was given. By this plan the visitor ... know[s] every member of the family and the individual family problems – they find out the wages earned, who is working, in fact by this plan every individual is known personally and the visitor is soon established as a friend of the family ... By the visitor entering the home each two weeks, it was easy to detect fraudulent cases ... [T]hese people ... soon confide in the visitor and reveal all their problems, hoping to and very often receiving help thereby.[4]

In return for this complete surrender of their privacy, most families on the dole could expect to receive relief in the form of food vouchers, not cash, since it was generally conceded, even among social workers themselves, that without greater 'intensive supervision,' relief in kind was far more 'effective and economical ... for that percentage of those dependent on social aid, who cannot be entrusted safely with the freedom of cash relief.'[5]

The food itself was invariably monotonous, high in carbohydrates, low in protein, and always never enough. Montreal's weekly voucher for a family of five, a total of $4.58, was typical (see Table I).[6]

Frequently, the distribution of even these rations was surrounded by shocking pettiness as Margaret McCready, nutritional expert for the Ontario Red Cross, explained:

TABLE I

Food	Quantity	Montreal cost approx.	Mr Russell's estimate	Miss Hiltz's estimate
Milk	13 qt	1.30	0.78	0.78
Tomatoes	3 tins, 6 lb	0.18	0.36	0.33
Potatoes	25 lb	0.25	0.20	0.18¾
Carrots or turnips	4 lb	0.16	0.06	(½ each 0.02½, 0.02½)
Cabbage	2 lb	0.05	0.02	0.02½
Onions	2 lb	0.08	0.05	0.04
Dried beans	1 lb	0.04	0.04	0.03
Dried peas	1 lb	0.06	0.04	0.08
Prunes or figs	1 lb	0.12	0.09	(½ each 0.03¾, 0.06)
Brown bread	10 loaves, 240 oz	0.60	0.60	0.75
Rolled oats or cracked wheat	3 lb	0.15	0.16½	0.15
Flour	2 lb	0.10	0.05	0.05
Rice or barley	2 lb	0.15	0.14	(½ each 0.07, 0.05)
Cheese	1 lb	0.15	0.16	0.16
Chuck roast	3½ lb	0.46	0.28	0.35
Beef or pork liver	½ lb	0.08	0.04	0.05
Butter	1 lb	0.26	0.20	0.21
Peanut butter	½ lb	0.08	0.07	0.06
Shortening	½ lb	0.08	0.05½	0.09
Molasses	1 pt	0.13	0.12	0.12½
Sugar	2 lb	0.10	0.15	0.11
		$4.58	$3.67	$3.84½

In one city with a medical man as mayor one finds the very poorest of relief food allowances, much lower than the government suggested scale. The mayor must have known of their inadequacy ... The poor food allowance was a matter of politics, and playing to the local taxpayers ... A southwestern city in this province in a fertile farming and dairying district, provided for no milk whatever to relief recipients except to infants and the sick ... One Public Welfare Board decreed no tinned tomatoes to be bought on relief orders except in cases of illness – the order then to be signed by the Public Health Nurse. Another Board allowed no butter and no canned goods to their relief recipients. Eggs have been taboo commonly. Even spices and seasonings [have] to be bought by special order only ... Another city has allowed only 25¢ per week for the feeding of an individual in any family over five in number. This is certainly a starvation allowance ... Above one dollar, everything earned is deducted from their food voucher. Naturally there is not much willingness to work.

Across Canada and within Ontario itself, McCready noted, the Red Cross had found 'everything from excessively inadequate to moderately inadequate relief food allowances with only a few that could be called adequate.' Despite this evidence, her own response was all too typical of social work professionals during the Depression. '[T]hose of us working in the capacity of nutritionists *are careful not to encourage dissatisfaction with the existing food allowances* but nonetheless understanding it, in many instances. We have been trying to show how to spend most wisely the amounts received.'[7]

As a final indignity, male heads of families on relief in almost all Canadian cities had to submit to 'work tests' each week in order to prove their genuine willingness to labour. James Gray in *The Winter Years* has eloquently described the effect of this 'boondoggling' on the unemployed themselves:

The closest any of us on relief ever got to socially useful labour was sawing cordwood, but we were drafted periodically for all the makework projects, like raking leaves, picking rock, digging dandelions, and tidying up back lanes ... It was all justified on the grounds that the exercise would be good for us, that working would improve our morale, and that, by providing us with a token opportunity to work for our relief, we would be freed of the stigma of accepting charity. None of these dubious propositions had much validity. The fatuous nature of the projects the authorities invented quickly brought the entire makework concept into disrepute ... No one tried to disguise them or make them into anything except what they were – organized time-wasting.[8]

These practices, which grew up alongside direct relief in most Canadian cities, although degrading, caused relatively little protest as long as they were confined to the unskilled – a class generally believed to lack the Protestant virtues of self-reliance, thrift, and sobriety.

However, the abandonment of relief works in favour of direct relief in the spring of 1932 came at a time when skilled workers and middle-class members of society had exhausted their personal assets after three years of unemployment and Depression. The result was a noticeable change in the type of people coming onto the dole. Applicants for relief, one RCMP officer noted in June, tended now to be 'the refined type, the educated person, men and women who have at some time or other held good positions and social standing.'[9] Yet, if relief standards were raised to meet the expectations of this new class of recipients, even more of the unskilled would be tempted to go on the dole. The situation was fraught with political tension. An RCMP officer noted: 'I have seen men come into the office with tears in their eyes suffering humiliation at being forced to apply for assistance and today the very same men are demanding increases in relief and adopting the attitude that it is their inalienable right to receive relief ... [A]s issued today ... it ... encourages them to develope [sic] socialistic ideas.'[10]

Bennett both feared and failed to understand this situation. To him, as to most

Canadians who never had to rely on public assistance, acceptance of relief meant a surrender of dignity. He could concede that most of the unemployed had lost their jobs through no fault of their own. What he could not accept was that so many, in order to survive, had no alternative but the dole. That hundreds of thousands of Canadians relied on the government for support seemed to him proof not of genuine hardship but of the fact that 'The people are not bearing their share of the load. Half a century ago people would work their way out of their difficulties rather than look to a government to take care of them. The fibre of some of our people has grown softer and they are not willing to turn in and save themselves.'[11] It was an attitude which infuriated Canadian social workers. At a conference on relief policy in April, some members of the profession, disgusted by the spectacle of 'families who had become sick on the miserable relief minima that had been paid,' urged their fellow workers to 'take [a] stand for adequate relief' and 'express their conviction that people could not be kept idle, dragged on the most miserable rations, from day to day.'[12]

Their most influential colleague disagreed. Although better known today for her tempestuous career in Ottawa municipal politics during the 1950s and 1960s, Charlotte Whitton in 1932 was acknowledged as 'one of the most outstanding women of her generation'[13] through her prodigious work in the area of child care. A short, pugnacious woman with fiery red hair, a raspy voice, and indefatigable energy (she was aptly dubbed the 'young cyclone' by one of her friends), Whitton was, without question, the most influential Canadian social worker of her era.

Born in Renfrew, Ontario, in 1896 into a family of modest means, she won scholarships to Queen's University from which she graduated with an outstanding academic record and an MA in 1918. For the rest of her life that institution along with social work, Conservative politics, the Ottawa Valley, and the cause of women would remain her most abiding passions. Whitton entered social work in 1918 when she became secretary to Dr John Shearer of the Social Service Council of Canada and assistant editor of that agency's journal, *Social Welfare*. Convinced that she was 'made of the stuff of a woman who could attempt things in [the] world,' Whitton lost no time moving to the top of her profession. In 1920 she was appointed honorary secretary of the newly formed Canadian Council on Child Welfare, a national federation of social agencies established to promote the development of child welfare programs across Canada. Starting with 'no office and no money,' she transformed the CCCW within six years (and with the help of federal government funding) into Canada's most respected social-work organization. For the remainder of the decade she worked tirelessly, arranging conferences, conducting sweeping research surveys, and publishing reports on the state of child care across the country in order to bring professional standards and prestige to the rapidly expanding field of social welfare. By the end of the 1920s Whitton had succeeded in placing her own network of hand-picked social workers in most of the nation's key private family welfare agencies.

As she once admitted in one of her candid moments, Whitton was driven by a 'desire to dominate and from there dictate.' A sense of 'lurking incompleteness' could drive her 'to the point of sheer temper.'[14] In the field of Canadian social work she found ample scope for both emotions. Even before the Depression struck, she was convinced that the growth of social aid programs such as old-age pensions and mothers' allowances was far outstripping the supply of trained workers who could capably run them. All too frequently, once such legislation was passed, 'a few hectic weeks follow ... "sorting out the plums" or selecting among the crowding hordes, the least unqualified of a miscellany of the faithful for the appointments from the superintendent, director, commissioner, etc. on down to the filing clerk in the inevitable local or district offices, which generally spring to spontaneous growth in areas where the foliage is of the same radiant hue as that of the "party in power." '[15]

As a result of such flagrant patronage in public welfare agencies across Canada, Whitton was hardly surprised when Bennett's first unemployment relief effort collapsed in disarray that spring of 1932. The problem, she wrote the prime minister in April, was not lack of money but rather the way it was being spent. At present, she noted, the provinces and municipalities were packing relief rolls with thousands of indigents who under normal circumstances would not be considered unemployed, simply to get a federal subsidy. In Quebec, relief funds were being distributed according to the 'racial or religious proportions of the population,' not actual need. She pointed to the wide variations in relief expenditure among Canada's six largest cities (from 84¢ per person in Montreal to $6.80 in Winnipeg) as evidence of the need for imposing a 'more rigid schedule of conditions' on the way federal money was spent. And here her profession could help. Social workers had a 'wealth of knowledge in the annual administration of hundreds of thousands of dollars' for social aid, a knowledge that was 'open and ready' for Ottawa's benefit if it seriously wanted to bring relief costs under control.[16]

More than generosity lay behind Whitton's offer. Her outrage over the waste and inefficiency surrounding relief reflected a strong sense of professional alarm at the rapid changes overtaking Canada's welfare structure. Thousands of untrained and frequently patronage-appointed personnel now staffed municipal and provincial relief offices. Unless her profession could somehow gain control of this 'sudden avalanche,' Whitton argued, its future looked bleak. '[The] question ... that has come upon us in Canadian social work today [is] will it survive or be engulfed in popular acceptance of a great corps of personnel, staffing ... the huge public welfare services of this country suddenly come to life and ... never knowing [their] loss of classification as social workers. That has happened in Great Britain to a marked degree. The great public social services are manned by thousands who, proud of their status as civil servants, would not know themselves as social workers.'[17] This threat to their professional status was all the more acute now that investigative casework, the skill on which social workers rested their occupational identity, was being undermined by the sheer volume of applicants for aid.

The abandonment of public works as Bennett's chief form of unemployment aid seemed to offer social workers a golden opportunity for 'professionalizing' the dole. The 'whole aspect' of relief, Whitton argued, had now changed 'from one of ... registration and employment to one primarily of social welfare.' Such a 'changed situation' demanded 'different procedure ... knowledge and experience' and, presumably, different administrators as well. 'Social work has its own technique as have engineering and construction,' she pointed out to Bennett a few months later, 'and the processes and personnel of the one cannot be automatically interchanged with the other without serious mismanagement and loss.'[18]

Coming at a time when Bennett was gravely worried that the ballooning cost of relief might bankrupt the country, Whitton's arguments could not have been more *à propos*. While Cassidy's study with its recommendation for a 'large increase in relief expenditure' was returned unread from the Prime Minister's Office, Whitton was called to a meeting with Bennett in early April 1932 in order to 'talk over' the contents of her memo. A month later she was hired by the federal government to 'work as quietly as possible' on a study of unemployment relief in western Canada, the area of the country hardest hit by the Depression.[19]

After four months of extensive travel throughout the Prairies, Whitton submitted a 200-page report that autumn. Since it was the only detailed unemployment relief study that Bennett ever commissioned during his five years in office, it had enormous influence in conditioning his subsequent response to the Depression – although in ways that Whitton hardly suspected at the time.

Her most startling conclusion from her tour was that almost 40 per cent of those then receiving relief in the West did not really need it. In fact, over the past two years, Bennett's relief work program had succeeded in actually 'raising ... the standard of employment and living of the great volume of the underemployed.'[20] Farmers and their sons, for example, had been employed on relief projects in large numbers 'when there was no actual question of the need of food, fuel, clothing or shelter for themselves and ... when ordinarily the winter was a period of idleness.' In southern Alberta the widespread availability of direct relief had 'arrested ... any natural disintegration' of dying mining communities and 'served to "suspend" them on direct relief.' The same was true of 'dead communities' in the northern fringes of all provinces that had been 'swept back or left behind as settlement moved elsewhere.' The plight of their people was pitiful but it was 'not one deriving from the present emergency' and therefore should not be supported by federal relief.

Jobless women fell into the same category. Their problems arose primarily from desertion, death, and illegitimacy, not from unemployment; therefore they did 'not form a justifiable charge on ... [relief] legislation.' Direct relief was also raising the living standards of unemployed single men and immigrant families. Too many of the former, who could have stayed on farms during the winter, were 'going to the cities where "they could get two good meals and a bed a day on relief" and "have a real rest for the winter."' Immigrant families were receiving 'supplies on a scale neither attained nor desired by these people from their own resources or efforts.'[21] In short, lax standards of administration were allowing thousands of casual workers who were *normally* unemployed six to eight months of the year to 'swarm ... into relief ... on a "year round basis"' and thus raise their standard of living 'beyond anything that they have ever known.'[22]

Whitton concluded that the problem lay with the western municipalities who had neither the incentive nor the expertise to restrict relief to only the genuinely unemployed. Fear of bankruptcy had acted as a deterrent to generosity in the past but now many cities were so hopelessly in debt that there was a real danger they might 'cut loose' from all fiscal restraint in order to avoid social unrest,[23] particularly now that Ottawa was paying such a large share of their costs. More important, municipal administration of relief had subjected it to 'the most contemptible type of local ... politics.' Relief offices were being staffed 'on the ... basis of party preferment' and, as a result, most of the people she found in charge of the dole 'would never be considered by even a small business for any responsible position.'[24]

Not surprisingly, her principal recommendation was to place trained professionals in charge of relief administration throughout the entire country. This had to be made the '*sine qua non* of any continuance of federal aid.' By attaching rigorous conditions to relief grants, demanding 'minimum standards of education, experience and similar qualifications for all appointments in provincial or municipal relief offices,' Ottawa could in effect 'professionalize' the dole, improve its efficiency, and thus reduce its cost. Unlike Cassidy, Whitton counselled against any national minimum of relief itself. This would make the dole too attractive in too many communities. Her object was to tighten up relief administration before the casually unemployed became 'permanently dependent at a scale of living which they never had and never will be able to provide for themselves.'[25]

Whitton's October report with its confused distinctions between 'casual' and 'genuine' unemployment confirmed Bennett's worst fears that widespread abuse of the dole lay behind its escalating cost. This was certainly no coincidence. Exaggerating the extravagance of the present system was Whitton's most effective means of stressing the importance of her profession's administrative skills to the government. However, although her analysis made an impact on Bennett, it was not in the way she hoped. With his suspicions of waste now confirmed by 'the most capable woman engaged in social welfare in the Dominion,'[26] the prime minister still did not believe that forcing the provinces to hire trained social workers was the answer. He opted for a quicker remedy. If the provinces and municipalities were wasting federal money, the solution was simply to give them less money to waste. Rather than spurring him on to exert bold new leadership in the relief field, Whitton's report merely increased his desire to get out of the whole business as soon as possible. By emphasizing the extravagance rather than the suffering surrounding the dole, she destroyed any chance that it might be reformed.

Out of all the recommendations in this 200-page report, Bennett implemented only one. Whitton had warned that there were over 100,000 transients in the West who were beginning to form a 'movement [that] is organizing itself, comparing treatment in different centres, demanding conferences with public bodies, putting forward demands for service and standards and generally becoming a menace to law, order, property and security.' She suggested that Bennett place an 'experienced military administrator' in charge of a system of 'concentration camps' where these men could be put to work under 'semi-military discipline' while being paid a 'small allotment for essentials.'[27] During the autumn of 1932 the federal government followed up on this idea by entering into negotiations with the provinces to establish relief camps for unemployed single men in the West.

The pressure of events, not the cogency of Whitton's arguments, forced Bennett to act. The switch in policy to direct relief provided the main impetus. One of the specific goals of the 1931 Relief Act had been provincial road-building programs designed to draw transients out of urban areas during the winter months. Now that federal funding was no longer available for these projects, the men returned to the cities expecting direct relief. No western provincial or municipal government wished to contemplate this prospect. At the same dominion-provincial conference in April 1932 which ratified the new direct relief policy, the provinces proposed setting up relief camps 'where work could be done ... food and other necessities ... given and some amount of cash subsistence advanced by the dominion and the provinces.' W.A. Gordon, Bennett's labour minister, claimed that he was 'not in disagreement' with such a proposal but, in the end, only the farm-placement scheme emerged from the conference as a solution to the problem of single men.[28]

Throughout the spring and summer, to the growing frustration of the western municipalities, Bennett continued to delay making a decision on relief camps. The local governments had long since denied any responsibility for single men and, in response both to the continued federal refusal to help them with this burden and their own imminent bankruptcy, the mayors of the West's largest municipalities held a conference on 6 July 1932. They produced a new demand that Ottawa assume 'entire responsibility for the administration of direct relief not later than 1 January 1933.' The dominion would pay 65 per cent, the province 25 per cent, and the city only 10 per cent of relief costs under this proposed arrangement.[29]

Perhaps in response to this demand or to Whitton's warning that the 100,000 transients were 'bitter and ready for action,' Bennett finally acted. In mid-July, less than two weeks after the conference of western mayors, the RCMP began to remove transients from the trains. The municipalities were not told why this was happening and, as the men poured into cities at crucial railway junctions, the howls of outraged mayors descended on Ottawa. The RCMP allowed these men to enter their cities. Why were they refusing to let them leave? Bennett replied, for their private information only, that this action had been taken pending a cabinet decision as to 'how and what assistance' should be given to the transients.[30]

He first toyed with the idea of assuming the costs of returning the transients to their original homes where they could legitimately qualify for relief. The railways, however, raised strong objections to this proposal. Most men, they argued, would choose to go to the larger cities and it would be extremely difficult to investigate whether they told the truth about their origins. Meanwhile, the cities 'where the men are so dumped' would put up serious protest. As R.J. Manion, minister of transportation, concluded, there would be a 'great danger of joy-riding on a vast scale, as each municipality will be only too glad to take any opportunity of keeping these men moving.'[31]

With the harvest over and winter fast approaching, something had to be done. Unemployment stood at 28 per cent and was climbing. As a result of financial crisis, large western cities such as Calgary and Edmonton cut off relief to single men after 1 July. This blow, coupled with the RCMP crackdown on railway travel, placed transients in an impossible position. They were trapped in cities which refused to give them assistance. Small wonder that Whitton had noticed the men were beginning to organize to demand better services. By October, Bennett finally conceded that his government would have to 'take some steps to deal with unemployed homeless men so that discipline may be enforced.'[32]

Relief camps seemed the only logical solution. The provinces had suggested them in April; the municipalities had demanded them in August; Whitton had recommended them in her report. So there was a wide consensus in favour of placing single men in camps on a subsistence basis. The only remaining question was whether these camps should be administered by the provincial or by the federal government. To this point Bennett resisted all suggestions that Ottawa take a direct hand in relief administration. When the House of Commons met in early October he again repeated that there could be 'no valid, legal exercise of power by this Parliament in the administration of these matters.'[33] How could an exception be made for single men without puncturing the doctrine of provincial constitutional responsibility? Obviously the provinces would take no initiative without financial assistance from the dominion, but if Ottawa simply handed the money over, what guarantee would it have against a repetition of British Columbia's relief-camp fiasco of the previous winter?

Bennett opted for a compromise. Earlier that summer General Andrew McNaughton, chief of the army General Staff, had been appalled during the course of his travels across the country to discover thousands of unemployed single men roaming the nation. An imaginative, outspoken, and forceful individual with exceptional organizational abilities, McNaughton had practised as an engineer in British Columbia before entering the Canadian army during the First World War. By 1918, at age thirty-one, he was a brigadier-general. Eleven years later 'Andy' McNaughton was chief military adviser to the Canadian government.

The enormous waste of labour and morale embodied in the jobless single men offended McNaughton's sensibility as an engineer. The potential menace they represented to law and order alarmed his instincts as a soldier. If riots broke out it would quite possibly be up to the military to restore peace. Why not instead forestall such unrest and at the same time utilize the men's labour by establishing work camps under the army's control which transients could enter at their own request? In return for labour they would be provided with food, shelter, clothing, and medical care until employment conditions improved.

By 1932 McNaughton had become 'perhaps the most powerful public servant in the country.' He had a close working relationship with Bennett, serving as chief organizer of the Imperial Economic Conference held in Ottawa that summer. He was also the key member of the government's interdepartmental advisory committee on the St Lawrence Seaway. With little scope for his ambitions within the conventional role of a Depression army, McNaughton was anxious to expand that organization's capabilities in new directions. He was also in an excellent position to make suggestions in an area where the government was clearly groping for solutions.

Back in Ottawa in September the general proposed his scheme for work camps to labour minister Gordon, who expressed his interest. Nothing was done, however, for a month. Then, at the opening of Parliament on 6 October, Bennett leaned over to McNaughton and whispered that the cabinet liked his plan and wanted a draft proposal from him for examination by 9:30 AM the following day. McNaughton complied and, on 8 October, PC 2248 made his scheme a reality.[34]

The Department of National Defence camps for the unemployed represented Ottawa's first direct participation in the administration of relief and, in keeping with his cautious approach to the whole question, Bennett wanted this experiment limited initially to only 2000 men. The cost of their care, he informed

McNaughton, should not exceed $1.00 per man per day including food, shelter, clothing, a 20¢ daily 'allowance,' and some part of the overhead involved in their construction projects. On a trial basis, McNaughton proposed restoration work on the Quebec City and Halifax citadels and clearing fields along the proposed route of the Trans-Canada airway. By November, as testimony to the general's organizational abilities, the DND camps were in operation.

McNaughton's camps served only 2000 men in eastern Canada, while the main transient problem was in the West where the municipalities refused to provide any relief for 100,000 single men. To deal with this problem Bennett reluctantly agreed, in late October, to accede to the long-standing western municipal and provincial demand that Ottawa assume 100 per cent of the cost of transient relief. However, as in Saskatchewan where the federal govenment paid the total cost of relief in certain drought-stricken areas, Bennett refused to hand the money directly over to the provinces. He insisted that the four provinces establish commissions composed of provincial residents chosen by Ottawa to supervise the care and feeding of single men. These commissions would operate 'subsistence camps' close to major urban areas to which all single homeless men would be sent. None of the men would be eligible for relief in the cities. The federal government would assume the cost of their care to a limit of 40¢ per man per day and work would be provided 'wherever possible.' Federal funds for these camps were to be 'placed in a separate account ... preferably in a separate bank ... [and] used for no other purpose.'[35]

Although scarcely flattering to their political egos, this offer relieved municipal and provincial leaders of a burden they denied was theirs. Consequently, by late October, they agreed to the proposal subject to two modifications. Apart from sending men into the camps, the commissions should have the option of either placing them on farms at a wage of $5.00 a month to be paid by Ottawa or of turning them over to charitable organizations for urban relief at the rate of $6.00 per month, also to be paid by Ottawa. Although Gordon wanted to see all transients in the camps, he reluctantly agreed to these concessions. At the end of October the total cost of transient relief until 31 July 1933 passed over to Ottawa.[36]

Transients had been Bennett's most pressing problem since the beginning of the Depression. They posed the main threat to public order and represented the weakest link in the federal argument that unemployment was primarily a municipal responsibility. But Bennett's hopes that the relief-camp solution would remove the pressure for direct federal responsibility for unemployment were rudely shattered by an astonishing jump in relief totals between October and November. The cumulative impact of an unemployment rate that had not dropped below 25 per cent in almost a year began to show. The number of individuals receiving relief, which had inched upward from 600,000 in May to almost 900,000 in October, suddenly leaped 28 per cent in one month to 1,114,000. To make matters worse, the price of wheat plummeted to 40¢ a bushel in December, the lowest price ever. Unemployment once more began to rise from 28 per cent in October to an all-time high of 30 per cent by the end of March. By then, roughly 1,500,000 Canadians were receiving relief in some form.[37] The Depression struck rock bottom, destroying any lingering hopes that the Imperial Economic Conference held in Ottawa the previous summer might mark a return to prosperity.

Municipalities across the country bore the brunt of the impact. By the end of the year nearly every large city was funding its relief costs through public borrowing. Yet the incidence of the Depression at this level was grossly uneven. In the Toronto area, for example, taxpayers in Scarborough or East York, where 27-30 per cent of the population was on the dole in 1933, found themselves paying per capita relief costs of $18.00 to $21.00 per year. Yet wealthier suburbs such as Forest Hill or Swansea, where only 5-8 per cent of the population was on relief, faced costs of only $4.00 to $6.00.[38] As John Taylor has noted, the cities' fiscal predicament by 1933 was acute. 'Traditional modes of support, like the private sector, had fallen away and non-traditional ones, like the senior governments, were adamant in their repeated refusal to assume any responsibility. The local governments were alone with their dependents and their bankruptcy.'[39]

The cities' response was to attempt to shift as much of the relief burden as possible from their shoulders by enforcing residency requirements in order to cut down the numbers on the dole. The tragic case of Edward and Rose Bates and their nine-year-old son Jack graphically illustrates the devastating consequences of this policy for one Depression family.

Edward and Rose Bates for years ran a butcher shop in Glidden, Saskatchewan. Early in the Depression the business went under and rather than face the humiliation of applying for relief, Bates sold all his remaining possessions in order to raise the money for one more try in the grocery business in Vancouver. Within months of moving to that city, his new venture failed as well. At this point, having lost everything, he and his wife had no alternative but to apply to the city for relief. They were refused on the grounds that they were not Vancouver citizens. The local Salvation Army volunteered to pay the family's way back to Saskatoon. A former neighbour related the rest of the story in a letter to the prime minister: 'Arriving at Saskatoon the City refused to put them on winter relief but did pay a few days board and room for them, understanding that they would get out of the city and return to Glidden. Hiring a car and selling their last belongings to pay for gas they started for Glidden. Overcome by the shame of returning to Glidden destitute, reports state they decided on a suicide pact by allowing engine gasses [sic] to overcome them. The plan failed although the boy died and the parents attempted other measures to end their lives and failed.'[40] Discovered on the roadside in this condition by the RCMP, Bates and his wife were charged with the murder of their son. The story would simply be another sad Depression vignette were it not for the response of the Glidden townspeople. Before their departure for Vancouver, the Bates were a well-known and well-respected local family. As a result, their neighbours refused to hold them responsible for Jack's death. A community defence fund was started on their behalf and a nearby coroner's jury refused to hand down a verdict of murder in the case. At the same time, the town council held a mass meeting which resulted in resolutions being forwarded to the prime minister. These first blamed the Bates's desperation solely on the Depression, then stated that the dominion government should accept all responsibility for relief and that such relief should be proffered wherever application for it was made so to ' ... avoid any person being placed in a position where they have to be moved long distances before they could secure relief, with no certainty that relief would be granted when they reached their destination.'[41] In the eyes of Glidden it was the Depression, not the Bates, that had murdered their young son and it was R.B. Bennett's unemployment policy, with its insistence on local responsibility for the jobless, which was a direct accomplice.

The deepening unemployment crisis during the winter of 1932–3 forced Bennett to take precipitate action on two fronts. The first was in response to a new crisis in relief financing. The previous year Ottawa had loaned over $4 million to the four western provincial governments to help them pay for their municipalities' share of relief works. One of the main reasons for switching to direct relief in the spring of 1932 was to avoid a repetition of this provincial dependence on federal credit. Unfortunately, the savings anticipated from the new policy quickly disappeared because of the steady increase in those dependent on the dole. By late autumn it was clear that the provincial governments would have to come to Ottawa once more for help. They needed to borrow their own as well as their municipalities' share of relief costs. However much Bennett raged against the fact that people were 'abandoning their sense of self-reliance and imposing too greatly on all the governments of the country,'[42] he realized that he could not allow a single province to default without endangering the credit rating of the dominion in financial circles.

His October decision to assume the total cost of transient relief represented his first response to this crisis but the staggering jump in relief totals the next month made it evident that this was not enough. On 21 November western Labour MP A.A. Heaps introduced a motion in the House calling on the government to appoint a federal commission to investigate the entire unemployment problem including 'jurisdiction as between [the] federal and Provincial governments.'[43] A federal unemployment commission was, of course, Mackenzie King's pet panacea for the

Depression and he and Bennett had debated the idea for the past two years, Bennett insisting it was beyond federal jurisdiction and King arguing that it was not. After three years of Depression, Bennett's insistence that unemployment was a temporary condition began to wear rather thin. Moreover, as both Cassidy's and Whitton's studies demonstrated, there was a growing unwillingness throughout the country to continue tolerating the shocking variation in relief conditions, especially now that over 200,000 families were dependent on the government for survival. Moreover, the inability of the western governments to pay their share of relief costs negated Bennett's argument that constitutionally the problem was their responsibility.

Despite the untenability of his position, Bennett publicly would not abandon his argument that unemployment in any legal sense was 'not a national emergency' and that to appoint a federal unemployment commission was beyond the power of his government.[44] Privately, however, he began to muster non-constitutional arguments to defend his policy of keeping Ottawa at arm's length from unemployment. An anonymous memo prepared in response to Heaps' motion pointed out that in a 'country of such widely varied conditions,' unemployment relief could not be administered 'with any standardized methods across the Dominion.' It had to be 'met on the basis of need existing in each district' and for this reason the municipalities must be allowed to 'adopt different and varying means to cope with the situation.'

In other words, because wage rates and standards of living differed so drastically throughout the country, any move by the federal government to enforce uniform conditions of relief or a 'national minimum' would distort the labour market by making low-paying, intermittent seasonal work less lucrative than relief or, in the language of the 1834 Poor Law Report, 'less eligible' than the dole. Relief must be kept below the living standards available from the worst-paying seasonal or unskilled work 'in each district' in order to prevent people in those areas from preferring the dole. The federal government could not administer one standard of relief in Gloucester, New Brunswick, and another in Toronto, Ontario. Municipal governments could do so; therefore, they must be kept constitutionally responsible for unemployment even though financially they were unable to bear the burden. Regional variations in relief rates were not an unfortunate by-product of Ottawa's policy. They were the reason for it. Any commission or 'general inquiry' into this situation would be 'highly embarrassing' to the provinces and municipalities. 'Comparisons,' the memo pointed out, 'are always odious and dangerous' and in this case might give 'discontented and subversive elements' an 'opportunity ... to attempt to create in the public mind any [sic] feeling of disatisfaction.' Further, 'in these days of easy and rapid communication' the publicity generated by a commission on unemployment relief might penalize relatively generous communities by creating 'an inrush of needy persons from other municipalities where less generous treatment was being accorded.'[45]

A federal commission was out of the question for political, not constitutional reasons. None the less, the sharp rise in relief totals, combined with the worsening unemployment, demanded some federal initiative if only to stem growing criticism that Bennett had lost control of the situation. Consequently, in the same speech in which he rejected Heaps' proposal, Bennett once again promised action on unemployment insurance. He announced that he was calling another dominion-provincial conference early in the new year to determine whether the provinces would agree to a constitutional amendment giving the federal government authority to enact a contributory system of unemployment insurance. Lack of jurisdiction and lack of information prevented his government from acting on this matter earlier, he insisted. In the new year the census department would complete its analysis of the 1931 unemployment figures and work could then begin on a legislative 'skeleton' of an unemployment insurance act. Now, he argued, was time to make a 'satisfactory arrangement' with the provinces in order to remove any constitutional impediments to action once this legislation was ready. Bennett would not say how long it would take to complete the 'skeleton' but he did vow that it would be 'no fault of ours' if the constitutional problem was not cleared up before the end of January 1933.[46]

In fact, Bennett once again used unemployment insurance as a diversionary issue to take public attention away from the real crisis posed by the number of people on relief and by the impending bankruptcy of the western provincial and municipal governments. Paying for the care of the existing unemployed was the single most important issue facing all Canadian governments. Yet, although willing to include questions of relief financing and taxation on the agenda, Bennett insisted that jurisdiction over unemployment insurance be the main topic of discussion at the upcoming conference. Unemployment insurance was an excellent means of dealing with future depressions, but for the provinces and the unemployed the real crisis was current relief. Even Bennett's advisers admitted that unemployment insurance would 'do nothing to meet the present difficulty.'[47] Realizing this, the provinces were hardly willing to cede authority without receiving some concessions in return to help them meet their relief obligations. The magnitude of the dependency problem posed by the Depression inextricably linked together the issues of social insurance, relief, and taxation. One could not be discussed without reference to the others, especially when problems of conflicting jurisdiction were involved.

This was clear to two of Bennett's key advisers, W.C. Clark and Rod Finlayson. Finlayson, a young Winnipeg lawyer, was Bennett's principal speech writer and personal executive assistant. He also co-ordinated the activities of the Prime

Minister's Office. His sharp political judgment and easy access to Bennett gave him a great deal of influence in shaping the government's legislative priorities. Clark, who became deputy minister of finance in 1932, was one of Bennett's most outstanding appointments. A brilliant economist with keen political intelligence, Clark had attended Queen's University along with Bryce Stewart in the pre-war years and had worked closely with Stewart in the development of the Employment Service of Canada in 1919, specializing in unemployment statistics. Like Stewart, he migrated to the United States in the 1920s, where he became a successful investment banker in Chicago and New York. When the Depression struck he was appointed to Herbert Hoover's advisory committee on unemployment before moving back to Canada to take up teaching at Queen's. As deputy minister, he would shape the course of Canadian economic policy for the next two decades.[48]

Neither Finlayson nor Clark was enthusiastic about forcing immediate action on unemployment insurance. To Clark the most pressing issue was to secure a 'major change in policy' over relief financing because of the fiscal crisis in the West.[49] Unemployment insurance threatened to repeat the 'old story of soldier's pension legislation, once you get started there is no end to the pressure for more and more assistance.' Given the present fiscal crisis, now was the least opportune time for assuming any new financial burden. None the less, if Bennett was determined to make this issue the main subject of discussion at the conference, Clark wanted it related directly to relief. '[If] you segregate ... unemployment relief from the insurance scheme,' he advised the prime minister before the conference began, 'you will make it much easier for your provinces to give you the new constitutional powers for which you are asking. To-day they are naturally hesitant about accepting a share in the cost of unemployment relief when the size of that burden is entirely uncertain. If you merely say to them that you will take care of the unemployment insurance programme, but that they must not expect such an insurance programme to do everything, particularly in the initial stages and in times of unprecedented depression, they will, I think, be prepared to accept the major responsibility which they now have for unemployment relief.'[50]

Finlayson offered identical advice. He too was unhappy with Bennett's decision to make unemployment insurance the most important topic on the agenda. 'Calling the Conference,' he warned, '... implied that it is with a view to action being taken to put unemployment insurance into effect.'[51] He and Clark both knew, however, that Bennett made virtually no preparations. Even the census material on unemployment would be unavailable until 10 January, only one week before the conference was to begin. Bennett could not expect the provinces to hand him a constitutional *carte blanche* to proceed with unemployment insurance without any knowledge of what such a scheme would imply. Yet no one in the federal government had any concrete information or plan. The dominion superintendent of insurance, although personally favourable to the principle of social insurance, could make no positive recommendations because of the 'lack of adequate volume of data regarding unemployment in this country' and of the 'overwhelming moral hazard arising from the indisposition of a minority of people to work.' Until the uncertainties presented by these two problems were cleared up, there was no way of knowing whether unemployment insurance could be administered in Canada on an 'actuarial basis.'[52]

Finlayson argued that Bennett must be prepared to place a 'definite plan of action' before the provinces if he wanted their consent to a constitutional amendment. Unemployment insurance at present was 'fraught with such dangers' to the country's credit standing abroad that its enactment simply had to be preceded by a royal commission investigation directed by the 'best minds available in Canada or elsewhere before committing the country to any definite plan.' If Bennett placed this proposal before the provinces, then perhaps they would agree to 'leave the Dominion Government free to act upon the report of the Commission, and obtain without further reference to the Provinces such constitutional amendments as may be required.' If they did agree and if the federal government assumed 'total responsibility' for unemployment insurance and at the same time greatly expanded its relief-camp scheme for single men, then 'it would help to escape the charge that it has accepted a policy of dole.' Moreover, once Ottawa accepted complete responsibility for unemployment insurance and the problem of single men and introduced a new program of federal public works, 'the administration of direct relief could then be entirely decentralized and its responsibility relegated to the provinces.'[53]

Although wary about rushing too quickly into an unemployment insurance scheme, both Finlayson and Clark agreed with their prime minister about its long-term political potential as a means of extracting Ottawa from the morass of relief. They hoped that the federal government, by accepting this new responsibility, could rid itself of its more onerous involvement with the dole.

Some businessmen had also begun to see unemployment insurance in a new, more favourable light because of the appalling inefficiency and wastefulness of direct relief, although recent claims that businessmen provided the major impetus behind this reform are certainly exaggerated.[54] In fact, Canada's business community was badly divided over the issue. As one recent study has shown, the overwhelming proportion of business communications with Bennett before the 1933 dominion-provincial conference were hostile to the idea of unemployment insurance. Canadian manufacturers, represented by the Canadian Manufacturers Association, produced the most vocal opposition. Such a scheme, they maintained, would increase their costs of production, erode the work ethic, and impede labour mobility throughout the country,[55] all arguments familiar from the 1920s. In effect, unemployment insurance would increase unemployment, Stelco president Ross McMaster stated, by ' encouraging idleness instead of spreading work by the levelling of wages to a point which stimulates production.'[56]

But a significant minority of businessmen, especially in banking, finance, and real estate, responded to Bennett's announcement of a conference on unemployment insurance with cautious enthusiasm. Vancouver's Board of Trade cabled its unanimous endorsement of the idea three days before Bennett's 22 November speech. In their view, the waste and inefficiency in the existing relief set-up already cost the country more than any possible insurance scheme. Thomas Bradshaw, a Toronto insurance industry spokesman and president of North American Life, told Bennett that, given 'intelligent leadership,' a system of unemployment insurance could be created on 'reasonable and sound principles.' He offered the assistance of his industry to help enact a plan that would 'safeguard the interests of the country.' Finally, Canadian Chamber of Commerce president and textile magnate A.O. Dawson assured the prime minister that his organization was 'very anxious to assist the Government and to ... lead the thought of businessmen of Canada along the lines followed by our premier.' Like Bradshaw, he gave cautious approval to unemployment insurance but urged Bennett to 'move very slowly' on the matter.[57]

As relief increasingly threatened the solvency of municipal and provincial governments, their banking and insurance industry creditors came to see unemployment insurance as a more rational means of financing the cost of future depressions. Real estate spokesmen, viewing the effects of relief on property taxes, came to the same conclusion. In a nation with 30 per cent of its labourforce unemployed, some form of job insurance seemed inevitable. In the eyes of business leaders like Bradshaw and Dawson, this very inevitability made it essential that businessmen exercise leadership in the early stages of investigation to ensure that in its final form the legislation would not repeat the British fiasco of the 1920s. Consequently, they added their voices to Finlayson's in urging the formation of an independent commission of 'experts' to scrutinize the entire question before any action on it was taken. In short, by 1933, although by no means in the forefront of the campaign, some important businessmen were willing to support Bennett's tentative moves towards unemployment insurance provided, as Dawson said, he reached no 'hasty conclusions.'

Despite this modest encouragement and continued pressure from business, organized labour, and the municipalities, Bennett's chances of securing provincial approval for the necessary constitutional amendment were slim. Given the lack of preparation within the federal government and the demand from business and from within the government itself for a royal commission investigation to precede definite federal commitment, the provinces felt no immediate need to amend the constitution.

The real crisis in dominion-provincial relations lay in relief financing. Two weeks before the conference began, the four western provinces stressed this fact by presenting Ottawa with a united demand that the federal government accept both the cost of financing the municipalities and their own share of relief. Canadian banks refused further credit and neither the British nor the American bond markets looked favourably on western Canadian flotations. Then, in mid-December, finance minister Edgar Rhodes also refused to extend them any more federal credit. In desperation they warned Bennett that 'unless funds are provided from some source immediately, [the] only alternative is to discontinue relief.'[58] This issue, not unemployment insurance, was the one that required action at the upcoming conference.

Nevertheless, federal officials remained inflexible. Clark, although willing to admit their financial dilemma, argued that to continue indefinitely financing western provincial relief would result in 'abominable ... waste and inefficiency.' He suggested a tough approach. The banks should force them to take 'a more realistic attitude in regard to their present financial position.' Belt-tightening, although politically unpopular, was the only solution to the problem. Insolvent provinces had to 'commit themselves to some definite programme for putting their financial houses in order in the very near future.'[59]

Even before the conference began, then, the federal government and the provinces were working at cross purposes. With Ottawa unyielding over relief financing and the provinces unable to see the urgency for unemployment insurance and tampering with the constitution, the conference was doomed to fail. Bennett's behaviour ensured that it did.

The conference convened on 17 January 1933. The western provinces opened the gathering by suggesting that Ottawa take over a larger share of relief costs. Bennett and labour minister Gordon would have nothing to do with this proposal. Already too many people were living off the dole because 'sufficient emphasis was not being placed upon the responsibility of the individual to maintain himself,' Gordon claimed. If Ottawa took over more of the relief burden and the cities were 'charged with little or no cost, administration will be without restraint.' Instead, the labour minister suggested, 'the land offers the best prospect for maintenance and independence of those who cannot find employment in the cities.'[60]

Having so dismissed the relief issue, Bennett and Gordon next turned to unemployment insurance with an even more insulting proposal. The prime minister not only wanted to know if the provinces would surrender jurisdiction on the matter but also how much they were prepared to contribute towards such a scheme. Had Ottawa any idea of the cost? Quebec's Premier Taschereau asked. 'No plan has been formulated,' Bennett replied. '[T]he question was what percentage the provinces would be prepared to contribute and then the Dominion would have to deal with the problem.' Bennett was either unbelievably arrogant or wanted deliberately to sabotage the proposal. He certainly did not help matters by admitting that 'all forms of social insurance were largely incompatible with the spirit of freedom' or by arguing that the only reason for proceeding with unemployment insurance was to honour Canada's commitments to the Versailles Treaty, 'however lightly they might have been entered into.'[61]

Not surprisingly, both Ontario and Quebec refused consent to a constitutional amendment on these terms. This suited Bennett fine. As Grant Dexter of the *Winnipeg Free Press* observed: 'On unemployment insurance, without doubt, he hoped that Taschereau and others representing the provinces would baulk [sic] at the transference of jurisdiction, thus enabling him to drop the policy without unpleasant political consequences. In this regard, therefore, he was not only willing but eager to concede the provinces the right to veto constitutional amendments.'[62] For Bennett the 1933 dominion-provincial conference was a success. It provided a convenient excuse to bury the potentially embarrassing unemployment insurance issue and it warned the provinces not to expect any increased federal financial help.

As a solution to the crisis in relief financing, however, the conference was a disaster. Although unemployment now stood at 30 per cent and almost a million-and-a-half people were on relief, Bennett refused to believe that the financial plight of the western provinces was beyond their control. Belt-tightening, retrenchment, and other fiscal catchwords might save some dollars but the fact remained that, for the past two years, the four western provinces had fallen over $13 million short of meeting their own $21 million share of relief costs and over $38 million short of meeting their total expenditures.[63] Only last-minute federal loans had rescued them from bankruptcy and the Depression promised no release from this financial stranglehold. Yet the conference produced no remedy as Ottawa refused to offer any more aid.

Bennett announced his new policy in a letter to the four western premiers on 9 March 1933. In effect it was an ultimatum. Noting that there was as yet little evidence to indicate that the western provinces were making a whole-hearted attempt to place themselves in a 'position of self-reliance,' the prime minister warned that any future request for federal financial assistance would be considered only if the province concerned pledged itself to present a balanced budget in the upcoming fiscal year through increasing taxation and reducing expenditures. If this was totally impossible, then Ottawa would tolerate a deficit of no more than $1 million. Otherwise, the province would have to place all its future expenditures under the supervision of a financial controller acceptable to Ottawa before receiving any federal loans. The new policy was harsh but 'obviously some limit [had to] be placed upon western borrowings from the Dominion,' Bennett concluded.[64]

This hard-line approach stemmed from two factors. The first was the federal government's own fiscal crisis – a $156 million deficit over the past year brought about by a combination of declining revenues and ballooning costs of relief and the debt-burdened railways. To remedy this situation, Ottawa drastically slashed expenditures and raised corporate and personal income taxes to achieve a balanced budget (exclusive of relief costs) for the next fiscal year. Bennett's 9 March ultimatum was his way of forcing the western provincial governments to do the same.

Second, this blunt threat reflected a growing sentiment in Bennett's cabinet that the western provinces were postponing unpleasant political decisions by borrowing from Ottawa. In effect, they were using the spectre of default to hold the federal government for ransom instead of, to use Clark's phrase, 'putting their financial houses in order.' This goal could be achieved only by getting people off relief. Federal ministers such as W.A. Gordon were firmly convinced that one of the most fundamental causes of the Depression was the 'decidedly disproportionate situation with respect to our urban and rural population.'[65] The relief-settlement, relief-camp, and farm-placement schemes initiated by the federal government over the past two years represented the one consistent theme in Bennett's unemployment policy – the necessity of forcing the excess urban population 'back to the land.' Yet to date these schemes had achieved only meagre results while the numbers receiving direct relief in the cities continued to spiral upwards.

If Whitton's 1932 report on unemployment in western Canada were accurate, loose relief administration was actually attracting people from the country to the cities. Unless the western provinces planned to be forever dependent on Ottawa, this trend had to be reversed. As Gordon warned the House, only with the 'gradual turn towards other vocations than those which have afforded a certain sense of security to our people in the past' could relief be phased out. The federal government had to encourage the provinces to force their people back to the land where they could become 'self-sustaining.' Despite perceptive criticism from Labour MP Angus MacInnis that such a policy represented an attempt to create a Canadian 'peasantry' that would 'form a labour reserve to be called upon at a time when working conditions in the cities improve,'[66] 'back to the land' became the Bennett government's only long-range solution to the relief crisis.

The western provinces understandably were outraged by Bennett's intrusion on their fiscal autonomy but, under the circumstances, they had little choice but to go along. As Bennett's comptroller of the Treasury Watson Sellar pointed out after a two-week tour of the four provinces in early April, their budgets were 'balanced on Hope.' Interest on their respective provincial debts alone would absorb 55.7 per cent of Manitoba's, 42.7 per cent of Saskatchewan's, and 38.5 per cent of British Columbia's total anticipated revenue during 1932–3. These provinces had made a 'real effort' to cut expenses, Sellar conceded, but any savings were eaten up by increased interest charges. Any new federal loans should thus be 'wisely treated as grants.'

Despite this sympathetic analysis, Sellar was unable to offer any constructive solution for the western provincial fiscal crisis. Placing a federal controller over provincial finances, as Bennett had threatened, would be a 'thankless task' since it would drag Ottawa into controversial areas such as education policy, a particularly sensitive issue in the West. Yet to adopt the provincial solution of providing federal loans to finance relief would be to invite disaster. ' If money became too easily available to the Province, pressure would be taken off the municipalities,' with the inevitable result that the numbers on relief would increase.

Faced with these two alternatives, Sellar could only recommend a continuation of the present policy of indirectly controlling both provincial expenditures and the unemployed by maintaining maximum fiscal pressure from Ottawa. Relief scales should be reduced, a limit should be placed on federal contributions, and first priority in any future provincial borrowings should be given to repaying existing federal loans. No new federal loans for relief purposes should be contemplated. Sellar admitted that his suggestions were 'arbitrary' and might endanger the solvency of the municipalities. He also conceded that the present provincial pledges to balance their budgets were based on expectations of rising revenues which might not materialize. But he justified his conclusion by arguing that the federal government had to 'preserve its resources until the maturities of 1933 and 1934 are arranged.'[67] Ottawa's refunding plans and the necessity of keeping a tight rein on the unemployed took precedence over finding a permanent solution to the fiscal disaster overtaking the West. Like a good accountant assessing an investment prospect, Sellar protected the interests of his client. However, he did not provide an answer as to how the insolvent western provinces could continue to pay for relief without substantial federal help.

One month after Sellar completed his report, Manitoba fell victim to his tough recommendations. The province was over $100 million in debt; it owed over the same amount to Winnipeg, which had not received its share of relief costs from the provincial government since May 1932; and it had been cut off further credit by the Royal Bank. Already 55.5 per cent of its current revenue was needed to pay interest charges on its debt. The province expected to run a deficit of over a million-and-a-half dollars on current expenditures for the upcoming fiscal year and, together with its municipalities, would fall $4,649,000 short of meeting the cost of unemployment relief. It had only three choices: to borrow the difference from the dominion at a low interest rate; to float a new bond issue at the abnormally high rate of 6½ per cent; or to default on interest altogether and use existing revenue only to pay for relief and essential services.[68]

The Progressive-Liberal government's first request for a federal loan was rebuffed with the argument that Ottawa already had loaned more money to Manitoba proportionately than to any other province. What followed during the first two weeks of June was an elaborate poker game between federal and provincial officials. Premier John Bracken insisted that his province would default before borrowing money at 6½ per cent on the bond market and that public opinion in his province would support him. Why, he asked, should Manitoba lock itself even deeper into long-term debt at abnormally high interest rates when Ottawa could borrow the necessary money at 4 per cent to tide the province over this emergency period?

Ottawa replied that the dominion had its own very large refunding program scheduled for the fall which might be jeopardized by continued loans to the provinces. The federal government was not responsible for the fact that Manitoba had to pay such high interest for its money. In the end the provincial premier's bluff was called. The federal government would loan the money only on condition that Bracken sign a statement declaring that his government would default without it. If he could get the money anywhere else 'at any rate' there would be no federal loan.[69] Bracken must decide either to float a bond issue at 6½ per cent or to default deliberately. Ottawa would provide no financial help until the province was unconditionally insolvent. Within the space of six months, when the Depression was at its nadir, Bennett's government not only rejected western proposals for solving their staggering financial problems and refused to consider increasing Ottawa's share of direct relief from one-third to one-half but it also refused to loan the provinces their own share of relief costs on easy terms.

To the *Winnipeg Free Press* the issue was clear. By telling Manitoba to borrow 'at any rate,' Ottawa ignored the special burden of the Depression on the West and in effect told the West to 'stagger along as best it can.'[70] At bottom the issue proved more complex. To federal officials, easing the burden of western municipalities and provinces 'did not result in a shifting of the burden from the ultimate taxpayer ... consequently, there was the utmost need of impressing upon the municipalities that relief must be curtailed and the fact brought home to the individual that responsibility for caring for himself and his dependents devolved solely upon himself.' Ottawa's intransigence on loans was an indirect means of forcing western governments to reduce the numbers on relief. Yet as Bracken pointed out in pleading for his loan, 'We have been threatened with riot if we did not increase relief. What would it be if we cut relief?'[71] This was the crux of the matter. To Ottawa, reducing the relief rolls was financially essential. To the western premiers it was politically impossible. As long as the two levels of government continued to respond to different pressures, there could be no solution to the relief crisis.

This deadlock over relief financing was symptomatic of a broader paralysis which gripped the country's political institutions after four years of Depression. There was no longer any talk of a 'temporary emergency,' but permanent solutions seemed in short supply. Conservative unemployment policy was now reduced to three essentials: maintaining law and order, forcing as many unemployed as possible out of the cities and back to the land, and preserving the country's credit rating.

For their part, the Liberals had little to offer in opposition. In an effort to appease inflationist sentiment within his party and to counter the potential threat of a new socialist party, the Cooperative Commonwealth Federation, Mackenzie King endorsed the concept of a central bank to regulate the nation's currency and credit. In a sense this did move the Liberals closer to the idea of central economic planning to combat depression but other statements by King during the 1933 session left grave doubts that the Liberal leader had learned anything from the economic collapse. His continued call for a national unemployment commission had been reduced to a version of the Patriotic Fund that supervised relief to dependents of war veterans during the First World War. The goal was to ensure closer federal supervision of relief expenditures, not to direct federal administration of relief or to investigate unemployment. Relief recipients throughout the country must have been surprised to learn that Bennett was indulging in an 'orgy of public expenditure' on their behalf. Nor could they find much hope in King's analysis that the Depression was the result of human greed which could be remedied by a return to the principles of the Sermon on the Mount. And they most certainly must have found his call for a balanced budget hard to reconcile with his argument that the state should provide work for all those able to work.[72] The Liberals were as bewildered by the Depression as the Conservatives and had as little to offer in the way of solutions.

As for the Ginger Group of left-leaning farmer and labour MPs, although able to offer penetrating critiques of Bennett's relief policies, they seemed divided over whether inflation or socialism was the answer to the Depression. Moreover, their inability to agree on whether to support the 1933 Relief Act did not augur well for the success of the new CCF which they were in the process of forming.[73]

Only two developments in 1933 held any promise of change. The first was the dramatic achievements of the new American president, Franklin Delano Roosevelt, in his first one hundred days in office. The second was the move to centralize responsibility for single homeless men under the auspices of the Department of National Defence. Both would greatly affect Bennett's final years as prime minister.

The Department of National Defence relief camps represent one of the most tragic and puzzling episodes of the Depression in Canada. They also provide a useful subject in comparative history. Both the Canadian and American federal governments initiated large-scale programs to care for the single unemployed at approximately the same time – July 1933 – and through essentially the same method – relief camps run by their defence departments.

While the American scheme, the Civilian Conservation Corps, initially provoked opposition from forestry groups and organized labour, the Canadian relief-camp experiment began with almost universal praise from trade unions, the social-work profession, the press, Parliament, and local governments.[74] The Winnipeg *Tribune*'s description of a camp for draining swamps at Lac Seul made the whole operation sound like an expensive resort.

The camps provide just such an outing as a young man's heart should long for – an outdoor life, as a man among men; plenty of time for sport, and plenty of sport at hand; an allowance sufficient for tobacco money and little comforts; work enough to keep the young men alert and interested, but not overdone, and tempered to their physical fitness; and a clean, pleasant, cheerful camp life. Those who have visited the camps say the young men already there could not be induced to leave by anything less than the prospect of a really good job at good wages. They are enjoying life to the full, and work more eagerly than well paid workmen ... [P]rovision is being made for winter sports – hockey, curling, snowshoeing, skiing, as well as for the fishing, swimming, and other sports available in the summer months ... [S]o far there has been no evidence of any desire to depart. On the contrary, the boys are writing their unemployed friends to 'come on in.'[75]

Within two years, however, the CCC was widely recognized as Roosevelt's most popular New Deal program while the DND 'slave camps,' as they came to be called, symbolized everything wrong with Bennett's approach to the Depression and eventually provoked the most violent episode of the decade, the On-to-Ottawa Trek, which culminated in the Regina Riot. Why was this so? Why did such similar methods of caring for the single unemployed produce such starkly contrasting results in the United States and Canada?

The success of the American relief-camp scheme and the failure of its Canadian counterpart can be traced to two related factors: the different nature of the single unemployed problem in the two countries and the difference in purpose behind the two schemes. The single man, as noted previously, played a much greater role in the Canadian than in the American economy in the years immediately prior to the Depression, a reflection of the much greater importance of seasonal, resource-extractive industry in this country. Because of this fact, Canadian immigration policy had been geared to importing large numbers of mostly single unskilled labourers from Britain, Europe, and the US to work on the nation's farms, in its mines, its lumber camps, and its railways.

By contrast, the US closed its doors to most unskilled workers after the First World War. Even during the so-called roaring Twenties, unemployment among this group had bedevilled Canadian governments and, when the Depression struck, the staple resources industries in which they worked (mining excepted) were the hardest hit. From 1930 onwards, therefore, Canada faced an unemployment problem which was not only proportionately more concentrated on single men than that in the US but which was also concentrated more heavily on recent immigrants. Both factors made the single unemployed a more menacing political phenomenon to Canadian than to American governments.

As a result, the provincial and federal governments in Canada very quickly developed programs for dealing with this group. The early emphasis on provincial road-building projects from 1930 to 1932 represented one attempt to draw the single men out of the cities by using the state as a substitute for private enterprise. When these projects proved too expensive, the farm-placement scheme and provincial relief camps operated by single-man commissions – both completely funded by Ottawa after 1932 – were substituted to deal with the problem in the West where it was most acute. During the winter of 1932–3, when the single unemployed in the US were still completely at the mercy of private charity, the Canadian federal government was paying the costs of caring for over 46,000 men.[76] Even before relief camps became the sole responsibility of the Defence Department in 1933, they had become a natural state substitute for the bush camps which had played such a large role in the Canadian economy.

This difference in the nature of the problem produced a corresponding difference in the purpose behind Canadian and American relief-camp schemes. The CCC, as its name implies, was related to a specific problem – conservation – and aimed at a specific group – unemployed, unmarried youths between the ages of eighteen and twenty-five. It was one of the few New Deal programs pledged by Roosevelt during the 1932 election campaign and it expressed his lifelong interest in reforestation and conservation. As most New Deal historians agree, resource management represented the one consistent theme in an otherwise bewildering series of New Deal schemes. This clear sense of purpose which emanated directly from the president permeated the entire CCC organization and contributed greatly to its success. As one Canadian external affairs analyst noted at the time, the CCC's greatest strength flowed from its 'practical fulfillment of William James's idea of providing a moral equivalent for war.' Recruits 'enlisted' for six months at a time, served under oath, wore uniforms, lived in army tents, and in general were subjected to 'quasi-military discipline enforced by the military personnel.'[77]

This resort to military discipline (often complained of but seldom actually present in the Canadian camps) was possible because the CCC was confined to an age group susceptible to idealism and generally considered to be in need of discipline and sense of purpose, and because it was directed at a cause that enjoyed widespread public support. As well, to ensure that CCC workers received a genuine sense of fulfilment from their work, $20.00 to $25.00 a month out of their $1.00 a day pay was allotted to their families. CCC recruits enjoyed the dual satisfaction of working for their parents as well as for their country. By concentrating on two popular social problems – conservation and youth (or, perhaps most important, the conservation *of* youth) – the CCC struck a genuinely responsive chord in the hearts of most Americans. At the same time, it removed a potentially dangerous class of unemployed youths from the nation's cities in a way that always seemed incidental to the main purpose. Small wonder then that the communists made little headway in Roosevelt's relief camps.

The contrast with the Canadian DND scheme could hardly be more striking. Unlike the CCC with its concentration on the emotionally charged problems of conservation and youth, the motives behind the creation of Canada's Defence Department relief camps were far more prosaic and, in the end, contradictory. Basically they were designed to serve four conflicting goals. The first was jurisdictional. We have seen how the mobility of the single unemployed caused contention among the three levels of government as to which authority was responsibile for their relief. Although Ottawa finally assumed the total costs of caring for this group in the West in the fall of 1932, this solution pleased no one. It did not solve the problem in the eastern provinces; it did not resolve who was responsible for interprovincial transients; it left the federal government to pay the total cost of programs it could not administer. By the spring of 1933 social workers, provincial governments, and federal officials pressed for centralized control of the single unemployed problem under one federal department.[77] As a Defence Department memo explained, 'from the surveys which were carried out it was clear that the problem of ... single homeless men could not be dealt with adequately either municipally or Provincially. Uniform action throughout Canada was needed so that there would be no inducement to the men ... to wander about the country in search of more favourable treatment.'[78] The Defence Department acceptance of this role was not a new policy so much as the final step in a three-year process which saw the federal government reluctantly accept responsibility for transients.

Moreover, the DND camps were designed to serve the economic function of removing single men from the urban labour market and thus reserving existing jobs for married men with dependents.[79] In this sense, the economic rationale for the camps was essentially negative – to restrict competition for jobs rather than to create necessary employment. The Defence Department's policy manual upheld this hardheaded approach by defining the 'primary purpose' of the camps to be 'the care of the maximum numbers possible of single homeless transients with the funds which have been made available, with a view to their return to the economic life of the Country ... at the earliest date that conditions permit. Incidentally, in order to justify the care which is being given by providing some return to the Country for the money expended and to command support for increases in the number to be looked after, it is important that as much useful work as possible be executed.'[80] The relief camps in short were just that – camps designed to provide relief, not to construct needed public works. They were holding operations whose essential economic function was to keep the single unemployed in limbo until the Depression ended and, if possible, to repay the cost of their care through a minimal amount of work.

Ironically, the third aim of the camps was to preserve the work ethic. Unlike their American counterparts, Canadian homeless men, especially in the West, had been receiving relief through government-funded hostels and subsistence relief camps operated by the provinces. As a result, by 1932 federal officials fretted that a 'dole mentality was creeping into the minds of the single unemployed' and that many had 'acquired the mental attitude that such assistance from the State was their inherent right.' Consequently, the camps had a 'moral purpose' to remedy this 'state of mind diseased by the demoralizing effect of compulsory idleness' by subjecting single men to the influence of 'steady work, wholesome food and congenial surroundings.' The camps were an attempt to reimpose a work test on the single unemployed. As W.A. Gordon noted, '[I]f the ... usefulness of this large number of men [was] to be preserved,' it was 'essential' to demand that 'work ... be performed by those in receipt of relief from the State.'[81]

Finally, the camps served an overriding political objective which was never lost on their sponsor, General Andrew McNaughton. 'By taking the men out ... of the cities we were removing the active elements on which the "red" agitators could play.' Without relief camps, the general argued, it was 'only a question of time until we had to resort to arms to restore and maintain order.' Bennett's chief adviser, Rod Finlayson, agreed. The 'main objective' of the camps, in his view, was to 'keep urban centres clear from such single men as more readily become amenable to the designs of agitators.' On this point at least the government and the communists agreed.[82]

In sum, what separated the CCC from the DND relief camps was the former's assumption that work was a means to an end. In a society which could no longer offer the reward of economic gain or potential self-advancement, the CCC offered work for a cause which had high social prestige as well as support for one's family. By so investing its work with meaning, the CCC offered its recruits an opportunity to preserve their individual self-respect and minimized their potential for rebellion.

Canada's relief camps, in contrast, offered work only for the sake of work or, at the very least, work for the barest means of personal subsistence. Projects were only 'incidentally' of public value and there were no wages, only a 20¢ daily 'allowance' which was kept ridiculously low in order to 'encourage' the men to 'return to normal industry as soon as opportunity offers.'[83] The camps were little more than a 'workhouse test' designed to enforce the nineteenth-century Poor Law principle of 'less eligibility' on single men. With no government-sponsored facilities for education and recreation (one internal Defence Department memo boasted that 'not one cent of public money has been spent ... on reading material and recreational equipment'), the camps offered only sheer physical survival to the men living in them. To the men working on farms for $5.00 a month, they stood as a constant reminder that the state would offer no free hand-outs. While seeming to solve problems of political and social discipline for the government, the camps offered nothing to the men themselves. As one resident noted, '[Y]ou come in broke, work all winter and still you are broke. It looks like they want to keep us bums all our lives.'[84]

Lacking the economic incentive of a 'stake' which had made the hard work, primitive conditions and isolation of the bush camp endurable to past generations of 'bunkhouse men,' the relief camps, unlike the CCC, ultimately debased the work ethic they were intended to preserve. One veteran of the system even years later could recall the distinction clearly:

Down the line the CCC ... did good work ... because they paid their guys and had decent leaders and discipline that made sense but you know what, I think down there a guy, well he didn't mind working in a camp. They had pride, they gave their guys pride. Parks built, dams built, roads a fellow could drive over years later and say to his wife, 'I helped build this road' just like a guy could take his wife to Europe and drive through a little French town and say 'I helped liberate this town.' But in Canada not on your blinking life. It was 'get those dogs off the street before they offend the people' ... Everything about those camps was wrong, but the thing most wrong was they treated us like dirt. And we weren't. We were up against it, broke, tired, hungry, but we were farm boys who knew how to work ... We were slaves. What else would you call a man who is given twenty cents a day and is expected to believe their bullshit that he is an important part of the country. They just wanted us out of sight, as far out of sight as they could manage.[85]

It was this kind of contradiction which made the camps such a fertile breeding-ground for unrest. As one of their inhabitants noted in his diary, '[I]t is not only the conditions ... that make us get up and howl for something to be done about our state. It is really the fact that we are getting no place in the plan of life – we are truly a lost legion of youth – rotting away for want of being offered an outlet for our energies. Something to do and something for that doing.' Relief camps, he observed, brought out 'the worst that is in you ... If you ever thought of committing suicide, you might choose a worse place, but not a better instigator.'[86]

The camps did not even solve the basic jurisdictional question of who was responsible for transients, the issue which had bedevilled dominion-provincial relations since the beginning of the Depression. If anything, they only exacerbated it. The problem arose from McNaughton's insistence that the DND camps would only accept responsibility for physically fit single men. All those who were unfit, who became ill in the camps, who were discharged for insubordination, or who left voluntarily were a provincial responsibility. The care of single men was still primarily a provincial concern. The Defence Department was only assisting the provinces in this duty by employing those fit enough to work on specially selected projects.[87]

This narrow definition of responsibility enraged the western provinces. Under the 1932 Relief Act the cost of caring for all transients to a maximum of 40¢ per man per day had been assumed by the dominion. Now Ottawa claimed it would pay only for those in the DND camps while leaving the provinces with half the cost of caring for those who remained outside, for whatever reason. As one provincial official complained, '[I]t looks as if the Dominion were going to hand pick the men for the camps and leave everyone who can't handle a pick and shovel on our hands.'[88]

The western provinces refused to play this way. British Columbia charged that too many men were being discharged from the federal camps for 'trivial reasons' while Alberta simply claimed that those accepted into the DND camps became a permanent federal responsibility unless they became ill. Both refused to accept responsibility for those who left or were thrown out for insurbordination. To provide these men with relief would only encourage those still in the camps to 'leave of their own accord,' while convicting them of vagrancy would be legally difficult and politically unpopular.[89] Moreover, in both cases the provinces would be saddled with the cost of caring for men whom they had always felt were an exclusive federal problem.

Despite continual public assurances by the Defence Department that there was 'no compulsion for a man either to enter or to remain in a camp,' both levels of government realized that the only way to keep men working at 20¢ a day was to jail those who left. Simply denying them relief outside the camps was not enough deterrent since, as BC's labour minister noted, they could not be allowed to starve without becoming a 'menace to the community.' Large numbers of men who left a camp on strike, one DND commander warned, 'could by publicly parading their condition and grievances, *put the wind up* local authorities, who would be bound to weaken on the *stand pat* policy [of no relief].'[90]

To deal with this contingency, McNaughton drew up an emergency plan in case the problem of strikers got out of hand. In early April 1933, he suggested that it might be necessary for the federal government to establish 'camps of discipline' – in effect, concentration camps – to deal with 'incorrigible' and 'dangerous agitators.' Once legal assurances were received that such disciplinary camps would indeed be within the federal government's authority to ensure 'peace, order and good government,' a draft order-in-council was drawn up in June. Under its terms, the minister of defence was given the power to establish 'camps of discipline' outside of towns and cities across Canada where all unemployed, physically fit, single men who either 'unreasonably refused to accept employment on [relief] works' or who, once in the DND camps, 'unreasonably refused to perform the duties required of them,' could be sent. He was also granted 'complete administrative power over such camps and the persons detained therein ... including the infliction and remission of penalties, and the remission of terms of detention.' Men convicted of 'unreasonably' refusing work could be confined in the camps of discipline for 'not less than fourteen ...and not more than sixty days.' In every case, a certificate from the relief-camp commander was the only '*prima facie* evidence' needed to determine that a man's conduct merited imprisonment.[91]

Once the order-in-council was drafted, McNaughton asked his district officers to begin considering 'where and how these camps will be established in the event of necessity.' They should be equipped to hold approximately 100 men each, the general noted, and should be made up of 'separate mechanically locked rooms for each person.' Within the camps, a rule of silence would prevail. Communication would be allowed only 'to persons under detention ... who have earned the necessary marks for good conduct, which they can do at the end of 14 days.' Anyone guilty of misconduct would 'lose the privilege of communicating.' Old Fort Henry in Kingston seemed to McNaughton an ideal site for such a camp, but it would 'probably be necessary to enclose the whole Fort with barbed wire entanglements.' Of one thing the general was convinced. '[N]o man who serves a term in such a camp,' he assured British Columbia's labour minister, 'will want to enter it again.'[92]

Throughout the winter of 1933–4, as the Communist-organized Relief Project Workers Union became increasingly successful in organizing strikes, walk-outs, and protests within British Columbia camps, the provincial government became more insistent that Ottawa should immediately establish camps of discipline in order to deal with a situation that was 'becoming acute.' The 'number of agitators in BC is small,' provincial officials pointed out, 'but [they] ... are of a particularly dangerous type.' McNaughton remained sceptical. From his perspective, men dismissed from the DND camps for insubordination were as yet receiving only 'trivial punishments' at the hands of provincial governments. British Columbia's request for the creation of camps of discipline was simply an attempt by that government to 'evade' its 'proper constitutional responsibilities.' Bennett's government thus refused to act. Detention camps, Gordon wired back to the province, would be established 'only as a last resort' because their implementation 'virtually means that your Province is either unable or is failing to administer the law.'[93]

At bottom, neither level of government wanted to take the political responsibility for jailing men whose only crime was unemployment and neither wanted to admit in principle that the care of single, homeless men was primarily its concern. The result was stalemate. The western provinces continued to insist that Ottawa establish camps of discipline, while federal officials demanded that provincial governments enforce their vagrancy laws.[94] Single men outside the camps remained in a state of legal limbo and the communists obtained a perfect issue for playing off one level of government against the other. This situation would bear bitter fruit during the relief camp strikes of 1935.

However flawed in their conception, the camps represented the only new initiative undertaken by Bennett's administration on the unemployment front in 1933. In this sense, W.A. Gordon correctly called them the 'one bright and constructive measure' carried out during his term of office.[95] The remainder of Bennett's social policy for that year was simply a continuation of his attempt to tighten up provincial relief administration. It was a hopeless task. By December 1933 over 1,225,000 people were still on the dole and unemployment hovered at 25 per cent of the labourforce. The prime minister's attempt to limit federal expenditures under the 1933 Relief Act to $20 million failed miserably. Instead, Ottawa spent more than $42 million caring for the unemployed during the fiscal year 1933–4. As Charlotte Whitton noted, costs were now rising faster than the increase in those on the dole because families entering their third and fourth winters on relief were 'absolutely bereft of resources.'[96]

Despite these gloomy statistics, Whitton noted in November that 'the tendency [in Ottawa] is all to optimism and ... the belief that the participation of the federal power may not be required much longer.' Convinced that the widespread existence of urban relief itself was attracting an unskilled seasonal and rural labourforce into the cities, Bennett determined to find some way of severing Ottawa's connection with the dole at the first opportunity. All he required was some sign that the economy was beginning to recover. It was a dangerous gambit. As Whitton warned, the 'patience and hope [of people] entering the fourth winter of gnawing misery ... is slowly disintegrating, and there are signs that its collapse, once begun, may be sudden and overpowering.'[97] The attempt at reform might prove too little and too late.

4

The attempt at reform: Bennett and the Depression, 1934–5

Since the spring of 1932 Bennett's administration had drifted almost helplessly. Only crisis situations – the threat from organized single men and the potential default of the western provincial governments – had provoked any significant extensions of federal power and in both cases the response reinforced, not reformed, existing policies. Federal relief camps were established not only to control transients but also to ease financial pressure on provincial governments. At the same time, federal loans to the western provinces were designed to prevent bankruptcies that would not only threaten the nation's credit standing in international money markets but would also compromise the dominion doctrine of local responsibility for the unemployed. By the beginning of 1934 these policies were clearly no longer tenable. Pressure for change came from the dynamic example of Roosevelt's New Deal, from public dissatisfaction with the local administration of direct relief, and from the prospect of a general election.

During the first three years of the Depression Bennett's unemployment policies, although limited to supplementing local relief efforts with federal funds, seemed more responsive to the plight of the unemployed than those of the American president, Herbert Hoover, who categorically refused to provide any federal money for direct relief. With Roosevelt's accession to office in March 1933 this favourable comparison changed. Although Roosevelt's National Industrial Recovery and Agricultural Adjustment Acts received much speculative comment in Canada, it was his public works program which, as Bennett's chief adviser conceded, was 'so much now in discussion.'[1] From Washington in January 1934 Bennett's brother-in-law, W.D. Herridge, agreed: '[W]e must do something even if it involves ... taking a chance ... [T]he issue before the government is employment and the government's worth will be decided by its capacity to deal effectively with it ... We cannot dodge the issue. We should not wish to do so. My belief is that, therefore, we should raise it ourselves.' Herridge proposed a comprehensive but 'financially sound' program of public works large enough to 'do no more than ... cut the present unemployment in two.' Otherwise, Bennett's 'laissez-faire' policy would 'assuredly ... prove to be the tombstone of the present government.'[2]

The prime minister conceded that the New Deal 'would profoundly affect Canada' because of its 'geographical location.' For Bennett, however, this was a truly frightening prospect. Roosevelt in his eyes was conducting a 'greater revolution ... in the United States during the last few months than was accomplished by Lenin and Stalin in Russia.' For once he and Mackenzie King agreed. The Liberal leader also confessed that the president's 'mad desire to bring about State control & interference beyond all bounds makes one shudder.'[3]

Whatever their private reservations, neither party leader could deny the enormous impact of the American president's first hundred days in office on Canadian public opinion. The United States now embarked on a massive project to provide jobs through public works. England was in the midst of completely overhauling its system of unemployment insurance. Only Canada seemed committed to fighting the worst industrial depression in modern times with an antiquated system of poor relief whose inherent contradictions, tolerable on a short-term basis, were becoming increasingly irrational after four years of collapse.

To counter some of this pressure, Bennett did promise construction industry spokesmen in November 1933 that, given signs of continued economic improvement, his government would embark on a 'reasonable policy of public works' in the spring. In the same month his office received draft copies of England's new unemployment insurance act and, in addition, asked Arthur Steel-Maitland, who was the minister responsible for the measure in the Baldwin government during the 1920s, to lecture Canadian businessmen on its virtues during a late autumn tour of the country.[4]

But the most insistent demands for change centred on relief. In January 1934 Bank of Montreal president Sir Charles Gordon warned Bennett that the present method of financing the dole was eroding municipal, provincial, and even national credit. Cities and provinces were borrowing so much for relief that attempts at refunding or new capital investment were becoming impossible. To Gordon the conclusion was obvious. Canada now faced the 'urgent desirability of invoking some system of unemployment insurance,' if only 'for our general self-preservation ... [and] ... if it can be done soon, so much the better.'[5]

More important to social workers like Harry Cassidy was the fact that the dole eroded self-respect. Direct relief actually 'breeds the very conditions it seeks to relieve – it generates poverty and pauperism,' Cassidy wrote in an article that same month. Since complete destitution was the one key qualification for the dole, the system 'penalizes the thrifty workman, for it denies him aid until his savings and property are exhausted; while it gives relief promptly after loss of his job to the man who was careless with his wages while he was at work. It protects and sustains only the very lowest standards of living, not those to which workmen of the better type were accustomed. Thus it denies the worthy and rewards the unworthy – with results that are not hard to imagine.'[6]

Even Charlotte Whitton, who had so far used her influence to keep the Canadian Council on Child and Family Welfare from direct criticism of Bennett's unemployment policy, confessed to a growing 'sense of futility and frustration' at Ottawa's continued indifference to the chaotic state of a relief system administered by over 4000 municipalities. There was a 'great deal of worry, anxiety and restlessness,' she stated early in 1934, not only among social workers and the unemployed but 'among many of the bigger financial groups' as well over the failure of Bennett's government to show any leadership on this issue.[7]

But while most social workers agreed that any attempt at reforming the dole presupposed a 'much greater degree of Dominion participation and control' than in the past, there was less consensus on the purpose of this leadership. To those on the left, such as Leonard Marsh and Harry Cassidy, a stronger federal presence was essential simply to make relief 'as adequate and as fair as possible.'[8] In their view, municipal administration of the dole had led to partisanship, discrimination, and a shocking disregard for the health and welfare of the unemployed by the most financially beleaguered unit of government. Nowhere was this neglect more glaring than over the plight of unemployed single women, a politically powerless group whose problems were ignored by all levels of government throughout the 1930s. As one of their number pointed out to the prime minister during one of his infrequent interviews with the unemployed:

[We] have very little to eat and ... have no clothing what [sic] you might say at all ... The conditions under which we are living compel a girl that she must be classed as a prostitute because she cannot get the things she needs. They put you in a room and you have to take it ... You are forced to go into a dirty, dilapidated room, where there is no heat ... [W]e are allowed a very small allowance for food. It is not enough to keep us three days, let alone a week. We are not living, we are just getting along. A young girl wants to be respectable. She cannot go on the street with no clothes or looking miserable and terrible. She would sooner stay in her room. She has nothing to look forward to.[9]

Whitton took a very different approach to the relief crisis, however. In two draft memos sent to Bennett's office in early January, she argued that the principal victim of municipal control of direct relief was not the unemployed but the taxpayer. Distribution of unemployment relief had been left to 'the unit of government most susceptible to direct political control and manœuvre.' Because of their four- to five-year terms of office, provincial and federal governments had a 'comparative freedom from direct pressure from the electorate' which allowed for a certain 'continuity of policy.' Municipal governments, in contrast, had their mandates renewed every twelve months and thus were 'directly accessible to local influence.' The result, as one relief administrator complained, was that cities such as Calgary, where labour exerted a strong political influence on the city hall and thus maintained a high level of relief, were 'giving us all a lead which the unemployed cannot be blamed for urging we should follow and which 50% of the members of our City of Winnipeg Council are trying hard to catch up and pass.'[10]

Multiplied across the country, this 'wide open' system of municipal relief administration actually 'penalize[d] the province or municipality which attempt[ed] to set up efficient and scientific control' while encouraging 'loose organization and lavish expenditure.' Even more ominously, according to Whitton, this system also penalized the low-paid seasonal worker because in many Canadian cities a man on relief with a family of small children was 'really far better off than the low paid wage earner in the same situation, with uncertainty and insecurity of wages. Especially is this true with the appearance of cash relief, which wipes out the last distinction between the family on relief and the struggling low paid wage earner's family, except that the latter, of course, enjoys the privilege of taxation for the former.' As a result, it was 'not surprising that there is a growing tendency to seek relief and to stay on it over an increasing period of time. The system has bonussed such developments.'[11]

To remedy this situation, Whitton returned to her 1932 solution: the social work profession, operating through independent provincial commissions or a provincial government department, must be given control of relief. The federal government could compel this change by attaching strict 'scientific' conditions of administration to future relief grants – conditions defined and implemented by professional experts. In return for this federal support, the profession would provide more efficient relief administration – for governments, not the unemployed. Unlike Cassidy, she specifically ruled out any attempt to define national standards of eligibility or allowances, as this might 'imply a right to relief.'[12]

To emphasize the importance of her argument, Whitton made two other points which raised a storm of controversy within her own organization. The first denigrated the utility of unemployment insurance. Such a scheme would 'remove very few persons from the direct relief lists' and even in the best of times would not 'provide social protection against the casually employed – always and even at the present our heaviest unemployment relief load.' Her message was clear. A national unemployment insurance system was no answer to the unemployment problem. To create one without first rationalizing relief would invite a repetition of the British experience of the 1920s. The pressure from the uninsured majority on poor relief to receive benefits equivalent to those enjoyed by an insured élite would in the end bankrupt the scheme.[13] Second, Whitton argued that Ottawa could reform the relief system from above without assuming any permanent responsibility for the problem. The Dominion Bureau of Statistics, she pointed out, now knew that unemployment between 1920 and 1930 averaged 'somewhere between 12% and 13%.' This could safely be regarded as a normal unemployment burden, 'the costs of which must be met by each province within provincial and municipal resources.' Only when the number of jobless exceeded this 'average unemployment incidence' should Ottawa contribute to relief. During such periods, the federal government could attach strict administrative conditions to its relief grants while at the same time it preserved its argument that dominion participation was only justified 'on an emergency basis.'[14]

Tom Moore, president of the Trades and Labour Congress and labour's representative on the CCC&FW governing board, was incensed at Whitton's memo because she had left the 'strong impression' that unemployment insurance was of 'very little real benefit' and because she suggested that Ottawa was responsible for the jobless 'only ... in case[s] of extreme emergency and ... only for definitely limited periods.' He pointed out that this policy had been opposed by all provincial and municipal governments in the West and ran counter to the 'strong feeling throughout the country that both employment and unemployment should become more and more centralized in federal authority.'[15]

Leonard Marsh and Harry Cassidy voiced identical complaints. While both agreed with Whitton on the urgency for reform in relief administration, they also echoed Moore's opinion that her memo might 'be taken as justification for delaying action on public works and unemployment insurance,' measures which they believed held more potential for relieving the major burden of unemployment in the future. Moreover, both men took serious exception to Whitton's argument that federal participation in relief should be limited to emergency periods. As Cassidy noted cryptically, 'Isn't the point to stress that the emergency method of attack should be discarded?' In assigning responsibility for relief, the real question was not whether unemployment averaged 12–13% in normal times but rather whether the provinces and municipalities had, in the long run, the 'capacity to pay' for it. The Depression proved they could not without pushing their expenditures 'beyond reasonable limits.' For this reason, Cassidy wanted 'Dominion power in this field, permanently.'[16]

Whitton made only token attempts to meet this criticism from Moore, Cassidy, and Marsh in the published version of her memo which appeared in early March. Unemployment insurance received a minor role as a means of meeting the future costs of unemployment and she clung to her argument that Ottawa should contribute to relief costs only when unemployment rose above an agreed-upon 'average unemployment incidence.' Her essential message remained unchanged. Relief administration had to be placed in the hands of social workers before an unemployment insurance or public-works program was launched if the perils of the British experience were to be avoided. Paradoxically, the federal government was expected to initiate these permanent reforms while limiting its own contribution to 'emergency periods'[17]

When Whitton first proposed her arguments for major federal relief reforms in 1932, Bennett rejected them all except for one recommendation which dealt with an immediate problem – the establishment of federal relief camps for single men. In the same way he now accepted only the suggestion which offered what he wanted – the proposal of an acceptable level of unemployment. In early January, after conferring with Whitton, his adviser Rod Finlayson asked R.H. Coats, head of the DBS, to devise an average incidence of unemployment for the 1920s in order to establish 'the point at which the Provinces and Municipalities might again undertake direct relief without assistance from the Dominion.'[18] Finlayson also wanted a forecast of when this period might be reached.

Exactly as Cassidy warned, federal officials were more interested in avoiding relief altogether through the implementation of an 'average unemployment incidence' than in reform. Moreover, Whitton's main argument that the present 'lavish' administration of relief wasted the taxpayers' money and lured people on to the dole confirmed Bennett's view that federal participation in itself was responsible for loosening the bonds of fiscal restraint among the local governments. Despite the cogency of her argument that relief administration had to be 'professionalized' and subjected to principles of 'scientific' control, Whitton could provide no convincing reason why this reform should be initiated by federal rather than provincial officials since she accepted Bennett's central premise that Ottawa had only an 'emergency' responsibility for unemployment. Ironically, the only effect of her memos was to strengthen Bennett's desire to extricate Ottawa completely from relief – the very development they were destined to prevent.

In mid-January 1934 the prime minister called another dominion-provincial conference on unemployment. Ostensibly its purpose was to find some solution to the relief crisis. How should the dole be financed now that four provincial governments and many more municipalities staved off bankruptcy only through federal loans? How could some sense of order and uniformity be imposed on a system administered by over 4000 city councils? Quebec's Premier Taschereau suggested removing relief totally from the hands of the municipalities and financing it equally between the provinces and the dominion. This idea was rejected by labour minister W.A. Gordon. Already too many people were developing the attitude that the 'state owed them a living.' If the cities were relieved of their share of the relief burden, he argued, 'those unemployed would increase in numbers. To keep these numbers down, the essential thing, responsibility, should rest first on the individual and secondly on the municipalities; even if at times this might result ... in individual hardship.' Taschereau's proposal implied that 'the care of the unemployed was a social service which devolved upon the Federal Government' – something federal officials could not accept.[19]

But if the care of the unemployed was to remain in municipal and provincial hands, how was it to be financed? By the end of the fiscal year the four western provinces would fall over $13 million short of meeting their necessary expenditures. Only last-minute federal loans saved them from defaulting earlier and they now owed Ottawa almost $51.5 million.[20] The real question facing the conference, Grant Dexter of the *Winnipeg Free Press* observed, was whether Bennett would continue to 'undertake the job of financial guarantor of the provinces.' The correspondent predicted a 'show-down.' Opposition to Bennett's position that provincial and dominion credit was 'indivisible' was building among a 'very powerful' group of cabinet ministers including Rhodes, Cahan, Gordon, and Guthrie. Bennett had secured their approval to the last series of loans only with the 'greatest difficulty' and Dexter noted that this group now demanded 'that there be no more loans unless the provinces accept federal supervision and control.' For their part, the four western provinces were 'in no mood to argue about this' and would 'just as soon default as go on.' The result, Dexter thought, would be some 'serious fighting.'[21]

He was right. Perhaps to appease the cabinet opposition, Bennett had considered placing the western provinces under the control of three-man commissions responsible to Ottawa but had rejected this idea as politically unfeasible.[22] Now he swung to the other extreme. When the conference opened, Gordon shocked the provincial delegates by informing them that Ottawa would withdraw totally from direct relief in the spring. At that time, it would launch a program of 'useful' public works and relief would be 'restored to the municipalities.' While the eastern premiers with the exception of Taschereau greeted this news with mixed feelings, their western counterparts exploded. Alberta premier J.E. Brownlee, head of a beleaguered and aging United Farmers of Alberta government, argued the case most succinctly. Given the high cost of relief, the low price of wheat, and their 'primitive state of development,' the western provincial governments had no choice but to appeal to Ottawa for aid. The easiest and most popular alternative was default but that 'might put them in the position of South American states, with no capital market available for future development. Further, their default might threaten the financial future of the whole country. Therefore ...

their financial problem could be reduced to this: they must get assistance from the only source where they could get it – the Federal Government – or else default. No other alternatives were possible.'

Bennett would not agree. The West was 'living too expensively.' Could it really afford four separate legislatures? Could it not discontinue expensive public services such as old-age pensions, telephones, and electric power which 'were suitable and within means of old established communities but which were ... difficult to justify in new ones'? Did the premiers not realize that the 'same body of taxpayers' bore the cost of relief whether it was financed by the municipalities, the provinces, or the dominion? Finally, would the continued use of federal credit to preserve provincial financial integrity 'not lead to a situation in which the dole was accepted as a fixed policy?'

There were no answers possible to such politically outrageous questions. Western voters would choose default invariably before sacrificing public telephones, electric power, pensions, or their own legislative autonomy. 'Fixed policy' or not, both the dole and federal loans must continue until 'existing conditions' improved – or so claimed British Columbia's newly-elected premier, Thomas 'Duff' Pattullo. The conference ended in stalemate. Bennett did not retract his proposal to withdraw all federal support of relief in the spring nor would he give any pledge to continue providing financial support for provincial credit. 'The problem,' he candidly concluded, 'was simply – could the Dominion take the risk to its credit caused by the default of a province or provinces or should the federal government remove this risk by financial assistance?'[23] For Bennett, at least, the endless complications that relief had created for dominion-provincial relations had been reduced to this one simple question.

Between March and July he struggled for an answer with the reformer from British Columbia, Duff Pattullo. Pattullo was one of the most colourful and certainly the most creative of Canada's Depression premiers. Born in Woodstock, Ontario, in 1873 into a well-known Liberal family, he worked as a journalist in neighbouring Galt before migrating west in the 1890s Yukon gold rush. He did not strike gold but, thanks to his family's political connections, he did become the Yukon's gold commissioner, noted throughout Dawson City for his snappy grey fedora and white flannel suits. After running a brokerage firm in Dawson for a number of years, Pattullo moved to Prince Rupert, BC, where he soon followed his father's footsteps by becoming first the town's mayor and then its representative in the provincial legislature. Throughout the 1920s he worked effectively as minister of lands in three Liberal administrations, acquiring an excellent reputation for conservation planning and political organization.

Pattullo was a gambler and optimist by nature (his favourite Presbyterian hymn was 'Dare to be a Daniel') and a fiercely proud British Columbian who was convinced that 'the West understands the East better than the East understands the West.' He was also one of the first prominent Canadian politicians to advocate massive deficit spending as a solution to the Depression. During the 1933 provincial election Pattullo campaigned boldly for an $800 million national 'work and wages' program to put the jobless back on their feet. Ottawa, he argued, should initiate a $200 million public works program on its own and, in addition, issue $600 million in non-interest-bearing securities which it could then loan to the provinces to finance their own job-creation schemes. Pattullo also called for immediate adoption of state unemployment and health insurance and a comprehensive system of old-age pensions to guarantee everyone an 'existence as far above the sustenance line as we can achieve.' 'If you ... [had] ... another war,' he insisted during the election, 'they would use the last dollar and the last man. They'd use the national credit to the ultimate limit. That's what we propose to do. We will use the national credit for a war on poverty.'[24]

Like Franklin Roosevelt to the south, Pattullo was no Keynesian. His calls for vigorous government spending and social reform was motivated by fear of the socialist CCF on the left, which became the official opposition in BC after this election, and by his own optimistic faith buoyed by his experience as gold commissioner and minister of lands that Canada's 'immense' natural resource wealth could finance such a sweeping recovery program.

His own government clearly could not. With only 700,000 citizens, British Columbia was already $165 million in debt when Pattullo took office and Ottawa was its sole remaining source of credit. The previous March, Bennett had forced the disintegrating administration of S.F. Tolmie to the brink of default before providing a last-minute federal loan. In December 1933 he repeated the same tactic with Pattullo in order to break down the premier's 'stand and deliver' attitude.[25] But it was Pattullo's attempt to implement his sweeping election promises during the early months of 1934 that finally drove Bennett and his finance minister Edgar Rhodes into a fiscal showdown with the recalcitrant premier.

No part of Pattullo's 'work and wages' program could be implemented without a complete reversal in federal fiscal and monetary policy. Since Bennett was facing a $135 million deficit for the latest fiscal year, he clearly felt the nation's credit already had reached its 'ultimate limits.' In fact, the prime minister had decided on his own 'new deal' for British Columbia.

Contrary to the guidelines for federal loans set the previous spring, Pattullo budgeted for a deficit of over $2 million for the following fiscal year and included no provision for the province's sinking fund or unemployment relief. At the same time, the premier also attempted to use the threat of growing communist strength in his province to scare Bennett into loaning him money to finance a public works program. Federal cabinet minister H.H. Stevens warned that the BC premier was proceeding under the assumption that Bennett 'would not permit any default on ... Provincial bond issues.' In that case, the prime minister replied, Pattullo was 'due ... for a rather unpleasant surprise.'[26]

Not only did Bennett refuse to finance the premier's election program but he also refused to provide federal loans to BC unless that province's projected deficit was brought below $1 million. Pattullo replied by warning that unless a federal loan for that amount was received before the end of March to cover the provincial share of unemployment relief, the province would default on 2 April. To reduce the provincial deficit would provoke 'chaotic conditions.'[27]

Bennett refused to be bullied. 'If we provide the money we have at least the right to impose some conditions as to its expenditure,' he wrote. The premier appeared to assume that the federal government 'had no option but to accept your programme in its entirety.' This was nonsense. If Pattullo continued to ignore federal advice, he would have to assume 'entire responsibility for the consequences.'

In response to Bennett's obstinacy, Pattullo ordered the province's agent, the Bank of Commerce, to cancel all interest payments on the maturing obligations on 2 April.[28] At this point, worried that the bluff had gone too far, bank officials stepped in to mediate a compromise. A provincial default, they claimed, would create a 'national calamity.' To avoid it, the bank would advance Pattullo the money needed to meet the interest payments as long as he went to Ottawa to work out some solution with Bennett. However, the officials warned that responsibility for avoiding any future default would lie with the federal and provincial governments, not with the bank. Commerce president S.H. Logan added a further warning to Bennett against the perils of brinkmanship. At present, he said, Canada was the favourite place next to Britain for investing American securities, but 'if we allow one member of the family to default ... this country is going to pay the penalty in the end.'[29]

Pattullo visited Ottawa in April but failed to reach agreement with the federal government. Finance minister Rhodes refused to modify his stance on the question of reasonable deficits – to give in on this matter would be to lose any hope of forcing the provincial government to 'take a firmer grip as to their finances.' For his part, Pattullo justifiably argued that Rhodes was attempting to assume 'Dominion control over Provincial expenditure.' In a 'far flung' country such as Canada, he warned, such 'centralized control' would never work. If accepting Rhodes's terms was the only way to get the money, then the premier would 'do without' and default.[30]

The deadlock lingered on into early July. Two more federal loans were provided to avert default. Each time the warning came that there would be no more federal funds until the province submitted a 'revised' financial program. Finally, the economic upturn during 1934 provided a face-saving compromise. On 6 July Pattullo informed Bennett that the province's position had improved 'by about one million dollars' over the anticipated $2 million deficit, enabling it at last to conform to Rhodes's fiscal guidelines.[31] No disagreement ensued over future loans for the rest of that year.

Only British Columbia's creditors emerged unscathed from this bitter struggle. Despite irreconcilable viewpoints, neither Bennett, Pattullo, nor the Bank of Commerce wished the province to default. No one won the game of bluff. On one side, the BC premier discovered that he could not plan his own budget let alone implement the 'work and wages' program he had promised the electorate. In spite of his fiery rhetoric, he was essentially powerless in combating the Depression alone. On the other, Bennett gained nothing, for the struggle exposed the ultimate contradiction of his policies. His attempt to preserve the nation's credit by preventing provincial default was drawing him deeper and deeper into provincial affairs despite his desperate attempts to keep Ottawa's involvement with unemployment at a minimum. Ironically, his insistence that relief policy was a provincial responsibility now forced him to assume control of it and other provincial expenditure as well. Pattullo had been elected with a clear mandate to replace the dole with public works – a mandate which Bennett vetoed on the grounds of national credit. As the premier warned, such 'centralized control' would not work. Bennett could not insist that the provinces should maintain law and order while denying them the means to prevent unrest. He could not claim that unemployment policy was a provincial responsibility when he prevented a provincial premier from implementing his mandate to change it. With relief the largest item in provincial budgets, it was in fact if not in theory a primary federal responsibility as long as Bennett maintained that provincial and national credit were 'indivisible.' One way or another, control of the nation's credit demanded control of relief.

The interdependence of national credit and relief costs was obvious to Canadian businessmen. In May the Montreal Chamber of Commerce warned that since 'numerous municipalities [were] on the verge of bankruptcy,' Ottawa should take over the entire cost of relief as a 'national problem,' a position soon endorsed by Wendall Clarke, secretary of the Canadian Chamber of Commerce.[32] Joseph Piggott, a prominent Hamilton businessman and important Conservative supporter, reached the same conclusion. In a fifty-mile radius around Toronto, he said, the monthly per capita cost of relief ranged from a high of $25.00 to a low of $4.00 in Forest Hill. 'There is no doubt that the residents of Forest Hill to a large extent are the employers of the people on direct relief in these other districts where the costs are running so high, yet because they can draw four lines around themselves they shift the burden that is rightfully theirs on to the shoulders of their more unfortunate employees, or the employees of those who have saved enough to be taxable.' Financing the dole in this way was simply 'unfair,' Piggott concluded. 'The cost of carrying the unemployed ... during a depression should be levelled over the whole country [and] that can only be done through the Dominion Government.' Even backbench Tory MPs began to worry how their party could justify the 'unequal distribution of food, fuel, clothing and shelter' by the nation's cities during the next election.[33]

Had Bennett seen the crisis in these terms, he would have accepted complete control of relief as a logical solution. With Ottawa administering and financing the dole, there would be no danger of municipal or provincial insolvency nor any reason to tolerate such shocking discrepancies in relief benefits. A close friend of Rod Finlayson pointed out that, in Winnipeg, the relief allowance for a transient family of four was only 5¢ per person per meal. '[H]ow is it humanly possible,' he wrote, 'to raise a family under such conditions and what can we possibly expect from the rising generation when we are trying to bring up children at the rate of 15¢ a day apiece?' Finlayson replied: 'The basic problem is this. On the one hand, you have social economists, dieticians and others prescribing what people have to receive in order to live decently and on the other hand, you have those who estimate what industry can pay, or in short when you have a large portion of your population unemployed, how much can those who have jobs pay towards the livelihood of those who have not?'[34]

Finlayson had placed his finger on the essential dilemma surrounding Canadian unemployment policy. Should the level of relief provided to the jobless be governed primarily by moral or market criteria? As far as Bennett and his advisers were concerned, the answer was never in doubt. From DBS statistics federal officials knew that, although 300,000 new jobs had been created over the past year and unemployment had dropped by 6.3 per cent, the total number of families on the dole remained virtually unchanged. To the prime minister, the reason was obvious. People had become 'more or less relief-conscious and were determined to get out of the Government, whether it be municipal, provincial or federal, all they could.'[35] If life on the dole was made decent according to some arbitrary social-work standard, would not even more people be attracted to it?

Bennett's government opted to move in the opposite direction. '[I]f we hope ever to overcome the present difficulties,' one of his spokesmen stated, '... some pressure [must be brought] to bear in order to get as many as possible ... off the relief lists and supporting themselves.'[36] Pressure could be employed most effectively by restricting, not increasing, Ottawa's contribution to the dole. In this way, the government which actually administered it would have no alternative but to crack down on the unemployed. As a result, in the early summer of 1934 the government announced that all federal support for direct relief would end on 15 June.

The decision provoked massive criticism. From the premiers came the warning that the prime minister was 'trying to do something that cannot be done'; mayors argued that they could neither assume a larger burden of relief nor cut down their 'already very meagre relief allowances'; the RCMP pointed out that the decision would provoke 'serious trouble' throughout the entire West and requested an extra reserve. Even backbench Tory MPs argued that the decision was a 'neglect of duty' that would 'spell disaster.'[37]

In response, a wavering cabinet postponed the cut-off date to 15 July. When the pressure for continued federal aid refused to let up, cabinet opposition to the decision mounted. By mid-July only labour minister Gordon remained adamant that all federal support be ended. The other ministers now wanted a reduction in federal support from one-third to one-quarter of the total cost of relief for a three-month trial period, pending a review of the entire situation. Reluctantly Bennett authorized a continuance of federal aid on a 25 per cent basis, but for one month only. After 15 August the new federal policy would allow support to the provinces based on 'necessity,' not on a fixed percentage share. At the end of July the premiers were summoned to Ottawa to learn of this change.[38]

Direct relief, Bennett told them, had become a 'racket.' Municipalities were now 'relief conscious' and, by paying out so much money, had accustomed the unemployed to a 'hitherto unknown' standard of living. Once those on the dole were able to obtain a better sustenance than tax-paying workers, he warned, 'collapse was inevitable.' Moreover, relief was being used as a wage subsidy for seasonal and casual workers. As much as 20 per cent of direct relief expenditures went not to the genuinely unemployed but to 'partially employed' workers whose wages were as high as before the Depression. Minimum wages were a provincial, not a federal matter and Ottawa 'would not pay a subsidy' for low-paid workers. Use of relief for this purpose was simply an attempt to blur responsibilities.

Finally, Bennett argued that nearly every province was attempting to 'scrap the constitution' by packing the relief rolls with dependents who in normal times were clearly recognized as provincial and municipal responsibilities. As long as Ottawa continued to contribute to relief on a percentage basis, it would inevitably absorb part of this load. In the future, therefore, federal relief grants would be based on a 'means test.' As of 1 August each province would receive a fixed monthly grant-in-aid of relief determined on the basis of 'necessity' instead of on a fixed percentage of costs.[39] And Ottawa would be the sole judge of necessity.

Up to this point Bennett merely repeated arguments long used by Whitton. But to the CCC&FW director the logical conclusion of this analysis was to place relief under the control of the social-work profession by attaching strict conditions of administration to the federal grants. Even McNaughton and Finlayson agreed with this argument and had urged Bennett to attach 'specific conditions as regards the scale of relief to be afforded' on the proposed grants-in-aid. Bennett rejected this advice. '[D]ivided authority,' he told the premiers, 'was not efficient.' There would be no conditions attached to the grants 'except that it be used for relief.'[40]

Unlike Whitton, who argued that the abuse of relief could be cured only by closer federal supervision, Bennett concluded that 'the proper method was to make the grant-in-aid and to place the whole responsibility upon the Provinces and Municipalities.' Up to now the local governments had 'not taken any steps to prevent abuses.' Limited to a fixed federal grant, they might. In effect, Whitton was hoist on her own petard. Using her arguments, Bennett opted for a 'reform' of relief policy which, as she ruefully admitted, was 'almost directly contrary' to her suggestions.[41] The ledger, not the social work profession, would provide the 'efficient' check on fiscal extravagance.

At first the premiers supported the replacement of Ottawa's percentage contribution with a fixed grant. As long as the municipalities initiated relief spending, the percentage policy inflated provincial costs as well. In contrast, a fixed grant would place the premiers in charge of how much the cities should receive. All they asked was for more time 'to work out what should be a fair amount.' Ontario's newly elected Liberal premier, Mitch Hepburn, suggested that the meeting should reconvene in September when the provinces would have such figures worked out. The premiers then received their second surprise. There would be no bargaining. Bennett had decided already what each would receive. At this point the Quebec delegation walked out.[42] The following day the federal cabinet met separately with the remaining provincial delegations to inform them how much they would get under the new policy of fixed grants.

No evidence remains as to what formula Bennett's administration used to determine the 'need' of each province. On an across-the-board basis, federal spending on direct relief per month dropped by 22 per cent after 1 August for the remainder of the 1934–5 fiscal year. In contrast, the average monthly relief load over the same period remained virtually unchanged, dropping by less than 1 per cent. Bennett had shifted almost a quarter of Ottawa's relief costs on to the shoulders of the provinces and municipalities.

Nor was the burden shifted fairly. Whatever formula Bennett used to determine need must have included a fair amount of political calculation. The Maritime provinces, for example, all received more federal money than before, in New Brunswick's case a whopping 78 per cent increase. Because that province's relief budget was only 1.4 per cent of Ontario's, however, Bennett could afford to be generous. Alberta and Manitoba received negligible cuts of approximately 3 per cent. The big losers were the biggest relief spenders – Ontario, Quebec,

Saskatchewan, and British Columbia. Quebec and Saskatchewan suffered identical 11 per cent cuts in support. Bennett's real wrath was reserved for Ontario and BC, whose premiers had been his most vociferous critics over the past year. Pattullo saw federal support for relief in his province shrink by 34 per cent; Hepburn was astounded by a 37 per cent cut.[43]

The brash thirty-seven-year-old onion-farmer from St Thomas, Ontario, had ended eleven years of provincial Tory rule that June by crushing George Henry's government at the polls. A chubby, balding, and hard-drinking politician with a folksy manner, Hepburn had a well-known fondness for fast women, earthy language, and the company of *nouveau riche* northern Ontario mining millionaires such as George McCullagh, J.P. Bickell, and 'Sell 'Em' Ben Smith. He was also a devastatingly effective platform speaker who swept normally staid Ontario with a vicious populist campaign that accused the Tories of personal corruption, spendthrift administration, and insensitivity to the needs of the unfortunate. Once in office, Hepburn promised to put the province back on its feet through slashing the cost of government administration by 50 per cent. True to his word, he fired all civil servants hired after October 1933; auctioned off forty-seven government limousines in Varsity Arena; unilaterally cancelled two power contracts negotiated with Quebec hydro utilities; and threatened to abolish the post of lieutenant-governor.[44]

While his intentions, unlike Pattullo's, were fiscally conservative, Hepburn and the BC premier did share a similar rhetorical style. Both men delighted in standing up for the 'little man' against predatory 'big interests,' which they invariably associated with Bennett's Tory government. Such attacks won them little favour in Ottawa. Although it was logical that significant savings on relief could only be made in the provinces spending the most on the dole, the severity of Bennett's cuts to BC and Ontario can only be explained by the prime minister's personal belief that Pattullo and Hepburn were irresponsible premiers. When W.A. Gordon complained a week before the dominion-provincial conference in July about '[l]oose talkers, even those who think even more loosely [sic] & some of them in high places' who were 'seeking to consolidate their political fortunes in the provinces by constantly and persistently dwelling upon the whole problem [of relief] as a federal one,' he obviously had Hepburn and Pattullo in mind. Presumably after 1 August they would have a more chastened sense of their responsibilities. So too would the municipalities for, as the *Edmonton Journal* stated, 'the fixed budget plan ... will have a tendency to make cities think twice before they increase relief scales for, hereafter, the whole burden of such increases is likely to fall on their own taxpayers.'[45]

Bennett attempted to cushion this severe cut-back in relief with two other unemployment initiatives. The first was a modest policy of federal public works.

In January 1934, in response to the strong pressure for jobs created by consideration of the success of Roosevelt's New Deal programs, Bennett asked his relief-camp director, General Andrew McNaughton, to prepare an estimate of how much it would cost to put the employable unemployed on relief to work. Assuming that there were approximately 379,000 men capable of work who were currently on the dole, McNaughton estimated that 'at the least, the programme for 1934 should envisage the provision of work to care for 200,000 wage-earners.' Assuming a one-to-one ratio of direct to indirect employment, this meant placing 100,000 relief recipients on the government payroll. To do this, the general suggested a range of projects including trans-Canada highway and airway construction, dams and irrigation development to reclaim drought areas, housing, reforestation and work in the national parks, construction of public buildings, aid to municipal and provincial public works, and work on the St Lawrence Seaway. As a 'safe margin over minimum requirements,' he recommended a monthly wage of $60.00. The total cost of such a program would be $165 million annually compared to the $26.5 million Ottawa would spend on direct relief under the 1934 act.

As an alternative, McNaughton also drew up a 'modified program' that would employ only 60,000 men at a total annual cost of $70 million. However, it would leave 107,000 employable unemployed on direct relief. The price was steep but the general argued, in somewhat Keynesian fashion, that it would 'give a substantial impulse to help the general economic system of the country to pass from a period of balance forward into a progressive revival.' If given permission to proceed, he promised he could organize his program in three to six months.[46]

Despite McNaughton's enthusiasm, Bennett had no intention of embarking on a public-works program of such magnitude. The first six months of 1934 did give grounds for hope that the Depression was lifting. In April finance minister Edgar Rhodes presented a budget which, for the first time since 1930, marked a reversal of the downward trend. Employment was up by 250,000 and the federal deficit was down over $20 million. It was a 'year of recovery,' Rhodes told the House.[47]

If anything, this trend made Bennett more wary about taking any action that might jeopardize this improvement, regardless of public enthusiasm for the New Deal. As he complained to one corporate president, 'we live side by side with the rich United States that can spend money literally by the hundreds of millions of dollars while we find it difficult to get along at all. Our real problem is a financial one and ... those who compare us with the United States ... do not realize the financial limitations imposed upon us by ... our relative poverty.'[48]

As a result, the Public Works Construction Act introduced in June 1934, although quite large by pre-Depression Canadian standards, was a very modest affair compared to the American example. Forty million dollars was appropriated for the construction of a series of federal public works such as wharves, post offices, and improvements to existing buildings. Although the bill received much praise in the House for marking a return to public works instead of relief, its limited scope emasculated most of its political or economic utility. It was the most Bennett thought the country could afford but it was not enough to 'answer [the] demand ... for ... public works,' 'accelerate recovery,' or 'reduce expenditures for relief,' the three stated purposes of the Act.[49]

Bennett's second initiative gave the green light to the preparation of a draft unemployment insurance bill. The decision was made in late January 1934 after the dominion-provincial conference. It was not an easy move. Although Bennett had pledged his government to unemployment insurance as early as April 1931, he was never fully convinced that such a scheme was feasible for Canada. As late as December 1933 he still feared that Canada's seasonal economy made the measure problematic. Apart from these considerations, there remained the problem of securing the constitutional amendment which every federal official deemed necessary before it could be enacted. Above all, his administration wanted some sign of significant recovery for, as R.J. Manion pointed out that February, 'in the midst of a depression ... like this it would be impossible to create such a scheme.'[50]

However, with a federal election approaching, Bennett could not delay his promise forever. By 1934 unemployment insurance commanded a wide range of support from labour, the social-work profession, municipalities, five provincial governments, and important sections of the business community. After four years of depression, the degradation and irrationality of relief had convinced most Canadians that an insurance scheme was necessary. Only the manufacturers, for clearly self-interested reasons, remained adamant in their opposition. Because of this broad consensus, Finlayson warned against delay: 'If we take it that such measures are inevitable from a political point of view, the important problem for this country is to enact a scheme which will be deprived as far as possible of the socialistic elements that are taking command of public thinking in the matter and enact legislation with due regard for industry and the necessity of not too severely inflicting it with burdens of this nature.'[51] Manufacturers had to be saved in spite of themselves. The longer unemployment insurance was put off, the more it was likely to cost, especially if enacted by an administration less friendly to business concerns. Moreover, such a scheme would have a calming effect on the public temper. As Bennett pointed out to one recalcitrant businessman: 'Great Britain has avoided revolution when other countries have had to face practically civil war, because Great Britain is so far ahead of other countries in socialist legislation. I am not unmindful of the differences between Great Britain and Canada but I have not forgotten the circumstances under which Bismarck introduced the legislation in Germany and the effect of such legislation in Australia.'[52]

Finally, there was the intimate relationship between insurance and relief. The longer Bennett delayed enacting an unemployment insurance scheme, Finlayson said, 'the more difficult it will become as a political undertaking.' Modern social and economic thinking, as represented by the CCC&FW, was now 'definitely of the view that this is only a first line of defence and that a well-organized national form of relief must be established as a last line.' This argument enjoyed a 'great deal of support.' However, at the moment, 'relief [was] ... repulsive ... to this country.' If Bennett brought down his public-works bill, 'followed by insurance legislation, you have selected the most opportune time to get this job behind you as far as the political values are concerned. This spring it could be done ... without raising the relief question. A year from now I am not quite sure that it could.'[53]

Thus, despite the difficulty in securing a constitutional amendment, the continued depression, and the danger of applying British precedents to what the DBS termed Canada's 'peculiar' situation,[54] unemployment insurance was politically essential. It might calm political unrest, reverse the decline in Conservative fortunes, and provide a convenient excuse for severing Ottawa's connection with relief. As with the public-works bill, the only remaining question was its scope.

From the outset Bennett's administration looked to Britain for guidance. During the summer of 1933, while Bennett and Finlayson were at the Imperial Economic Conference in London, they consulted extensively with officials from that country's Department of Labour which was then in the process of drafting a new unemployment insurance act to restore the British scheme to actuarial soundness. Both men came home with far more confidence in the feasibility of the idea.[55]

Consequently, once Bennett gave his approval for a Canadian act, F.G. Price, who had worked closely on the reformed British bill, was brought to Canada to advise the federal government. Rod Finlayson headed the project team whose other members included A.D. Watson, chief dominion actuary; Hugh Wolfenden, an independent insurance consultant; and Leonard Marsh, head of McGill University's School of Social Research and one of the country's authorities on unemployment statistics.

From the beginning they realized that unemployment insurance in Canada might prove a risky venture given the country's wide expanse, the 'extreme fluidity' of its labour market, and the seasonality of its economy. During the boom years of 1922–30, Marsh pointed out, unemployment averaged 10.6 per cent, while 30 per cent of the labourforce lost some time each year and the average spell of joblessness was eighteen weeks.[56] Even in 'normal' times, unemployment insurance was likely to prove more expensive than most thought.

As a result, Bennett's advisers initially determined on quite a restricted version of the British scheme, applied only to workers in manufacturing, trade, transport, communications, and some service industries – roughly half the labourforce. Later this coverage was extended in the final draft to cover an estimated two-thirds of the workers. The 'heaviest incidence of unemployment,' the Insurance Department stated, occurred among 'manual and unskilled workers,' which was why they recommended leaving out construction, logging, and farm labourers from the plan. On this limited base, the department estimated unemployment insurance would cost $50 million in a normal year or $85 million if all the labourforce were included.[57]

There were other 'non-actuarial' reasons for ignoring the plight of unemployed seasonal workers. As Price said, the purpose of unemployment insurance was the 'provision of maintenance for the unemployed, without the loss of self-respect.' Relief, because it was based on need, reduced all the unemployed to a common level. It made no distinctions between the worthy and the unworthy, between those whose savings were exhausted and those who had nothing to save. In this sense it was truly subversive, for it eradicated class differences among the unemployed. That was why the RCMP had noted that 'men and women who have at some time or other held good positions and social standing' soon developed 'socialistic ideas' when exposed to the relief system.[58] To avoid this development, the unemployment insurance scheme would offer the skilled and semi-skilled workers an alternative to dependency on relief. The unskilled, with less distance to fall between normal and relief living standards, could be left to the traditional poor-relief methods for preserving their 'morale.'

The question of benefits possessed distinctly non-actuarial dimensions as well. For the sake of administrative simplicity, the Insurance Department decided to use the uniform 'flat-rate' benefit practised by the British. In theory this rate could be established anywhere between the 'minimum costs of living and existing wage rates.'[59] In practice, because of the absence of minimum-wage legislation for males throughout Canada, there was little distance between the two. As a Toronto study on relief allowances pointed out:

... a minimum of $28.35 a week [is] required to cover the bare essentials for health and self-respect for a family of five with two adults, a boy aged 6, a girl aged 10, and a boy aged 12 ... Comparisons available indicate that $28.35 is far above prevailing wages; for example, a survey of 398 wage-earning families given service by one of the social agencies ... reveals that 305 were earning below $22.00 a week with 116 of these between $15.00 and $19.00. Figures obtained at the time of the 1931 Census showed that of 448,000 Ontario families with male heads, the earnings in 67% were less than $1500 per year. It would appear to be evident that the earnings of a substantial part of the population are below the level suggested as desirable.[60]

Even a more sharply reduced emergency budget of $17.50 per week for a family of five, worked out by the Montreal Council of Social Agencies in 1933 dollars, was rejected by the consulting actuaries as far too generous a standard for benefit levels. '[U]nemployment insurance in itself increases ... unemployment,' they argued, because of the 'temptation ... to malinger.' This was proof enough why 'anything like generous benefits [would be] dangerous and undesirable.'[61]

As a result, a benefit level lower than the worst-paying unskilled wage was agreed upon. The scheme would pay $6.00 a week to every insured unemployed male over twenty-one, $2.70 to his fully dependent wife, and 90¢ for each child. The total of $11.40 for a family of five was well below the $17.30 recommended by the Montreal Council of Social Agencies, yet federal officials still fretted that it might exceed the earnings of some workers. Consequently, the further stipulation was added that in no case could the payment exceed 80 per cent of wages. Unemployment insurance would have a ceiling but there would be no floor. If complaints were received that such benefits were inadequate, the government could answer that 'wages must be out of alignment.'[62]

Had Bennett been inclined towards a more ambitious measure, however, the pessimism of Watson and Wolfenden would have dissuaded him. For despite the fact that both actuaries produced an exceedingly cautious insurance bill, neither would guarantee it would work. For them, as for the prime minister, the key criterion remained that contributions cover benefits without recourse to government loans. In actuarial terms, this meant that existing rates of contributions and benefits must be based on projections of future unemployment. And here was the dilemma, Watson noted: 'The only guide to future unemployment of workers is necessarily past experience of unemployment; but can past experience be a reasonably safe guide to the future? For example, who in the early part of 1914 could have forecast the course of unemployment for, say, the succeeding ten years, even if accurate and satisfactory data ... had been available? Or who in 1924 could have indicated the course of unemployment up to 1934?' Since unemployment first became an issue in Canadian politics, politicians from Borden to Bennett had postponed action on unemployment insurance on the grounds that satisfactory statistics were not available to attempt an 'actuarially sound' scheme. Yet, as Watson finally conceded, this was a meaningless concern: 'For practical purposes ... it may be assumed that unemployment data will never be a very satisfactory guide to future claims ... The plain fact is that until means are found of effecting greater stability ... in social and economic conditions, an unemployment insurance fund is liable to be called upon to bear burdens so uncertain and so incalculable as to set at naught the best considered rates of contributions.'[63]

This point was nicely illustrated by the fact that calculations for the 1934 scheme were based on the 12 per cent average unemployment rate between 1921 and 1931. Yet during the four months it took to prepare the plan, unemployment did not drop below 23 per cent. In short, Bennett's advisers designed an insurance bill for a world that no longer existed! Small wonder that Wolfenden confessed that the problem was 'extremely baffling and ... almost entirely unpredictable.'[64] To a prime minister constantly fretting over the danger of national bankruptcy, these were not comforting words. Unemployment insurance, both his experts implied, was at best a shot in the dark.

By the end of April a first draft of the bill was completed. Although in principle it copied the British scheme, in practice it differed greatly. The benefit levels were approximately equal but the Canadian conditions were 'much stricter.' Whereas the British scheme provided coverage for virtually the entire labourforce, the Canadian legislation excluded both unskilled seasonal workers and professionals such as nurses, teachers, civil servants, or anyone earning more than $2000 a year. The Canadian plan offered neither sickness nor 'transitional' benefits for those who had exhausted their coverage, nor did it provide any alternative to the uninsured except relief. Compared to the British government's one-third contribution, Ottawa would pay only one-fifth of the scheme's cost. Finally, while the British scheme was administered by the Ministry of Labour, the Canadian plan set up a commission which was itself supervised by an advisory committee – the 'financial watchdog' of the plan. The idea, Finlayson argued, was to 'keep control of the measure as far as possible out of Parliament.'[65]

In sum, Bennett's bill was a cautious, conservative document which closely resembled the original British legislation of 1911. Above all, it reflected the fears of its creators that the same pressures which made unemployment insurance politically inevitable might in turn lead to its bankruptcy. Once it was generally accepted that the federal government was responsible for the living standards of the unemployed, it might prove impossible to resist the pressure for larger benefits and wider coverage. To forestall this, Bennett duplicated his relief policy. Costs would be limited by keeping federal involvement to a minimum. Unemployment insurance, like relief, would neither be administered nor financed directly by the dominion. Moreover, the criterion of 'actuarial soundness' would serve an identical function to that of municipal solvency as an arbitrary limiting factor for benefits. In this way, unemployment insurance, like relief, would be insulated as much as possible from the political process.[66] Seen in this light, the insurance bill was an attempt to limit, not to expand, Ottawa's responsibility for unemployment.

Once the unemployment insurance legislation was drafted by mid-June 1934, two questions remained. When should it be introduced? How could a constitutional amendment be secured? At no point during the preparation of the bill had it been assumed that such an amendment was not necessary. In April, in a clear reference to the insurance legislation, Bennett admitted that his government had enough information to give a 'fairly complete' picture of the unemployment situation. However, there was 'not the slightest doubt in the world,' he argued, that 'unless there is a rearrangement of the powers of this parliament and the legislatures of the provinces ... the problem cannot be dealt with.' Consequently, he favoured an 'early revision' of the British North America Act but hinted that it would have to wait until after an election.[67]

In Quebec, this announcement precipitated a reply from Premier Taschereau that his government would oppose any constitutional change that did not receive the unanimous consent of the provinces. When asked whether he believed unanimous consent was necessary, Bennett answered that from a legal standpoint it was not but that politically any attempt to 'impinge on the rights of provinces that were the original partners to the confederation pact is a matter that would require careful consideration.'[68]

Despite this constitutional problem and the economic advantages of delaying implementation until 1935 when recovery, presumably, would be more advanced, Finlayson thought it expedient politically that the bill should be introduced at once. Convinced the legislation would be a 'political liability' until benefits began to be paid, which he felt would take 'at least one year,' he insisted that the plan be operational before the next election, due in 1935. Moreover, the longer the legislation was delayed, the more difficult it would become to resist pressure to accompany unemployment insurance with a 'well-organized national form of relief.' Since one of the goals of the bill was to afford an excuse to hand relief back entirely to the provinces, it was essential that it be enacted now so that, together with the public-works bill, it would provide a perfect political cover for the federal withdrawal from relief planned for mid-summer.[69]

Bennett rejected Finlayson's advice. He attempted to eliminate Ottawa's relief responsibilities in mid-July with only the public-works bill and the slight economic recovery as justification. The reasons for this decision are obscure. Perhaps he agreed with his chief adviser that economically it was not the right time to introduce such a costly measure. More likely, he disliked the idea of passing the legislation before trying to settle the constitutional issue. If so, it was an ironic mistake. Although the Quebec premier was unlikely to assent to an amendment anyway, Bennett's highhanded attempt to cut off federal support for relief made his co-operation inconceivable, especially after his stormy exit from the July dominion-provincial conference. Moreover, Taschereau's rage was echoed by Mitch Hepburn of Ontario. As a result, Finlayson's strategy was destroyed. The insurance bill was intended to make the withdrawal from relief palatable. Instead, the attempt to withdraw from relief wrecked any chance of constitutional agreement on the insurance bill. After July, Bennett remained linked to relief yet was farther than ever from securing the authority necessary to enact unemployment insurance.

None the less, plans still went ahead for another dominion-provincial conference in the fall. At the end of August, a draft letter was prepared asking the premiers whether they were 'prepared to surrender their exclusive jurisdiction over legislation dealing with such social problems as old age pensions, unemployment insurance, hours and conditions for work, minimum wages, etc. to the Dominion Parliament.'[70]

From the outset, the endeavour was hopeless. Although the financial plight of the western provinces gave them little choice but to concede some transfer of responsibilities to Ottawa, Hepburn and Taschereau were under no such pressure and, after the blow-up over relief, were in no mood to make concessions to Bennett, especially since both anticipated his imminent replacement by a more congenial Liberal administration. To make matters more complicated, there was no agreed-upon formula for constitutional amendment.

Bennett's enthusiasm for the conference quickly waned. On the same day the invitations were sent to the premiers, he authorized acting prime minister Sir George Perley to announce that the government planned to introduce unemployment insurance legislation in the next session of Parliament. As Finlayson noted, the announcement 'renders somewhat futile the discussion with the Provinces if the Government ... is going to bring down this measure anyway.' Faced with five crucial by-elections that month, Bennett was under strong pressure from backbench MPs to make some statement on the issue they felt was 'more vital than any other one question.'[71] By November, with four of these elections lost, Bennett cancelled the conference. Realizing he would not be granted the authority needed to enact his unemployment insurance bill, he decided instead to seize it.

In early January 1935 the prime minister electrified the country with a series of five 'New Deal' radio broadcasts promising a reform of the capitalist system and an end to 'laissez-faire.' For his first five years in office, Bennett told Canadians, his government's energies had been totally absorbed with preventing economic collapse. Now with recovery proceeding, he could strike out for reform in order to provide full employment and an end to relief. The dole 'was a condemnation, final and complete, of our economic system. If we cannot abolish the dole,' he continued in an echo of his 1930 campaign promises, 'we should abolish the system.'

The remaining four broadcasts outlined his plan of action. Included were promises for national minimum wage and maximum hours-of-work legislation; a more progressive tax system; consumer protection against monopolies and 'unfair trading practices'; an 'economic council'; reorganization of the civil service; an early start to the Bank of Canada; and contributory old-age pensions and health and unemployment insurance. The goal, the Speech from the Throne announced on 17 January, was 'to ensure to all classes and to all parts of the country a greater degree of equality in the distribution of the benefits of the capitalist system.'[72]

The content of Bennett's New Deal proposal was actually quite tame. Virtually everything he promised had already been put in place in either Great Britain or the United States. It was the language of the speeches which caught public attention. Borrowing a page from Hepburn and Pattullo, Bennett promised to eliminate 'economic parasites' who preyed on farmers and to 'stamp out ... evil in corporations'; he warned of 'selfish men ... corporations without souls and without virtue' who would 'whisper against us' in order to protect what they regarded as their 'immemorial right of exploitation.' Liberals like Mackenzie King, Bennett declared, were believers in industrial laissez-faire and therefore tended to fascism – 'and there is no place for Fascism in Canada.' It was pretty strong language coming from the millionaire prime minister and it left many staunch Tory supporters in the Montreal business community aghast. '[W]as the communist Tim Buck ... sentenced to five years in Kingston Penitentiary for saying much more than the P.M. said last night?' asked Henry Borden of his uncle Sir Robert, the former Conservative prime minister.[73]

While in public Bennett justified his New Deal in terms of this political threat from the right, in private correspondence to Conservative supporters across the country he claimed, in equally apocalyptic language, that the real danger was from the left. '[U]nless we are prepared to immediately grapple with the social and economic problems of our country,' he told the editor of his hometown newspaper, the *Calgary Herald*, 'the solution of our difficulties will be entrusted either to the Communists or the Socialists.' His New Deal was an attempt to 'forestall that possibility.'[74]

Bennett's New Deal was an act of sheer opportunism born out of political desperation. With the exception of Rod Finlayson, his speech writer, and his brother-in-law, W.D. Herridge, no one in the cabinet, the caucus, or the party had been consulted before the prime minister aired his new ideas, and none of the proposed legislation, with the exception of the Employment and Social Insurance Act, had even been drafted. Instead, the ideas and much of the language of the broadcasts came from Herridge, a former advertising executive who was now Canadian minister to Washington and greatly enamoured of Roosevelt's public relations genius. 'This New Deal,' he had written to Bennett in April 1934 describing the American president's first year in office,

is a sort of Pandora's box, from which, at suitable intervals, the President has pulled the NRA and the AAA and a lot of other mysterious things. Most of the people never understood the NRA or the AAA any more than they understood the Signs of the Zodiac, but that did not matter very much: they were all part of the New Deal, and the New Deal meant recovery because the President had so promised ... Therefore the spirit of the New Deal is what has really mattered. The mechanics of the New Deal are a lesser thing ... We need a Pandora's box. We need some means by which the people can be persuaded that they also have a New

Deal and that that New Deal will do everything for them in fact which the New Deal here has done in fancy ... Sometimes a promise is of more value than its fulfillment.[75]

For the next six months Herridge continued to pester the prime minister with memos on the need to announce a similar bold recovery program to win back public confidence. He insisted that '90 per cent of the potential power of the CCF is decent, respectable, constructive and as such, the stuff out of which Conservatism can build ... support.'[76] By November, with his hopes for constitutional reform in tatters and facing both a revolt led by former cabinet minister H.H. Stevens from within his own party and imminent defeat in the upcoming 1935 election, Bennett was convinced. Herridge was called home to begin work with Finlayson on the radio broadcasts.

The bold rhetoric of reform, however, could not disguise the fact that most of the New Deal was unconstitutional. The Judicial Committee of the Privy Council had, in the past year, awarded the federal government jurisdiction over radio broadcasting and civil aviation on the grounds that section 132 of the BNA Act gave Ottawa authority to carry out treaties between the British empire and foreign countries. Consequently, in introducing the Employment and Social Insurance Act to the House of Commons in January 1935, Bennett claimed that this 'widening sense of the power of the central authority' would also legally justify most of his New Deal legislation because of Ottawa's commitment to secure humane conditions for Canadian workers under the Versailles Peace Treaty of 1919. In private, however, even he conceded that there were 'grave constitutional difficulties' with respect to some of the legislation.[77]

This was certainly true with unemployment insurance, which the prime minister as late as August 1934 was still insisting lay within the 'exclusive jurisdiction' of the provinces. The federal government eventually justified its case for legal supremacy in this field in two ways, neither of which rested upon an expanded interpretation of section 132. First, by claiming that unemployment was now a national emergency, federal officials argued that unemployment insurance fell within Ottawa's residual authority to ensure 'peace, order and good government.' Second, on the basis of what has since become known as the 'spending power,' they argued that Ottawa's right to raise money by 'any mode of taxation' and its exclusive jurisdiction under section 91 (1A) of the BNA Act over 'public debt and property' gave it the right to give money away directly to Canadian citizens even in areas of provincial jurisdiction.

In no recent decision had the JCPC given any indication that it supported such an expanded interpretation of federal powers under these parts of the BNA Act. As the justices eventually pointed out in their 1937 decision, legislation that was 'intended to be permanent ... could not be supported upon the suggested existence of any special emergency.' And to concede that federal control of public debt and property and its authority to tax took precedence over provincial control of 'property and civil rights' would 'afford the Dominion an easy passage into the provincial domain,' something which in fact occurred after World War II when Ottawa began to use the spending-power argument extensively to justify new initiatives such as family allowances and grants to post-secondary education. In 1935, however, even Finlayson was willing to admit the weakness of Ottawa's case. '[O]n the whole,' he advised acting prime minister Sir George Perley in March, it was 'better not to close with Mr. King in a debate on its constitutional aspects.'[78]

Nevertheless, Bennett counted on opposition objections to the constitutionality of his New Deal legislation as the pretext to dissolve Parliament and call a snap election during which King and the Liberal party could be portrayed as the opponents of reform. If he won, Grant Dexter of the *Winnipeg Free Press* observed, Bennett probably intended to 'make the constitutional changes' by putting a grant of general power through the House of Commons and the Senate and to tell 'the provinces to go climb trees.'[79] Anticipating this gambit, King wisely refused to be drawn. Instead, he persuaded his party to support the New Deal legislation while reserving judgment on its constitutionality. In this way, Bennett's bluff was called. Rather than calling an election, the Tory leader had to bring forward his legislation. As a result, the Employment and Social Insurance Act speedily passed through Parliament in early March with only three dissenting votes – an effective testimony to its broad public support.[80]

Yet unemployment insurance was not really part of Bennett's New Deal. While his other measures had neither been prepared or 'even reduced in broad terms to paper' at the time of the January broadcasts,[81] the Employment and Social Insurance Act was ready as early as June 1934. Its origins lay not in Bennett's desperate acceptance of Herridge's pre-election advice but in the three-year struggle to find some credible federal alternative to relief. Furthermore, while the other reform legislation was designed in part to foment a constitutional crisis and thus to provide an acceptable election issue, unemployment insurance was premised on the possibility of a constitutional settlement.

It was fitting, then, that Bennett's carefully crafted unemployment insurance scheme should suffer the same fate as his hastily contrived New Deal since both attempts at reform were animated by the same approach to dominion-provincial relations. As Christopher Armstrong has noted, Bennett 'refused to negotiate with the provinces in good faith. Instead, he simply demanded that they accept his terms.'[82] At one point or another during Bennett's five years in office, Leonard Marsh, Harry Cassidy, W.C. Clark, and Rod Finlayson had all pointed out the crucial connection between unemployment insurance and relief. Although differing in certain essentials, the four men at least agreed that the two issues could not be separated and that negotiations with respect to unemployment insurance could not proceed in isolation from bargaining over relief. Yet Bennett attempted to do just that. While making almost no concessions to the provinces over relief policy, he expected them to surrender jurisdiction over unemployment insurance and other essential social services on his terms and to suit his convenience. A compromise agreement on the two issues might not have been possible. The important point is that it was never tried.

As Finlayson had warned the previous spring, Bennett's postponement of the Employment and Social Insurance Act to 1935 only directed attention to the shortcomings of his relief policy. For despite the bravado of the New Deal reforms, not one of them related to the existing unemployment crisis. To Herridge, author of the radio broadcasts, there was no need to discuss 'measures for the cure of unemployment, such as housing and so forth, because this step comes, if at all, in the later stage of the reform programme.'[83] Yet for the 1.24 million Canadians still dependent on relief, it was precisely the cure that was essential and that was lacking in Bennett's promises. 'We listened with much interest and hope to your radio talks,' observed one relief recipient speaking on behalf of twenty-five others, 'We thought at first that we could see some light but developments since have made us again doubtful. We cannot reconcile your promises made five years ago that you would end unemployment. We do not see that any definite move has been made in this direction. We look askance at your unemployment insurance bill ... We are wondering where our forty weeks of employment is coming from before *we* can benefit ... [W]hat we want and must have is some measure that will help *us*, we the army of the unemployed, *right now*, not at some vague future time.'[84]

But Bennett offered only increased hardship. At the same time that his New Deal measure passed through Parliament, the 1935 Relief Act simply repeated the fixed grants-in-aid adopted at the July 1934 dominion-provincial conference even though in major cities such as Winnipeg the proportion of federal aid now stood at only 20 per cent. As for work-and-wages or a housing program, both were out of the question, as Bennett and other government spokesmen argued, because they would attract too many people not on relief and limit foreign investment by impairing the nation's credit.[85]

For many this was not a convincing explanation. Why could Bennett not assume authority over relief under the same legal basis he now claimed dominion jurisdiction over unemployment insurance? the CCF asked. If the British experience was any indication, some form of unemployment assistance 'should have been the very crux of the act.' Bennett's response was revealing. 'Relief,' he said, 'is one thing, insurance is another.' The dole, he argued, was an 'entirely different matter ... [than insurance because it] ... cannot be the subject of actuarial computations. There is not the scientific data upon which to predicate any degree of assistance.'[86]

While this distinction had nothing to do with the BNA Act, it did show why Bennett did not press for jurisdiction over relief as well as over unemployment insurance. By 1935 there was, in fact, a great deal of 'scientific data' as to how much minimum assistance was needed to maintain health and decency on relief. Unlike unemployment insurance, however, there was no actuarial argument for setting a maximum. For five years Bennett had relied on the threat of provincial and municipal fiscal insolvency to keep relief benefits down. If relief became a national obligation, he was convinced that there would be irresistible pressure for a national minimum because the burden would be transferred to the strongest fiscal unit of government. To Bennett, this was the lesson of the British experience. National responsibility for unemployment relief might lead to national bankruptcy. Consequently, there could be no 'New Deal' for the unemployed.

This failure to reform the dole aroused widespread protest, but for somewhat different reasons. From the social-work profession came yet one more appeal for the 'removal of relief standards, practices and administration from the realm of political influence and manœuvre.' Throughout the country, Charlotte Whitton argued, there was a growing 'despair and sense of futility' among welfare administrators at the 'increasing core of permanent dependency developing from the tendency to exploit the vote of the dependent unemployed and to offer more and easier relief.'[87]

Whitton, of course, had been using this argument for years. When she realized after July 1934 that Bennett was ignoring her advice, she concentrated her efforts on the business members of her governing board. As a result, in 1935 important Canadian business organizations turned against Bennett's relief policy. In mid-April the Canadian Chamber of Commerce sent a letter to all members of Parliament arguing that, while the organization of unemployment insurance would be a 'lengthy' process, the 'question of unemployment relief is immediate.' The dole was now the 'heaviest burden on ... government treasuries ... [yet it was] ... loosely integrated [and] ... subject in many cases ... to political influence.' Consequently, the Chamber insisted that Ottawa should 'immediately ... lift ... control of relief administration and financing directly out of the field of local political influence' in order to 'conserve public funds.'[88]

This sudden concern among the business community over the care of the unemployed was a direct response to the impact of the Depression on municipal politics. As John Taylor has noted, 'In the 1930s there emerged in most, but not all of the major centres of western Canada successful or nearly successful bids for municipal power by left-wing parties usually, by 1935, connected with the CCF.

Again, there also emerged in most, but not all of these centres, charismatic populists as mayors.[89] Alberta premier J.E. Brownlee vividly outlined to labour minister W.A. Gordon the consequence of such left-wing power in Calgary, the city with Canada's most generous relief rates. '[T]he unemployed ... are very thoroughly organized,' he complained bitterly,

and have the complete support of the Labour Organizations which, in turn, are very strong in the City administration. There is no doubt at all that any attempt to reduce the standards of relief in that City will be most bitterly fought and we can anticipate a very great deal of trouble, with the possibility of rather violent outbreaks before the matter is finally adjusted ... [I]n the light of the unemployment situation ... I have personally hesitated to take any action in view of the pronounced feeling of the City Officials against any reduction in the standard of relief.[90]

Nor was such political activity confined to the West. Ontario cities from 1932 onward witnessed frequent relief strikes and angry parades to city halls by the jobless. In Welland, Ontario, during the spring of 1935 hundreds of relief strikers engaged in vicious hand-to-hand fighting with police over an attempt to break their picket line around the municipal tool shed in protests against inadequate relief rates. Dispersed by tear gas, 300 of the men later marched to the homes of civic officials and pelted their houses with rocks and bricks. In East York, where 46 per cent of the population was on the dole, 2700 families took part in a bitter two-month struggle with local officials over attempts to cut back cash relief. Eventually, they elected their leader, Arthur Williams, reeve of the township in local elections.[91] The ascension to power of flamboyant mayors such as Jimmy Simpson in Toronto and Camillien Houde in Montreal was further testimony to the volatility of local electorates by the mid 1930s.

Alarmed by this leftward turn in municipal politics as well as by the success of unconventional provincial politicians such as Duff Pattullo and Mitch Hepburn, Canadian businessmen turned to the federal government as the last bastion of political and financial stability. Like Whitton, their demand for a federal 'reform' of relief was motivated by profound distrust of municipal democracy and by a desire to level down the living standards which some of the unemployed had won through hard-fought urban political action.

The left also demanded national control of relief, and once more unemployed single men provided the symbolic issue. From the time federal relief camps had been established in 1932, the transient problem quietly simmered in the background of other events. Three years later this tension exploded in a relief strike which demonstrated graphically the inadequacies of Ottawa's relief program. The details of the BC relief camp strike which began in April 1935 and which culminated in the On-to-Ottawa Trek and the Regina Riot have been well documented and need not be repeated here.[92] However, the basic cause of the strike and the breakdown it produced in intergovernmental relations deserve close attention as both directly highlight the weakness of Bennett's unemployment policy.

Virtually every investigation of the relief camps during 1934 and 1935 reached the same conclusion. The problem was not so much the physical facilities, which on the whole were adequate although not generous, but rather the 'mental attitude' of the men. The Macdonald Commission, which began its inquiry of the camps at the beginning of the 1935 strike, put the matter best. 'Camp life,' the commissioners explained, 'is not a normal condition under which men desire to live. Men are attracted to mining, logging and construction camps because of a wage paid for labour. It was pointed out by the men that usually there is some goal at the end of a period of employment, and men put up with the discomforts and lack of social contacts associated with camp life because in due course, there will be a substantial pay cheque, and a way open to some other form of living.'[93] The 20¢ daily allowance paid to the men in the relief camps gave them no possibility of saving a 'stake' and getting out – the rationale for bunkhouse work. Consequently, as strike leader Arthur Evans said, 'it is the hopelessness of life these people are kicking about, not the camp conditions.'[94] 'The men feel that they are hostages, prisoners,' *Vancouver Sun* reporter Bob Bouchette pointed out in a devastating series of articles on camp life. '[T]aking them as a class [they are] about as merry and bright as men I have talked to in penitentiaries. Not miserably unhappy ... but utterly without hope.' In some ways this attitude was deliberately fostered by camp authorities. Unlike the American CCC which was restricted to those under the age of twenty-five, the DND relief camps rejected age segregation out of fear, Bouchette noted, that 'the young gathered together in one group constituted a charge of dynamite.' Instead all DND camps were 'carefully balanced ... [with] 50% ... oldsters' for their 'steadying influence.' Bouchette went on, 'Which is it now? ... A steadying influence or a stupefying influence? Which is the better: hotheaded and headlong in its expression, or a youth meekly submitting to their fate with the bovine resignation of the more aged for whom ... the fire of hope and ambition burns low?'

The mens' deprivation of women was also 'unnatural and inhuman.' With 'plenty of time on their hands and few amusements,' their thoughts 'naturally ... centre on sex' yet there was no 'set time limit on their isolation.' As a result, the men lived in a 'neurotic condition' which kept them perpetually 'on edge and ready for any sort of action.' Bouchette's conclusion effectively captured the relief-camp irony. 'The federal government is administering as efficiently as is humanly possible a system which is vicious and subversive in essence.'[95]

Nowhere was this more obvious than over the wage question. The payment of a

20¢ daily 'allowance' made labour discipline the major problem of camp life. Most of the commanders and foremen had been chosen from unemployed men who had held similar supervisory positions in railway, logging, and mining camps. Accustomed to simply firing unco-operative workers, they found themselves perplexed by a situation in which men who had 'voluntarily resorted to the camps for purposes of relief ... were entitled to a different treatment.' Not surprisingly, by mid-1934 camp commanders began complaining that 'our set-up does not provide a motive for good conduct.' As one declared, 'practically every man in camp asserts that he would sooner work at a given rate per hour, buy his own clothes and pay his board than work under the present system ... The present allowance system gives the agitator all the ammunition he needs to stir up strife and trouble in a camp.'[96]

Since it was well known, even within the Department of Defence, that the lack of a wage structure was the major cause of discontent in the camps, why was the 20¢ allowance maintained? Why did McNaughton and Bennett continue to believe they could maintain order among the most difficult class of workers and under the most trying conditions without the major disciplinary agent of private industry?

In the first place, unlike private employers, neither man cared about the work performed. According to McNaughton, 'the whole of the work has been directed from a relief and not from a departmental point of view. Our advantage has come not primarily from the works created, which are useful for our purposes, but most importantly from the fact that by breaking up the congestions of many thousands of single, homeless and desperate men in our larger centres of population ... we have avoided the use of troops and firearms to quell disturbances, which many besides myself regarded as otherwise inevitable.'[97] Since the importance of the camps was not what they built but where they were, the quality and efficiency of the work performed were not important enough to justify higher wages. It was enough to have the men out in the bush. While this made perfect sense to McNaughton and Bennett, it was, of course, incomprehensible to the men themselves. 'Here we are playing at highway building where men once did things,' one of the camp workers wrote in his diary. 'What a joke we are! You Mr. and Mrs. Taxpayer should come up and see how your money is being wasted. We make a ditch one day and then change the plans and find that it is in the wrong place. And this is called construction!'[98] More than communist agitation, it was this government-sponsored perversion of capitalist values which radicalized the men in the camps.

Second, federal officials were convinced that to place the camps on a wage basis would subvert government relief policy. Unlike the American government which maintained a network of relief camps in tandem with a policy of public works, the Canadian relief camps were established only after public works had been abandoned. Since the married unemployed were eligible only for direct relief, it was essential that single men be treated on the same basis, even though they were required to work. If a work-and-wages program were established, Sir George Perley claimed, it would be impossible to restrict it 'to persons now in the relief camps. If it were introduced, it would certainly result in drawing in many thousands of citizens who at present are not on relief ... [O]nce started, the policy of work and wages would grow into a task quite beyond the power of the people of Canada to support. And further, it might result in retarding the gradual but steady revival of business.'[99]

This last point was essential. Above all, Bennett and McNaughton were convinced that placing the relief camps on a wage basis would impair the proper functioning of the labour market. When board, lodging, medical services, clothing, transportation, and tobacco were added along with the daily allowance, the men in the camps received the equivalent of $7.84 per week which, in the general's view, made them 'considerably better off than many men now in employment ... [I]t would take only a very slight increase in our cash allowances or standard of living to upset the balance of our system so that men would not have a definite incentive to leave for ordinary employment.'[100]

The general's point was well taken. In late autumn 1934 the United Farmers of Manitoba at their annual convention denounced the government relief camps which, they claimed, were 'robbing farmers of necessary help through offering leisure with wages.'[101] In this sense the camps presented a problem similar to unemployment insurance benefits. In an economy highly dependent on low-paying unskilled work, any form of relief for the unemployed constantly ran the risk of becoming more attractive than work. McNaughton attempted to circumvent the problem by paying most of the relief in board with only a meagre cash allowance. As he explained to one critical Tory MP, the camps 'never aimed at making the men self supporting.' Their purpose was simply to 'meet an emergency situation and to care for many thousands until they could be re-absorbed in industry not to set up a wholly new and socialistic substitute for the ordinary methods of organization of the economic life of the country.' The government would not compete with private industry for labour for fear of perpetuating unemployment.[102] In short, relief camps could not be placed on a wage basis for the same reason that direct relief could not be raised to a national minimum and unemployment insurance benefits had to be kept below the living standards of the unskilled. Behind every one of these unemployment policies lay the Poor Law doctrine of 'less eligibility.'

But while the 20¢ daily allowance explains the cause of the unrest, it does not account for the breakdown in dominion-provincial-municipal relations once the men left the camps. Not one provincial or municipal government prior to 1935 had voiced disapproval of either the principle behind the federal relief camps or the basis on which the men were paid.[103] The refusal of Vancouver, British Columbia, and Saskatchewan authorities to co-operate with the federal government during the relief strike was rooted not in sympathy for the men's actions but in revenge against Bennett's refusal to accept total responsibility for the relief of all single unemployed men.

Since 1932, General McNaughton had in effect counted on provincial and municipal governments to enforce discipline among transients. As he constantly pointed out, 'the only means we had of keeping the men in our camps was the guarantee that they could not obtain relief elsewhere.'[104] Western provincial and municipal authorities had never been happy with this role. When the communists organized the mass walk-out from BC's camps in May 1935, these governments were placed in an impossible position.

To grant the striking men relief would only encourage others to leave the camps and would create a larger relief burden and a more dangerous political situation. To jail them for vagrancy, as the federal government wished them to do, meant accepting responsibility for the failure of a federal policy. Although the men were striking in protest against the federal camps, the provincial and municipal governments were expected to discipline them – a task which neither Premier Pattullo nor Vancouver mayor Gerry McGeer would accept. '[P]rimary responsibility unemployment situation rests with Dominion,' Pattullo tersely telegraphed to Bennett after an abortive December 1934 relief camp walk-out. 'In administration relief camps your government is acting for yourselves and not the provinces. Responsibility rests with your Government to justify its own administration in defence camps.' Once the strikers' intention to travel to Ottawa became apparent, the other three western provinces adopted identical positions. They would not discipline men who were protesting against a federal policy which they themselves did not accept.[105] As a result, Bennett had no choice but to violate his own doctrine on provincial responsiblity for law and order by intervening directly in Saskatchewan to stop the trek. In this way, responsibility for the crisis rested where it belonged – on the shoulders of the federal government.

The On-to-Ottawa Trek provided a fitting conclusion to Bennett's five years in office for it symbolized the failure of the unemployment policies pursued by his administration. Not only was the country facing a serious demonstration of political unrest but relations between the federal and local authorities had deteriorated to the point where no one was willing to deal constructively with the situation. Owing more than $117 million in relief debt to the dominion[106] and with every budgetary action subject to federal approval, the four western provinces used the transient crisis as an opportunity to force Ottawa to accept total responsibility for the unemployed. Once the men left the camps, neither the provinces nor the municipalities would care for them in spite of the desperate federal appeal that such men were no longer under dominion jurisdiction. This breakdown in dominion-provincial affairs turned a localized relief strike into a national crisis. The communists could not have been handed a better weapon than the spectacle of three levels of government abdicating responsibility for the unemployed. In the midst of the debacle even British Columbia's Conservative Association concluded that the relief strike had 'crystallized' public opinion 'in the belief that unemployment has become a National responsibility.'[107] As the men headed for Ottawa, this point was symbolically driven home.

By mid-summer 1935 Bennett's administration was completely discredited. Its dismal legislative performance quickly dissipated the brief initiative gained by the January New Deal broadcasts. When Herridge complained to Bennett in mid-May that he did 'not know now where you stand,'[108] he undoubtedly echoed the bewilderment of the entire country. In October, having clung to office as long as possible, Bennett appealed to the electorate with the fiasco of the relief strike still fresh news. He was also faced with a splinter Reconstruction party headed by H.H. Stevens, former minister of trade and commerce in his own cabinet, who was instigator of the muck-raking 1934 Royal Commission on Price Spreads and the most popular Conservative politician in the country.

Above all, there remained the legacy of the last campaign. Bennett won office in 1930 by promising to 'end unemployment.' Five years later there were still almost one million people on relief who the prime minister claimed were not the 'primary' responsibility of his government. It was an indefensible contradiction. The Tories lost all but forty seats. 'Democracy is Democracy. That is all that can be said,' Bennett reminisced bitterly four years later. 'I slaved for the People [but] they rejected me and all my plans and ideas and hopes.'[109]

In fact, Canadians rejected the Tory leader's continued insistence that the care of the unemployed was a local responsibility. By concentrating the burden of the Depression in the areas where its impact was the greatest, this reliance on Poor Law tradition produced progressive municipal and provincial insolvency which only weakened the bonds of fiscal responsibility that Bennett was so anxious to preserve. More ominous for businessmen was the placement of relief administration in the hands of local governments that were most susceptible to the left-wing political sentiment which seemed to be spreading throughout the country. Finally, Bennett's unemployment policy turned dominion-provincial relations into a continuing fiscal battleground which made co-operation on other issues such as unemployment insurance or the need for constitutional reform virtually impossible.

The result was a broad consensus, reflected in Bennett's defeat, on the need for a national reform of relief and a sweeping change in the basis of Canadian federalism itself. In 1930 Bennett had promised to tackle unemployment as a national problem. The man he defeated then had now to implement this mandate.

5
King and chaos:
unemployment policy, 1935–7

Mackenzie King came to power in October 1935 on the crest of what then constituted the largest electoral victory in Canadian federal politics. It was a decisive mandate for change. Unfortunately, no one was quite sure what direction this change would take, for King made almost no specific promises during the campaign. '[P]eople vote against, rather than for something,' he shrewdly noted to his caucus before the election;[1] consequently, the Liberals simply made Bennett's leadership the central issue, with devastating results. The 1935 election was more a referendum against the policies of the past five years than a clear indication of what alternatives should be put in their place.

None the less, King did inherit four key domestic issues which demanded immediate action. The first was a crisis in dominion-provincial financial relations signified by the $115 million which the four western provinces now owed to the federal government because of their inability to pay for their share of direct relief.[2] The second was relief administration itself, a confusing tangle of overlapping responsibilities between the three levels of government which seemed to guarantee maximum suffering for the unemployed and a minimal check on how money was spent. Next was the problem of constitutional reform, exacerbated more than ever by Bennett's arbitrary seizure of authority for his controversial New Deal legislation. Finally, looming in the background, was the menace of unemployed single men, now back in the hated relief camps after their spectacular but unsuccessful attempt to march on Ottawa. Linking these four problems together was one key question: who was responsible for the unemployed?

At first King appeared more willing to tackle this central question of responsibility than had Bennett. Within two months of taking office, he called a dominion-provincial conference whose agenda seemed to promise a new approach to the unemployment crisis. The delegates would discuss the problems of dominion-provincial financial relations, unemployment relief, and constitutional amendment. The connection between these three vital issues appeared to be recognized. Moreover, King's opening address to the conference displayed a promising flexibility. He had no intention of imposing a 'rigid, preconceived programme of action' upon the provinces but instead sought to open up a 'new era of harmonious relations' between the two levels of government.[3] Since nine of the ten administrations present were Liberal, King's chances of success seemed good.

Appearances were deceptive. Underneath the surface harmony there remained the same fundamental differences which had plagued intergovernmental relations during Bennett's administration. It soon became clear that King's basic attitude towards the fiscal plight of the provinces and the responsibility for the care of the unemployed was little different from that of his predecessor.

In fact, as Blair Neatby has noted, despite five years of opposition during the Depression, King's own views 'about politics as well as economics ... had undergone little change.' If anything, one business journalist noted at the time, the Depression had moved him to the right. Why was the author of *Industry and Humanity* so barren of new ideas in the face of the worst industrial crisis of the century?

Part of the answer comes from his record during the 1920s. King had clearly shown that, regardless of the sentiments expressed in his book, he was not predisposed to push for social reform. Although the political climate of the 1920s perhaps left him little option, a politician truly influenced by the new English Liberalism would not have so carelessly presided over the destruction of Canada's first national employment service. His response to the unemployment problem in the past left little grounds for expecting much innovation in the present crisis.

His record also showed that King did not perceive recurrent mass unemployment as a structural problem of modern capitalism that required a significant expansion of the state's role in economic life. Here the links between the King of *Industry and Humanity* and the 1930s are clear. His natural talents were as a conciliator. He responded to the threat of conflict and, in this sense, his ideas and his actions showed him to be sensitive to the menace of working-class unrest. But the causes of that unrest he consistently saw in moral terms. Class conflict was the result of 'that certain blindness' in human affairs which placed self-interest above the public good. Unemployment fell into the same category. It was 'due more to the greed of individuals, to human selfishness and greed,' King argued in 1933, than to 'defects in the system.' Small wonder then that during the 1935 campaign he maintained, 'what is needed more than a change of economic structure is a change of heart.' To King, the Depression posed the necessity of moral, not institutional change. Roosevelt's New Deal seemed more a move towards 'dictatorship' and 'state socialism' than an attempt to save capitalism through pragmatic reforms. Even more than Bennett, King was philosophically averse to expanding the role of the government. Only the threat of serious working-class unrest could provoke a 'change of heart' in the Liberal leader.[4]

At the same time, King's political strategy for the next four years predisposed him to take a hard line towards the provinces. He saw his task as being similar to that of his first administration in 1921. Then too he had taken office in the midst of a depression and led the country out of it through balancing the budget, reducing the national debt, increasing trade, and avoiding expensive social reforms – policies all designed to restore the confidence of business.[5] Now he would repeat this scenario by cutting back the cost of relief, eliminating loans to the provinces, and avoiding the assumption of costly new responsibilities. It was not a formula which offered the provinces much hope of easing their own financial difficulties.

However, they should have been forewarned. At no time during his five years of opposition had King given any hint of sympathy for their plight. Instead, his constant criticism of Bennett's relief policy was that it allowed the provinces to waste vast sums of federal money, a view which scarcely implied they were particularly hard pressed. Nor were he and his finance minister, Charles Dunning, predisposed towards more liberal loans. Instead, Dunning had specified the 'prevention of provincial raids upon the federal treasury' as one of his key tasks on re-entering government.[6] Finally, although the Liberals had frequently castigated Bennett for his failure to treat unemployment as a national problem during their period of opposition, at no point did they demand that Ottawa should assume exclusive or even primary responsibility for the relief of those out of work. Consequently, the presence of a new administration in Ottawa by no means implied a new approach to the care of the unemployed, the heart of the crisis in dominion-provincial relations.

This soon became apparent from the inconclusive results of the 1935 conference. Only the provinces seemed willing to link the three issues on the agenda. Their central concern was to ease their financial plight and to do this they proposed that Ottawa could refund their debt at a lower rate of interest, surrender the field of direct taxation, or take over the principal responsibility for unemployment relief.[7]

Like Bennett before him, King approached the issues of constitutional reform, financial relations, and unemployment relief as if they were in separate compartments. Thus, the subcommittee on constitutional reform was instructed to discuss only the general question of an amending formula as King had no specific suggestion for changed responsibilities. The only result was an agreement to continue discussions. The subcommittee on financial relations bogged down when Dunning refused to consider a compulsory refunding of the public debt or a surrender of federal revenue from direct taxation. Ontario retaliated by rejecting his proposal for a voluntary loan-council scheme to supervise provincial finances.

The wealthier provinces had little interest in increasing federal control over their affairs when the only prospect in return was an increase in their indebtedness. Once again the only agreement was to continue discussions.[8]

The subcommittee on unemployment relief, however, did seem to make significant progress. Ontario wanted the federal government to place relief on the same footing as old-age pensions by assuming 75 per cent of the burden. Quebec went even further, arguing that Ottawa should 'regard the question as a national problem and ... pay the entire cost.' While not willing to go as far as that, finance minister Dunning did not simply dismiss the provincial proposals. Instead, perhaps to their surprise, he promised that the government would 'substantially increas[e]' the present level of its assistance. Shortly after the conference ended, Ottawa announced a 75 per cent jump in its monthly relief grants to the provinces, effective until the end of that fiscal year.[9] This was the most tangible evidence of a new flexibility in dominion-provincial relations and it stood in marked contrast to the arbitrary cuts at the previous conference in 1934.

King agreed to the increase only with the greatest reluctance and afterwards regretted the decision bitterly. Only pressure from a cabinet anxious to pay off political debts to friendly provincial administrations and eager to 'meet what they thought was expected by the public and the provinces at this time' had forced him away from his natural inclination to 'get down to rock bottom' on the question of relief financing.[10]

In addition, the decision was palatable to King only because, in turn, the provinces agreed to co-operate with the National Employment Commission he proposed to establish to supervise their relief expenditures. The creation of such a body had been one of King's few specific proposals for dealing with unemployment during the recent campaign and had formed the core of his unemployment policy since 1930. Its origin lay in King's conviction that the provinces had been grossly wasting federal money and would continue to do so unless subjected to close supervision, something Bennett had not done. Consequently, although tied to the increase in grants-in-aid, the NEC was in fact designed to reduce Ottawa's expenditure on relief over the long run by ensuring its administration would become more 'efficient and economical.' Like Dunning's proposal for a loan council, it was part of King's strategy of balancing the federal budget by increasing Ottawa's control over provincial expenditure. Anxious only for the extra funds, the provinces failed to notice this implication. Nor did they realize that by insisting on the 'added precaution' of a National Employment Commission, King was actually condemning their ability to administer relief.[11]

With the conference over, King immediately set to work determining the scope and composition of the NEC. His discovery that federal relief spending would top

$50 million for the past fiscal year, the highest total since the beginning of the Depression, gave an added urgency to this task. King's chief adviser on the project was Norman Rogers, his minister of labour, who would be responsible for supervising the work of the commission.

Rogers and King had been close associates since the late 1920s when the young university professor took a two-year sojourn from academic life to work as King's personal secretary. At that time Rogers' brilliance, capacity for hard work, and intense idealism had reminded the Liberal leader of his own youthful career in the Department of Labour. King developed, as Blair Neatby notes, a kind of 'paternal pride' in Rogers whom he saw 'almost [as] a protégé.'[12]

After leaving King's employ in 1929, Rogers taught political science at Queen's University where he gained a reputation as one of Canada's leading experts in constitutional law. Throughout this period he continued to serve as a close adviser and speech writer for King while the latter was leader of the opposition. In addition, he represented his native province, Nova Scotia, before the 1934 Royal Commission of Economic Enquiry into fiscal woes. Rogers also developed a close intellectual friendship during these years with socialists such as Frank Underhill, F.R. Scott, and Harry Cassidy of the League for Social Reconstruction but he rejected their endorsement of the CCF. 'I have a high regard for Mr. Woodsworth's character ... [and] some of his objectives,' he told a CCF supporter, but the party itself 'lack[ed] .. a sense of political realities.'[13]

In 1935, convinced that the 'next five years are certain to bring up problems ... in which I have been deeply interested for a long time,'[14] Rogers took the plunge into politics by running successfully for the Liberals in his home riding of Kingston. As a personal favourite of the prime minister, he was quickly appointed minister of labour in King's new cabinet.

Rogers took up his portfolio with a passionate interest in two issues. The first was constitutional reform. '[O]ne of the first tasks that will confront [the] new administration,' he told Cassidy, 'will be a redistribution of powers under the British North America Act.' Nowhere was this change more urgent than in the second area where reform was essential – unemployment relief. 'There has been no clear sense of direction on the part of those who have been responsible for the administration of unemployment relief at Ottawa,' he argued privately during the election. 'They seem to have proceeded on the theory that unemployment and its attendant ills is a temporary obligation and not a continuing responsibility of the state.' With the Liberals in power, it would be possible to make a 'new beginning.' If private industry were 'unable to increase its wage rolls materially,' it would be up to Ottawa to 'undertake long range developmental schemes in order to provide work and wages for at least the young and able-bodied of the unemployed army.'[15] Rogers clearly saw the work of the NEC in this light.

But King had no intention of making unemployment relief a federal responsibility or of using large-scale public works as an anti-depression strategy. He viewed the NEC as simply a supervisory body which would save Ottawa money by keeping a very close watch on provincial and municipal relief administration, much as the Patriotic Fund had supervised but not actually administered the relief of needy families of veterans during the First World War.

In fact, King's choice of the Patriotic Fund as a model for the NEC was revealing. It showed that, like Bennett, he too viewed Ottawa's involvement with relief as a temporary responsibility justified only by the 'exceptional' circumstances of the Depression, in the same way that the Patriotic Fund had been created to deal with an unusual wartime emergency. It also indicated that the prime minister was not expecting the NEC to come up with drastically new methods of relieving unemployment.

This was readily apparent from the National Employment Commission Act which received royal assent on 8 April 1936. The preamble instructed the seven commissioners to 'find ways and means of providing remunerative employment, thus reducing the numbers at present on relief, and lessening the burden of taxation.' The last phrase was the punch-line, for it ruled out reducing the relief rolls through a massive public-works program as Roosevelt's Works Progress Administration Bill had done in 1935. Instead, the three principal tasks of the NEC were of the 'watch-dog' variety: to register and classify those on relief; to attach stricter conditions to the grants-in-aid to the provinces; and to supervise and audit provincial and municipal relief expenditures in order to 'avoid overlapping and abuses.' The act gave the NEC only the vaguest administrative duties which specifically did not include the right directly to administer unemployment relief itself.[16]

The *Globe and Mail*'s assessment of the NEC's mandate was apt: '[T]he Commission [does not have] unlimited resources and ... powers to go New Dealing all over the country with elaborate work projects and farm rehabilitation schemes. It must proceed within the framework of the present system and confine its plans to sound and meritorious schemes ... within the limitations of the public purse.'[17] The seven people appointed to the NEC certainly reflected this conservative thrust. Rogers had argued previously that if the commission was to 'do its job satisfactorily' it needed the 'service of men who possess technical knowledge and who have first hand experience with relief administration.'[18] With the exception of Rogers' colleague W.A. Mackintosh, a Queen's University economist, none of the seven appointees to the NEC fit this description. Instead, they were chosen to represent important economic and regional constituencies. Alfred Marois, the Quebec representative, was a shoe manufacturer; Neil McLean, a small businessman from New Brunswick; E.J. Young and Mary

Sutherland were both from rural areas of western Canada; and Tom Moore, the sole trade unionist on the commission, was president of the Trade and Labour Congress and well known throughout the country as the senior statesman of Canadian labour.[19]

The NEC's chairman was a prominent Montreal industrialist, Arthur Blaikie Purvis. Described by the press as a 'dynamic personality' who could 'dominate [a] gathering' without seeming to do so, Purvis was something of a star in Canada's small corporate élite. A Scottish immigrant who had carved out a distinguished career in the burgeoning chemicals and explosives industry in Glasgow during the war, he migrated to Canada in 1925 at the age of thirty-five to become president of the chemical complex, Canadian Industries Limited. By the time of his appointment to the NEC eleven years later, Purvis was a bastion of Montreal business, holding directorships in General Motors, Bell Telephone, Sun Life, and British American Oil in addition to his presidency of Dunlop Tire and Rubber and CIL.[20]

Formerly a staunch Tory, Purvis was seriously disillusioned with his party by Bennett's inflammatory New Deal rhetoric and he now saw the Liberals as 'our only hope ... to continue the same line of action ... which ... [until 1935] Mr. Bennett [had] done so well.' Not surprisingly, his approach to the NEC was decidedly low-key. 'We don't want to go off at half-cock, we don't want a lot of ballyhoo and we hope ... the people will not expect us to work wonders overnight,' Purvis warned the press. 'My experience in industry has been that it is better to analyse the problem ... in the laboratory and make sure the correct solution has been found before galloping off without knowing anything about the objectives or how it is to be attained.'[21]

King, for his part, took great pride in the creation of the NEC for which he felt he was 'almost wholly responsible.' By finally bringing to light the 'obvious abuses, rackets, overlapping and the like' surrounding provincial and municipal administration of relief, he was convinced he would 'save the Treasury & ... the taxpayers many millions of dollars.' It would also give Ottawa the non-partisan statistical information it needed to begin scaling down its grants-in-aid. 'Municipalities and provinces will soon find the truth of the saying that "every man must learn to earn his bread by the sweat of his brow," ' King noted in his diary on the day the NEC act passed Parliament. How this would promote their 'effective co-operation' with the commission remained to be seen.[22]

The opposition parties were less enthusiastic. From bitter experience Bennett asked how the NEC could possibly lessen the cost of relief without the 'power and authority to determine how many shall be on [it]' or to define 'just what amount is to be paid ... to Halifax ... or London, or Winnipeg or Calgary?' From the other side of the political spectrum came even more scathing criticism as CCF spokesmen noted that the bill did nothing to clarify who was responsible for the unemployed, held out no hope of providing immediate jobs, and was silent on whether those on relief would be ensured a decent minimum of food, clothing, shelter, and medical care.[23] As the *Canadian Forum* pointed out,

The government speeches contain the implication that without a scientific classification of the unemployed into their age, sex, occupational groups and the like, the exact nature of the problem cannot be known, and hence a solution cannot be formulated. This is ... the crudest kind of empiricism ... For the unemployed, no matter how carefully they may be classified, represent the effect and not the cause of the problem. Given a policy, such information as the government seeks would help towards its effective administration. Without a policy the information will not mean one day's work or one cent in wages.

The only policy the *Forum* could discern was that 'nothing must be done which is likely to tread on the toe of private business; relief and public works are to be kept at that minimum which will prevent tax payers from kicking and the unemployed from starving.'[24] Despite Rogers' early hopes, this was an accurate insight into the NEC's mandate.

Apart from the dominion-provincial conference and the formation of the NEC, there remained one other pledge from the 1935 campaign. This was King's promise to provide wages, education, training, and work that would 'give them pride' and be of 'service to the state' for the 20,000 men presently in the relief camps. Significantly he did not promise to abolish the camps but only said that they would be transferred from the Department of Defence to the NEC.[25] Beyond these vague pledges, he took office with no specific idea of how he would deal with the dangerous problem of unemployed single men.

Consequently, a month after the election, a three-man commission made up of R.A. Rigg, director of the Employment Service, Dr Edmund Bradwin, head of Frontier College, and Humphrey Mitchell, a former Liberal MP and trade unionist, was appointed to investigate the entire relief-camp situation and to recommend whether the camps should be maintained, modified, or closed down. After conferring with Civilian Conservation Corps' administrators in the United States and visiting over forty relief camps in western Canada, the commission submitted its report in early January 1936.

Its main recommendation was to close the camps 'as soon as possible,' although the commissioners 'regretfully' noted that they had to be maintained for the time being because of the lack of alternative employment. The camps contained too many young men of 'thwarted ambitions' who had now become 'viciously rebellious against and defiant to authority' with the help of communist agitation.

Moreover, if maintained much longer, there was a 'serious danger' that they would become 'accepted as a fixed, national institution akin to the Poor Law Work Houses of Europe.' For both reasons, the commissioners wanted them replaced by an immediate job-creation program in industry and agriculture.[26]

Two weeks after receiving this report, the cabinet decided to close down the camps 'as quickly as possible.' On 25 February Rogers informed the House that they would be phased out completely by 1 July. Through an agreement with the two national railways, track maintenance jobs would be offered to 10,000 men at normal wages over the four summer months. The other 10,000 would be assisted in finding farm work. In the interim, wages in the camps would be raised to $15.00 a month effective 1 March, half of which would be deferred until the men left in order to provide them with 'some means of support while ... seeking industrial re-establishment.' Rogers also gave a third reason for the government's decision to close the camps which was, perhaps, more decisive than the two provided by the Rigg Commission. They were too expensive. For the same amount that it cost to keep 20,000 men in the camps in 1935, the government could have maintained 73,000 men on farms at a wage of $10.00 a month. Thus, the 'true condemnation of the relief camps,' Rogers told the House, 'is that the government ... has not obtained fair value for its money.'[27] It was not an argument which boded well for single men.

It was one thing to state that the camps would be closed. More difficult was the task of getting the men to leave, especially once wages were raised from $7.50 to $15.00 a month. As army chief General Ashton pointed out, 'most young men prefer camp life to that on an isolated prairie farm.' Consequently, despite a concerted campaign by the Soldier Settlement Branch to find over 4000 farm jobs, only 650 of the more than 20,000 men in the camps picked this option. As one frustrated district superintendent observed, the men preferred to stay where they had 'regular hours' and 'good food' than leave for farms where 'they have to work harder, longer hours, and for lower wages with a possibility that they may not collect their wages in the fall.'[28]

Since most men would not voluntarily choose agricultural labour, the government simply used their refusal as an excuse to throw them out of the camps. By mid-April all commanders were instructed that if any man 'refuses to accept farm work, he will be discharged from the project.' From the government's point of view, a refusal was just as valuable as a placement for it put Ottawa 'in the position of being able to meet any challenge that jobs are not available for all who are sincerely desirous of getting off the relief rolls.'[29] What the men gained was less clear.

The offer of railway work at regular wages of 25¢ an hour was more attractive. By the end of June, 8700 men had left the camps to pursue this activity. However, the government had no plans for their care once the jobs expired in autumn. The money they earned over the summer, Rogers explained, 'ought to enable them to provide for themselves during the coming winter.' As CCF spokesmen quickly pointed out, this was a ridiculous expectation. The government had made no arrangement for deferred payment of wages so there was no guarantee that the men would have any money when they left the railway camps. Moreover, they would be charged the going rate for room, board, and clothing while working so that at the most they could be expected to save $100, not nearly enough to get anyone over the winter without relief. The men were no longer 'wards of the government,' transport minister C.D. Howe replied, but were 'on their own ... If they want to squander their money ... they will have to reap the rewards of that sort of thing.'[30]

By the time the relief camps closed on 1 July, the makings of a new transient crisis were readily apparent. Fewer than half of the 20,000 men had been placed in jobs. As the other 10,000 began drifting toward the cities in search of work or relief, new fears of disorder began to grow. By abolishing the relief camps, the King administration made its sharpest break with the policy of the previous government. It was not designed to improve the lot of single unemployed men.

On the most important question affecting the unemployed – relief – the new Liberal government displayed a remarkable adherence to the approach of Conservative R.B. Bennett. The new 1936 Relief Act introduced in March contained no important modifications of previous policy. Like his predecessors in the Labour ministry, Rogers simply reaffirmed that the care of the unemployed was 'primarily a responsibility of the provincial and municipal authorities.'[31]

Throughout the 1936 session the labour minister continued to resist any suggestion that federal responsibilities for relief should be expanded. Large expenditures for public works were out of the question because of their 'deterrent effect' on private investment. It would take $300-$400 million per year to put the 332,000 employable on relief to work, Rogers told the House, and this was inconceivable outside of a 'philosophy of socialism.' At the same time, although he did concede that the scale of relief should be 'just and reasonable,' he refused to use his authority to ensure that a national minimum standard of support was adopted by the provinces and municipalities. 'Different standards of living prevail in different parts of the Dominion and even in different areas in a province,' he declared. For this reason, 'some disparities must continue to exist ... with regard to relief scales.'[32] Under the Liberals the doctrine of 'less eligibility' would remain intact.

In only one area was there any attempt at innovation. The new government was determined to get a complete classification of those on relief. Since the administration already made it quite clear it had no intention of putting them to work or of improving their standard of support, the only question was why. Rogers, of course, claimed that the information was needed so that the relief problem could be tackled in a 'scientific way,' although he would not specify what this meant. However, there were hints. Referring to the 'lack of balance' between the urban and rural populations, he noted that knowledge of how many on relief had agricultural training would be indispensable for 'far-reaching schemes of agricultural re-settlement.' Better data would also reveal how many seasonal workers 'whose wages were sufficient to carry them through the remainder of the year' were taking advantage of the dole as well as the number of unemployables the municipalities were loading onto relief.[33] In short, although it would not help the unemployed, such a classification would be a useful bureaucratic device for saving Ottawa money. Consequently, even before the 1936 Relief Act was passed, federal officials began collecting detailed information on what kind of people were on relief and how long they had been on the rolls. The only question not asked was how much support they received.

This concern for economy also surfaced in the 25 per cent cut in grants-in-aid which the cabinet agreed to at the end of March. King had never been reconciled to the 75 per cent December increase. Now that the provinces had given their consent to the NEC, there was no pressing reason to continue being generous, especially since he was determined to cut the federal deficit by almost $60 million over the next fiscal year. None the less, the fact that the decision was made without provincial consultation came as a rude shock to the premiers who had quite reasonably expected no action would be taken until the NEC had had a chance to establish their 'actual needs.'[34] King's promise of 'effective cooperation,' it seemed, was little different from the arbitrary style of R.B. Bennett.

The prime minister, however, was indifferent to provincial outrage or the fact that the credibility of the NEC had been severely compromised. '[U]nless we let the municipalities and the country see that we are going to cut down on these outlays there never would be a tightening up of the indiscriminate relief process,' he noted in a passage that could have been written by Bennett himself.[35]

For his part, Ontario premier Mitch Hepburn simply passed these cuts down the line. 'I'm sorry but the cut is not our responsibility. The municipalities must fight it out with the federal government,' he told a protest demonstration organized by the Ontario Federation of the Unemployed. 'We are reluctant to have the impression get across that every time the federal government gets out of the picture ... Ontario takes up the slack.' If Ontario cities felt their relief scales were inadequate as a result of these cutbacks, they had the consent of the province to raise them, Ontario welfare and municipal affairs minister David Croll told the reeve of York Township, 'but the increased rate must be at [their own] expense ... Spending other people's money put the municipalities where they are today. They'll have to get out of the habit.'[36]

The city of Ottawa took the lead in implementing this relief crackdown. In 1933, with the creation of its Public Welfare Board, Ottawa became one of the first Canadian communities to employ professional social workers in the distribution of relief. Over the next three years, they gradually liberalized the dole. Casual earnings of the jobless were no longer routinely deducted from their relief allowances; clothing provisions were implemented for the first time and grants for rent and fuel became the highest in Ontario. As a result, by 1936, the city dispensed a scale of relief that was relatively generous by provincial standards. Of the six Ontario cities with more than 100,000 persons per year on the dole, Ottawa ranked third overall in total per capita relief expenditure, spending $8.62 per month for each of its citizens on welfare.[37]

Complaints had been growing within the local press and on city council against the steadily rising cost of relief and the federal cut-back in the spring of 1936 brought the whole issue to a head. In order to make up the difference, the city was forced to hike property taxes stiffly. The result was an immediate backlash against the city's new Welfare Board. Social service was an 'evil,' one city controller charged, that was 'creeping into the Public Welfare Board which had been appointed to administer Relief, not to build up a body of social workers.' The local press agreed. Social workers in the Welfare Board, the *Ottawa Citizen* pointed out, had tended 'to treat those on relief as chronic help-receivers, as public charges and as a class apart, [which] leads on the one hand to a recognition of a class of professional relief beneficiaries and on the other to a class of professional social workers whose career is to treat the unfortunate according to well defined principles.' '[T]he number of those who want relief and not work is increasing,' the *Ottawa Journal* claimed. 'A habit has been created and habits are hard to change,'[38]

In response to these criticisms, the city council, over the course of the summer, fired forty women social workers from the Public Welfare Board. Eleven male detectives were installed in their place to reinvestigate the board's caseloads and to root out chisellers. 'Women were good for social service work,' Ottawa's mayor pointed out in justifying the move, but it was the city's intention to 'divorce direct relief from social service ... [T]he men investigators did better work than women; they were not interested in social service but in seeing that those on relief gave the city the right information and reported their earnings.'[39]

This purge sent shock waves throughout the ranks of Canadian social work. In Ottawa, Bessie Touzel, staff supervisor of the Welfare Board and the person most responsible for building up its professional staff, resigned in protest against the arbitrary dismissal of her female colleagues and the destruction of relief policies she had worked so hard to establish. '[O]ur social work future rests ... on the standards which we can maintain in our public departments,' Touzel argued in defence of her action. Since the profession believed that 'adequate standards of assistance are essential if we are to avoid social catastrophe,' then it had a 'first obligation to stand guard here.' Her resignation quickly became a cause célèbre amongst her colleagues. For too long social workers had accepted with 'comparative calm' the 'continued pressure to economize in the administration of relief' at the expense of their clients, charged *The Social Worker*, monthly journal of the Canadian Association of Social Workers. Touzel's 'courageous stand' had now 'brought the situation more or less dramatically to a head.' Did Canadian social workers 'wish to make the professional association a force in its own field, or not?'[40]

The answer was unclear. All members of the profession were outraged by the events in Ottawa, but there was no agreement over what they could or should do about it. '[I]t would be worse than futile,' wrote one CASW member from Victoria, 'for the four ... members attached to private agencies [in my city] to take any overt group action on such a matter. After all, a statement in a newspaper from a group about which the average citizen knows nothing is not going to affect his views to any great extent.' A CASW writer from Winnipeg probably summed up the feelings of most in the profession: Touzel's protest resignation had 'failed' because it 'only left the field vacant to be filled by inexperienced workers. In such cases any social worker would be well advised to hold a position and argue the points to a conclusion, meanwhile, calling on the CASW for moral support and public education.'[41] The sad truth was that Canada's 500 social workers scattered across the country possessed no force other than moral suasion to defend collectively either their professional standards or the interests of their clients. After a brief flurry of indignation within the CASW, Touzel's resignation and the gutting of Ottawa's Welfare Board were forgotten.

Within the city itself, the much-heralded search for relief chisellers quickly degenerated into farce. 'The detectives set to work,' Marjorie Bradford reported from the Canadian Welfare Council national office, 'and I think the net results have been two or three prosecutions for unreported supplementary earnings. The total amount involved was something like $400.00 in all ... but in no case could the family be removed from the relief rolls. There has also been one assault case involving an irascible husband and father who said his family had been insulted. The cost to the city of this investigation will be $1400-$1500, but I can say with certainty that there will be nothing in the press telling what the city has to show for [it].'[42] The 'real racket in relief,' Muriel Tucker, Bradford's colleague in the CWC office pointed out, 'came not from the few families who endeavour to "get by" the relief investigator by concealing a few dollars of savings, but through ... the graft practiced by local merchants [through relief vouchers] which is more or less connived at by city or township councils in order to secure votes.'[43] This form of relief chiselling, although widespread throughout Canadian cities, remained relatively immune from investigation during the 1930s.

By the spring of 1936 the outlines of King's unemployment policy were beginning to take shape. The closing of the camps, the classification of those on relief, the arbitrary cutbacks in grants-in-aid, and even the creation of the NEC were part of a determined campaign to reduce the numbers on relief without resort to the costly expedient of providing public works. There was also a renewed emphasis on the 'back-to-the-land' philosophy. Convinced that not enough had been provided 'for replacement of men on the land,' King personally saw to it that federal expenditure on relief settlement was boosted to $408,609, a staggering increase from the meagre $2496 spent in 1935. As he explained to his party caucus at the end of April, the government 'intended to meet [unemployment] by getting men back to work, not to have [sic] in the State a trough for idle or worthless people to feed out of.'[44]

However, the unemployed were not the only ones feeding from Ottawa's 'trough.' Since the inconclusive end of the dominion-provincial conference in December, King had cast about desperately for a way of stopping the seemingly uncontrollable flow of federal funds to the provinces in the form of loans and grants-in-aid. They were necessary, of course, because the provinces' tax base was insufficient to support their primary responsibility for the care of the unemployed but the Liberal government continued to approach the questions of debt, taxation, and relief as if they were three separate issues.

This was readily apparent from two constitutional amendments which Ottawa placed before the provinces between January and May of 1936. Both were pet proposals of King's minister of finance, Charles Dunning. The first, a national loan-council scheme, was designed to stem the steady growth in the national debt which had risen by almost a billion dollars in the years since 1930. It offered a federal guarantee for all provincial loans providing each one was first approved by a loan council which included the federal minister of finance. The proposal was aimed directly at the four western provinces and, like Bennett's earlier demand for a million dollar ceiling on their deficits, it was intended to give Ottawa a veto power over provincial fiscal affairs. Participation in the scheme was to be voluntary, except there would be no more federal loans until the provinces agreed to the amendment. The loan council, in short, offered the premiers little hope of easing their financial plight since its ultimate goal was to cut down the extent of their borrowing.[45]

For that very reason both British Columbia and Alberta refused to agree. Pattullo quite rightly suspected that no loan council which included Dunning would finance his 'work and wages' schemes. In Alberta, opposition to any federal control of provincial credit was even more extreme. The previous August, voters in that province had astounded North America and seriously shaken the financial community by electing to office the world's first Social Credit government, led by Calgary high-school principal and radio evangelist, William 'Bible Bill' Aberhart.

Aberhart, a simplistic interpreter of the unorthodox monetary theories of Scottish engineer Major C.H. Douglas, believed that inadequate credit or purchasing power was the root cause of the Depression, particularly the parasitical activities of banks. His solution was to advocate provincial issuance of monthly 'social credit' dividends of $25.00 to each citizen in order to restore consumer spending power. 'Where does all the money come from? We don't use money. Then where does all the credit come from? Why out of the end of a fountain pen,' the Calgary preacher promised Alberta voters. In a debt-ridden and highly sectarian province, Aberhart's clever mix of inflation, religion, and the hope of salvation caught on fast, particularly through the enormous radio audience of 350,000 people who tuned in weekly for his bible broadcasts.[46] In 1935 his newly organized Alberta Social Credit party easily swept the UFA government of J.E. Brownlee out of office.

Once in power, Aberhart quickly realized the difficulties that Dunning's loan-council scheme would pose for his attempt to implement Social Credit. Pattullo, by 1936, at least had the option of raising money elsewhere. The Alberta premier did not. The result was a return to a familiar scenario from the Bennett years – a fiscal showdown between Ottawa and the provinces.

On 1 April Alberta had an interest payment due which it could not meet without a federal loan. Since Aberhart refused to give his consent to the loan-council amendment, the province was allowed to become the first to default since the beginning of the Depression. Aberhart retaliated by reducing the interest rate on Alberta bonds by 50 per cent. Both govenments had shown admirable toughness but there was still no loan-council scheme nor any other formula for providing fresh federal loans.

Saskatchewan became the next test. Without a loan, it would default in May. This time, however, federal money was provided despite King's previous stand that there would be no more loans without a loan council. Like Bennett, the prime minister finally discovered that Ottawa's veto power on loans was really illusory because a series of provincial defaults would endanger the whole country's credit rating abroad. In the eyes of Canada's creditors, at least, federal and provincial finances were linked; therefore, with or without a loan council, Ottawa would have to stand behind the solvency of the provinces. By mid-May a chastened King was regretting 'the effort even indirectly to "control" the provinces in any of their acts.'[47]

Paradoxically, the other amendment introduced along with the loan-council scheme would have had the opposite effect of reducing Ottawa's fiscal authority over the premiers. This was Dunning's idea of giving the provinces the right to levy an indirect sales tax – a field previously occupied by the dominion. The revenue from the federal sales tax roughly equalled Ottawa's expenditure on relief and

Dunning apparently felt that a surrender of this field would give the federal government a perfect excuse for abandoning the hated system of grants-in-aid. The scheme had obvious appeal for King because it would permit a return to his cherished goal of 'responsible government,' in which governments only spent money they raised themselves.[48]

Desperate for any extra revenue, the provinces were more than willing to go along with the idea, although they were given no indication that it implied a federal withdrawal from relief. Nevertheless, it was killed in the Senate along with the loan-council amendment by a Conservative Senate majority which feared that differential provincial sales taxes might be used as indirect tariffs to impede inter-provincial trade. By then King, perhaps because of the loan-council fiasco, was convinced that the whole idea of surrendering revenue was a mistake. 'We would have been better off with Tory Govt's in the provinces ... It is a case of doing too much for our friends,' he noted bitterly when the measure went down to defeat.[49]

By the spring of 1936 King's hope of restoring 'harmony' to dominion-provincial relations lay in shreds. His two attempts to amend the constitution contained contradictory objectives – a consequence perhaps of his refusal to devise serious alternatives to Bennett's policies while in opposition. Moreover, they failed precisely because they were designed to cut down Ottawa's financial obligations at a time when the real fiscal crisis lay with the provinces.[50] Finally, both the loan-council and taxation amendments, along with the cutbacks in grants-in-aid and the closing of relief camps, skirted the central problem. Only the federal government had the financial capacity to care for the unemployed; yet the central thrust of King's policy was to shed this burden as quickly as possible. It was a contradiction which guaranteed a return to conflict with both the provinces and with the unemployed.

There was one bright spot in this sombre pattern. In mid-May the NEC was officially appointed, although by now a harried King confessed that he was 'so fatigued & so engrossed in so many things that I just cannot give myself to its work.' For the next eighteen months the NEC would look to Norman Rogers for political direction.[51]

The NEC's first task was to register those on relief. A complete registration of all unemployed people was ruled out for fear that they 'would expect, in return, quick results in securing employment and failure to give them this would possibly bring disastrous reaction.' In its first important political decision, therefore, the NEC ensured that it would obtain only a partial view of the unemployment problem. For help in straightening out the relief mess, it hired Canada's foremost authority on the subject, Charlotte Whitton. Whitton had now the chance to put into effect all the recommendations for reform of relief which she had urged so fruitlessly on Bennett. She wasted no time in returning to her familiar theme. '[T]he most important phase of the whole problem,' she warned the commission, was the 'continuous interference and exploitation of the situation' by the municipalities. Consequently, the first step in reforming relief was to guarantee the social work profession 'administrative freedom and adequacy of personnel' by attaching strict conditions to the new relief agreements with the provinces. Whitton was soon at work devising yet another comprehensive memorandum on how this should be done.[52]

Reform of relief was only part of the NEC's mandate. More important was to get people off the dole. Here the commission's approach followed the thinking of its most influential member, economist W.A. Mackintosh. A brilliant academic and a prolific writer on Canadian economic problems, he was yet another example of the growing influence of Queen's University on the federal government. A pioneer, along with Harold Innis, of the staples approach to Canadian economic history, Mackintosh's rise within the university was meteoric. In 1926, at the age of thirty-two, he became chairman of the Department of Economics and Political Science which would later include another equally young and ambitious political scientist, Norman Rogers. During the latter half of the 1920s, Mackintosh got his first taste of government service by acting as a member of Ottawa's Advisory Board on Tariffs and Taxation. When Rogers made the decision to run for office in 1935, Mackintosh provided political advice and moral support from the sidelines. With Rogers's victory, he was the logical first choice of fellow Queen's colleagues O.D. Skelton, W.C. Clark, and of course, Rogers himself, for the NEC. His appointment to that commission marked the intensification of an advisory career in Ottawa that would shape the course of Canadian economic policy for the next three decades.[53]

To Mackintosh, economics was a discipline that was above politics. It 'prescribes no policy and enunciates no doctrine,' he argued, 'apart from the analysis of the particular facts of the moment.' Not surprisingly, his first task on joining the commission was to apply his staples analysis to the country's current economic plight. Canada, he argued in a decisive July 1936 memo that would fundamentally shape the NEC's approach to unemployment, was an exporting nation. For this reason, the Depression had been largely communicated to it from abroad. Consequently, little could be done to reduce unemployment beyond working for an increase in trade. The monetary and tariff policies of the present government were now 'favourable to recovery.' The chief task of the NEC was thus to 'endeavour by every means to clear the channels of investment of all removeable obstacles.' In short, private, not public investment was the key to recovery and the commission would recommend nothing that might disturb the confidence of business such as extensive spending on public works. Instead, the NEC's role would be to 'see ... that employables are brought into the jobs which have been opened for them.' Since recovery was already underway, the chief concern of the commission should not be employment but employability.[54]

Within these somewhat limited parameters the NEC set about finding work for those on the dole. By September 1936 four important recommendations lay on Rogers's desk. The first suggested a national employment service run exclusively by the federal government. It was not a particularly new suggestion since the same proposal had been contained in Bennett's Employment and Social Insurance Act. Given the NEC's stress on employability, however, a new labour-exchange network to replace the patronage-ridden Employment Service of Canada was an obvious first step in finding jobs for those on relief.[55]

The second recommendation for a 'broad Housing policy' was a more significant departure. The idea originated with Mackintosh. Although at this point he opposed public investment in general as an anti-depression strategy, he felt that housing was one area where the government could spend directly without fear of competing with private industry. There was already a backlog of 75,000 homes which were needed but had not been built because of the slump in the construction industry. Moreover, from its registration of those on the dole, the NEC knew that 13 per cent of employable males on relief were in construction and 32 per cent were general labourers. A housing policy offered a chance of 'striking at the root of present unemployment.' Because there was an appalling lack of low-cost rental accommodation in slum areas, which contained the greatest number of unemployed, this had a 'direct relationship not only to unemployment but to public health.' Now was the time to do something about the problem, Mackintosh argued, before 'we have moved into a period of higher building costs.'

The proposed attack included renovation of existing homes through a Home Improvement Act modelled on a similar scheme in the US; a new Dominion Housing Act to encourage new housing starts by making more federal funds available for mortgages; and a low-cost housing and slum-clearance scheme which would provide direct federal subsidies for the construction of low-rental units. Public opinion was 'ripe for ... bold leadership in this field' and the announcement of such a comprehensive program would 'go a long way toward creating a public belief that the problems of relief and unemployment could be overcome in the near future.' Purvis agreed. A 'considerable measure of public support ... would be lost if the programme is allowed to go out piecemeal,' he warned when forwarding the recommendation to Rogers on 2 September.[56]

The third set of recommendations came from the Youth Employment Committee of the NEC. Having visited several CCC camps in the United States as well as the headquarters of the National Youth Administration in Washington, its proposals were heavily influenced by the New Deal approach to the problem of youth unemployment. There were 75,000 young people between eighteen and twenty-five on relief, the committee pointed out, and another 100,000 were unemployed and living with their parents. They were desperately in need of jobs at a wage 'which would make the workers feel that they are doing work of real significance.' To provide this incentive the committee proposed the creation of a National Volunteer Conservation Service modelled along the lines of the American CCC.

The service was designed to train workers in Canada's primary industries. It would contain three branches: a Volunteer Forest Service employing 12,000 men which would work on a national program of forest conservation; a Volunteer Mining Service of 8000 which would develop mining areas and provide 'practical experience' in mine labour for 'young unemployed from city areas'; and a Volunteer Agricultural Service of 5000 to train 'inexperienced' youth in farm work. The volunteer nature of the service was strongly emphasized. Like its American counterpart, it would sign up youths for six-month stints during which they would not be allowed to leave except to take up work. Refusal to sign would not constitute grounds for being cut off relief as had been the case with the relief camps. Wages would be geared to the 'normal' rate for inexperienced labour in the industry and area. The total annual cost of caring for 25,000 men in the service was placed at $9.4 million.

In addition to this proposal, the committee also recommended that Ottawa embark on a 'national plan of apprentice or probationary training in industry in the skilled, semi-skilled and specialized trades.' Only a few of the provinces had passed apprenticeship legislation and the Employment Service existed 'like an island in mid-stream, having absolutely no contact on the one hand with its source of supply [the school] and very little contact on the other hand with industry.' Consequently, there were almost no facilities either for training skilled workers or placing them in industries where they could be trained. Even if recovery opened up skilled jobs, there was no guarantee they would be taken up by young people on relief. For this reason, both a new Employment Service and a national apprenticeship program were essential. As a first step the committee recommended the creation of twenty-six Young Men's Training Centres in major cities to provide recreation, guidance, and job skills to 7500 men at an estimated cost of $400,000 per year.[57]

The final set of recommendations came from the Committee on Land Settlement. Of all the NEC's suggestions, these were the ones most likely to receive a sympathetic hearing in cabinet. By his dramatic boost in funding for relief settlement, King had made no secret of his 'back-to-the-land' bias and Rogers had earlier referred to 'far-reaching schemes of agricultural resettlement' as one of the benefits to be gained from the registration and classification of those on the dole.

Moreover, the committee was chaired by E.J. Young, a western Liberal MP who was known within the party for his right-wing, laissez-faire beliefs.[58]

Instead of supporting land settlement, the committee came out staunchly against 'making agriculture the dumping ground for all those who have failed in other walks in life.' The present relief settlement scheme into which King had just poured an extra $477,000 was 'essentially unsound,' Young argued passionately. In the first place, it used taxpayers' money to 'start people up in private business ... in a line ... that has never been profitable in Canada.' Secondly, it reserved land for relief settlers which was not available to those who had avoided the dole and provided them with 'advice and guidance ... while letting their self-supporting neighbours fend for themselves,' a policy which had only created 'bad feelings between these two classes.' Finally, there were already over 30,000 farm families in the dried-out districts who were now on relief. Until something was done to place them back on their feet, it was 'difficult to justify the placing of new settlers on the land.'[59]

By coming out so strongly against relief settlement, Young's committee was giving vent to widespread rural resentment at governments which seemed more anxious to rid cities of their surplus unemployed than to help experienced farmers become self-supporting. The real 'back-to-the-land' problem was not relief settlement but resettlement: placing farmers on land they could farm instead of attempting to solve an urban crisis at the expense of the countryside. It was sound advice but obviously not what King expected.

The NEC was off to a good start. Within three months it had placed a number of specific and well-conceived suggestions before the government. Taken together they hardly constituted a New Deal but they did imply a moderate increase in federal spending and responsibility. This point was lost on King when he commented on Purvis's cabinet presentation in early September: 'We had Mr. Purvis in for an hour. He outlined the Board's recommendations re policy to be adopted as regards single homeless unemployed, (rehabilitation & employment) & also re Housing, a program including renovation & repairs, general building & low cost (rental) building. Purvis made an exceptionally fine presentation – all tending in direction of getting back to voluntary effort. He admitted most of our problems was [sic] undoing the mistakes of the last few years' mistaken policies – Bennett's reckless spending, etc.'[60] King simply continued to see the NEC as a body that would save him money. Three months of hard work by the commission could not shake his conviction that the key to recovery was a reduction in federal responsibilities. As a result, by the end of the year only one of the proposals, the Home Improvement Plan, had been approved.

In one other area the government did act quickly. When the relief camps closed on 1 July, Ottawa still had not announced any alternative plans for the care of single men during the winter. Originally, federal officials assumed that the wages earned on railway maintenance, farm employment, and extra jobs created by the pace of recovery would provide the men with sufficient savings. Ottawa wanted to get them off relief and the $3 million spent on the railway scheme was intended as its last big splurge on single men.[61]

The provinces saw things differently. As the summer wore on, they began to suspect that Ottawa's real intention was to 'entrap them into some sort of ... responsibility for transient men' and however 'unjustifiable' the attitude, Purvis warned Rogers, the provinces definitely still felt that this was 'a sole Dominion responsibility.' With the memory of the On-to-Ottawa Trek less than a year old, NEC officials became increasingly nervous as the deadlock continued. By the end of July, one employee noted, the 'ugly spectre of the transient problem' was threatening to 'frighten into disorder almost every meeting of those who are studying relief problems.'[62]

The commission had good reason to worry. Transients were the most visible sign of unemployment, one that was 'brought to the attention of every person several times a day.'[63] They were also the most dangerous. 'What do we see while putting in hours? What do we think about?' one of their number wrote to the *Vancouver Sun* in 1935. His answer undoubtedly typified the sentiments of many:

We see a great many people going to shows, to this and that. Young couples who seem to be enjoying themselves, well-dressed and acting as if the world isn't so bad after all. People who have homes and kids and all the rest of it. People who seem to have faith in the future. We think that something is wrong. We can't do as they do. We must go around lonely and dejected. No home life to enjoy, shut off from all social existence ... We see wonderful things in the stores. Food! Clothes! Books! And shiny cars line the streets. But none such for us. Outside looking in! Or in jail looking out ... We think of marriage and homes, just like others have ... Shunned like lepers of early times, we are left to our fate ... Because we have the guts to fight for our inherited rights we are put in jail. Called Reds and a lot of other meaningless names ... We see Red ... and we think Red. Can you blame us? Would you like to have us lie down lie a bunch of spineless whelps and be contented as slaves?[64]

As the On-to-Ottawa Trek vividly demonstrated, the patience of transient single men could no longer be taken for granted, particularly in the first formative months of the new King administration. 'Any outbreak this winter in the big cities,' Purvis warned the government, 'particularly in Vancouver, or the Prairie Province Centres ... or even the visual evidence that large bodies of such men are still in the cities, will be used to prove to the public as a whole that the government's policy is non-existent or ineffectual. Further in the likely event of local disturbances the opportunity for the National Employment Commission to function on long range plans will be eliminated or seriously impaired because of the unfavourable public atmosphere obtaining, and again financial outlays of a serious nature will ... be forced upon the government in handling the emergency situations therein involved.'[65]

Both the credibility of the government and the success of the NEC depended on getting the single men out of the cities and out of sight without provoking unrest. Yet the present policy promised exactly opposite results. To expect the men to live on their summer earnings guaranteed that they would congregate in the cities over the winter. Violence could be almost assured now that the provinces refused to accept responsibility for their care. As a result, the commission decided to 'seize this particularly pricking nettle and deal with it at once.'[66]

The solution was not very original. The NEC proposed that Ottawa should extend the farm-placement plan which paid $5.00 a month to about 10,000 single men in western Canada to include the entire country and to care for up to 100,000 unemployed. The new scheme would be open to both men and women and would pay a $5.00 monthly stipend to both the farmer and the person he hired. In addition, there would be an extra $2.50 deferred bonus for each month worked during the winter in order to 'keep the men from drifting back into the cities.'[67]

This was a clever and cynical idea which accomplished several objectives at once. It met the essential need to get the men out of the cities. The camps, of course, had done this too but, as one NEC official noted, they also 'drew the people together and ... permitted a lot of demonstrators to act and get into an advantageous position.' It would take Arthur Evans a long time to organize another On-to-Ottawa Trek from 45,000 men scattered on farms the length and breadth of Canada! Moreover, it was cheap. Although it paid the men no more than what they made in Bennett's relief camps (with no guarantee of comparable food, clothing, accommodation, and medical care), it cost the government only one-quarter as much – $13.00 per capita per month compared to $42.00 in the camps.[68] It also defused agrarian criticism that relief camps had made it almost impossible to attract farm labour. The $5.00 monthly payment and the prospect of free labour were additional political plums in rural Canada at a time when farm income was low.

Finally, the farm-placement plan did not conflict with King's goal of cutting single men off relief. This had been one of the key reasons for closing the camps. Purvis made it quite clear that the jobs provided through farm placement were to be considered 'not relief work in the ordinary sense, but really more or less of an offer of normal work under normal working conditions and approximately normal rates of pay for the work to be accomplished. The reason behind this ... is that if some of the men refuse to take positions under the Farm Placement Plan ... the Government concerned would have public opinion behind it if no further effort were made on their behalf.'[69]

To make this work test more politically acceptable as well as to provide jobs in

BC where there were many single men and few farms, the NEC also asked the provinces to devise a limited number of 'alternative employment schemes' in other primary product industries such as forestry, mining, and tourism, the cost to be split equally between the provinces and the dominion. These jobs paid more ($4.00 a week in deferred pay compared to $7.50 a month on the farms) but they were few and far between. '[I]f the idea got abroad that other schemes were contemplated,' the NEC warned the provinces, 'men would hang around the cities with the end of securing employment other than on farms.' Thus the announcement of the alternative plans was deliberately withheld until after the farm-placement scheme was well under way. Only 6700 men found work on such alternative projects. Their function was to allow government to claim the men had been offered two jobs before being cut off from relief in order to 'obtain public support if and where jobs are refused.'[70]

Although he ignored the NEC's other proposals, King quickly approved the farm-placement plan in September. With thousands of transients flowing into Alberta hoping to register for a $25.00 Social Credit dividend and with 6000 more in Vancouver, even King began to realize the 'great danger of this whole Western situation developing into a serious conflict between classes.' After refusing loans to Aberhart and Pattullo, he could no longer count on their co-operation to maintain law and order among single men. The idea of placing the unemployed on farms meshed nicely with the 'back-to-the-land' bias of his administration which had already sharply increased funding for relief settlement.[71]

The new farm-placement plan was not implemented without opposition. The four western provinces were angered at having to pay half the cost of the scheme when Ottawa had provided 100 per cent of the funding for the relief camps and the old farm-placement system. As a result, British Columbia once more resumed its stand that it would not care for any transients under the scheme who were not provincial residents. Ontario ostensibly objected to the small wages paid to the men and refused to participate. Despite these protests, federal officials remained intransigent. Relief grants overall were still 34 per cent higher than in 1935; therefore, the provinces, in their view, had no grounds for complaining about paying half the cost of caring for transients. Furthermore, Ontario's refusal to participate was really a blessing in disguise since it 'had the effect of keeping the transients in the Prairie Provinces.'[72]

More serious was the protest from the men themselves, particularly in Alberta. When the plan went into effect in October, over 5000 transient men were in Calgary attracted, as one federal official put it, by 'the lure of SC dividends and the sense of nearer kinship ... with the Alberta Government than with other governments who do not attack financial institutions so vigorously.' Instead of collecting $25.00 per month, however, they soon found themselves faced with the choice of working on a farm for $5.00 per month or being cut off relief. The result was a series of 'parades to the Legislative Buildings and mass meetings held every day in ... Calgary and Edmonton.' By the end of the month, eight men had been jailed 'for creating a disturbance when refused relief, after they had refused the Farm Placement Plan.' Calgary's city council, which already provided the most generous relief scales in Canada, also vigorously protested against the small pay, long hours, poor clothing, and 'coercion' surrounding the farm-placement plan.[73]

It was all to no avail. By the end of the year the scheme was in effect in every province except Ontario and Nova Scotia and was caring for some 37,000 homeless men and 5000 women. Officials of the NEC were quite pleased with this result. Everywhere but Alberta the transient problem was now 'stable' and in the other two prairie provinces the 'degree of criticism and disturbing influence' had been 'reduced to the minimum.' They safely concluded that 'on broad lines the situation as it affects [the] single unemployed is on a better footing than since the beginning of the Depression.'[74] The men might have given a different answer.

While the transient problem seemed well in hand by the beginning of 1937, almost every other aspect of dominion-provincial relations was rapidly deteriorating. In December, King learned that the Judicial Committee of the Privy Council was going to declare the bulk of Bennett's New Deal legislation, including the Employment and Social Insurance Act, *ultra vires*. Although immensely satisfied that the JCPC had vindicated his position, King was also convinced that the 'whole cause of social reform has ... been delayed for years.' Bennett's attempt to 'force the pace' had made the provinces 'very restive and assertive of their so-called "sovereignty"' and he was sure they would now oppose the constitutional amendment needed to implement unemployment insurance 'more vigorously than ever.'[75]

It is not clear whether King was altogether displeased by this outcome. Of course since 1919 he had been committed to the principle of unemployment insurance and it would have been impossible to admit, perhaps even to himself, that he was in no hurry to see it actually become law. Yet there is strong evidence that this is what he felt. His economic strategy, as we have seen, explicitly duplicated that of his first administration, which sought a balanced budget through reducing existing federal responsibilities and postponing the assumption of new ones. From this standpoint, any reason for delaying what was certain to be a costly unemployment insurance system was not to be lamented.

Also, although anxious to secure constitutional amendments on the loan-council and indirect taxation proposals, which would have saved Ottawa money, King was strangely lackadaisical in pushing for provincial agreement on a general amending formula. After the breakup of the 1935 dominion-provincial conference, a committee of provincial attorneys-general along with federal justice minister Ernest Lapointe had been called together to work on this question. In February, they came up with an amending formula which satisfied every province except New Brunswick. Yet, as Blair Neatby points out, King 'made no effort to force the issue' and the committee's report was 'filed away and forgotten.'[76] Despite his conviction that Bennett's unemployment insurance legislation would soon be declared unconstitutional, King was content to deal with the problem through the cumbersome and time-consuming process of securing unanimous provincial consent for the necessary amendment.

As in the 1920s, the BNA Act once more afforded King a convenient excuse for delaying legislation that would make the task of balancing the budget more difficult and promised only to lighten the provinces' burden at Ottawa's expense. From this angle, his initial reaction to the 1936 Quebec election is explicable. 'On the whole,' King noted on learning the result, 'I am not sorry to have a Conservative government in power in Quebec. It is easier to govern at Ottawa with the provinces *contra*. Also it will help us in dealing with provinces and in meeting constitutional questions.' Either he mistook Maurice Duplessis for a centralist or King was fundamentally uninterested in the reform of Canadian federalism.[77]

Paradoxically, the provinces were interested despite King's initial assumption that Bennett's New Deal legislation had made them warier than ever. After the failure of the loan-council and taxation amendments, Dunning had established a National Finance Committee composed of himself and the provincial finance ministers to try to come up with a new approach to the growing chaos in dominion-provincial financial relations. At its one and only meeting in December 1936 the committee ventured two suggestions. The first, endorsed by all the provinces, was that Ottawa should 'take over all or a larger share of the cost of unemployment relief.' The second, suggested by the three prairie provinces but opposed by none of the others, was the creation of a royal commission 'to enquire into the broad question of the economic and financial basis of Confederation' and to determine 'whether any adjustments in the allocation of revenue sources and governmental responsibilities' were now warranted.[78]

Although uninterested in the first proposal, King soon found himself pushed towards the second by the pressure of events. In early January it became apparent that Manitoba and Saskatchewan were once again headed for default without fresh federal financing. Half the cabinet was willing to let them go under on the grounds that their bankruptcy was inevitable and that the only alternative seemed to be a never-ending succession of federal loans. In December this had been King's view as well but when the time came for a decision both he and Dunning were convinced that the loans should go through. The reasons were familiar. There was the ever-present danger that 'unrest in Canada might assume alarming proportions at any time' even without the stimulus of provincial bankruptcy. More important was the fact that Ottawa was contemplating a vast refunding of its war debt in London money markets and two provincial defaults, along with the threat of a general repudiation of debt throughout the West, would have a depressing effect on the nation's credit.

Thus the new federal guarantees for the necessary provincial bond issues were tentatively approved. At the same time, however, King and Dunning both picked up on the suggestion made by the National Finance Committee and argued 'very strongly' for the appointment of a royal commission on dominion-provincial financial relations. There was some cabinet opposition and the matter was 'allowed ... to stand' but six weeks later, when final approval was needed for the Manitoba and Saskatchewan loans, the cabinet agreed 'inside of half an hour' to appoint the commission. This decision was provoked by a detailed report from the Bank of Canada which conclusively established that both provinces could neither reduce expenditures nor raise additional revenue through taxation. Without continuous federal help, they were bankrupt.[79]

In actual fact, this had been the case for the past five years but loans had always been made reluctantly on an ad hoc, last-minute basis and only because of the constant threat which provincial default posed for Ottawa's own credit rating abroad. They had always been accompanied by threats that the provinces must 'put their houses in order' and eliminate 'wasteful practices.' Neither Bennett, King, nor their ministers of finance had believed that the loans were really necessary for any reason other than political expediency. Successive 'raids upon the federal treasury,' according to Dunning, had allowed the western premiers to avoid unpleasant political decisions and federal officials generally viewed provincial politicians, in Hepburn's view, as 'so many burglars.'[80]

Now it seemed that this attitude was beginning to change thanks to the authoritative advice emanating from the Bank of Canada – a federal institution. When he announced the new loan guarantees in February, Dunning conceded for the first time that 'the revenue-raising powers assigned to the provinces do not appear to be commensurate with the responsibilities which they were given or which they have assumed in an age of increasing provision for governmental social services.'[81] It was a long overdue admission which seemed to clear the way for a coherent attack on the interrelated problems of debt, unemployment relief, and constitutional reform.

It was not to be. The Bank of Canada report may have jolted King and Dunning into recognizing that there was something fundamentally wrong with the structure of Canadian federalism but they were in no hurry to find out what it was. Although the decision to establish the royal commission was taken in mid-February, it was not appointed until mid-August, six months later. In the meantime, King continued to approach the relief problem – the heart of the crisis – with the same single-minded determination to cut costs that he had shown since taking office. To his chagrin, he discovered that the National Employment Commission, which was supposed to aid him in this endeavour, instead was 'turning out to be a spending body instead of one to effect economy.'[82] Despite six months of hard work, the NEC had not turned up evidence of gross abuse of relief by the provinces, the municipalities, or the unemployed (apart from a recommendation to cut off relief to seasonal workers and marginal farmers in northern Ontario who were using it to avoid 'sav[ing] for winter need').[83] What it had done, however, was to devise programs which, in their original form, would have cost Ottawa $20 million a year.

By February 1937 the NEC had developed a coherent approach to the Depression. It was based on two key assumptions, both of which were only partially correct. The first claimed that recovery was proceeding naturally. The second saw that this improvement was by-passing those on relief because they were not qualified for the jobs that were opening up. These assumptions seemed to be borne out by a gloomy set of statistics which Dunning presented to the House at the end of the month. Reflecting the new economic sophistication being developed in the Department of Finance, Dunning was able to point out that in the past year the national income had increased by 10 per cent. Unfortunately, employment had risen by only 5 per cent and, 'still more disheartening,' the total number on relief was down by only 5 per cent – a 'discouragingly small' decline. The new jobs were being filled by the unemployed who were not on relief and by young people entering the labourforce for the first time, leaving Dunning to conclude that 'a hard core of unemployment and relief will always remain.'[84]

The proposals which the NEC submitted to cabinet in the early months of 1937 were designed to tackle what was now perceived as a problem of structural unemployment. Public employment was ruled out. Since the commission assumed that recovery was underway and that unemployment was more structural than cyclical, it called instead for 'very substantial reductions in expenditures for public works' in order to increase business confidence to invest and reduce competition for skilled labour which was felt to be in short supply.[85] Clearly, the commission had little use for Roosevelt's approach to the Depression.

Had it coupled this recommendation with a call for equally substantial reductions in relief spending, the NEC would have fulfilled King's fondest expectations. Instead, it argued that the savings resulting from this cutback in public works should be ploughed back into specific long-term programs designed to increase the 'employability' of those on relief and to provide a stimulus in areas where recovery was lagging.

The three areas singled out for attention were the same ones pinpointed in September – housing, retraining, and job placement. Despite Purvis's earlier warning that the NEC's housing program should not be allowed to go out 'piecemeal,' this was exactly what King had done by approving only the Home Improvement Plan which called for no actual federal spending but only a federal guarantee of 15 per cent of the value of private loans for home renovation. Therefore, in February, Purvis repeated the request for a low-rental housing act to provide a one-third federal subsidy for the construction of this badly needed accommodation. Mackintosh had originally set the price tag at $10 million a year but the NEC's final proposal was scaled down to half that amount to overcome cabinet resistance to moving into this new field.

Once again, however, King's administration refused to act, even though it knew that construction was almost the only area where employment was lower than in 1935, that it provided jobs for more of those on relief than any other industry, and that only half the number of new houses needed were being built. The reason was by now familiar. '[T]he provision of low rental housing,' Rogers lamely explained in August when nothing had yet been done, 'is primarily a municipal and provincial responsibility,'[86]

The pattern was repeated with the rest of the NEC recommendations. The Youth Committee had originally asked for $9,400,000 for its youth-training and rehabilitation schemes, but this too was reduced, first to $3 million and finally to $2.5 million, before Rogers presented it to cabinet. The last cut was the hardest, for by then the commission wanted to broaden the reconditioning and rehabilitation proposals to include a 'broader section of the community than is covered by the Youth age group' in order to increase the employability of the hard-core unemployed on relief. At the last minute, therefore, Purvis pushed for more money.[87]

Rogers asked for only $2.5 million, however, and got a meagre million dollars, roughly 10 per cent of the original proposal. The cabinet meeting is preserved in King's diary: '... attended a meeting of the Cabinet at which we had an extremely difficult time discussing estimates. Rogers wanted two and a half millions for youth education. This on the recommendation of the National Employment Commission ... I took the position and was supported by the Cabinet, that technical education and vocational training etc. were not in the Federal field, but were matters to which the Provinces should give their attention. That voting this amount simply meant helping manufacturers to get skilled mechanics, that they themselves should put up the amount to train the men that they need. On getting an opinion from the Cabinet as a whole, Rogers was left without a supporter and the amount was reduced to one million dollars.'[88]

Since King also condemned the youth-training appropriation as 'round about effort to bring an employment system into being,' it is not surprising that Purvis's third request for half a million dollars to operate a 'nationalized' employment service never got past Rogers. Yet it was the most important of the NEC's proposals, for once the commission defined the central problem as structural unemployment and its own role as increasing the 'employability' of those on relief, an efficient national labour exchange network became the linchpin around which its other recommendations hinged. If, as Mackintosh argued, the main task was 'seeing that employables are brought into the jobs which have been opened for them,' how could this be done without any adequate contact with the jobs? The government, however, remained adamantly opposed. Employment offices were a provincial responsibility and it had no intention of moving into this field until other questions of constitutional reform had been settled.[89]

For all intents and purposes, the NEC was dead by the end of February. Purvis had wanted $20 million, had asked for $9 million, and got a begrudging one million dollars from a cabinet which, apart from Rogers, was totally unsympathetic to its work. Soon afterwards even the labour minister was threatening to resign because of the lack of progress on social reform.[90]

Why did the commission's recommendations meet such fierce resistance? In the first place, Purvis proposed to spend money when King had expected him to save it. When the NEC recommendations came forward, King was making a determined effort to slash Ottawa's deficit in half. Relief was the area slated for the deepest cuts and he had counted on the commission to act as a 'buffer' in this politically difficult task of reducing grants-in-aid to the provinces. Instead, Rogers, on Purvis's advice, asked for an extra $9 million and seemed 'unequal to the task of getting the Commission to report upon overlapping and expenditure.'[91] At bottom, King shared Bennett's simplistic view of the relief crisis. There were too many people on the dole because administration was so lax; this laxity was a result of the availability of federal money. Cutting back on grants-in-aid, then, would not only help to balance the budget, but would also get people off the dole.

After half a year of studying the problem, Purvis and Rogers both realized that it was not so simple. The greatest waste surrounding relief was not money but lives. Half of the 1.1 million people on the dole by December 1936 had been collecting direct relief 'fairly steadily for nearly three years,' Charlotte Whitton pointed out, and fear was growing among the ranks of government officials and social workers that these people were rapidly becoming permanent psychological casualties of the Depression, a 'highwater line of broken, dispossessed men and women, most of them in upper age groups, who with their dependents will form the solid core of our needy for much time to come.' Others in the profession were convinced that public attitudes towards the jobless were themselves contributing heavily to the breakdown of morale. 'Ignored, bullied, accused of "not wanting work," "chiselling on relief," "preferring to bum on relief rather than to do an honest days work," [these accusations] destroy a man's self-respect and tend to encourage the practice of those subterfuges of which critic[s] accuse [the unemployed],' Frieda Held, a Toronto social worker, observed.[92] To the members of the NEC, one fact at least seemed clear. The only way to get the jobless permanently off the dole was to establish specific federal programs to make them 'employable.' Otherwise, Purvis argued, 'the relief jam will not be dislodged by good times and we may find ourselves entering a period which may lead to serious social unrest.'[93]

Herein lay the second problem. Each of the NEC proposals demanded a significant extension of federal responsibilities. To ease unemployment Purvis was suggesting that Ottawa get directly involved with housing, manpower retraining, vocational education, rehabilitation, and job placement, fields which constitutionally belonged to the provinces but which in practice had not been deeply probed by any level of government. This aspect of the commission's recommendations disturbed the cabinet more even than their cost.

NEC member Mary Sutherland made this point explicitly. Sutherland was ostensibly the representative of women on the commission. As Mary McCallum she had acquired a reputation as a 'well-known speaker on farm problems' during the 1920s through her work for the *Grain Grower's Guide*. Her task on the NEC was to co-ordinate the activities of the committee on women's unemployment, a job she performed with little sensitivity or imagination. In her view, the problem of unemployed women was simple but frustrating. There was still an 'unfilled demand for domestic workers in most ... cities' yet over 26,000 women were currently 'eke[ing] out an existence on ... relief ... and prefer that to working in homes.' Should they not, perhaps, be 'compelled to accept ... housework as an alternative to obtaining relief?' At the very least, government should subsidize training for domestic work in order to give it 'the prestige of a profession.'[94]

Apart from her 'back-to-the-home' recommendations, Sutherland performed another role on the NEC. Through her work for the federal Liberal party in western Canada during the 1920s, she had developed connections with prominent prairie Liberals such as T.A. Crerar and Jimmy Gardiner and, more importantly, she had come to know King as well. In fact, unlike most of the NEC members, she was the personal choice of the prime minister who had pushed for her appointment despite some cabinet opposition. It was these political qualifications above all which secured Sutherland's membership on the NEC and, throughout her tenure on that body, she played an explicit political role in providing Crerar, Gardiner, and King with a direct pipeline to what the other members of the commission were about to recommend.[95]

When she first saw the package of proposals which Purvis was about to submit, Sutherland exploded. The problem was not their cost but their implications. Purvis had asked that the NEC be granted the authority to administer the programs it was recommending. He also wanted grants-in-aid to be placed on a three-year instead of a one-year basis to ensure more 'continuity' in relief administration. The cabinet would be 'shocked and terrified' by these two proposals, Sutherland warned, because they would 'fasten on the Dominion Government permanently a policy of granting unemployment relief.' At present the cabinet was proceeding on the assumption that 'unemployment would continue to be a temporary thing with which it properly might deal from year to year' and no one had given the commission the slightest indication that the government was 'now ... willing to assume larger administrative obligations or longer term responsibility.' The NEC was already 'not in too high repute with some Members of the Government,' she continued. If it continued 'proposing measures we have reasons to believe are not in accord with Government policy,' its usefulness would be 'minimized.'[96]

To his credit, Purvis ignored this advice. Nevertheless, Sutherland was right. The cabinet curtly rejected the NEC recommendations because they cut across the grain of government policy – to reduce Ottawa's involvement with unemployment as quickly as possible.

Nowhere was Ottawa's desire to reduce its unemployment obligations clearer than with relief. Throughout 1937 King cut into the dole with a tenacity and determination that even Bennett would have admired. During the life of the 1937 Unemployment Assistance Act, total federal spending on grants-in-aid to the provinces was cut from $28,929,773 to $19,272,150 or by 34 per cent. The reduction was justified, Rogers claimed, because of the 'marked economic recovery in the past year' and was made on a 'rational basis and in such a way as to ensure for us the continued cooperation of the provinces and municipalities.'[97]

This was nonsense. There was recovery to be sure throughout most of 1937 but, as the NEC had warned in February, its impact on those on relief bore no relation to the reduction in federal spending on the dole. The average monthly relief load throughout the life of the 1937 act dropped by only 16 per cent compared to the same period in 1936.[98] The federal cuts were arbitrary, not rational, and were designed to throw more of the burden of the Depression on the backs of the provinces, the municipalities, and ultimately the unemployed themselves.

The result was not co-operation but outrage. It made no sense to increase the provinces' relief costs when the government had already conceded that their revenues were not equal to their responsibilities. Yet this was precisely what was done. Ontario's Mitch Hepburn complained that his government was being 'sandwiched between a reluctant federal government and increasing demands from the municipalities.'[99] Single unemployed men in that province bore the brunt of the premier's wrath. In the autumn they were totally cut off winter relief for the first time since the beginning of the Depression. '[They] ought to be ashamed to apply for relief,' Hepburn told the press. 'There are jobs available for them in the bush if only they will take them.'[100]

By cutting off loans to British Columbia and Alberta, King had already made enemies of Pattullo and Aberhart. Now he added Hepburn and Duplessis to their ranks. Through his determination to balance the federal budget, he succeeded in fatally compromising the work of the newly appointed Royal Commission on Dominion-Provincial Relations, chaired by Newton Rowell, before it had even got started. (The commission was finally appointed in mid-August 1937.)

He had certainly made a mockery of the NEC. In August the commission released an interim report of its work to counter 'the prevalent feeling that [it] has been inactive.' Much of the report simply made public what the NEC had been urging privately on the federal government without success for the past year, including the proposals for vocational training, a volunteer conservation service, a national employment system, and subsidies for low-rental housing. Of twenty specific recommendations listed in the report's appendix, only eight carried the designation 'approved.'[101]

It was a sorry record for King's much-heralded 'body of experts' but the urgency of the NEC's call for federal action was undermined by its own acknowledgment that, during the past year, there had been a 'natural' and 'very material' improvement in economic conditions even though none of its principal recommendations had been adopted. With the economy already on the upswing, why should the government pay serious attention to the NEC?

It was a difficult question to answer, particularly since much of the interim report was an argument against state intervention as a depression remedy, either through bonuses to private industry or direct spending on public works. The commission's emphasis on 'rehabilitation' and 'employability' was a necessary corollary to its rejection of public employment. The Depression, Purvis realized, had created a lot of 'loose thinking' about 'human versus property rights,' in particular the 'theory that those willing to work should be provided with a job or its near equivalent.' This had undermined the work ethic of the unemployed in three important ways. Instead of trying to find a job himself, the man out of work now expected 'the Government to obtain it for him.' He was also developing the idea that he had a right 'to take the *kind* of job he wants, or stay on accepting aid.' Finally, many seasonal workers were now using the dole as a '*supplement* to existing income' instead of using summer earnings to tide them over the winter. Public employment would exaggerate all these tendencies by creating 'a feeling of dependence upon Government for the supply of work opportunities.' This was one of the principal reasons why the NEC had rejected this option so emphatically.[102]

By emphasizing 'employability' rather than employment, however, the commission could reassert the traditional emphasis on the individual's personal responsibility for finding work while at the same time satisfy the widespread public demand for government action to end unemployment. In this way the work ethic – so essential to the proper functioning of a market economy – could be preserved in a time of mass unemployment.

In addition, by stressing that it was the unemployed and not private enterprise which needed to be 'rehabilitated' before recovery could proceed, the commission could counter the growing criticism of capitalism produced by the Depression. At bottom, the stress on 'employability' continued to blame the unemployed for their plight, albeit in a much more subtle fashion. It implied that 'natural' recovery was slow not because of any failure on the part of business but because the unemployed were no longer suitable for the type of jobs business was offering. In this sense, employability was as much a mask for the lack of employment as it was an attempt to find work for those on relief.

Rehabilitation, however, was only half the task of getting people off the dole. Equally important was ensuring that they would take the kind of jobs offered. This problem was addressed by Charlotte Whitton in her section of the report devoted to unemployment aid. Her ideas had changed little from her first report to Bennett in 1932. The dole, she told NEC commissioner Tom Moore when the interim report was released, was providing many people with a 'regularity of income' they had 'not known in their usual occupation.'[103] Not surprisingly, then, the thrust of her recommendations was to tighten up control over those on relief.

Whitton suggested three ways this could be done. The first was to divide those now on the dole into two categories, those who could work and those who could not. Ottawa would assume partial financial responsibility for the first group. In this way the federal government would both limit its expenditure and concentrate its efforts on getting the employable unemployed off relief. Second, the actual administration of unemployment aid should remain with the provinces and municipalities. Although this suggestion flew in the face of current British practice as well as the growing sentiment for federal control in Canada, Whitton was convinced that a nationally administered relief system could not effectively keep payments to the unemployed below regional and local wage rates. In short, a national dole would erode the work ethic.[104]

While these two proposals would have limited Ottawa's responsibilities, Whitton's third recommendation involved an important extension of federal authority. The present unconditional block grants for relief, introduced by Bennett in 1934, should be replaced by new agreements which attached strict and comprehensive conditions to all federal aid. The goal, Whitton argued, was to 'make it certain that those unemployed ... will move into employment as rapidly as employment opportunities offer.'

To ensure that this would take place, she recommended surrounding local administration of relief with close federal supervision to guarantee that work was kept more attractive than the dole. The new relief agreements, she argued, should contain provincial 'standards of eligibility,' a 'limitation of shelter allowances to a definite relationship with assessments,' and procedures for maintaining a 'running record of earnings' of those on relief in order to 'facilitate the acceptance of casual employment' through quick 'cancellation of aid.' In addition, there should be reports on 'schedules of allowances, costs of living and average earnings of unskilled workers' as well as those 'in receipt of Aid continuously for 12 months.' Above all, constant 'investigation' should be conducted into the 'circumstances of individual relief recipients.'

But while all these recommendations called for increased standardization of unemployment aid across the country, in one crucial area flexibility would remain. The new relief agreements, Whitton stressed, should enforce 'the principle of maintenance of incentive to accept employment by relating the *maximum* Aid to actual earnings of unskilled labour in each centre or regional division.' There was to be no national minimum. The goal of reforming relief was not to abolish the Poor Law doctrine of less eligibility but to make it work more effectively by removing control over relief rates and eligibility from the unit of government 'most susceptible to every wind of popular demand.'[105]

The NEC's interim report was thus a conservative and in many ways contradictory document. On one level it called for a significant extension of federal authority in order to make work more attractive to the unemployed and the unemployed more attractive to work. But the underlying purpose was to limit state intervention in the labour market. The reform of relief was designed to reduce overly generous local policies that were interfering with the 'incentive' to find work. At the same time, enhancing 'employability' was the only way Ottawa could get people off the dole without providing a system of public works, an alternative which would undermine both the work ethic and the private incentive to invest. Somehow both these reforms were to be accomplished without linking the federal government to any permanent responsibility for the unemployed. Ottawa's sole initiative would be a national employment service to provide a 'source of local information independent of Province or Municipality in respect to unemployment assistance.'[106]

By September, Arthur Purvis was a deeply disillusioned man. He had released the interim report in a desperate bid to goad the King administration into enacting recommendations that had been sitting before cabinet for over a year. Instead, the government responded by pointing out that most of the commission's proposals lay beyond its jurisdiction.[107] By the end of the year only the Farm Placement and Home Improvement plans along with a drastically scaled-down version of the

Youth Training scheme testified to the NEC's work. Their total cost was $4 million, less than half of what Bennett had annually spent on relief camps.

In anger, Purvis moved towards open criticism of the government. For over a year the NEC had campaigned against public works as a solution to unemployment but when Maurice Duplessis proposed a public-works program that autumn to replace direct relief in his province, an embittered Purvis gave the idea his support. Had the King administration provided the funds 'to implement the NEC programme recommended early this year,' such an expensive expedient would not have been necessary. However, Ottawa had 'failed to head off the suggestion by having an attack of its own.' Anything, Purvis argued, was better than simply keeping people on relief.[108]

Publicly he repeated the message. In 1936 the King administration had drafted a National Employment Commission Act which called unemployment 'Canada's most urgent national problem.' Yet compared to the 'vigorous governmental action ... being applied to Western drought regions,' the federal government had 'only scratched' the surface of the relief problem. Surely the continued demoralization of those on the dole was a crisis 'as vital and urgent as that of the drought?'[109]

As 1937 ended there was little indication that Ottawa shared this view of the relief crisis. In early November King did send a letter to all the provincial premiers asking for their consent to a constitutional amendment empowering the federal government to enact a national system of unemployment insurance. If they were agreeable, he promised to introduce the legislation in the next session of Parliament. This was hardly a new initiative. Almost a year had passed since the Judicial Committee had declared Bennett's Employment and Social Insurance Act to be unconstitutional and, since the Liberals were committed to the legislation in principle, some such action was long overdue. Moreover, while unemployment insurance would be a blessing in future depressions, it would do little for the victims of this one. Otherwise, King had little to offer the unemployed. He was not pre-pared to fund provincial public-works programs because of the 'unwisdom of giving federal money for work & leaving it to provinces to administer.' The NEC's recommendation that Ottawa reduce its own expenditure in this area was one of the few that King took to heart. Ruthless economy was the key to continued recovery and King ended the year 'determined to see that we get our budget balanced and expenditures curtailed with taxes reduced ... parallel to picture of our previous administration.'[110]

Unfortunately, recovery was not continuing. By the fall of 1937 the economy was once again sliding into recession in response to Ottawa's deflationary policies, western drought, and the effect of the Roosevelt recession to the south. Once more the numbers on relief climbed towards the million mark. As a result, even within his own cabinet, King could find 'hardly a word of support' for his determination to balance the budget.[111] Consensus was breaking down.

Since taking office in October 1935 King had tried to duplicate the economic policy of his first administration. His principal strategy for balancing the budget was to reduce Ottawa's costly responsibilities for unemployment as quickly as possible. Spending on relief was cut faster than the drop in the numbers on the dole, public works were avoided, half the cost of transient care was handed back to the provinces, and no action was taken on unemployment insurance for almost two years. When the NEC turned out to be a 'spending body instead of one to effect economy,' its recommendations were ignored.

As long as King could point to evidence of recovery, it was a harsh but tenable approach. Although it heightened dominion-provincial conflict to a level unsurpassed even during the Bennett era, there was no indication that King's own popularity was waning, regardless of how he was viewed by the premiers or the jobless.

Nevertheless, King's unemployment policy had devastating consequences for those on the dole. An Ottawa welfare administrator summed up the state of Canadian relief administration in 1937 in words almost identical to those written by Harry Cassidy five years previously. Responsibility for the unemployed was 'nebulous and ill-defined'; financial assistance for municipal relief existed, because of continual federal and provincial cut-backs, 'on a hand to mouth basis'; home-visiting of the jobless had 'degenerate[d] into an inquisition'; and municipal councils, 'haunted by the spectre of an increased tax rate,' had allowed their relief policies to be 'dictated ... by political expediency or ignorant prejudice.' His conclusion was blunt. '[L]ocal relief grants to families are not adequate to maintain health and malnutrition is rapidly spreading.' In Toronto Dr R.A. Blye made the same point. Families of more than four on relief in that city had 'only enough food to last them for five days of the week and for the remaining two are either without food or on a minimum.' Because of price increases, relief scales were '25% to 30% ... below [the amount needed for] medical safety.' As a result, 'hundreds of families in Toronto [were] threatened with malnutrition.'[112]

Apart from the suffering it caused for those on the dole, King's unemployment policy was also short-sighted because it tried to reverse the momentum which had been building since 1930. If for no other reason, the fiscal crisis of Canadian federalism was convincing proof that only the national government had the financial capacity to care for the jobless. Transients – the most visible evidence of a national labour market – were additional signs that unemployment was Ottawa's responsibility. Finally, after the events of the past seven years, few seriously claimed that employment offices or unemployment insurance could best be administered by provincial governments. Even housing and manpower training, the NEC argued, were areas in which the number out of work demanded federal action.

Since Bennett won office by promising to 'end unemployment,' the Depression had pushed a reluctant federal government ever closer toward assuming exclusive responsibility for the jobless. For a brief period, King had tried to reverse this momentum but, once recovery collapsed, he too would find it impossible to resist the demand that Ottawa take over the care of the unemployed.

6
Towards the welfare state: unemployment policy, 1938–41

On 20 December 1937 Arthur Purvis presented King with a political bombshell. On that day the National Employment Commission met for apparently the last time to discuss and sign its final report. For the next month the contents of that report would provide King with his 'greatest embarrassment ... in public life,' precipitating a crisis which, he was convinced, might 'conceivably occasion the overthrow of the government.'[1]

Why was King so upset? Because, in a complete reversal of the assumptions which had governed both its interim report and federal unemployment policy since 1920, the NEC recommended that Ottawa assume total financial and administrative responsibility for aid to the unemployed. In its final act the commission thus brought to a head the underlying tensions and contradictions which had surrounded Ottawa's involvement with the unemployed since its first contributions to relief at the end of the First World War. A federally appointed body was finally going to suggest what the provinces, municipalities, and the unemployed had been urging without success throughout the Depression. The result was a sequence of events which pitted the civil service against the cabinet on a major issue of government policy and led to an incredible attempt, on King's part, to use every political pressure at his command to suppress the recommendations of the commission he had been responsible for creating. His consternation was understandable, for the NEC's final report marked a watershed in the Canadian welfare state.

The decision to recommend federal control of relief was the work of four men – NEC members W.A. Mackintosh, Tom Moore, Purvis himself, and labour minister Norman Rogers – who had known what the commission was going to propose since mid-November but had not told King or any other cabinet minister. Three factors influenced their break with previous policy.

The most important was unemployment insurance. As noted already, in

November King asked for provincial assent to a constitutional amendment that would allow the federal government to enact unemployment insurance legislation at the next session of Parliament and, in the process, he also consented to a new national employment service. As with Bennett's Employment and Social Insurance Act, the Department of Labour relied heavily on the British experience in preparing the legislation and British expert Dr Christie Tait was brought over from Geneva to give the department the benefit of his advice.

By pressing for a national system of unemployment insurance coupled with an employment service, King signalled his intention to follow the mother country's example. Consequently, when Tait recommended that Ottawa establish an unemployment assistance scheme as well, the NEC leaped at the suggestion.[2]

Once again the British experience in the 1920s provided the rationale. To create an insurance plan without providing for the assistance of those who were not eligible for its benefits would 'almost certainly lead to a complete breakdown,' the NEC argued. Unemployment insurance would always leave a large number of unemployed outside its framework. If they were forced to depend on poor relief, 'there will be continued pressure of public opinion to force extended benefits under the Insurance Scheme even though these may not be actuarially sound.' Moreover, if the provinces and municipalities were left responsible for their care, they would only add their own 'interested pressures' to the 'popular agitation for extended Insurance benefits.' The result, as in Britain, would be the threat of national bankruptcy. For that reason alone, Purvis argued, an unemployment assistance scheme 'follows logically ... upon the ... decision to institute a national system of unemployment insurance.'[3]

Moreover, as Rogers pointed out, the present system of grants-in-aid 'was ... impossible.' The Depression had created a variety of financial problems for the provinces, of which care of the unemployed was only one. Yet Ottawa had singled it out as the sole reason for providing grants-in-aid. As a result, the provinces had been forced to use federal funds ticketed only for relief to solve all their financial woes. Ottawa in turn interpreted this as an abuse of its money.

The sole way out of this morass was to separate financial assistance to fiscally weak provinces from aid to the unemployed. This could best be done if Ottawa assumed total responsibility for the jobless. As the Depression had demonstrated, unemployment was a 'highly fluctuating' problem which, averaged over all of Canada, was much less severe 'than for individual regions or localities.' Only the federal government possessed a sufficiently flexible revenue base and a civil service with the 'broader experience' needed to deal with the matter properly.[4]

A final reason for pushing Rogers and the NEC towards this sharp break with past policy was undoubtedly King's failure to act on most of the commission's previous recommendations. For both Purvis and Rogers the past eighteen months had been very frustrating. Both men had been attracted to government service in the first place by the possibility of achieving significant reforms. Instead, King had virtually ignored their work. Almost every suggestion for even a moderate expansion of federal power had been rebuffed with the argument that it was beyond Ottawa's constitutional responsibilities. The release of the NEC's interim report in August was one response to this stalemate. When no action was forthcoming, the final report scheduled for release just before the opening of the 1938 parliamentary session must have seemed like the last chance to force King's hand. Certainly, frustration was not the only reason why Purvis and Rogers decided to push for federal control of relief. But King's constant use of the constitution as an excuse for not acting on the NEC's recommendations must have increased both men's determination to bring the issue of responsibility for the unemployed to a showdown.[5]

A showdown was precisely what they got. On the day the NEC met to sign its final report, Mary Sutherland left the meeting to tell King what the commission was about to recommend. Throughout the NEC's work she had been the one member who consistently opposed any move towards increasing Ottawa's responsibilities. She was about to oppose this recommendation as well, she told the prime minister, except that Purvis, Mackintosh, and Moore insisted that both Rogers and the government were behind it.

King exploded. With Sutherland still in his office, he phoned Rogers to find out what was going on. To his amazement, Rogers confirmed that with his consent the commission was indeed going to propose that Ottawa take over relief because an assistance scheme would be needed for those not covered by unemployment insurance. Of course, the labour minister added it would mean a reallocation of taxation revenue as well.

In shock King retorted that the 'principle was wrong,' there was 'not a member of the Government who would support it,' and 'the row we were having with Hepburn was a small thing to what this other business would amount to.' Rogers may have thought he was trying to 'please labour' but he would end up 'defeat[ing] the Liberal Party entirely by attempting something its members will not adhere to for one moment.' In a rage King ordered Rogers to see Purvis at once and tell him that the government would be 'opposed very strongly' to such a recommendation. Next, he phoned Dunning to find out whether he was behind the idea since Purvis was his appointee. Dunning replied that he was 'equally amazed' and agreed that the recommendation was 'wholly indefensible.' Now confident that the commission's cabinet support ended with Rogers, King determined to nip its recommendation in the bud. As a last resort he got Sutherland to promise that she would submit a dissent rather than sign the final report as it now stood. His main goal, however, was to change the report itself.[6]

The next day King told the cabinet what the NEC was about to recommend. Rogers again defended their position by arguing that it followed logically on the British experience with unemployment insurance and also allowed the government to abolish an 'impossible' system of grants-in-aid. The commissioners were 'adamant' in this view and their report would be 'unanimous.'

King listened with mounting anger. He already thought it 'outrageous' that Rogers should have known what was in the NEC final report for the past few months without telling the cabinet, especially since they had discussed the unemployment insurance issue in November. To make matters worse, Rogers was continuing to defend an idea to which he knew King was utterly opposed.

King raked his labour minister over the coals. If grants-in-aid were bad, the provinces should be given 'additional sources of income but held responsible for relief.' As for the supposed 'unanimity' of the commission, King 'knew for a fact' that Sutherland would not sign their final report nor would her colleagues E.J. Young and Neil McLean, the Maritime representative on the commission. Purvis had exceeded his mandate. Somewhat illogically King argued that the NEC had only been empowered to examine the 'concrete situation in Canada,' not the 'problem of unemployment generally.'

The rest of the cabinet sided with the prime minister. Minister of agriculture Jimmy Gardiner pointed out that the NEC was really trespassing on the territory of the Rowell Commission. As a possible compromise, he suggested that their final report might simply be forwarded to that body for consideration. King, however, was not interested in a compromise. Instead, he ordered his ministers to get the NEC members they had been responsible for appointing to change their minds. The commission was an 'arm of Government,' King argued, and would 'not be used to destroy the body that had created it.'[7]

While cabinet minister Joseph Michaud was set to work on fellow New Brunswicker Neil McLean and Power and Lapointe lobbied with Alfred Maurois, the NEC's Quebec representative, King concentrated his attention on Rogers himself. As long as Rogers continued to defend the original report, there was little hope of getting Purvis to back down.

At first the labour minister remained adamant. The recommendation was 'logical'; he had personally asked the commission to look into unemployment insurance; Purvis would not reconsider it; and so on. King, however, was not interested in being 'logical.' Purvis, Mackintosh, and Moore were 'really seeking to stab in the back those who had given them their opportunity of public service.' If Rogers continued to defend them, he would 'find not only every Member of the Cabinet but every Member of the party down on ... himself in particular for the mistake that had been made.' The message got through. Rogers agreed to see Purvis again and this time persuade him to meet with Rowell to see whether the NEC had invaded the jurisdiction of the latter's commission.[8]

Beyond this Purvis would not budge. King's crude pressure tactics deeply angered the NEC chairman and stiffened his determination to persist. When he finally met with Rowell on 18 January, he agreed only to minor changes in the commission's final report. The basic recommendation that Ottawa should establish a 'unified' and 'nationally administered' system of unemployment aid remained unchanged.[9] As a result, King concentrated his efforts on seeing that 'no step would be left unturned to secure the support of the other Commissioners Young, MacLean [sic] and Maurois' for Mary Sutherland's minority report. In this way Purvis, Mackintosh, and Moore would be outnumbered four to three and the commission's final report, although embarrassing, would at least 'show how divided opinion is.'[10]

Sutherland's dissent was King's one source of comfort throughout this difficult period. 'No public document,' he confessed on reading it, had ever given him 'the same relief of mind and satisfaction of heart. It expresses admirably the correct point of view and causes me to feel that I do not care in the least what Purvis, Mackintosh and Moore do or say in their report.'[11] What did Sutherland say to earn such unqualified praise? In effect, her dissent was a plea against the centralizing tendencies of the welfare state which finally put into words many of the unstated assumptions that had lain behind Ottawa's tenacious resistance to accepting permanent responsibility for the unemployed. 'The further removed and more centralized government becomes and the less direct its taxing power,' Sutherland wrote, 'the less easily can the individual relate his own responsibilities to its functions. No matter which government is responsible for and administers relief ... there will be constant pressure to increase the benefits and to enlarge the base of admittance to benefits. If responsibility is centralized in the Dominion Government, the counter-pressure from local tax-payers will be eased. The irksome, unwelcome and hard check provided by necessity by municipal officials, harrassed by mounting demands on diminishing revenues, will be removed.' Moreover, as long as Ottawa contributed to relief on an emergency basis only, grants could be terminated when conditions improved. If the federal government accepted complete responsibility for the unemployed, the 'blight' of a permanent dole would become 'inevitable.'[12]

This was the heart of the matter, the 'human factor' which King believed that Rogers and Mackintosh had 'left ... out of consideration' because their 'academic mind[s] ... saw only ... theory and ... logic.' From a theoretical standpoint, a 'functional division of responsibilities' which left Ottawa in charge of the unemployed might make perfect sense. Politically, however, its implications were 'more disturbing' than anything King had seen 'apart from the upsetting conditions ... occasioned by war.' The problem was not provincial rights, King confessed, for the premiers would be 'only too ready to turn over the whole burden of unemployment relief to the Dominion.'[13] His real fear stemmed from Sutherland's basic point that the threat of local bankruptcy, although 'irksome' and 'unwelcome,' had served as the only check on the 'constant pressure to increase the benefits' for the unemployed. If this check were removed by making relief a responsibility of the government with the strongest financial powers, the logical conclusion – as the British experience in the 1920s seemed to prove – was the threat of national bankruptcy.

This was the reason both Bennett and King so fiercely resisted any suggestion that Ottawa take over the dole. No matter how much it complicated dominion-provincial relations or created suffering for the unemployed, local responsibility seemed to provide the only limit on the maximum benefits available from relief. It was a vital counterpart to the Poor Law doctrine of 'less eligibility' because it ensured that relief could be kept below real wage rates for unskilled labour. Without this check, King was convinced, the 'whole situation' would be in 'chaos ... for years to come.'[14]

Had he read their final report more closely, King would have realized that the NEC commissioners had no intention of abandoning the 'less eligibility' principle. Instead, they built it into their proposed unemployment assistance scheme. '[I]ndividuals in need,' they argued, ' ... would not be entitled by statutory right to stated amounts, but ... the Aid given would be modified in proportion to the means which the applicant had for providing for his own needs. In establishing the maximum amounts, it would be essential to observe the principle of maintenance of incentive to accept employment by relating the maximum Aid to actual earnings in each centre and regional division.' National administration of relief did not mean a national minimum. Moreover, 'as far as possible' the beneficiaries of this unemployment assistance scheme would 'be required ... to work for the Aid received.'[15] In short, the new proposal with its means and work tests and a limit on maximum support geared to local wage rates was almost identical to the dole it was replacing. The only difference was the recommendation that Ottawa, rather than the municipalities, would be enforcing the work ethic on the able-bodied unemployed.

In the final analysis, the disagreement between Purvis and Rogers on the one hand and King and Sutherland on the other came down to this one basic question: which level of government could best enforce the 'less eligibility' principle? The Poor Law heritage and their own political intuition told King and Sutherland that it was the government closest to the individual taxpayer. This was why they continually viewed Ottawa's involvement with relief as an aberration which had to be kept to a minimum so that it could be terminated as soon as the Depression ended.

Rogers, Purvis, and Mackintosh, however, knew that the days of limited central government were gone forever. For one thing, unemployment insurance and a national employment service, to which the prime minister had already agreed, would give the dominion a permanent responsibility for the jobless regardless of when the Depression came to an end. It would also, for the first time, give Ottawa a far better administrative apparatus for ensuring that the unemployed were kept looking for work than anything the municipalities or provinces could provide. Moreover, if those governments were left responsible for the uninsured unemployed, they would only seek to shake the burden by pressing for an expanded insurance scheme and this might prove more of a threat to 'less eligibility' than the existing relief system.

Apart from this danger, the Depression had also exposed the financial weakness of local government. As Charlotte Whitton was so fond of pointing out, saddling local taxpayers with a responsibility they could not afford encouraged apathy, not vigilance. Municipalities which in effect paid only one-sixth of the cost of relief no longer had the same incentive to keep benefits down, especially when they were most subject to political pressure from the unemployed. The only alternative to federal control of relief, it seemed, was a system of grants-in-aid and, as the Depression had further shown, divided responsibility did not encourage efficient and economical control of relief. In sum, the only way to enforce the 'less eligibility' principle under conditions of modern industrialism, the NEC's final report argued, was to centralize responsibility for the unemployed. Ottawa had to take over relief not because local administration was inhumane but because it was inefficient.[16]

It was this insight which pitted Rogers and the NEC against the political instincts of King and his other cabinet colleagues. As King soon discovered to his horror, it was an insight that was shared by the top levels of his civil service. At previous cabinet discussions of the NEC's final report, King had been perplexed by Dunning's failure to 'show the back-bone he should have, in this matter.' Soon he found out why. On the advice of deputy minister W.C. Clark, the Finance Department had already approved the expenditures involved in making relief a federal responsibility. To make matters worse, O.D. Skelton, the under-secretary of state for external affairs, told King that he also agreed with the NEC's recommendation.[17]

Now King saw 'the whole picture in one minute.' There was a conspiracy within the federal civil service. Rogers, Skelton, Mackintosh, and Clark

all of whom are Queen's University, Department of Economics, have come together, and have been working jointly to seek to bring about change in constitutional relations which will lead to a centralization of power and away from the present order of things. The Rowell Commission will be doing the same thing; with Skelton's son as Secretary, and with Clark, will be working toward the same end. I told Council, quite frankly ... that these University men who had this inside opportunity, thought they had more in the way of wisdom than the rest of us put together ... The impression I think created on the Cabinet was that Rogers had played with the Queen's people rather than the Government in this whole matter. Doubtless, from the best of intentions and the belief that the Department of Economics, at Queen's, knows more about these matters than any corresponding group in Canada.[18]

Although somewhat paranoid, King's instincts were essentially correct. The NEC's final report had created a split, not within the cabinet (Rogers excepted) but between the cabinet and the civil service, on one of the most important questions of policy posed by the Depression. As such it marked a turning-point in cabinet / civil service relations. King's disparaging remark about 'University men who ... thought they had more in the way of wisdom than the rest of us put together' was really the gut response of a political veteran to an emerging mandarinate whose power derived from the growing complexity of government itself. Unlike King, they had no fear of an activist social service state. Moreover, for reasons they understood better than their political superiors, Ottawa had to take the lead in its creation and the first step was taking over care of the unemployed.

For the moment, however, this remained unwelcome advice. The knowledge that the NEC's final report was supported by the two most powerful deputy ministers in the civil service did not moderate King's opposition. Nevertheless, his attempt to stampede the other commissioners behind Sutherland's minority report failed. Despite last-minute wavering by Young and McLean, both men sided with Purvis eventually and signed a final report that was modified only slightly from the original version. Sutherland, who was not invited to the NEC's last meeting, remained alone in her dissent.[19]

Unable to change this outcome, King did his best to 'spike ... more than one gun' by deciding the report would not be tabled until it was translated into French. Through this cynical ploy, he ensured that the NEC's conclusions would not be available for the opening of Parliament when press coverage would be at the maximum. By the time the House did get hold of the final report, it would be 'under way in discussion of many things' and the impact of the controversial suggestions would be minimized.[20]

Strangely enough, despite their consternation over the recommendation on relief, the cabinet passed over the NEC's partial endorsement of Keynesianism without a comment. Yet it was this aspect of the final report which has received the most attention from historians.[21] In a section clearly written by Mackintosh, the report argued that there was 'sound economic ground for urging a policy under which public expenditures might be expanded and contracted to off-set fluctuations in private expenditures.' The goal was to use public investment as a balance wheel so that '*total expenditures* (public and private) may be made more stable.'

Consequently, the government 'should not violently contract expenditures' during the initial downswing of the business cycle but instead it should strive for greater public spending 'combined with unimpaired credit and tax reductions rather than increases during depression.'[22]

Needless to say, this was a radical reversal of the economic policy which both Bennett and King had followed for the past eight years. However, this Keynesian approach was qualified by Mackintosh's knowledge that an economy so dependent on staple exports did not allow the government much room to bring about recovery on its own. As long as its customers were subject to depressions, so too was Canada, and that meant government policy had to facilitate a 'reduction rather than an increase in the disparity that will develop between export prices and those of goods for sale to exporters and others in the domestic market.' In other words, if the incomes of Canada's primary producers dropped, then so must those of wage-earners in the protected industrial sector. At the onset of depression, therefore, spending on public works had to be 'kept to a minimum' and the unemployed assisted only through insurance or relief.[23] It was a conclusion which owed more to the work of Harold Innis than John Maynard Keynes.

Moreover, as Leonard Marsh pointed out, the Keynesianism of the report was somewhat suspect when it argued that the one-fifth to one-quarter of Canada's national income that was 'withdrawn by taxation' had 'restrictive and harmful effects ... upon private expenditure in productive industry, and, therefore, upon employment.' This assumed, as Keynes did not, that taxation revenue was somehow 'withdrawn' from the economy and that public investment was incapable of creating 'productive' employment. As Marsh noted, the only state expenditures the commissioners specifically endorsed were in areas such as tourism, mining, roads, afforestation, land settlement, manpower training, and slum clearance which did 'not compete with private enterprise.' In short, as far as the NEC was concerned, Marsh argued, the role of the state was to 'entice private capital' into fields 'where it has been particularly timid,' not to create work itself.

Yet how long, he asked, would it take 'for private capital to restore even moderate levels of employment?' What guarantee was there that by restoring business confidence the government could assure 'balanced economic development'? The commission was silent on both questions. While willing to press for a 'national lead in social security administration,' Marsh concluded, it was 'much more hesitant on the subject of national economic control.'[24] In this sense, at least, it was a fitting harbinger of the welfare state.

By mid-March King had delayed the publication of the NEC's report as long as he could. Now his administration had to decide what stance it would adopt towards the controversial proposal that Ottawa take over relief. His instinctive response was to 'fight it at once,' but he also realized, 'viewing the situation politically,' that it would be 'fatal to come out openly and oppose what our own Commission has recommended.' Instead, he decided to 'wait developments on Unemployment Insurance, and the Royal Commission and not permit ourselves to be drawn.' The government would neither denounce nor endorse the suggestion. It would simply ignore it.[25] Rogers was handed the unpleasant task of telling the House that 'since the subject of unemployment aid is bound up with the larger questions of redistribution of responsibility for social services and reallocation of revenue sources,' the government had to 'reserve judgement' on the matter until the Rowell Commission submitted its report. As one Tory aptly quipped, it was 'very much like a double play in a baseball game, "Rogers to Purvis to Rowell".'[26]

Yet it worked. The crisis King had so feared simply failed to materialize once the report was made public. Although the CCF strongly endorsed the NEC's recommendation and the press gave it 'wide approval,' the Conservatives, much to King's relief, did not make it an issue. Instead, along with the newspapers, they accepted the explanation that the matter was best postponed until the Rowell Commission had finished its work. Although he still regretted creating the NEC in the first place, for the moment King was safe.[27]

This scare over relief made King warier than ever about proceeding with unemployment insurance. The decision to go ahead with this legislation at the 1938 session had been made in the summer of 1937. In November, before he knew what the NEC was about to recommend, King asked the premiers for their consent to the necessary constitutional amendment.

Six premiers including Hepburn said that they were willing to surrender jurisdiction to Ottawa but three–New Brunswick's Arthur Dysart, Aberhart, and Duplessis–expressed reservations.[28] Dysart wanted to wait until the Rowell Commission had made its report before agreeing to any change of responsibilities. Aberhart, after two years of fiscally orthodox government, had finally been pressured into action on his Social Credit promises by a revolt within his party's caucus. In a special session that September he introduced sweeping legislation which required the licensing of all bank employees in Alberta. The object was to give his government the authority to compel banks to lend money on terms dictated by the will of the province. Local citizens' committees were to be established throughout the province to supervise bank activities. Bankers who failed to perform to their satisfaction would lose their licences.[29]

The legislation provoked outrage and charges of 'communism' from business, press, and government spokesmen across Canada. In response to intense political pressure, King was forced to use the seldom invoked federal power of disallowance to squash Aberhart's bill. As a result, the Alberta premier was hardly in a generous mood two months later when King asked him to concede federal jurisdiction over unemployment insurance. What his province needed was crop, not unemployment insurance, Aberhart replied. Under no circumstances would he agree to a constitutional amendment unless he could see the legislation first.[30]

Maurice Duplessis was equally unco-operative. In 1936 his newly formed Union Nationale party, a coalition between provincial Conservatives and a group of breakaway reformist Liberals known as Action Liberal Nationale, swept the scandal-ridden government of Louis-Alexandre Taschereau from power and so ended thirty-nine consecutive years of Liberal rule in Quebec. During the election campaign Duplessis' dependence on ALN supporters had given some grounds for hope that he shared their mild interest in social reform. Once in office, however, the UN leader proved to be every bit as conservative as the premier he had just replaced. Key ALN spokesmen were shut out from the cabinet and Duplessis turned his back on legislation designed to confront the urban catastrophe caused by the Depression. Instead, agricultural and resource development, anti-communism, and a vigorous defence of provincial autonomy became the three key policy concerns of his first administration.[31]

In each area he found a close friend in Mitch Hepburn and throughout 1937 the two men forged an increasingly open alliance against the King administration. Apart from their fondness for hard drinking, they had much in common. Both men were angered at King's cut-backs in relief funding, at his refusal to cede greater taxing power to their governments, and at his decision not to allow Ontario and Quebec to increase their power exports to the United States. They also resented federal aid to the bankrupt western provinces which, in their view, was financed out of the pockets of central Canadian taxpayers. As a result, neither Hepburn nor Duplessis was particularly sympathetic by 1937 to proposals for constitutional reform emanating from Ottawa.[32]

Given the broad public support for unemployment insurance throughout Ontario, it would have been political suicide for Hepburn to have opposed such a measure openly on constitutional grounds but in private the Ontario premier expressed 'regret' that he had endorsed the amendment. King was 'simply asking for a blank cheque insofar as amending the British North America [Act] is concerned and is using unemployment insurance as the thin edge of the wedge,' he complained to Duplessis. 'It is clear to me that with the western provinces hopelessly bankrupt, any national scheme of unemployment insurance will have to be borne by the two central provinces, and if unemployment insurance is necessary, it probably will be better to run our own show.'[33]

Duplessis faced no qualms over publicly opposing the amendment. Any constitutional change which involved a surrender of some of Quebec's power could be portrayed as an attack on provincial autonomy and hence a threat to French-Canadian culture. For this reason, Duplessis had already denied that

Ottawa even had the right to appoint a Royal Commission on Dominion-Provincial Relations. He now added unemployment insurance to his list of attempted federal incursions on provincial affairs. Why was a constitutional amendment necessary at all? he asked. Concurrent legislation similar to that governing old-age pensions, which provided federal funding but left the administration of unemployment insurance in provincial hands, would afford a far stronger guarantee of Quebec's autonomy.[34]

This negative response from Dysart, Aberhart, and Duplessis left King with three options. The draft bill, which was already prepared, could be passed and used as a club to force the three recalcitrant provinces to agree to the needed amendment. Alternatively, the government could simply proceed with the amendment, despite their objections, in the confidence that the British Parliament would not refuse to act on a joint request from both Houses of Parliament 'regardless of any opposition offered by the provincial authorities.'[35] Or King could simply do nothing by arguing, as he had in the case of the NEC's recommendation on relief, that any change in constitutional responsibilities should be postponed until the Rowell Commission had submitted its report.

Rogers, not surprisingly, pressed for the first option. Before Parliament opened, the premiers should be asked point blank whether they would say yes or no to an amendment giving Ottawa jurisdiction over unemployment insurance and employment offices. Then the government should 'go ... ahead at all costs' with the legislation.[36] However, his advice was no longer to be trusted. King knew that Rogers saw unemployment insurance as the key to federal control of relief. For that reason alone the prime minister now viewed every suggestion emanating from the Labour Department with extreme suspicion.

More important, prior to the commission's final report it had not occurred to King that there were strong arguments why the two responsibilities should go together. Now he knew differently and this affected his entire attitude towards the insurance question. In November he had been the one who 'sought to hold Council to its decision to have the Employment Insurance Bill introduced ... at the forthcoming session.' By January, in the midst of the NEC crisis, he had changed his mind and, over Rogers's objections, won cabinet support for a decision not to proceed with the legislation until there was agreement on the amendment.[37]

One reason for this turnabout was the objections of Aberhart, Dysart, and Duplessis. But King's fear that Rogers's approach might smack of 'coercion' because it would 'throw a very heavy onus on the Province that would decline to permit a national insurance scheme to be introduced' was unconvincing.[38] The prime minister had not hesitated to use 'coercion' in attempting to win provincial assent for his loan-council amendment. Nor was there any reason after eight years of depression why a 'heavy onus' should not be placed on any province that would oppose such a scheme.

More revealing of King's real motive was the decision to drop any reference to a national employment service in the proposed draft amendment because of the danger that responsibility for finding jobs might 'be used by Provinces and municipalities as [an] argument for [the] Dominion assuming sole responsibility for relief.' The NEC's final report had clearly acted as a catalyst stimulating all King's latent fears of centralization. Convinced that 'people generally would be against centralization of authority at Ottawa,' King decided to 'let matters get to the point where [the provinces] will come to beg of us to take over some of the obligations that they today pretend they are ready to assume.'[39]

In early June 1938 King announced that, since some of the provinces had not agreed to the necessary amendment, there would be no unemployment insurance legislation until the Rowell Commission submitted its report. Under no circumstances did his government intend 'in any way to coerce any province of the Dominion.' By accepting the doctrine of unanimous consent King was, in effect, postponing unemployment insurance indefinitely.

When Rogers raised the issue once more at the end of the year by arguing for legislation that would apply only to provinces which had agreed to the amendment, King remained adamant. The government would 'hold to the position we have already taken, and point out at a general election wherein we had been prevented by the Provinces from introducing a Bill.'[40] This was stretching the truth. To be sure, three provinces had opposed the amendment. Unlike Rogers, however, King displayed not the slightest interest in either securing their support or proceeding without it. Behind his decision to avoid 'coercion' lay the final report of the NEC with its implications. In a cruel irony, the 'logic' which drove Rogers to press for federal control of relief just as surely drove King away from unemployment insurance. As a result, by the end of 1938 both reforms seemed as far away as ever.

Paradoxically, at the same time King was forced to accept almost all the NEC's other recommendations because of the growing economic crisis. Since coming into office his unemployment policy had been harsh but consistent. Except for his initial 75 per cent increase in relief spending in 1935, he had progressively scaled down the extent of Ottawa's contribution to the dole and had resisted all suggestions of programs that might expand the federal government's responsibility for the unemployed. As long as the economy continued to show signs of recovery, it was a tenable policy which allowed him to ignore both the recommendations of the NEC and the anger of the provinces, municipalities, and the unemployed.

Unfortunately for King, recovery did not continue past the summer of 1937. In autumn there were unmistakable signs that unemployment was once more on the rise and by mid-winter 1938 the spill-over effects of the Roosevelt recession were obvious throughout Canada. To make matters worse, drought had burnt out the

1937 wheat harvest so that the numbers dependent on relief in the West were increased.

Since recovery had afforded King an excuse for cutting back Ottawa's contributions to relief, it might have been expected that the recession would prompt an increase. This was not the case. In early January, over some cabinet resistance, King committed his government to a balanced budget for the next fiscal year which meant cutting $70 million off current expenditures. The 'danger of a temporary depression' only made it 'more imperative ... [to] ... economize as much as possible.' Since spending on relief was the 'most wasteful of any, particularly on grants and aid [sic],' King was determined to cut deeply into the dole. Rogers, perhaps still smarting from his wrath over the NEC, promised to produce 'substantial savings.'[41]

He did this in two ways. Although the number on relief rose from 802,046 to 1,044,726 or 30 per cent between October 1937 and March 1938, Ottawa's spending on grants-in-aid was frozen at the October level – the point at which the last cut had been made. In addition, a new proviso was inserted into the agreements from January to March which limited Ottawa's contribution to no more than 30 per cent of the total in any one province provided this did not exceed the maximum level set in October.[42] In short, the brunt of the recession was thrown on the backs of the provinces and municipalities who in turn passed it on to the unemployed.

The response, of course, was predictable. Hepburn charged that King was 'trying to shelve the jobless on to us entirely'; the Duplessis administration accurately claimed that Ottawa was 'attempting to balance its Budget at the expense of ... Quebec'; and Pattullo privately warned King that his government was courting unrest.[43] All these pleas fell on deaf ears. In a statement released in March, Rogers expressed 'every sympathy' with the plight of the municipalities but argued that his refusal to increase grants-in-aid reflected not 'indifference' but 'a conviction that larger grants of themselves do not lead toward a solution but may tend to aggravate the situation.' Past experience proved that 'costs would inevitably rise under such an arrangement and the taxpayer instead of getting relief from relief costs, would have his burden considerably increased.' The new agreements had 'but one object in view – a reduction in magnitude of the problems of unemployment and distress by the most efficient means at our disposal.'[44] However pleasing to taxpayers, this was small comfort to the unemployed.

Rogers's second technique for cutting costs was even more ruthless. In a direct application of the 'less eligibility' principles put forward by the interim and final reports of the NEC, federal grants-in-aid, as of January 1938, contained the stipulation that 'material aid given to any family head or individual ... must be less than the normal earnings of an unskilled labourer in the district as averaged over the preceding year.' When CCF spokesmen denounced this change as an attempt to reduce the living standards of the unemployed, Rogers denied that the government had 'in any way brought pressure to bear upon provincial government with respect to any change in relief scales.'[45] This was simply untrue. While not interested in ensuring a minimum standard of support, the federal government was now actively placing a maximum on the level of relief provided by any community. Whitton's advice had finally triumphed at the expense of those on the dole.

This attempt to reduce Ottawa's support for the jobless in a time of rising unemployment provoked such a storm of criticism and unrest throughout the country that, by the end of March, King found himself faced with a full-scale cabinet revolt. On one side stood Dunning and himself, both determined to produce a balanced budget for the next fiscal year. Against them was pitted the rest of the cabinet 'all for more in the way of expenditures, to save a situation of which they have grown very fearful.'[46]

Despite his sympathy for Dunning's position, King could not ignore their fears. He too recognized that the 'unemployment problem [was] becoming again critical' and that there was the possibility of a 'very serious conflict in our cities' if his government did nothing to stop it. At the same time, there was 'mounting up as well a formidable demand on the part of our own following in Parliament' for some federal initiative, especially after Roosevelt announced his billion-dollar expenditure on emergency public works to counter the new recession.

To meet these pressures, King appointed a cabinet subcommittee on 'Unemployment Coordination' on 1 April. Its task was to come up with suggestions for a series of exclusively federal unemployment relief projects, for the cabinet had 'all agreed we must cease to make grants ... or carry on joint undertakings with the Provinces.' By the spring of 1938 King had come full circle to the position adopted by Bennett in 1934. Rogers was chosen as chairman of the subcommittee and this gave the labour minister the opportunity he craved. For over two years King had used recovery and the need for a balanced budget as an excuse for not implementing the suggestions of the NEC. Yet although the last budget was only $13 million shy of being balanced, recovery had failed. Now, armed with the quasi-Keynesian arguments of the commission's final report, Rogers adamantly rejected 'any suggestion of seeking to have the budget even approximately balancing.' Instead, his subcommittee returned to the cabinet in early May with suggestions for expenditures totalling over $75 million.[47]

Dunning and King were appalled. For the next week a vicious cabinet struggle took place between them and Rogers' subcommittee over whether the emergency spending should be limited to $25 million or $75 million. At one point both Dunning and Rogers threatened to resign; a caucus spokesman visited King to complain that there was a 'strong feeling' within the party that 'the government was not doing enough'; and King himself warned that he would dissolve

Parliament and hold an election rather than 'remain ... at the head of a Government which was unable to hold together.' In the end a compromise was struck. The supplementary estimates would contain an extra $40 million for expenditures on a national program of conservation and development.[48]

Although a significant reversal of policy, this was hardly a 'tacit acceptance of the Keynesian policy of conta-cyclical budgetting.' With the exception of Rogers, the rest of the cabinet was motivated more by fear of unrest, 'displeasure encountered at moments of visits of their constituents,' and the chance of increased spending for their own departments than by any new-found commitment to 'pump-priming.' Moreover, the $40 million agreed to was no more than what Bennett spent on his Public Works Construction Act of 1934, hardly a Keynesian initiative. Finally, despite this emergency measure, Dunning forecast a deficit of only $23 million for the next fiscal year. 'Attempts to stimulate consumption by government expenditure,' he argued in his budget speech, '... have been tried on more than one occasion but in every case they have been found wanting.' It was 'of little use to prime the pump of business enterprise ... if at the same time we dry up the springs of private enterprise which feed the well.'[49]

More significant than the sum of money were the projects themselves. Apart from the traditional round of road, wharf, and office building, much of the recovery program did significantly expand the range of federal responsibilities. Most of the ideas came from the NEC's final report. The commission's argument that public spending should be directed to Canada's primary industries was reflected in the $1,310,000 appropriated for mining roads, the $3 million for tourist highways and national parks, the $450,000 for the restoration of historic sites, and $650,000 to develop the fishing industry. In addition, the youth-training budget was expanded from $1 million to $2.5 million, concentrated mainly in the areas of afforestation and conservation and in occupational training courses.[50] It was a small step but one which firmly committed Ottawa to a responsibility for manpower training.

Equally significant were two new pieces of legislation designed to aid the construction industry. Shortly after the supplementary estimates were brought down at the end of May, the government introduced the Municipal Improvements Assistance Act which for the first time offered federal loans directly to the municipalities for the construction of projects that would eventually pay for themselves over the life of the loan. It was a dual-purpose bill designed both to provide jobs and to allow cities to establish public services which had been much neglected during the past eight years of depression. $30 million in federal loans were set aside for this purpose at the 'exceedingly low interest rate of 2%.'

It was an ironic departure. For years the municipalities, crippled by falling revenues from property taxation and soaring relief expenditures, had begged the federal government for just such help so that they could stave off bankruptcy. Each time Ottawa replied that, as the cities were the creatures of the provinces, it could have no contact with them. Now this excuse was swiftly thrown aside in order to 'assist in the revival of the construction industry,' even though Dunning conceded some might argue that the government was 'interfering with the autonomy of the provinces.'[51]

This precedent-breaking pattern was repeated a few days later when the National Housing Act was introduced. Apart from changes in the old Dominion Housing Act which provided easier terms for federally backed mortgages to prospective home owners, the government for the first time entered the field of subsidized housing for low-income earners. Ottawa would offer $30 million, again at the low rate of 2 per cent interest, to local authorities for the construction of low-rental housing, provided the houses were rented to families whose income was less than five times the 'economic rental' of the unit. The authorities themselves had to put up only 10 per cent of the total cost. In a final move to overcome the deterrent effect of high property taxation (itself a result of relief costs) on new home construction, the federal government offered to pay all the municipal tax for the first year, half for the second year, and one-quarter for the third year for any home built between 1938 and 1940.

Like the Municipal Improvements Bill, the National Housing Act embodied a dual purpose, both to provide homes and to create jobs. Moreover, as Dunning admitted, 'as we did the other day in connection with municipal improvements, we are stepping into a field which hitherto has not been a field of the dominion parliament, a field which, according to the opinions held by very eminent gentlemen, we have no constitutional right to occupy, and which we can justify entering at all only as primarily an attack upon our great national problem of unemployment.'[52] It was an ironic concession. The King administration had started the year determined to shed its involvement with unemployment. Instead, that problem had dragged it into an ever-widening net of new responsibilities. As King reluctantly conceded, the government had reached a turning-point in its unemployment policy:

In politics, one has to continually deal with situations as they are in the light of conditions as they develop from time to time. The world situation has headed ... countries ... more and more in the direction of the extension of State authority and enterprise, and I am afraid Canada will not be able to resist the pressure of the tide. The most we can do is to hope to go only sufficiently far with it as to prevent the power of Government passing to those who would go much farther, and holding the situation where it can be remedied most quickly in the future, should conditions improve.[53]

It was a telling insight into the Liberal welfare state.

Before King's recovery program could begin to take effect, the legacy of his past unemployment policy overtook him. All the provinces had suffered over the winter from Ottawa's decision to keep grants-in-aid at the October 1937 level. Nowhere was this policy more irritating than in British Columbia which had to care for an influx of transients from the rest of the country as well as for its own citizens. To make matters worse, during the past winter Labour Department officials reported that the number of non-resident single men in BC's forestry camps was up by 50 per cent from the previous year.[54]

Pattullo had never been reconciled to this supplemental employment plan which had replaced federal relief camps in British Columbia in the fall of 1936. In the first place, it forced his government to assume 50 per cent of the cost of transient care. Second, the wages offered in the forestry camps, which formed the heart of the scheme, were more than triple what the men could make under the Farm Placement Plan operating throughout the rest of the country. The effect was to draw transients into BC during summer months in the hope of obtaining one of the coveted camp jobs over the winter.[55]

King's decision not to increase Ottawa's support for relief during this new recession was the last straw for the volatile premier. In March, federal officials were informed that the BC government would close down the forestry camps by 30 April, six weeks earlier than in 1937. After that date the men would not be provided with relief of any kind. If they wanted to stay in the province, they would have to find work themselves. Otherwise, the government would pay their way back to their home provinces.[56]

Pattullo's decision worried Ottawa. Federal officials knew the men in the camps were 'well organized in the Relief Project Workers Union' and that its leaders intended to set in motion 'widespread agitation ... at the conclusion of the present plans in an effort to compel the Government to extend them.' Pattullo's gamble would succeed, they warned, only if the labour market was capable of 'absorbing the large numbers of men now congregated in British Columbia who were laid off at the end of the logging season.'[57] Under present economic conditions, this was doubtful. The Labour Department prepared for trouble.

They were not disappointed. On 30 April the camps were closed. By 15 May the men had exhausted their deferred pay. More than 1200 congregated in Vancouver but both the provincial and municipal governments refused them any relief and King's last-minute recovery program had not even reached Parliament. Stranded without support from any level of government, over 600 men occupied the Vancouver Post Office and Art Gallery to dramatize their plight. Another 600 launched a successful tin-canning campaign. As their *Sitdowners' Gazette* pointed out, the men were 'not criminals and do not desire to be such, but government policy gives them little choice.' The public agreed. Only a few days after the strike began, even Pattullo conceded that there was a 'great deal of sympathy' for the men and their demand for jobs, not train fare.[58]

Despite this public support, the BC premier was determined to stick to his decision that they not be given relief. Publicly, his labour minister told the men to 'get out and rustle' after the 'fifteen to twenty thousand jobs' that opened up every summer in the province. Privately, however, Pattullo was motivated more by a desire to force a showdown with Ottawa over responsibility for transients than out of any conviction that his province was overflowing with work. '[T]he people may suffer a little,' he told the *Vancouver Sun*, 'but it is best to get this thing over with. We are not going to yield. If we give in it will not be a matter of a thousand or fifteen hundred men but five to ten thousand men.'[59]

As the strike wore on into mid-June, Pattullo tried to use it as a means of pinning Ottawa with responsibility for all transients. Financially, his government was simply 'not in a position to set up works for all the single unemployed during the summer time and consequently is not going to attempt to do so.' However, Ottawa was. If it exercised its 'primary authority' by announcing a 'broad and expansive policy of public works construction' in conjunction with his province, Pattullo was sure the situation would be quickly cleared up. Otherwise, he warned King, 'you will find that agitation will become more severe each passing month.'[60]

In one sense he was right. When the men were forcibly evicted from the Post Office and Art Gallery by baton-wielding RCMP on 19 June, they organized an expedition to Victoria to continue their protest on the premier's doorstep. Soon hundreds were arriving in the BC capital and a panicky Pattullo warned King that the situation was developing into a 'highly organized effort on the part of radical and other subversive forces to break down constituted authority and government,' with the likelihood of 'serious bloodshed.' There was only one alternative. '[Y]our government must accept responsibility in meeting this transient problem.'[61]

This was precisely what King had no intention of doing. When the strike first began, his government offered to pay the cost of emergency relief for the men who had left the federally funded forestry camps if they accepted transportation back home. Once it became clear that the strikers had no intention of settling for this, King then said he would share half the cost of 'any reasonable measures which the government of British Columbia may decide are necessary for the provision of emergency relief.' Beyond this he would not go. Pattullo was 'trying to throw the burden on to the Federal Government in a very unfair way' and King would have no part of it. It was the BC government which had precipitated the crisis by cutting the men off relief; therefore, the whole matter was 'a question of relief administration within the control of the province.' The strikers' and Pattullo's demand that Ottawa meet the situation through public works was out of the question. As Rogers pointed out, how could the government create 'preferred conditions' for this group of single men 'without at the same time finding employment for married men, the heads of families on relief, for war veterans on relief, and for dependents on relief above the age of 16?' Ottawa had rejected large-scale public works as an anti-depression strategy. It could not change its mind simply because one group of men had 'adopted this novel and spectacular means of bringing their situation to the attention of this country.'[62]

For Pattullo this was not good enough. Ottawa already paid half the cost of transient care during the winter so this latest federal offer would leave him no farther ahead in his attempt to shed this burden entirely. 'To offer temporary relief,' he replied to King, 'would only aggravate and prolong [the] problem and encourage similar methods and this province will not under any consideration accept responsibility for transients.'[63]

As the strike lingered on into July and public criticism of both governments mounted, King finally made a modest concession. His government would pay the cost of relief for all non-resident transients, not simply those who had left the forestry camps, 'pending their return home or an offer to them of employment.' Although the strike leaders counselled refusal, the men themselves, weary from two months of fruitless struggle, accepted this offer and by 9 July the strike was over.[64]

Neither government emerged unscathed. Pattullo's decision to cut single men off relief appeared needlessly cruel at a time when unemployment throughout the province was rising. As a result, the strike marked the beginning of the end of his political career in British Columbia. However, King looked bad as well. The crisis had arisen in the first place because transients did not fit inside the doctrine of local responsibility for the dole. The solution of simply shipping them back home where there was no guarantee of work only succeeded in focusing attention on the contradiction of this policy. To the public, the whole episode appeared as a classic illustration of government buck-passing. Coming on top of the NEC's final report and the 1938 recession, it thus renewed demands that Ottawa assume full responsibility for the care of the unemployed.[65]

Perhaps the most eloquent statement of this view came from within the government itself. In October Jack Pickersgill, a new addition to the Prime Minister's Office, sent a comprehensive memo to the Department of Finance arguing that Ottawa should take over relief immediately before there was any general constitutional settlement between the provinces and the dominion. Unlike the final report of the NEC, Pickersgill's reasoning had nothing to do with unemployment insurance or the present system of grants-in-aid. Instead, perhaps reflecting his own Manitoba background, it anticipated many of the points that would soon be made in the Rowell-Sirois report.

First he made the obvious point that unemployment was 'not primarily ... the result of local conditions.' National, not provincial economic policies provided the main influence over the level of business activity and the flow of population in any one part of the country. Why then should local governments be held responsible for relief? '[I]f ... taxable wealth and ... unemployment were evenly distributed throughout all the Provinces,' there might be some grounds for such a policy. Instead, there was 'no such even distribution of wealth and unemployment'; therefore, it was 'impossible so long as ... relief ... is left to the Provincial and local authorities to distribute the burden equitably throughout the country.' In short, the West was paying for the costs of the Depression and the price was the ruined credit of its provincial and municipal governments. Giving the provinces access to greater taxation revenue would do nothing to alleviate this basic regional disparity. The poorer provinces would still be left without 'sufficient revenues to meet these extraordinary changes.' Only by making Ottawa responsible for relief could the burden of unemployment be shared equally throughout Canada.

There was a strong political argument for assuming this burden now, not later. The Rowell Commission would soon be submitting its report and presumably this would be followed by a conference to discuss a readjustment of constitutional and financial responsibilities. Under present circumstances, every provincial government was in worse financial shape than the dominion. The wealthier provinces could thus be expected to enter the conference arguing for an expansion of their revenue sources at the expense of Ottawa. This would 'obviously weaken the national government seriously and would do nothing to solve the problems of the poorer Provinces where taxation has already reached virtually prohibitive levels.'

However, 'the whole picture would be changed,' Pickersgill argued,

... if the Dominion, by assuming the whole cost of unemployment relief, could instead make a *prima facie* case for the enlargement of its sources of revenue and the further curtailment of Provincial revenues. The Federal government could do so much more convincingly if they had already assumed functions and obligations which made such a course necessary. If they were relieved of their present share of the costs of unemployment relief, the Provinces of Ontario and Quebec, and perhaps British Columbia, would probably have budgetary surpluses almost at once with the result that they would be in no position to insist upon the enlargement of their sources of revenue, and might not be able to offer any very effective resistance to their curtailment.

The premiers of all three provinces had already 'advocated the assumption by the Dominion of the whole cost of relief'; therefore, they could not really complain about an invasion of provincial rights 'if the Federal government accepted their advice.' Such a gesture would also give the public evidence that Ottawa had a 'new vision of its responsibilities ... in a field which touches closely the very existence of a large part of the population.' It would be difficult to think of another reform, Pickersgill concluded, 'more calculated to contribute to the national unity of Canada.'[66]

Pickersgill had given a new slant to the case for handing over care of the unemployed to Ottawa. Instead of arguing about what followed 'logically' from the British experience (which usually provoked the reply that Britain was a unitary state while Canada was not), he situated his conclusions within a uniquely Canadian framework. The Depression had gravely accentuated problems of regional disparity which could only be overcome by policies designed to promote a regional transfer of income. The most important such policy was federal control of relief. In short, 'national unity' demanded that Ottawa assume complete responsibility for the unemployed.

It was an 'ingenious' argument, deputy finance minister W.C. Clark conceded, but one which for the moment he could not accept, more for reasons of 'method and timing' than from any fundamental disagreement with the principle involved. For was it not 'equally plausible,' Clark replied,

to take precisely the opposite point of view, namely, that if the Dominion were now to assume the whole cost of unemployment relief without any quid pro quo whatsoever we would be in a much weaker position when a financial settlement with the provinces had to be made. In other words, we would have no bargaining power left ... [A]n expressed willingness to take over one hundred percent responsibility for the employable unemployed is by far the best bargaining lever we can have to obtain constitutional amendments giving us undisputed jurisdiction in the field of unemployment insurance and perhaps also in certain other fields. If we assume immediate responsibility for the whole cost of unemployment relief, the provinces will tell us to go ahead and deal with it as best we can without any change in the constitutional position.[67]

Thus, by the end of 1938 the question of whether Ottawa should assume control of relief had become one of tactics rather than strategy. Despite King's own strong opposition to the idea, he was surrounded by officials who accepted its inevitability and argued only over the most propitious moment for making the move. Pickersgill notwithstanding, the consensus was that nothing could be done until the Rowell Commission submitted its report. Until then, the present division of responsibilities would remain unchanged.

So 1939 became a year of stasis as far as federal unemployment policy was concerned. In one significant move which indicated the direction of federal thinking, Ottawa raised its share of relief costs to 40 per cent from the previous 30 per cent maximum imposed by the 1938 Relief Act. This was done despite the fact that the number dependent on the dole dropped to the lowest point since 1931.[68] At the same time, although recovery resumed its pace after the 1938 recession, the conservation and national development programs enacted the previous year were expanded for 1939 and the federal deficit forecast in that year's budget ballooned to $60 million. It was still not pump-priming but at least Dunning was deliberately moistening the leather. In a marked change from his 1938 budget speech, the finance minister now admitted that 'if the people as a whole and business in particular will not spend, government must. It is not a matter of choice but of sheer social necessity.'[69]

Throughout 1939 the King administration continued on the new course set in the previous spring. The policy of attempting to liquidate Ottawa's responsibility for unemployment was now totally abandoned. At the same time, however, the growing threat of war overshadowed all discussion of unemployment both within and without the government. Had the Royal Commission on Dominion-Provincial Relations submitted its report in the early spring, as King promised, this might not have been the case. Instead, plagued by the illness and forced retirement of its chairman and by an incredible volume of work, the commission was hopelessly behind schedule and would not complete its report until February 1940. King prepared to face the electorate in the autumn of 1939 lacking both an unemployment insurance bill and a general constitutional settlement.

The outbreak of war in September changed this situation. In the first place, it forced King to postpone the election and to face another parliamentary session in 1940. More important, as his new minister of labour Norman McLarty (Rogers had been moved to Defence) pointed out, the war itself had created a compelling new reason for unemployment insurance; namely, the need for 'affording a cushion when we are faced with the problem of demobilization and the cessation of war industry.' Yet McLarty could see no way such a bill could be introduced in the upcoming session. The Rowell-Sirois report would still not be available in time to make it part of a general constitutional settlement. In addition, the wartime demands on the Treasury would not leave enough money to establish a scheme that would not be 'disappointing to labour.' As a possible compromise, he suggested legislation creating a voluntary 'Profit-Sharing-Savings-Retirement Fund' in various industries.

King rejected this idea. It was 'like using [a] sprat to catch a whale,' he said.[70] Yet McLarty's basic point about demobilization and unemployment set him thinking. Two days after the cabinet rejected the profit-sharing idea, King wrote McLarty a four-page letter that marked a turning-point in federal policy. Throwing his labour minister's objections aside, King said he wanted the draft unemployment insurance bill introduced at the upcoming parliamentary session. 'The war has not only made possible immediate action on some measures of obvious social reform,' he wrote, 'but has made them more or less imperative.' It was 'clear that unemployment insurance will be indispensable in coping with the problem of re-establishment' and now was the time to get it passed. It would be two years before any benefits could be paid out so the financial problem was not as severe as McLarty thought and the contributions could be 'easily paid during the years of prosperity.' More important from a political standpoint, now was the 'right moment.' Duplessis had been defeated that autumn and replaced by a Liberal government headed by Adelard Godbout which, King was convinced, 'would ... be prepared to support an unemployment insurance measure.' Under the 'necessity which war has revealed,' King also expected the Hepburn administration would be 'ready ... to change its attitude of non-cooperation to one of cooperation' as well. The two cabinet ministers in the New Brunswick government who had most objected to the necessary amendment had been defeated at the last provincial election; therefore, he did 'not contemplate the slightest difficulty' in securing that province's consent. As for Aberhart, King confessed privately that he was pre-pared to 'go ahead notwithstanding' if the Alberta premier still refused to play along.

There was one final consideration more crucial perhaps than all the others. Passing unemployment insurance legislation would 'help to offset any feeling there might be that Parliament, at this session, should deal with some recommen-dations of the Dominion-Provincial Relations report.' It was clear that document would not be ready for the present session 'nor could we deal with it while [the] war was on.' With an election coming up, unemployment insurance could 'fill the gap.' For all these reasons he urged McLarty to give the measure 'precedence over all other matters.'[71]

Eleven days later King raised the issue in cabinet. It was not a smooth meeting. The war which now made unemployment insurance such an urgent matter to King also created strong opposition within the cabinet to going ahead with it. J.I. Ilsley and King's powerful new finance minister J.L. Ralston objected that the government had 'spent enough on socialistic legislation' through its relief and housing acts and 'needed the money for the prosecution of the war,' while C.D. Howe argued that the employer and employee contributions involved would force up wages and prices and thus contribute to inflation. From private discussions with Ernest Lapointe, King also knew that his Quebec lieutenant preferred to see the legislation postponed until after the Rowell-Sirois report was in the government's hands.

Despite this opposition, King was set on his course. It was 'necessary now to prepare for post-war conditions,' he told his colleagues, and there was 'now a chance to get all the provinces into line.' At the same time, money was 'flowing into the country for manufacturers'; therefore, it was 'the best of all times to begin a measure of unemployment [sic]. Employers and employees would be in a position to contribute. In a couple of years the war will be over and there will be much unemployment with the return of men to civil life. Benefits under the measure would save relief expenditure.' King also pointed out that the party was 'pledged to its introduction at the last campaign and before.' If the government did not introduce it before the next election, 'we would be confronted with a request from the Opposition and would be embarrassed.' Finally, there was the ever-present danger from the left. 'Labour, which was doing so much for the winning of the war, would expect us to make provisions for its needs once the war was over.' If they were rebuffed, there was always the CCF. King was 'anxious to keep Liberalism in control in Canada, not let third parties wrest away from us our rightful place in the matter of social reform.'[72] It was a powerful presentation which silenced the opposition of Ilsley, Ralston, and Howe. The war had filled King with a sense of urgency and opportunity that was notably absent during the Depression. Largely on the strength of his arguments, the cabinet agreed to introduce the unemployment insurance bill at the upcoming parliamentary session.

As King predicted, the war also cleared the way for provincial agreement to a constitutional amendment. Indeed, by basing his latest appeal entirely on the needs of the war effort, he left the premiers little choice. Since unemployment insurance would 'go far to prevent much of the insecurity and industrial dislocation which might otherwise be the aftermath of war,' King told them, he was sure 'you and your colleagues share fully our concern for the welfare of our people in the difficult days ahead.' In short, to oppose the amendment now would be unpatriotic. It was an argument no premier wanted to face. Quebec and New Brunswick quickly gave their consent, Ontario raised no objections, and, by the end of May, even Alberta gave in. Aberhart still could not see how the measure would help his 'largely ... Agricultural Province' but with Quebec and New Brunswick's opposition gone, he did not want to 'stand ... in the way of what the other eight provinces believe would be an advantage.'[73]

The needs of the war effort also made unemployment insurance essential in other ways. As a Department of Finance memo pointed out, 'during the expected brisk activity of the war period, the plan would act as a scheme of compulsory saving' which would not only provide workers with money for the anticipated post-war depression but would also make a large pool of savings 'available for Government use, just as if individual workers bought savings certificates.' In fact, it was 'one of the few forms of compulsory saving which could probably command public support in this country.' Because it would force people to save, the plan would also 'help to hold down consumption and make labour, equipment and resources available for the war effort.' Most important, unemployment insurance would necessitate an 'efficient and well-staffed employment service' that would soon become the 'informed field staff at the service of the Dominion' providing expert knowledge on the 'changes and conditions of employment.' Such an organization was 'immediately necessary if we are to make use of the available idle labour. On that will depend the possibility of meeting the next year's war effort out of increased production rather than out of decreased consumption and capital maintenance.' Of course, it would also be essential for dealing with demobilization. Even if one opposed the principle of unemployment insurance, the department concluded, the fact that it 'was a method of establishing an actual operating employment service' made it worthwhile.[74]

Once the decision had been taken to go ahead with the bill, there was no problem getting it ready since the legislation had been drafted in 1938. In fact, as McLarty readily admitted, the 1940 Unemployment Insurance Act was 'the same in principle' as Bennett's 1935 measure and both were based, for the most part, on the British legislation of 1934.

There were some important differences between the Bennett and King bills. Tait, the British consultant, had argued convincingly for making the scheme 'as generous ... as possible' in terms of coverage, eligibility, and benefit periods in order to reduce 'the amount of residual unemployment to be relieved in other ways.' To a certain extent the Department of Labour took his advice. Whereas the 1935 act aimed at covering two-thirds of the total labourforce, its 1940 counterpart intended to protect 75 per cent or a total of 2.1 million people. It too excluded seasonal workers in agriculture, forestry, fishing, lumbering and logging, transportation by air or water, and stevedoring. Domestic servants and anyone making over $2000 a year were left out of the 1940 act as they had been in 1935. Much of the greater coverage was provided by changes in the occupational composition of the labourforce than by any implicit generosity in the bill itself, although in one important modification the qualifying period for benefits was lowered from forty to thirty weeks worked over any two-year period.[75]

Unquestionably, the most significant difference between the two bills was the last-minute decision to provide graded rather than flat-rate benefits. This sounds like a technical question but in fact it cut to the heart of the most crucial dilemma in unemployment insurance. The 1935 act, like its British model, paid out a flat $6.00 weekly benefit (plus additional supplemental benefits for dependents) to every insured unemployed male over twenty-one in return for a standard weekly contribution of 25¢. The reason for this was administrative simplicity. It was much easier to run an insurance scheme which paid the same benefit to all workers than to try and grade both benefits and contributions to the highly complex variations in wage rates throughout the country.

There were two grave drawbacks to the flat-rate benefit, however. On the one hand, to prevent 'malingering,' the Labour Department pointed out, it had to be 'fixed at the lowest earnings of any worker in any part of the country.' The result was a weekly benefit that had 'no value ... whatsoever' to the 'high wage earner,' something that was bound to have 'political repercussions.' On the other hand, flat-rate benefits, small as they were, still ran the danger of 'over-insuring' the lowest third of the labourforce since they had also to include dependents' benefits. In other words, under this system, insurance living standards were at least roughly related to need in a way that wage rates were not.

For the department, this was the 'fundamental problem arising in any scheme of unemployment insurance; can you compensate need, or can you only compensate for something that relates to the normal standard of living of your worker?' Put differently, should unemployment insurance be used to redistribute income or to enforce the work ethic? The answer was clearly the latter. In the first place, the department argued, under any insurance system those most in need of benefits were least likely to get them because their poor employment record would disqualify them from frequent payments. Moreover, the constant danger of over-insurance (or less eligibility) made it impossible for the government to devise a flat-rate benefit that would both preserve the work ethic and provide an adequate standard of living across the country. '[T]he best that unemployment insurance can be expected to do,' the department concluded, 'is to relate benefits [and contributions] to actual earnings and therefore to the standard of living while in employment.'[76]

In the early months of 1940 both the flat-rate principle and dependents' benefits were scrapped from the 1938 draft scheme and replaced by a system which graded benefits and contributions according to previous earnings. The new bill created seven wage categories ranging from $6.44 to $32.24 per week. Contributions and benefits were graded according to these categories. The lowest-paid worker contributed 12¢ a week and could receive $4.08 in weekly benefits. The highest-paid worker put in 36¢ a week and received $12.24 in benefits. Married claimants were eligible for only a 15 per cent supplement to this base rate, regardless of how many dependents were in their family. On average, benefits under the new scheme equalled 50 per cent of wages, although as the federal government's *Report on Social Security for Canada* pointed out three years later, 'none of the [seven] categories ... reaches the "desirable" minimum or "living wage" standard.' Nevertheless, federal officials were happy with the changes. The revised bill was 'more definitely on insurance principles than ... the prior measure which ... was intended to deal with the problem of need,' a Labour Department spokesman testified. Moreover, there was 'no danger of over-insurance where you never pay the full amount of the earnings.' Finally, the graded system would allow high benefits that could 'take account of the higher standard of living of the worker receiving higher wages.'[77] In this way it would have less of a pauperizing effect and class differences among the unemployed could be preserved.

However, the graded system did have one consequence which seems to have gone unnoticed by Department of Labour officials at the time but which recently received much discussion. Because the benefit was geared to income while working, relatively high-paid skilled workers would be more inclined to exhaust their benefits waiting until comparable work returned rather than taking any work that became available. The flat-rate system had the opposite effect. Because it was geared to the lowest unskilled wage, almost any kind of work became preferable to insurance living standards. Either system, therefore, posed certain dangers to the less eligibility principle and it is the graded system which has recently come under such strong attack for encouraging people to be 'picky' about work.

On 12 July 1940 the British Parliament amended the British North America Act giving the federal government jurisdiction over unemployment insurance. By 1 August the bill itself had passed both Canadian Houses of Parliament and, a few days later, it became law. It was a landmark piece of social legislation.[78] Administratively, it was one of the most ambitious tasks undertaken to that date by a Canadian government. In one stroke 3000 new civil-service jobs were created and 1600 federal offices were opened in cities and towns across the country. More important, from this time on, in peace as well as war, the federal government would intrude into the daily lives of its citizens in a crucial way. Whether searching for work or cashing their insurance cheques, Canadians could no longer regard Ottawa in the same way as before 1 August 1940. Financially, the amounts involved seemed staggering as well. By 1941 the insurance fund would have an income of $58.5 million, made up of $23.4 million each in contributions from employers and workers and $9.7 million from the federal government. It would take an additional $5.25 million simply to administer the scheme.[79] In sheer administrative and financial terms, the Unemployment Insurance Act was a crucial milestone in the development of the Canadian welfare state.

Beyond these physical changes lay even more important political and social implications. King had always been able to keep a neat distinction in his mind between insurance and relief. The first held no terrors, but responsibility for the second was to be avoided at all costs. Only when the two became blurred, as in the final report of the NEC, did he begin to have second thoughts about unemployment insurance itself. Nevertheless, when the time came to act, King pressed ahead, confident that Ottawa's responsibility had been limited to only the insured unemployed.

The very circumstances which forced him to act made this a delusion. War, not the Depression, finally convinced King that unemployment insurance was an urgent necessity. In a pattern reminiscent of Borden's actions in 1918, the Liberal leader realized that a federal government which was about to demand great sacrifice from its citizens could not simply abandon them to fate once hostilities ended. Ottawa had passed through the Depression at arms' length from most of the unemployed. It would not be able to maintain this distance after the Second World War. Veterans would not willingly go back on relief. Neither would munitions workers.

Yet if demobilization and the fear of post-war unemployment made the insurance scheme politically necessary, they also made it obsolete. As federal officials pointed out the same month the bill became law, the measure now gave Ottawa 'an overhead administrative organization which should be adequate to handle the whole unemployment problem but which will, in fact, at any one time provide for no more than one-quarter of the unemployed.' This would not discharge the government's post-war obligations and would only 'leave the whole situation more confused than ever.' Provincial governments would have an incentive 'to press for a broader coverage ... and for more extended benefits, which could not be actuarially sound'; divided jurisdiction would cripple any possibility of 'dealing with unemployment by clear-cut national policies in any comprehensive and positive way'; and it was indefensible to 'leav[e] a major portion of the unemployed, and incidentally those least able to care for themselves, in the hands of provincial and local governments of widely varying financial capacity to support them.'

In sum, unemployment insurance without any provision for the uninsured unemployed was a 'backward' step: 'The general arguments ... favouring national responsibility for unemployment are greatly strengthened by the war and by the prospects of violent post-war readjustments. Unemployment resulting from the war is even more clearly a national responsibility than that resulting from the trade cycle, and the dislocation threatens to be on such a scale in some areas as to make any suggestion of local responsibility and planning and administration even more absurd than it has been in practice in the last decade.'[80] The Unemployment Insurance Act thus gave King more than he bargained for. There may have been sound actuarial reasons for limiting federal responsibility to only one-quarter of the post-war unemployed. Politically, there were none. Before the war's end the dominion government would be actively preparing a companion unemployment assistance scheme to bring all the employable unemployed under federal jurisdiction, although this initiative, ultimately, would not meet with success.[81] Nevertheless, August 1940 marked the point at which Ottawa became committed to accepting unemployment as a national responsibility.

The Unemployment Insurance Act marked another important turning-point. Prior to 1940, market considerations alone governed the income of working Canadians. Unemployment insurance gave the federal government a potential opportunity for introducing a new factor – one of need – in defining an adequate and decent social minimum in this country. As the conflict over graded versus flat-rate benefits revealed, this opportunity was rejected. Despite the horrendous dimensions of poverty revealed during the Depression, the most important piece of social legislation to come out of that decade refused to tackle the question of inadequate income. After 1940 the unemployed would simply receive a fixed proportion of what they earned when working. The less they worked, the less they were eligible to receive. Social insurance would mirror, not change the workings of the marketplace.

This process was repeated with the May 1940 publication of the report of the Royal Commission on Dominion-Provincial Relations. By now it came as no surprise that the commission's central recommendation was complete federal responsibility for unemployment relief. Moreover, like the final report of the NEC, the Rowell-Sirois Commission based its arguments on grounds of administrative and financial efficiency, not the abuse of the unemployed by local governments. 'Nothing in the history of Canadian government,' the report stated, 'has contributed more to the breakdown of our system of public finances or has been productive of greater waste in the economy than the attempt to hold local governments primarily responsible for unemployment as well as other relief.'[82]

Two key arguments underpinned the commission's case. The first was Keynesianism, muted in the NEC's final report and now fully embraced by Rowell-Sirois. Because of its wide monetary and taxation powers, the dominion was the 'only government' that could meet the 'large fluctuating expenditures due to unemployment' through a 'planned budgetary policy of deficits during depressions, and surpluses and debt repayment during prosperity.' For that reason alone, responsibility for the 'whole problem of unemployment' had to be 'brought under the single control of the Federal Government.' As long as it remained with the provinces and the municipalities, Canada would be 'unable to eliminate the avoidable economic wastes and social consequences of mass unemployment.'[83] It was a compelling new argument. Unemployment was 'avoidable'; only Ottawa could prevent it; therefore, it had to be made a federal responsibility. Keynesianism had changed the terms of the debate.

So too had the arguments for national unity. Canada, the report pointed out, possessed an 'intricate ... closely-knit ... [and] ... fundamentally national' economic structure which had been 'compartmentalized for the purposes of meeting the costs of widespread destitution and unemployment.' The result was to throw the burden of the Depression on the backs of communities dependent on the country's exposed primary industries, particularly in the four bankrupt western provinces. It was an irrational policy which endangered not only public finance but Confederation itself. The only logical solution was to make the whole cost of relief a national responsibility.[84]

Even this, however, was not enough to overcome the unequal burdens of confederation. In its most radical departure, the report argued that 'National economic policies adopted in the general interest, inevitably operate to impoverish some areas and enrich others. The only equitable corollary of this is national taxation which treats residents of all provinces equally, and thus provides for some redistribution of surplus income among provincial governments to enable them to perform their functions without imposing excessive taxation on their citizens.' As a remedy, Rowell-Sirois called for a complete federal takeover of the fields of personal and corporate income tax and succession duties from the provinces. In return, they would receive 'national adjustment grants' from Ottawa that would allow the poorer governments to raise their social services to a level consistent with the 'national average.'[85] Ottawa could use its broad financial powers not simply to prevent unemployment but to alleviate regional disparity as well.

The call for a federal takeover of provincial tax fields was not new. It had long been considered a necessary corollary of dominion responsibility for unemployment relief. But Rowell-Sirois did not put the case in these terms. Even without such a surrender, it still called for federal control of relief. Its justification for expanded federal revenues was not the added burden of unemployment but the need for a regional transfer of income. It was this call for a redistribution of the nation's wealth and the establishment of national standards in social services that earned Rowell-Sirois its reputation as the blueprint for the Canadian welfare state.

Without downplaying the report's significance in outlining a new deal for Canadian federalism, one qualification must be made. Nothing in the report implied a better deal for the unemployed. Although it deplored the existence of local relief standards which had 'emphasized immediate economy rather than adequacy' and had led to a 'probable increase of deficiency diseases,' Rowell-Sirois did not argue that unemployment relief should be raised to any national average standard. The redistribution of income it called for was between regions, not individuals. When it came to the question of relief scales, the report simply incorporated the 'less eligibility' principle into its recommendations.

'While unemloyment aid would aim primarily to maintain the employability of the worker,' its argument ran, 'minimum going wages in the community should be maintained above this rate.' Since the report recommended that minimum wages be left with the provinces, this meant a continuation of the existing variation in relief scales. In calculating the cost of a federal unemployment aid system, Rowell-Sirois simply 'assumed that the Dominion will provide for the maintenance of the unemployed on the scales adopted by the provinces.' Whether this aid 'should ... include relief for ... dependents' or 'should ... vary in accordance with local costs and standards of living' were ... 'details of policy and administration' which the commission felt were 'beyond its duty to advise upon.'[86]

In short, like the NEC, the Rowell-Sirois report did not assume that national responsibility for relief implied a national minimum. Its recommendations were designed to strengthen public finance, depressed regions, and the federal government, not to raise the living standards of the unemployed.

The Rowell-Sirois report was a peacetime document. Its arguments were based on the experience of Canada during the Depression. But it was completed after the outbreak of the Second World War and, as with unemployment insurance, the war forced the King administration to accept some of its recommendations. The cost of financing the war effort presented Ottawa with exactly the kind of immediate, large-scale responsibility that it had so deftly avoided during the past ten years. Moreover, unequal burdens that were barely tolerable during the Depression would be fiercely resented during a period of maximum national sacrifice. As the governor of the Bank of Canada pointed out, post-war workers would far more 'likely ... face unemployment ... with much greater resentment – to put it mildly – than displayed during the Depression years.' In the 'interests of peace, order and good government,' Ottawa would have to 'assume full responsibility' for the problem. If it did so without adopting the other recommendations of the Rowell-Sirois report, the financial situation would be 'chaotic.'[87]

The logic was unassailable. The federal government would be held responsible for the next depression in a way it had not been for the past one. After calling an abortive dominion-provincial conference in January 1941 during which Hepburn, Aberhart, and Pattullo predictably rejected the report's recommendations, the federal government raised its own taxes to a level which forced the provinces out of the fields of personal and corporate income tax and succession duties. In return, they received annual payments set at levels suggested by the Rowell-Sirois report. Ottawa now had the fiscal powers it needed to fight both war and depression.

It was a 'temporary [wartime] expedient' and the report's other recommendations, including dominion control of relief, were 'shelved' for the duration of the conflict, although by 1942 the economy was operating at full capacity and the burden itself was negligible. By the war's end, King hoped, the provinces would have 'come to see that the Sirois report is, after all, what is best for them as well as for us.'[88] Federal officials were soon at work on a comprehensive scheme of unemployment assistance to be presented at the 1945 dominion-provincial conference.

The Rowell-Sirois report and the Second World War thus brought a cycle to a close. In 1918, under the influence of war, Ottawa established the Employment Service of Canada – its first concrete connection with the unemployed. Twenty-two years later, again under the shadow of world conflict, the federal government moved towards the full acceptance of responsibility both for unemployment and the unemployed.

The report completed another cycle as well. Since 1932, when the Bennett government finally abandoned public works for direct relief as its principal depression remedy, the question of how to finance the cost of unemployment had increasingly overshadowed that of how to care for the unemployed themselves. Local responsibility for relief created two anomalies during the Depression. The first was the breakdown of public finance. The second was the unjustifiable variation in relief rates and a glaring failure to provide the unemployed with an adequate standard of living.

In recommending complete federal responsibility for the unemployed, the reports of both the NEC and the Rowell-Sirois Commission were responding only to the first problem. Neither argued that national standards of relief should accompany national responsibility for those out of work. Instead, both reports explicitly stated that unemployment aid, although administered by Ottawa, would have to be kept below the lowest rates for unskilled labour in each region. By 1940, then, the unemployed had become a federal responsibility in every sense but one. How much they received was still a function of the market. 'Less eligibility' had survived the passing of the Poor Law.

Conclusion

Between the beginning of the First World War and the end of the Second, Canada created a welfare state. In the process, no measure was so fiercely resisted or so long delayed as the assumption of national responsibility for the unemployed, signified by the creation of unemployment insurance and a national employment service in 1940. From the 1913-15 depression onwards, it was increasingly apparent within Canadian cities that the problem of unemployment, both in its origins and dimensions, was beyond the capability of local governments to handle. Despite this evidence, a succession of federal governments, backed by their provincial counterparts, insisted throughout the 1920s that the care of the jobless was primarily a matter for private charity and municipal poor relief. As a result, Canada entered the Great Depression totally unprepared for a crisis that would soon sever almost one out of every three Canadian workers from their jobs.

Throughout the 1930s Ottawa intensified the impact of mass unemployment by adhering to this poor-law tradition. From Bennett's first Relief Act in 1930 until the passage of unemployment insurance ten years later, the one consistent theme underpinning federal unemployment policy was Ottawa's insistence that the jobless were primarily a municipal and provincial responsibility. Although the federal government spent almost $400 million on relief during the Depression and lent the four western provinces more than $100 million to pay for their share of its costs, at no time during the 1930s did Bennett or King ever admit that Ottawa's contributions to the dole were anything more than the result of a temporary phenomenon.[1] The result of this policy was the fiscal breakdown of first local and then provincial governments; the 1935 explosion of unrest among transient single men for whom no one would assume responsibility; and, most importantly, the hardship and suffering endured by the jobless and their families who were abandoned to local governments that could nowhere provide adequate and decent standards of support.

Why did the poor-relief heritage last so long? Canadian historians, in writing about the Depression, have advanced two explanations. The first is constitutional. Measures designed to deal with the 'immediate needs of the country and issues raised by the Depression' W.L. Morton has written, were not possible because 'the national government had the means but not the authority and the provincial governments the authority without adequate means.' He concludes, 'what the provinces would not grant the power to do, could not be done.' This argument, first put forward by the Rowell-Sirois report in 1940, has been echoed by J.M.S. Careless, Kenneth McNaught, and H. Blair Neatby in their writing on the 1930s.[2]

This approach ignores the fact that throughout the Depression it was Ottawa, not the provinces, which consistently invoked the constitution and the sanctity of provincial rights as justification for its limited responsibility for the jobless. The premiers, in contrast, along with mayors, businessmen, labour leaders, two federal commissions, and of course the unemployed, insisted that the care of those without work was, or should be, totally a federal matter. As King himself conceded in 1938, the provinces were 'only too ready to turn over the whole burden of unemployment relief to the Dominion.'[3] Like his predecessor, R.B. Bennett, King had not the slightest intention of accepting it. On the most important issue of the Depression, it was Ottawa which jealously defended provincial rights while the premiers were centralists.

No legal barriers barred Bennett or King from providing work for the jobless. Nothing in the constitution stopped Ottawa from defining a national minimum standard of relief and making provincial compliance a condition of federal aid. No province ever took the dominion government to court for assuming responsibility for the relief of unemployed single men. The preoccupation with unemployment insurance, which did require a constitutional amendment but which offered little to the victims of the 1930s, has distracted attention from the important fact that neither the BNA Act nor provincial rights prevented the federal government from taking positive steps to improve the care of the unemployed. Instead, Ottawa's narrow definition of its own responsibility, by bankrupting the West and turning the premiers against the central government, was the principal factor pushing Canadian federalism to the brink of collapse.

Even with unemployment insurance, the constitution in the 1930s, as in the 1920s, provided more of a convenient excuse for delay than a barrier to action for both Bennett and King. Although Bennett pledged his government to such legislation in April 1931, he made no serious attempt to secure the constitutional amendment needed to bring unemployment insurance within federal authority before introducing it as part of his New Deal in February 1935. The Employment and Social Insurance Act was a well-crafted piece of legislation but Bennett used it as a pre-election ploy knowing that, in all likelihood, it would be declared *ultra vires* by the courts.

King followed a similar strategy. Although he knew an amendment was essential to its passage, he did not ask the premiers for their consent until November 1937. When three provinces raised objections, the matter was dropped until the outbreak of war in 1939 made unemployment insurance, in King's words, 'indispensable in coping with the problem of re-establishment.'[4] At this point, faced with the prospect of an election, King, like Bennett in 1935, acted decisively in introducing an insurance bill. Clearly, neither man during the 1930s was anxious to accept the costs or the risks of an unemployment insurance scheme launched in a time of heavy unemployment. The constitution provided a useful justification for delay.

The second explanation by historians for the tenacity of the poor-relief heritage is developmental. Simply put, it argues that Canada's recent industrialization before 1930 played a crucial role in limiting the subsequent response to mass unemployment in this country. On the one hand, as Linda Grayson and Michael Bliss claim, the Depression was the 'first major collapse of the new urban-industrial Canadian economy'; therefore, 'lack of knowledge and experience ... impeded every programme for recovery or relief.'[5] On the other, the continuing strength of rural traditions in the country meant that Canadians going into the Depression shared a 'pioneer mentality' which viewed reliance on public relief as 'a confession of incompetence or sinfulness, of friendlessness and failure.' '[R]ooted in rural life,' these attitudes, Michiel Horn argues, 'persisted in the towns and cities' and prevented any widespread acceptance of the 'full consequences of ... changing economic reality.'[6]

That Canadian governments at all levels lacked knowledge and expertise in their attempts to relieve the unemployed during the 1930s cannot be denied. The reason, however, was not lack of experience with unemployment. As this study has shown, two major depressions struck this country before 1930, one during the years 1913-15 and the other between 1920 and 1925. During the latter, initiatives were launched by the Union government in the areas of labour exchanges, unemployment research, and relief which made this country, for a short time, the North American pioneer in devising new methods of dealing with those out of work. These efforts were scrapped by the first King administration. Deliberate policy decisions, not simply inexperience, lay behind Canada's woeful lack of preparation for the 'dirty thirties.'

Inexperience is no excuse for Ottawa's failure, throughout the Depression, to make any contribution towards the costs of relief administration so that competent personnel could be hired by provincial and municipal governments. It does not explain why a general investigation into the problems surrounding unemployment relief was delayed by the federal government until 1936. Nor does it explain why the advice of the National Employment Commission was ignored. Questions of policy governed these decisions.

At the level of ideology, the developmental approach is more convincing. As this study has shown, the 'back-to-the-land' solution was a consistent response to the problem of unemployment throughout the interwar years, a testimony to the importance of agriculture to the Canadian economy. But more was included in shaping 'back to the land' as a panacea for unemployment than merely the persistence of rural attitudes. Beneath the nostalgic rhetoric and the fears of rural depopulation lay the sterner imperatives of a labour market that had to supply sufficient quantities of cheap unskilled labour to the agricultural and resource frontiers. At stake in the debate between proponents of 'back to the land' on the one hand and unemployment insurance or relief on the other was a controversy over the meaning of work. Was room and board and $5.00 a month on a homestead an acceptable offer of employment? Did the unemployed have the right to refuse such offers and to collect relief in the city? At bottom, this was as much a debate over living standards as over the existence or non-existence of work, a debate, moreover, in which the state could not avoid taking sides. Throughout the 1920s and 1930s the existence of a large agricultural labour market operated as a crucial check on the limits to urban relief. Any attempt to provide the unemployed in the cities with a decent standard of living quickly ran the risk of raising relief above what rural employers were able or willing to pay. These were the imperatives which turned the Progressives against the Union government's unemployment initiatives between 1918 and 1921. It was the same imperative which placed unemployed single men in the front line of the struggle against Ottawa's unemployment policy in the 1930s.

Beneath 'back to the land' lay the heritage of another more powerful tradition – the Poor Law doctrine of 'less eligibility.' This legacy ultimately shaped federal unemployment policy during the interwar years. As Frances Fox Piven and Richard Cloward have pointed out, relief arrangements in market societies 'are ancillary to economic arrangements. Their chief function is to regulate labour ... To demean and punish those who do not work is to exalt by contrast even the meanest labour at the meanest wages.'[7] Before the Depression, Canada's agricultural and resource sector provided low-wage unskilled jobs in abundance and during the 1930s their wages became even 'meaner.' The necessity of imposing a work ethic on this large mass of unskilled labour led Ottawa to insist that unemployment relief should remain a local responsibility. Municipalities were more in touch with local wage rates, which varied widely across the country, and thus they could justify politically keeping relief scales below these levels in a way the national government could not. In addition, the strain which the cost of relief placed on municipal finances, and consequently on local tax-payers, acted as a powerful check against generosity in setting minimum standards of living for the jobless. Finally, in the background lay the British experience with unemployment insurance in the 1920s – a constant stimulus to Bennett's and King's fears that national responsibility for the unemployed might lead to national bankruptcy.

By the end of the 1930s a variety of factors converged to erode the utility of local responsibility for relief. Most important was the fear that 'less eligibility' was breaking down because of it. By 1937 municipal governments paid, on a national average, only one-sixth of the cost of the dole. At the same time 65 per cent of the nation's relief load was concentrated in the ten largest cities,[8] allowing the unemployed, along with organized labour, to exert powerful political pressure on local governments to provide better relief benefits. As Charlotte Whitton pointed out ceaselessly from 1932 onwards, in Montreal, Toronto, Windsor, Winnipeg, Calgary, and Vancouver work incentives were being eroded through a combination of 'lax' administration and 'political' exploitation of relief. To save the work ethic, Ottawa had to step in.

It did. After 1938, maximum levels of support set below local wage rates for unskilled labour were written into every relief agreement the federal government signed with the provinces. Ottawa finally moved to enforce administrative and financial standards for unemployment relief in order to contract, not to expand, existing levels of expenditure.

The imperative of 'less eligibility' also enhanced the appeal of unemployment insurance to both Bennett and King. Unlike relief, the duration of insurance benefits was strictly related to previous contribution, not to need. Like any insurance scheme, the more one paid in, the more one was entitled to take out. In this way, unemployment insurance seemed to pose little threat to work incentives since those who were eligible for the most benefits were those who needed them the least – the regularly employed. Seasonal workers, in contrast, who suffered from severe unemployment on a regular basis, were deliberately excluded from both the Bennett and King insurance bills on the grounds that their occupations fell beyond the bounds of acceptable 'actuarial risk.'

The level of benefits was set below existing wage rates under both schemes so that in no case would insurance become more attractive than work. Indeed, neither scheme offered a benefit level sufficient to maintain the health of a family of five with no other source of income. Nor could these benefits be raised without increased contributions from the workers themselves. By so taxing labour for its own unemployment, it was hoped that the pressure for larger benefits, which had destroyed the 'actuarial soundness' of the British scheme in the 1920s, could be held in check. In short, unemployment insurance was designed to mirror the market distribution of income, not to change it. There was no attempt in either the Bennett or King insurance bills to define a national minimum standard of living based on need, not on existing wage rates.

Keynesian economics provided another powerful incentive for Ottawa to assume national responsibility for the jobless. Once the Department of Finance accepted the view that mass unemployment was avoidable through centralized control over fiscal and monetary policy, centralized control over the victims of unemployment followed logically. Governments, it seemed, could spend their way out of depressions, but only through efficient and co-ordinated policies. Since the goal of this expenditure was to put the unemployed to work, it made sense to entrust their care to the government which had both the financial power and administrative expertise to achieve this end. Otherwise, conflicting policies could frustrate the best anti-depression strategy. National responsibility for unemployment, in other words, implied national responsibility for the unemployed as well.

The same logic explains why war provided the final reason for centralizing in Ottawa control of the unemployed. Two decades before Keynesianism had made any impact on Canada, the federal government, because of its wartime control over the nation's manpower, was dragged into creating an employment service and paying one-third of the cost of relief. Although this early initiative was abandoned, the Second World War completed the cycle. When King finally pushed for speedy passage of the Unemployment Insurance Act, it was out of his own fear of post-war unrest. War made Ottawa directly responsible for the nation's labourforce in a way that trade cycles could not, since mobilization and demobilization linked the federal government directly to the fate of the post-war labourforce. If depression and unemployment followed the Second World War, as many thought they would, Ottawa would be held responsible. No one expected that veterans or unemployed war workers would queue up meekly in front of local relief offices. In the final analysis it was war and not depression which destroyed the poor-law heritage.

The 1930s was the last decade in which Canadians were forced to deal with the contradictions posed by long-term mass unemployment. Unemployment insurance which emerged out of that decade was not designed to deal with the problems a depression posed. Rather, insurance has worked best in combination with the full employment policy which emerged as the key response of Ottawa to the crisis of the 1930s – in easing workers over short-term spells of seasonal or cyclical joblessness.[9] Moreover, with the confidence bred of Keynesian counter-cyclical economics and an expanding economy, the federal government, as many earlier critics feared, has followed the British pattern of the 1920s by progressively extending the coverage of unemployment insurance to virtually the entire labourforce while, at the same time, reducing the eligibility requirements and extending benefit periods. With the 1971 reforms, unemployment insurance became in fact, if not in name, a welfare scheme with an explicit redistributive function.[10]

Ironically, the 1970s produced what most economists predicted would not happen again – long-term, large-scale unemployment combined with double-digit inflation, which has seemingly defied any easy Keynesian remedy. As we enter the 1980s with daily news of plant shut-downs, lay-offs, and 13 per cent of the labourforce or almost 1.5 million people unemployed, the spectre of another great depression stares us in the face. A new royal commission on the unemployment crisis has been announced. Ominously we hear talk once more of Canada's 'natural rate of unemployment.' The state's definition of full employment has steadily incorporated ever higher levels of joblessness. Once again economists, newspaper editors, and prime ministers have accused the unemployed of preferring relief to work. In response, unemployment insurance benefits have been reduced and eligibility requirements stiffened, even though the percentage of those without work has reached a level unprecedented since the Great Depression. Welfare rolls have reached crisis proportions and mayors and premiers are again complaining that Ottawa is trying to 'shift ... the burden of unemployment ... to the provinces and municipalities.'[11] To those who lived through the 1930s, it all must have a most familiar ring.

Appendices

APPENDIX I
Average annual unemployment rates in Canada, 1920–40 (per cent)

1920	4.6	1931	17.4
1921	8.9	1932	26.0
1922	7.1	1933	26.6
1923	4.9	1934	20.6
1924	7.1	1935	19.1
1925	7.0	1936	16.7
1926	4.7	1937	12.5
1927	2.9	1938	15.1
1928	2.6	1939	14.1
1929	4.2	1940	9.3
1930	12.9		

Sources: Census of Canada, 1931, XIII, 'Monograph on Unemployment,' 274–6, and W. Galenson and A. Zellner, 'International Comparison of Unemployment Rates,' in Universities National Bureau Committee for Economic Research, *The Measurement and Behaviour of Unemployment* (Princeton 1957), 455–6

APPENDIX II
Summary by months of numbers assisted on direct relief (food, fuel, clothing, and shelter), 1932–41

	Urban				Agricultural				Grand total direct relief
	Heads of families	Depen- dents	Indi- vidual cases	Total	Heads of families	Depen- dents	Indi- vidual cases	Total	
1932									
May	93,608	332,762	30,343	456,713	28,015	112,062	156	140,233	596,946
June	103,686	365,063	32,295	501,044	24,468	97,872	136	122,476	623,520
July	114,717	440,394	35,572	590,683	21,191	84,765	118	106,074	696,757
August	139,227	517,094	34,120	690,441	8,363	33,450	46	41,859	732,300
September	158,033	580,644	35,911	774,588	4,032	16,128	22	20,182	794,770
October	168,779	627,186	44,952	840,917	6,741	23,593		30,334	871,251
November	203,680	800,483	45,734	1,049,897	11,617	52,277	58	63,952	1,113,849
December	223,037	896,411	50,842	1,170,290	13,120	59,040	66	72,226	1,242,516
1933									
January	245,853	992,442	59,034	1,297,329	12,064	54,288	61	66,413	1,363,742
February	259,799	1,046,132	66,760	1,372,691	16,273	73,228	82	89,583	1,462,274
March	266,847	1,054,673	68,896	1,390,416	18,992	85,463	95	104,550	1,494,966
April	267,803	1,089,846	70,097	1,427,746	16,310	73,394	81	89,785	1,517,531
May	241,176	962,897	64,001	1,268,074	12,320	55,440	62	67,822	1,335,896
June	225,913	819,975	37,179	1,083,067	9,563	43,033	48	52,644	1,135,711
July	207,908	747,691	30,446	986,045	9,657	43,456	49	53,162	1,039,207
August	202,363	724,453	31,560	958,376	2,080	9,360	11	11,451	969,827
September	197,623	691,159	31,528	920,310	8,867	39,901	45	48,813	969,123
October	207,362	769,153	42,665	1,019,180	11,686	52,586	59	64,331	1,083,511
November	210,665	726,483	46,699	983,847	26,330	118,485	133	144,948	1,128,795
December	227,447	786,216	45,197	1,058,860	31,108	139,985	157	171,250	1,230,110
1934									
January	236,605	818,989	45,055	1,100,649	34,773	156,478	175	191,426	1,292,075
February	248,183	859,118	44,541	1,151,842	35,491	159,709	178	195,378	1,347,220
March	257,503	900,637	47,723	1,205,863	33,837	118,429	170	152,436	1,358,299
April	236,990	815,739	43,574	1,096,303	31,331	109,658	157	141,146	1,237,449
May	228,964	789,125	40,121	1,058,210	33,575	117,512	168	151,255	1,209,465
June	201,246	656,743	33,713	891,702	33,168	116,088	167	149,423	1,041,125
July	181,790	625,121	30,897	837,808	32,626	114,191	164	146,981	984,789
August	186,158	618,458	29,414	834,030	31,866	111,531	160	143,557	977,587
September	186,406	608,531	29,616	824,553	19,716	84,232	1,669	105,617	930,170
October	197,423	665,635	34,110	897,168	30,031	121,323	2,563	153,917	1,051,085
November	196,712	657,043	35,484	889,239	33,124	138,005	3,138	174,267	1,063,506
December	212,943	710,364	43,192	966,499	32,878	133,662	4,997	171,537	1,138,036

APPENDIX II continued

	Urban				Agricultural				Grand total direct relief
	Heads of families	Dependents	Individual cases	Total	Heads of families	Dependents	Individual cases	Total	
1935									
January	240,193	785,837	42,955	1,068,985	33,548	137,523	5,069	176,140	1,245,125
February	240,051	849,652	47,137	1,136,840	33,965	138,984	5,243	178,192	1,315,032
March	252,889	868,115	41,242	1,172,246	34,161	139,103	5,319	178,583	1,350,829
April	244,862	862,593	54,124	1,161,579	32,901	133,942	5,011	171,854	1,333,433
May	234,939	831,988	46,908	1,113,835	31,376	127,444	4,797	163,617	1,277,452
June	216,742	759,739	43,424	1,019,905	30,115	122,639	4,591	157,345	1,177,250
July	206,137	728,622	41,473	976,232	29,541	120,038	4,546	154,125	1,130,357
August	194,019	696,676	34,794	925,489	28,986	117,926	4,437	151,349	1,076,838
September	210,720	638,723	37,020	886,463	3,474	14,565	515	18,554	905,017
October	215,290	636,038	39,637	890,965	6,850	27,740	915	35,505	926,470
November	205,530	688,748	43,310	937,588	18,761	77,979	2,131	98,871	1,036,459
December	220,921	781,387	48,175	1,050,483	23,619	99,666	2,723	126,008	1,176,491
1936									
January	247,934	883,661	53,932	1,185,527	27,054	110,484	3,023	140,561	1,326,088
February	256,367	915,522	54,811	1,226,700	28,908	122,018	3,234	154,160	1,380,860
March	257,284	926,705	56,085	1,240,074	29,560	125,090	3,408	158,058	1,398,132
April	242,253	880,118	54,087	1,176,458	27,379	116,510	3,165	147,054	1,323,512
May	218,573	783,384	47,860	1,049,817	21,262	89,085	2,672	113,019	1,162,836
June	196,365	711,640	53,173	961,178	19,574	81,956	2,390	103,920	1,065,098
July	185,880	670,021	52,114	908,015	19,884	82,395	2,406	104,685	1,012,700
August	179,417	647,100	53,157	879,674	19,261	80,225	2,519	102,005	981,679
September	150,778	508,958	47,557	707,293	44,991	196,989	6,347	248,327	955,620
October	155,087	522,475	51,965	729,527	51,346	220,642	7,281	279,269	1,008,796
November	159,431	536,195	55,280	750,906	54,782	232,946	7,733	295,461	1,046,367
December	171,076	575,432	58,849	805,357	57,400	244,616	7,936	309,952	1,115,309
1937									
January	182,514	614,207	61,735	858,456	59,263	252,417	8,095	319,775	1,178,231
February	187,049	629,352	62,882	879,283	60,846	259,033	8,297	328,176	1,207,459
March	186,292	629,231	62,620	878,143	61,343	261,190	8,226	330,759	1,208,902
April	176,520	597,738	59,542	833,800	60,099	257,826	7,942	325,867	1,159,667
May	156,423	528,845	52,480	737,748	55,543	237,234	7,375	300,152	1,037,900
June	135,925	456,966	43,399	636,290	49,552	208,212	6,731	264,495	900,785
July	121,400	402,590	39,909	563,899	44,037	178,921	6,414	229,372	739,271
August	110,416	364,469	36,505	511,390	44,889	181,337	6,618	232,844	744,234
September	100,600	324,087	31,152	455,839	52,913	209,049	7,114	269,076	724,915
October	103,864	333,070	33,877	470,811	65,379	257,435	8,421	331,235	802,046
November	112,316	360,703	40,456	513,475	71,763	282,190	9,120	363,073	876,548
December	127,310	411,650	41,381	580,341	74,428	292,624	9,531	376,583	956,924

APPENDIX II continued

	Urban				Agricultural				Grand total direct relief
	Heads of families	Depen- dents	Indi- vidual cases	Total	Heads of families	Depen- dents	Indi- vidual cases	Total	
1938									
January	139,137	449,812	43,025	631,974	75,793	297,643	9,755	383,191	1,015,165
February	144,557	466,553	43,419	654,529	76,950	302,578	9,891	389,419	1,043,948
March	144,696	467,979	40,015	652,690	77,388	304,720	9,928	392,036	1,044,726
April	139,897	453,091	39,306	632,294	77,248	304,617	10,063	391,928	1,024,222
May	127,284	410,306	38,370	575,960	75,053	295,508	9,931	380,492	956,452
June	115,568	369,476	35,836	520,880	71,820	282,216	9,651	363,687	884,567
July	109,854	351,120	36,153	497,127	67,213	262,952	9,264	339,429	836,556
August	104,443	332,848	33,808	471,099	56,790	221,625	8,121	286,536	757,635
September	98,446	312,459	33,827	444,732	20,795	85,558	2,519	108,872	553,604
October	103,958	330,934	38,370	473,262	32,830	130,981	3,984	167,795	641,057
November	116,815	373,061	45,017	534,893	49,601	196,339	5,996	251,936	786,829
December	132,482	426,380	45,804	604,666	57,504	227,392	6,915	291,811	896,477
1939									
January	146,754	472,721	48,721	668,196	60,636	240,445	7,251	308,332	976,528
February	153,639	494,332	49,925	697,896	63,116	250,130	7,525	320,771	1,018,667
March	155,291	499,535	49,868	704,694	63,392	251,877	7,573	322,842	1,027,536
April	151,018	486,767	48,248	686,033	62,488	248,862	7,473	318,823	1,004,856
May	138,370	444,023	43,881	626,274	58,180	231,947	7,020	297,147	923,421
June	123,455	393,771	40,182	557,408	55,366	219,7^^	^ 77?	281,918	839,326
July	118,637	376,071	40,012	534,720	53,302	211,027	6,605	270,934	805,654
August	120,383	386,183	38,251	544,817	50,777	200,725	6,333	257,835	802,652
September	107,696	346,401	34,887	488,984	9,721	38,856	1,452	50,029	539,013
October	105,402	341,474	37,433	484,309	11,541	46,492	1,541	59,574	543,883
November	109,184	356,896	41,813	507,893	15,030	60,912	1,861	77,803	585,696
December	119,202	392,770	44,704	556,676	13,494	57,464	1,612	72,570	629,246
1940									
January	132,047	438,937	47,066	618,050	17,761	76,414	1,918	96,093	714,143
February	137,452	455,772	47,748	640,972	20,700	89,279	2,114	112,093	753,065
March	138,961	461,832	48,076	648,869	22,760	98,627	2,286	123,673	772,542
April	132,612	440,129	47,107	619,848	23,997	103,843	2,396	130,236	750,084
May	118,247	389,801	42,202	550,250	20,265	87,254	2,093	109,612	659,862
June	99,151	321,929	37,889	458,969	15,681	67,016	1,703	84,400	543,369
July	85,583	274,919	33,808	394,310	11,589	48,975	1,409	61,973	456,283
August	69,533	223,144	28,546	321,223	8,541	35,752	1,165	45,458	366,681
September	53,752	167,579	25,385	246,716	2,902	11,869	585	15,356	262,072
October	49,131	152,619	24,972	226,722	4,605	18,439	734	23,778	250,500
November	49,781	155,981	26,401	232,163	7,651	31,101	1,020	39,772	271,935
December	53,284	169,650	28,043	250,977	10,713	44,456	1,257	56,426	307,403

APPENDIX II concluded

	Urban				Agricultural				Grand total direct relief
	Heads of families	Depen- dents	Indi- vidual cases	Total	Heads of families	Depen- dents	Indi- vidual cases	Total	
1941									
January	56,784	183,160	28,901	268,845	10,030	42,563	1,236	53,829	322,674
February	57,746	179,469	33,785	271,000	10,828	46,840	1,332	59,000	330,000
March	56,254	174,404	33,342	264,000	11,215	48,429	1,356	61,000	325,000

Source: *Report* of the Dominion Commissioner of Unemployment Relief, 31 March 1941, Appendix D, 37–8

APPENDIX III
Classification of dominion disbursements under relief legislation Sept. 1930 to 31 March 1939 (in dollars)

Year	Direct relief (urban and agricultural) and grant-in-aid	Public works	Agricultural aid and other than direct relief	Farm employment plan	Relief settlement	Youth training and reha-bilitation	Total paid provinces	Federal departments and railways	Total
1930	3,431,557	11,887,216	2,001				15,320,774	2,364,604	17,685,378
1931	10,135,088	25,004,290	1,746,725	139,848			37,025,951	5,315,739	42,341,690
1932	19,579,670	1,139,045	3,603,527	104,873	519,370		24,946,485	981,088	25,927,573
1933	29,326,462	3,376,906	288,512	276,055			33,267,935	7,648,537	40,916,472
1934	26,414,649	3,071,397	2,244,048	167,964	242,651		32,140,709	8,398,280	40,538,989
1935	29,606,181	10,511,167	2,376,072	222,601	2,496		42,718,517	8,283,813	51,002,330
1936	34,062,935	11,220,851	257,262	1,375,969	480,609		47,397,626	608,942	48,006,568
1937	31,424,586	6,077,904	12,267,981	1,360,463	8,931	584,353	51,724,218	1,430,355	53,154,573
1938	25,853,059	2,196,182	360,000	561,983		874,382	29,845,606	2,733,972	32,579,578
Totals	209,834,187	74,484,958	23,146,128	4,209,756	1,254,057	1,458,735	314,387,821	37,765,330	352,153,151

Administration, Sept. 1930–31 March 1939   1,091,603
Grand total   353,244,754

Source: Department of Labour Records, Lacelle files, vol. 213, file 617, 'Dominion Unemployment Relief – Relief since 1930,' Jan. 1940, 34

Maximum monthly relief allowances for a family of five, selected Canadian cities, Sept. 1936

City	Food	Fuel	Rent	Total
Brandon	$18.20	$10.50	$10.00	$42.00
Brantford	27.08	11.00	11.00	50.00
Calgary	35.75	7.00	17.85	60.60
Cornwall	26.65	4.00	not provided	38.61
Edmonton	29.25	3.50	15.00	49.25
Fredericton	24.60	in kind	7.00	31.60
Guelph	26.87	11.00	15.00	52.87
Halifax	14.53	4.33	not provided	18.86
Hamilton	24.40	9.00	9.00	42.40
Hull	16.47	11.00	10.00	37.47
Kingston	23.19	9.00	5.00	38.19
Kitchener	27.08	9.60	11.25	56.63
Lachine	18.00	6.00	6.00	30.00
Lethbridge	26.35	4.00	12.00	42.35
London	26.39	in kind	14.00	40.39
Medicine Hat	20.40	5.50	13.50	39.40
Moncton	18.75	4.00	8.00	30.75
Montreal	21.88	3.25	10.50	40.83
Moose Jaw	24.90	12.00	15.00	51.90
New Westminster	29.00	not provided	8.00	37.00
Niagara Falls	27.10	10.00	not stated	40.35
North Bay	21.66	9.00	12.00	43.66
Oshawa	24.35	11.05	16.00	53.40
Ottawa	24.20	7.15	13.00	45.32
Port Arthur	21.67	12.98	15.00	49.65
Prince Albert	18.90	8.00	10.00	36.90
Prince Rupert	25.00	8.00	not provided	37.00
Quebec City	14.08	4.33	8.00	26.66
Regina	25.35	9.25	12.00	49.10
Saint John	16.47	2.25	not provided	18.70
St. Boniface	24.98	4.82	16.00	45.80
Saskatoon	19.50	in kind	12.50	32.00
Sherbrooke	16.25	3.60	6.00	30.07
Stratford	21.00	3.50	12.00	41.00
Sydney	17.32	7.56	10.00	34.88
Timmins	26.00	10.00	15.00	53.00
Toronto	25.74	12.13	20.00	58.87
Trois Rivieres	15.17	6.00	8.50	27.33
Vancouver	26.09	4.25	8.00	38.34
Verdun	16.16	4.80	11.00	31.96
Victoria	26.55	2.50	5.50	34.55
Windsor	29.36	9.32	9.77	48.45
Winnipeg	24.98	7.32	12.00	49.50

Note: Totals listed sometimes include clothing, medical, and other allowances when these were provided and thus can be greater than the three categories listed.
Source: CCSD Papers, vol. 128, 'Relief Schedules – the 45 Larger Cities, 1936–37'

Notes

ABBREVIATIONS USED IN THE NOTES

CCC & FW Canadian Council on Child and Family Welfare
CCSD Canadian Council on Social Development
CMA Canadian Manufacturers' Association
DLL Department of Labour Library
DND Department of National Defence
ESC Employment Service of Canada
NEC National Employment Commission
PAC Public Archives of Canada
PAO Public Archives of Ontario
RDCUR Report of the Dominion Commissioner of Unemployment Relief

INTRODUCTION

1 John A. Garraty, *Unemployment in History: Economic Thought and Public Policy* (New York 1978), 5
2 Judith Fingard, 'The Winter's Tale: Contours of Poverty in British North America, 1815–1860.' Canadian Historical Association, *Historical Papers*, 1974, 66–7; Census of Canada, 1931, XIII, 'Monograph on Unemployment,' 275–6
3 Sylvia Ostry, *The Occupational Composition of the Canadian Labour Force* (Ottawa 1967), 50–1
4 Donald Avery, *'Dangerous Foreigners': European Immigrant Workers and Labour Radicalism in Canada, 1896–1932* (Toronto 1979), 8
5 Leonard Marsh, *Canadians in and out of Work: a Survey of Economic Classes and their Relation to the Labour Market* (Toronto 1940), 328; Canada, House of Commons, *Debates*, 18 Feb. 1935, 934

6 Marsh, *Canadians in and out of work*, 457, 196, 471 Table XIV; W.A. Mackintosh, *The Economic Background of Dominion-Provincial Relations* (Toronto 1967), 82

7 Avery, '*Dangerous Foreigners*,' 27; David Jay Bercuson, *Fools and Wise Men: the Rise and Fall of the One Big Union* (Toronto 1978), 21; John Herd Thompson, 'Bringing in the Sheaves: the Harvest Excursionists, 1890–1929,' *Canadian Historical Review*, LIX, 4, Dec. 1978, 482; Marsh, *Canadians in and out of Work* , 166, 193; Edmund Bradwin, *The Bunkhouse Man: a Study of Work and Pay in the Camps of Canada 1903–14* (1928; Toronto 1972), 206

8 Melville Watkins, 'A Staple Theory of Economic Growth,' in W.T. Easterbrook and M.H. Watkins, eds., *Approaches to Canadian Economic History* (Toronto 1967), 72

9 H. Woods and Sylvia Ostry, *Labour Policy and Labour Economics in Canada* (Toronto 1962), 468, 370, 375; Avery, '*Dangerous Foreigners*,' 11

10 Donald Smiley, ed., *The Rowell-Sirois Report, Book 1* (Toronto 1964), 93

11 Avery, '*Dangerous Foreigners*,' 19, 31; Thompson, 'Bringing in the Sheaves,' 469

12 Robert Lekachman, *The Age of Keynes* (New York 1966), 85–6; Garraty, *Unemployment in History*, 71–3

13 S.G. and E.O.A. Checkland, eds., *The Poor Law Report of 1834* (Harmondsworth 1973), 335–6

14 Frances Fox Piven and Richard Cloward, *Regulating the Poor: the Functions of Public Welfare* (New York 1971), 34

15 Fingard, 'The Winter's Tale,' 79

16 Dennis Guest, *The Emergence of Social Security in Canada* (Vancouver 1980), 11–15; Toronto *Globe*, 26 Jan. 1877, cited in Michael Cross, ed., *The Workingman in Nineteenth Century Canada* (Toronto 1974), 196

17 See, for example, Herbert Ames, *The City below the Hill: a Sociological Study of a Portion of the City of Montreal, Canada* (1897; Toronto 1972).

18 Guest, *The Emergence of Social Security in Canada*, 37

19 Diane Matters, 'Public Welfare Vancouver Style, 1910–1920,' *Journal of Canadian Studies*, XIV, 1, 1979, 3–15; Paul Bator, '"The Struggle to Raise the Lower Classes": Public Health Reform and the Problem of Poverty in Toronto, 1910 to 1921,' in ibid., 43–50

20 Michael Bliss, *A Living Profit: Studies in the Social History of Canadian Business, 1883–1911* (Toronto 1974), 102

CHAPTER I

1 H. Blair Neatby, *The Politics of Chaos: Canada in the Thirties* (Toronto 1972), 46

2 Robert Craig Brown and Ramsay Cook, *Canada, 1896–1921: a Nation Transformed* (Toronto 1974), 199; Robert Craig Brown, *Robert Laird Borden, a Biography, 1854–1914*, vol. I (Toronto 1975), 222; John Herd Thompson, *The Harvests of War:*

the Prairie West, 1914–1918 (Toronto 1978), 47–8; House of Commons, *Debates*, 19 Jan. 1914, 18–19; Toronto *Globe*, 10 Jan. 1914; Irving Abella and David Millar, eds., *The Canadian Worker in the Twentieth Century* (Toronto 1978), 75; Ontario, *Report of the Ontario Commission on Unemployment* (Toronto 1916), 95

3 Horatio Hocken, 'The New Spirit in Municipal Government,' Canadian Club of Ottawa, *Addresses*, 19 Dec. 1914, cited in Paul Rutherford, ed., *Saving the Canadian City* (Toronto 1974), 207–8

4 *Toronto Daily Star*, 13 Jan. 1914; *Globe*, 29 Jan. 1914; Rowell's speech is reported in *Star*, 20 Feb. 1914, and the *Globe*, 20 Feb. 1914; Richard Allen, *The Social Passion: Religion and Social Reform in Canada 1914–28* (Toronto 1971), 30

5 *Star*, 13 Jan. 1914

6 House of Commons, *Debates*, 20 Jan. 1914, 67–8; Brown, *Robert Laird Borden*, vol. 1, 222; for the reaction of the Ontario government see W.J. Hanna, 'Social Problems and what the Whitney Government is doing to solve them,' 20 Feb. 1914, 7–8, Ontario Archives Library; for labour's response to the crisis see the *Industrial Banner*, 12 Sept. 1913, 30 Jan. and 6 Feb. 1914.

7 DLL, vertical files, 'Unemployed – Canada-Provinces-1920,' Thomas Crothers to all provincial premiers, 3 Oct. 1914

8 Philip Morris, ed., *The Canadian Patriotic Fund: a Record of its Activities from 1914 to 1919* (np, nd), 8–9

9 Ibid, 23, 271

10 'Unemployed – Canada-Provinces-1920,' Robert Borden to Thomas Crothers, 26 Aug. 1914; Delbert T. Haylock, 'The Historical Tradition behind the Establishment of the Employment Service of Canada, 1896–1919' (MA thesis, Dalhousie University, 1971), 53; 'Unemployed – Canada-Provinces-1920,' undated memo entitled 'Plan Suggested for Dealing with Unemployment in Canada,' Sept. 1914

11 'Unemployment – Canada-Provinces-1920,' Crothers to all provincial premiers, 3 Oct. 1914; undated memo entitled 'Steps Taken by the Department of Labour in View of the War and Resulting Conditions,' 1915

12 Ontario, *Report of the Ontario Commission on Unemployment*, 5, 9, 11–15, 28, 32, 42–3, 62, 80–2, 143; for the origins of the commission see PAO, G. Frank Beer Papers, N.W. Rowell to Beer, 16 Oct. 1914

13 *Report of the Ontario Commission on Unemployment*, 75–9, 50–1, 37–40

14 *Financial Post*, 29 April 1916; Udo Sautter, 'The Origins of the Employment Service of Canada, 1900–1920,' *Labour/Le Travailleur*, 6, 1980, 103

15 PAC, Borden Papers, MG 26 H, 63120–6, Rowell to Borden, 28 Oct. 1918

16 Canada, *Sessional Papers*, 1919, no 184b, Report of the Royal Commission on Industrial Relations, 5–7; DLL, *Minutes* of the Royal Commission on Industrial Relations, 1, 453, 469–71

17 DLL, 'Minutes of Conference of Dominion and Provincial Government Officials re

Demobilization of Troops and the Public Employment Service,' 19–23 Nov. 1918, 6; Canada, *Journals* of the House of Commons, September Session, 1919, Appendix 1, *Proceedings* of the Special Committee appointed by the House of Commons on the Amendment of the Department of Soldier and Civil Re-establishment Act, 319

18 Brown and Cook, *Canada, 1896–1921*, 322, 326; Glenn T. Wright, 'Rifles to Ploughshares: Veterans and Land Settlement in Western Canada, 1917–1930,' paper presented to the Canadian Historical Association, June 1982

19 On the origins of the Employment Service of Canada see Borden Papers, 'Minutes of Conference between Labour and Government Representatives,' 16 Jan. 1918, 54121–2; 'Conference of Dominion and Provincial Governments, Canada,' Feb. 1918, OC series, file no 529, conference paper no 11; PAC, Department of Labour Records, RG 27, Lacelle files, vol. 125, copy of Bill 57, 'An Act to Aid and Encourage the Organization and Coordination of Employment Offices,' 24 April 1918

20 Haylock, 'The Historical Tradition behind the Establishment of the Employment Service of Canada,' 111–13; Lacelle files, vol. 183, copy of PC 537, 12 March 1919; copy of PC 3111, 17 Dec. 1918; Sautter, 'The Origins of the Employment Service of Canada,' 109–10

21 For the fate of the United States Employment Service see Burl Noggle, *Into the Twenties: the United States from Armistice to Normalcy* (Urbana 1974), 72–3; Bryce Stewart, 'Administration of the Public Employment Service in Canada,' in Industrial Relations Counselors, eds., *Administration of Public Employment Offices and Unemployment Insurance* (New York 1935), 65

22 John English, *The Decline of Politics: the Conservatives and the Party System, 1901–1920* (Toronto 1977), 70

23 Margaret Prang, *N.W. Rowell: Ontario Nationalist* (Toronto 1975), 129, 132, 294–300

24 Lacelle files, vol. 183, copy of PC 3111, 17 Dec. 1918; vol. 184, 'Memorandum re. P.C. 3097, Section 5.'

25 *Who's Who in Canada*, 1943, 897–8; Richard Allen, 'The Social Gospel and the Reform Tradition in Canada, 1890–1928,' in S.D. Clark, Linda and Paul Grayson, eds., *Prophecy and Protest: Social Movements in Twentieth Century Canada* (Toronto 1975), 51

26 Bryce Stewart, 'Memorandum re. the Employment Offices Co-ordination Bill,' nd, in DLL, 'Miscellaneous Reports Relating to the Employment Offices. 1918'; Public Employment Bureaus and Unemployment,' *Canadian Municipal Journal*, Oct. 1916, 6, 20–1; 'The Employment Service of Canada,' *Bulletin* of the Departments of History and Political and Economic Science in Queen's University, no 32, July 1919

27 Stewart, 'Administration of Public Employment Offices in Canada,' 25, 66, 77, 79; 'The Employment Service of Canada,' 20–1; see also *Labour Gazette*, July 1919, 816.

28 Lacelle files, vol. 184, press release by the ESC, 1919; vol. 159, Stewart to F.A. Acland, 31 March 1922; DLL, Gilbert Jackson, 'The Survey of Unemployment in Canada,'

Proceedings of the International Association of Public Employment Services, Ottawa 20–22 Sept. 1920

29 Stewart, 'The Employment Service of Canada'; 'Unemployed – Canada-1920,' 'Memorandum on Government Employment as a Factor in the Prevention of Unemployment,' 1919. The memo was most likely written by W.C. Clark. On the other activities of the ESC see Lacelle files, vol. 184, memo from R.A. Rigg to Miss McCool, 14 Aug. 1925; DLL, 'Minutes of Dominion Conference of Employment Service Officials,' Ottawa, 12–13 June 1923; and DLL, *Proceedings* of the Employment Service Council of Canada, 1920.

30 Stewart, 'Administration of Public Employment Offices in Canada,' 36

31 Edmund Bradwin, *The Bunkhouse Man: a Study of Work and Pay in the Camps of Canada 1903–14*, (1928; Toronto 1972), 206

32 Canada, *Sessional Papers*, 1921, no 37, 'Annual Report of the Department of Labour, 1920,' 89; Stewart, 'The Administration of Public Employment Offices in Canada,' 70; DLL, J.A. Bowman, 'The Public Employment Service – its Weakness and its Strength,' *Proceedings* of the International Association of Public Employment Services, 1928, 81

33 DLL, W.C. Clark, 'Regularization of National Demand for Labour by Government Employment,' *Proceedings* of the International Association of Public Employment Services 1920, 12–13

34 *Labour Gazette*, 1919, 1173, 1426–36; Liberal Party of Canada, *The Story of the Convention and the Report of its Proceedings* (Ottawa 1919), 127

35 Borden Papers, Rowell to Borden, 28 Oct. 1918, 63120–6; *Report of the Royal Commission on Industrial Relations*, 5–7

36 *Social Welfare*, I, 5, I Feb. 1919; for the British experience with unemployment insurance see Bentley Gilbert, *British Social Policy, 1914–1939* (London 1970), chap. 2.

37 *Globe*, 28 Jan. 1921, cited in *Social Welfare* I Jan. 1922, 'What do the Papers Say on Unemployment Insurance?'

38 Lacelle files, vol. 167, memo to the minister, 31 Oct. 1920

39 DLL, 'Memorandum of Information and Selected List of References Respecting Unemployment Insurance,' prepared by the Employment Service of Canada, 15 March 1921; Lacelle files, vol. 167, Gerald Brown to Gideon Robertson, 1 Nov. 1921; 'Public Employment Bureaus and Unemployment'; 'The Problem of Unemployment,' *Social Welfare*, I March 1921

40 Department of Labour Records, acc 74-5/74, box no 15, International Affairs Branch, memo from Gerald Brown to Gideon Robertson, 17 Jan. 1920; Brown to Francis Gisborne, 29 Dec. 1920; Gisborne to Brown, 18 Jan. 1921; E.L. Newcombe to Newton Rowell, 16 April 1920

41 Roger Graham, *Arthur Meighen, I : the Door of Opportunity* (Toronto 1960), 295–6; English, *The Decline of Politics*, 189; Prang, *N.W. Rowell*, 345

42 For example, union membership in Canada dropped from 373,842 in 1919 to 260,643

by 1924 and did not reach its 1919 peak until World War II; Canada, Department of Labour, *24th Annual Report on Labour Organization in Canada 1934*, 8. For a good account of the demise of labour radicalism in the aftermath of the Winnipeg General Strike see David Bercuson, *Fools and Wise Men: the Rise and Fall of the One Big Union* (Toronto 1978).

43 *Industrial Canada*, Dec. 1919, 45; April 1920, 67; House of Commons, *Debates*, 24 Feb. 1921, 263–6

44 *Labour Gazette*, 1921, 1128–9; PAC, Meighen Papers, 18665, Meighen to the United Brotherhood of Maintenance of Way Employees and Railway Shop Labourers, 11 Nov. 1921

45 *Census of Canada*, 1931, XIII, 'Monograph on Unemployment,' 275; *Social Welfare*, 1 Feb. 1921, 126

46 Morris, ed., *The Canadian Patriotic Fund*, 334–6

47 Borden Papers, memo on the 'Re-absorption of the Demobilized,' 60773. Borden's comments were pencilled in the margin.

48 On the developing unemployment crisis in 1920 see Meighen Papers, Meighen to G.D. Robertson, 7 Nov. 1920, 18490; R.H. Gale to Meighen, 17 Nov. 1920, 29688; Gale to Meighen, 26 Nov. 1920, 29693; John Oliver to Meighen, 21 Dec. 1920, 29713.

49 Ibid., Meighen to C.A.C. Jennings, 4 Dec. 1920, 24935-6

50 Ibid., Meighen to Gideon Robertson, 7 Nov. 1920, 18490; Robertson to Meighen, 5 Dec. 1920, 18511–13

51 Ibid., Robertson to Walter Rollo, 14 Dec. 1920, 29697–8

52 DLL, *Proceedings* of the Employment Service Council of Canada, Third Annual Meeting, 31 Aug. – 2 Sept. 1921, 24–6. That the post-war depression was expected is evident from Borden's comment in July 1919: 'After the present period of inflation has passed, Canada in common with other countries will probably face a period of depression,' *Labour Gazette*, 1919, 918.

53 *Industrial Canada*, Dec. 1919, 45; Meighen Papers, E.D. Parnell to Meighen, 9 Sept. 1921, 18612–17, enclosing a copy of a report by the Industrial Relations Committee of the CMA on unemployment.

54 House of Commons, *Debates*, 16 Feb. 1921, 61–2; 30 March 1921, 1363, 1368–70, 1375

55 Meighen Papers, T.L. Church to Meighen, 31 Jan. 1921, 29748, enclosing letter from Toronto chapter of the Great War Veterans Association; *Minutes* of the Royal Commission on Industrial Relations, vol. 5, 3709–10; *Labour Gazette*, 1921, 1141; *Canadian Congress Journal*, Feb. 1922, 73

56 Borden Papers, Robertson to Borden, 16 April 1920, 3909

57 Ibid., Borden to Meighen, 7 July 1921, 65611; Meighen Papers, Robertson to Meighen, 1 July 1921, 24569

58 *Census of Canada*, 1931, XIII, 275

59 Lacelle files, vol. 208, 'Memorandum re. Unemployment Relief,' containing copy of PC 3831, 7 Oct. 1921. For background on the 'concentric circle' approach to relief see John Taylor, '"Relief from Relief": the Cities' Answer to Depression Dependency,' *Journal of Canadian Studies*, XIV, 1, 1979, 16–17

60 Desmond Morton, *Canada and War: a Military and Political History* (Toronto 1981), 76

61 Borden Papers, Newton Rowell to Borden, 4 July 1919, 63133–40; *Census of Canada*, 1931, XIII, 275

62 For an excellent analysis of this phase of King's career see Paul Craven, *'An Impartial Umpire': Industrial Relations and the Canadian State 1900–1911* (Toronto 1980).

63 W.L.M. King, *Industry and Humanity* (1918; Toronto 1973), 222

64 Prang, *N.W. Rowell*, 391

65 PAC, King Diary, 8 Dec. 1921

66 House of Commons, *Debates*, 2 Feb. 1923, 35–6; 24 Feb. 1921, 263–6; PAC, King Papers, MG 26, J 1, vol. 73, W.S. Fielding to King and all cabinet ministers, 9 Jan. 1922

67 DLL, Gilbert Jackson, 'Cycles of Unemployment in Canada,' *Proceedings* of the International Association of Public Employment Services, 14th Annual Meeting, 1926, 55; *Census of Canada*, 1931, XIII, 275; Lacelle files, vol. 208, copy of PC 191, 25 Jan. 1922

68 House of Commons, *Debates*, 24 April 1922, 1073

69 Lacelle files, vol. 119, 'Report of the Proceedings of the Dominion-Provincial Conference on Unemployment,' 5–7 Sept. 1922, 2–10; King Papers, J 1, vol. 31, King to J.E. Atkinson, 18 March 1916

70 'Report of the Proceedings of the Dominion-Provincial Conference on Unemployment,' 71–2, 86

71 Ibid., 151

72 Ibid., 152, 155

73 Ibid., 180–3, 175–8

74 Ibid., 195–6, 204–5, 180–3

75 King Papers, J 4, vol. 67, memo of conference with delegation of Soldiers' Aid Commission, 25 Jan. 1923; House of Commons, *Debates*, 9 April 1923, 1680

76 Donald Avery, *'Dangerous Foreigners'; European Immigrant Workers and Labour Radicalism in Canada, 1896–1932* (Toronto 1979), 98–9; House of Commons, *Debates*, 9 April 1923, 1679

77 Lacelle files, vol. 114, *Proceedings* of the 1924 Conference on Winter Employment, 18, 31–9, 5

78 Ibid., 92, 49–52; House of Commons, *Debates*, 23 March 1925, 1411, 1426

79 Canada, *Sessional Papers*, 1925, no 183, 'Correspondence between the Dominion Government and Municipalities on Unemployment,' copy of letter from Howard Ferguson to Mayor Hiltz of Toronto, 27 Oct. 1924

80 *Census of Canada*, 1931, XIII, 275; 'Correspondence between the Dominion Government and Municipalities on Unemployment'; the mayor of Winnipeg's statement is from the *Labour Gazette*, 1925, 982
81 Michael R. Goeres, 'Disorder, Dependency and Fiscal Responsibility: Unemployment Relief in Winnipeg, 1907–1930,' paper presented to the First Conference on Provincial Social Welfare Policy, Calgary, 5–7 May 1982, 26–7; DLL, R.W. Murchie, W.H. Carter, and F.J. Dixon, *Seasonal Unemployment in Manitoba: a Report*, 1 Feb. 1928
82 Lacelle files, vols. 208–9, King to John Bracken, 20 Feb. 1928; King Diary, 10 Feb. 1923
83 Lacelle files, vol. 114, *Verbatim Report* of the Sixth Annual Meeting of the Employment Service Council of Canada, 1924, 23–6; Stewart, 'Administration of Public Employment Offices in Canada,' 66
84 Lacelle files, vols. 185–6, James Murdock to J.G. Gardiner, 10 March 1924
85 Stewart, 'The Employment Service of Canada,' 20–1
86 House of Commons, *Debates*, 22 March 1923, 1424
87 On the change in immigration policy see Avery, '*Dangerous Foreigners*,' 99–100; Lacelle files, vol. 186, 'Co-ordination of Federal Government Activities on Employment Matters,' Murdock to King, 12 Feb. 1924.
88 Lacelle files, vol. 159, Memorandum from the deputy minister of labour to James Murdock, 3 April 1924
89 Ibid.; Beer Papers, Bryce Stewart to Beer, 9 Jan. 1933
90 Lacelle files, vol. 144, *Verbatim Report* of the Sixth Annual Meeting of the Employment Service Council of Canada, 1924, J-10; vols. 185–6, 'Employment Offices Co-ordination Act – Agreements and Correspondence between Federal Government and Provinces,' Alex Ross to James Murdock, 1 March 1924
91 DLL, J.A. Bowman, 'The Public Employment Service – Its Weakness and its Strength,' *Proceedings* of the International Association of Public Employment Services, 16th Annual Meeting, 1928, 81
92 See, for example, Michiel Horn, ed., *The Dirty Thirties: Canadians in the Great Depression* (Toronto 1972), 252.
93 Canada, House of Commons, *Report, Proceedings and Evidence of Enquiry into Questions of Insurance against Unemployment, Sickness and Invalidity*, 1928, iv–v
94 King Papers, J 1, vol. 106, James Murdock to King, 10 April 1924
95 'Report of the Proceedings of the Dominion-Provincial Conference on Unemployment,' 285–6
96 Gilbert, *British Social Policy*, chap. 2
97 *Industrial Canada*, July 1922, 156; July 1924, 108–10; Dec. 1919, 46; April 1920, 67
98 King Papers, J 1, vol. 106, Murdock to King, 10 April 1924; House of Commons, *Debates*, 23 March 1925, 1431; Peter Oliver, *G. Howard Ferguson: Ontario Tory* (Toronto 1977), 226–7

99 King Diary, 23 May 1929; *Report, Proceedings and Evidence of Enquiry into Questions of Insurance Against Unemployment, Sickness and Invalidity*, 1928, 19; Jackson, 'Cycles of Unemployment in Canada,' 49

100 *Census of Canada*, 1931, XIII, 276; King Diary, 8 Jan., 26 Feb. 1930; House of Commons, *Debates*, 3 April 1930, 1221–8

101 King Diary, 3, 8 April 1930; King quoting from *Industry and Humanity* in House of Commons, *Debates*, 3 April 1930, 1231

102 Stewart, 'The Problem of Unemployment,' *Social Welfare*, March 1921, 170

CHAPTER 2

1 PAC, King Papers, MG 26, J 4, vol. 142, speech on unemployment, 1 July 1930

2 Ibid., J 1, vol. 175, Heenan to King, 23 June 1930; King to Heenan, 4 July 1930; PAC, King Diary, 14 June 1930

3 H. Blair Neatby, *The Politics of Chaos: Canada in the Thirties* (Toronto 1972), 53–4; H. Blair Neatby, *William Lyon Mackenzie King, II: 1924–1932: the Lonely Heights* (Toronto 1963), 231

4 Neatby, *The Politics of Chaos*, 53; *Who's Who in Canada 1936–1937* (Toronto 1937), vi

5 Neatby, *The Politics of Chaos*, 53; Neatby, *The Lonely Heights*, 231; Richard Wilbur, *The Bennett Administration 1930–35* (Ottawa 1969), 3

6 *Census of Canada*, 1931, XIII, 'Monograph on Unemployment,' 276; House of Commons, *Debates*, 9 Sept. 1930, 21–7

7 King Papers, J 4, vol. 141, Heenan to King, July 1930

8 House of Commons, *Debates*, 16 Sept. 1930, 239; PAC, Bennett Papers, MG 26 K, vol. 797, Gideon Robertson to Bennett, Sept. 1930

9 *Statutes of Canada*, 21 Geo V, 1, 'An Act for the granting of aid for the Relief of Unemployment,' 22 Sept. 1930; House of Commons, *Debates*, 11 Sept. 1930, 91; 12 Sept. 1930, 174

10 House of Commons, *Debates*, 10 Sept. 1930, 77; 12 Sept. 1930, 141

11 Harry Cassidy, *Unemployment and Relief in Ontario, 1929–1932* (Toronto 1932), 85, 91; Bennett Papers, vol. 783, Robertson to Bennett, 27 Oct. 1930; Canada, RDCUR, 31 March 1933, 24, Appendix D

12 Cassidy, *Unemployment and Relief in Ontario*, 144–7, 91; Bennett Papers, vol. 778, Robertson to Bennett, 20 Dec. 1930

13 Elizabeth King, 'The Experience of some Canadian Cities from the Angle of the Private Agency,' Canadian Conference on Social Work *Proceedings*, Second Bienniel Meeting, 1930; Bennett Papers, vol. 798, Charlotte Whitton to Bennett, 9 April 1932, 'Memo Re The Distribution of Unemployment Relief.'

14 King, 'The Experience of Some Canadian Cities'

15 Harry Cassidy, 'Some Essentials in Canadian Social Welfare,' Canadian Conference on Social Work *Proceedings*, Sixth Meeting, 1938

16 Dorothy King, 'Unemployment Aid (Direct Relief),' in L.R. Richter, ed., *Canada's Unemployment Problem* (Toronto 1939), 94–5

17 A. Ethel Parker, 'Family Case Work goes through the Deep Waters of Unemployment,' *Social Welfare*, Sept. 1930, 266

18 Cassidy, *Unemployment and Relief in Ontario*, 91

19 P.W.L. Norton to R.B. Bennett, 5 Jan. 1931, cited in Linda Grayson and Michael Bliss, eds., *The Wretched of Canada: Letters to R.B. Bennett 1930–1935* (Toronto 1971), 5

20 *Census of Canada*, 1931, XIII, 274–6; PAC, CCSD Papers, MG 28, I 10, vol. 14, file 68, Ethel Parker to Whitton, 6 March 1931

21 Bennett Papers, vol. 791, H.B. Shaw of Winnipeg's Citizens' Committee on Unemployment to Bennett, 10 April 1931

22 Ibid., vol. 789, P.L. to R.B. Bennett, 4 March 1932

23 Ibid., vol. 778, G.D. Robertson to Bennett, 19 June 1931

24 Ibid., vol. 778, S.F. Tolmie to G.D. Robertson, 19 June 1931

25 Ibid., vol. 778, John Bracken to Bennett, 23 April 1931; vol. 791, Winnipeg Board of Trade to Bennett, 19 May 1931; CCSD Papers, vol. 706, 'Report of Round Table Conference on Present Employment Conditions and Related Social Problems,' 28-29 April 1931; Bennett Papers, vol. 778, Robertson to Bennett, 6 May 1931; Robertson to all cabinet ministers, 12 May 1931

26 David Bercuson, *Confrontation at Winnipeg: Labour Industrial Relations and the General Strike* (Montreal 1974), 135, 164–5

27 Bennett Papers, vol. 778, Statement concerning unemployment in Winnipeg prepared by Alderman Ralph Maybank for Robertson, June 1931

28 Ibid., vol. 778, Report of Saskatoon's Standing Committee on Unemployment, prepared for Robertson, June 1931

29 Ibid., vol. 778, Robertson to Bennett, 1 July 1931

30 Ibid., vol. 778, Robertson to Bennett, 11 June 1931; Robertson to Bennett, 19 June 1931; Robertson to Bennett, 1 July 1931

31 David Smith, *Prairie Liberalism: the Liberal Party in Saskatchewan 1905–71* (Toronto 1975), 205–6; House of Commons, *Debates*, 29 July 1931, 4278; 1 July 1931, 3249; *Statutes of Canada*, 21–22 Geo V, ch 58, 429

32 House of Commons, *Debates*, 29 July 1931, 4289; Bennett Papers, vol. 788, William Price to Bennett, 2 July 1931; House of Commons, *Debates*, 29 July 1931, 4281

33 Bennett Papers, vol. 778, R.B. Manion to Bennett, 1 July 1931

34 House of Commons, *Debates*, 29 April 1931, 1099–1104, 29 July 1931, 4280

35 Ibid., 29 July 1931, 4287, 4279; 12 Sept. 1930, 174

36 *Census of Canada*, 1931, XIII, 274

37 F. Deane to Bennett, 24 June 1932, cited in Grayson and Bliss, eds., *The Wretched of Canada*, 29

38 Bennett Papers, vol. 796, W.J. Bingham to Bennett, 4 Sept. 1931; vol. 793, telegram from all western ministers of labour and public works to Robertson, 3 Sept. 1931; vol. 796, Bennett to Vancouver Property Owners' Association, 11 Sept. 1931; vol. 778, Bennett to the four western premiers, 4 Sept. 1931

39 Ibid., vol. 778, Bennett to the four western premiers, 4 Sept. 1931; Robertson to Bennett, 9 Oct. 1931

40 Ibid., vol. 778, J.W. Jones to Bennett, 11 Sept. 1931

41 Margaret Ormsby, *British Columbia: a History* (Toronto 1958), 445; Bennett Papers, vol. 778, Tolmie to Bennett, 17 Oct. 1931; Bennett to Tolmie, 23 Oct. 1931

42 *Canadian Annual Review*, 1932, 303–4; Ormsby, *British Columbia*, 446–7

43 Bennett Papers, vol. 798, Bennett to R.B. Hanson, 22 Oct. 1931; vol. 793, Bennett to F.R. MacMillan, 21 Oct. 1931; vol. 778, Bennett to Robertson, 22 Sept. 1931; RDCUR, 1 March 1932, ii; PAC, Department of Labour Records, RG 27, vol. 614, 'Memorandum re Financing Approved Unemployment Works,' 25 Nov. 1931

44 Bennett Papers, vol. 798, R.W. Bruhn to Bennett, 23 Dec. 1931; vol. 569, J.W. Jones to Bennett, 21 Dec. 1931

45 Ibid., vol. 783, Michael McGeough to Harry Hereford, 19 Dec. 1931

46 Ibid., vol. 796, Union of BC Municipalities to Bennett, 28 Jan. 1932; vol. 779, Bennett to J.W. Jones, 29 Jan. 1932

47 Ormsby, *British Columbia*, 446–7

48 Bennett Papers, vol. 786, N.A.P. Garceau to Bennett, 7 Sept. 1931; Thomas Maher to Bennett, 11 Sept. 1931; Gustave Monette to Bennett, 17 Sept. 1931; Romeo Langlois to Bennett, 19 Sept. 1931; John Sullivan to Bennett, 15 Sept. 1931

49 Ibid., vol. 786, Bennett to Thomas Maher, 17 Sept. 1931; vol. 779, Bennett to C.B. Richards, 17 March 1932; vol. 778, T.G. Murphy to Bennett, 25 Sept. 1931

50 Toronto *Globe*, 27 Aug. 1931, cited in Cassidy, *Unemployment and Relief in Ontario*, 65, 145, 155

51 *Census of Canada*, 1931, XIII, 'Monograph on Unemployment,' 274–6; Derek Chisolm, 'How Essential was the Bank of Canada? the Interwar Gold Standard Reconsidered' (unpublished paper, University of Western Ontario, Department of Economics, Oct. 1980), 18–19; A.E. Safarian, *The Canadian Economy in the Great Depression* (Toronto 1970), 49

52 Cassidy, *Unemployment and Relief in Ontario*, 154–5; *Canadian Annual Review*, 1932, 44

53 The $50,000,000 figure is mentioned in a letter from R.J. Manion to Bennett on 1 July 1931 in the Bennett Papers, vol. 778; RDCUR, 30 March 1935, 32

54 Bennett Papers, vol. 778, T.G. Murphy to Bennett, 25 Sept. 1931; vol. 793, M.N. Campbell to Bennett, 16 Sept. 1931; vol. 779, Bennett to J.W. Jones, 29 Jan. 1932; vol. 789, Peter McGibbon to Bennett, 18 Feb. 1932

55 *Financial Post*, 14 Nov. 1931; House of Commons, *Debates*, 5 Feb. 1932, 2

56 House of Commons, *Debates* , 8 March 1932, 935

57 Ibid., 1 March 1932, 702–3; see also H. Blair Neatby, *William Lyon Mackenzie King,* III *1932–1939: the Prism of Unity* (Toronto 1976), 396–7

58 Bennett Papers, vol. 794, Edmonton City Council to Bennett, 13 Jan. 1932; vol. 791, Winnipeg City Council to Bennett, 2 Feb. 1932; both called on the prime minister to summon an 'Economic Congress' of representative organizations to formulate solutions to the unemployment problem. This had also been urged by the Trades and Labour Congress and the Social Service Council of Canada; on unemployment insurance see vol. 810, S. Baker, president of the Union of Canadian Municipalities, to Bennett, 22 Sept. 1931; vol. 789, Conference of Ontario Municipalities to Bennett, 23 Feb. 1932.

59 Carl Cuneo, 'State Mediation of Class Contradictions in Canadian Unemployment Insurance, 1930–1935,' *Studies in Political Economy*, 3, 1980, 41

60 House of Commons, *Debates*, 29 April 1931, 1099–1104

61 Ibid.

62 Bennett Papers, vol. 810, Bernard Rose to Bennett, 29 Jan. 1932; memo on Unemployment Insurance, c Jan.-Feb. 1932

63 PAO, G. Frank Beer Papers, R.H. Coats to Beer, 3 Dec. 1932; House of Commons, *Debates*, 29 April 1931, 1100; Bennett Papers, vol. 810, Bennett to Bernard Rose, 2 Feb. 1932; Bennett to the city clerk of East Windsor, 4 Feb. 1932

64 Bennett Papers, vol. 779, 'Report re Unemployment and Relief in Western Canada, Summer 1932,' 478127–8

65 Ibid.

66 Ibid., vol. 14, file 68, Judith Driscoll to Whitton, 8 Jan. 1932

67 Ibid., Whitton to Driscoll, 11 Jan. 1932

68 Ibid., Harry Cassidy to Whitton, 30 July 1931

69 Beer Papers, E.D. Macphee to Beer, 7 July 1931

70 Michiel Horn, *The League for Social Reconstruction: Intellectual Origins of the Democratic Left in Canada 1930–1942* (Toronto 1980), 23–4; University of Toronto Archives, Cassidy Papers, vol. 61, Cassidy to Victor Odlum, 3 Sept. 1928

71 Cassidy, *Unemployment and Relief in Ontario*, 183–8, 160–3, 280

72 Ibid., 183–8; A.E. Grauer, 'Public Assistance and Social Insurance,' Appendix G, Canada, *Royal Commission on Dominion-Provincial Relations* (Ottawa 1940), 23

73 Cassidy, *Unemployment and Relief in Ontario*, 202–4, 211, 256; Roger Riendeau, 'A Clash of Interests: Dependency and the Municipal Problem in the Great Depression,' *Journal of Canadian Studies*, XIV, 1, 1979, 54

74 Ibid., 276–7, 279–85

75 Ibid., 279–85, 288–9

76 Bennett Papers, vol. 798, W.F. Nickle to Bennett, 16 March 1932; vol. 789, Nickle to Bennett, 13 April 1932

77 House of Commons, *Debates*, 28 April 1932, 2452

78 Ibid., 2445; 9 May 1932, 2748; 3 May 1932, 2632

79 Ibid., 9 May 1932, 2736
80 *Canadian Annual Review*, 1932, 42
81 Department of Labour Records, vol. 213, file 617, memo on 'Dominion Unemployment Relief Since 1930,' Jan. 1940, 111; RDCUR, 30 March 1935, 39
82 *Canadian Annual Review*, 1932, 419; House of Commons, *Debates*, 28 April 1932, 2453. See also Bennett Papers, vol. 779, Premier Harrington to Gordon, 19 Sept. 1931.
83 *Who's Who in Canada*, 1936–7, 1682
84 Bennett Papers, vol. 779, Gordon to Bennett, 25 Sept. 1931
85 Ibid., vol. 783, memo to Gordon re 'Unemployment Relief – Land Settlement,' 29 March 1932; vol. 783, Gordon to Bennett, 6 April 1932; House of Commons, *Debates*, 28 April 1932, 2452
86 House of Commons, *Debates*, 28 April 1932, 2448; Bennett Papers, vol. 783, 'Memo on Land Settlement,' 29 March 1932
87 House of Commons, *Debates*, 28 April 1932, 2447
88 Cassidy, *Unemployment and Relief in Ontario*, 81

CHAPTER 3

1 PAC, Bennett Papers, MG 26 K, vol. 793, 489188, undated, unsigned letter (c March 1932), from a Saskatchewan MP to Bennett
2 Barry Broadfoot, *Ten Lost Years: Memories of Canadians who survived the Depression* (Toronto 1973), 70
3 Roger Riendeau, 'A Clash of Interests: Dependency and the Municipal Problem in the Great Depression,' *Journal of Canadian Studies* XIV, 1, 1979, 54
4 A.P. Kappele, 'The Administrative Set-up for Local Welfare Services,' *Canadian Conference on Social Work Proceedings*, 6th Conference, 1938, 193–4
5 'Problems in the Social Administration of General and Unemployment Relief,' Discussion and Findings of a Conference on this subject, called at Ottawa from 1–4 May 1933 and reprinted in *Child and Family Welfare*, IX, 1, 1933, 25
6 Bennett Papers, vol. 780, and reproduced in Michiel Horn, ed., *The Dirty Thirties: Canadians in the Great Depression* (Toronto 1972), 284
7 Margaret McCready, 'Relief Diets,' *Canadian Conference on Social Work Proceedings*, 4th Bienniel Meeting, 1934, 54–7
8 James H. Gray, *The Winter Years* (Toronto 1966), 38
9 Bennett Papers, vol. 780, R.C. Rathbone, 'Report on Unemployment Relief in Edmonton,' 10 June 1932
10 Ibid., 'Report on Unemployment Relief in Edmonton,' 4 July 1932
11 Ibid., vol. 794, Bennett to J.G. Bennett, 21 Oct. 1931
12 Ibid., vol. 706, 'Summary of the proceedings of the Second Bilingual Conference on Family and Child Welfare,' Montreal, April 1932

13 *Canadian Welfare*, XVII, 7, 1942. Whitton's pre-eminence was revealed when she became one of seven Canadian women to receive a CBE upon the resumption of the Crown's Honour List in Canada in 1934. See *Child and Family Welfare*, IX, 5, 1934

14 Patricia T. Rooke and R.L. Schnell, '"An Idiot's Flowerbed": a Study of Charlotte Whitton's Feminist Thought, 1941–1950,' *International Journal of Women's Studies*, V, 1, 31; Phyllis Harrison, 'In the Beginning was Charlotte ... ' *Canadian Welfare*, LI, 2, 1975, 14–15; Rooke and Schnell, '"Making the Way More Comfortable": Charlotte Whitton's Child Welfare Career, 1920–1948,' *Journal of Canadian Studies*, forthcoming 1983

15 PAC, CCSD Papers, MG 28; I 10; vol. 25, Charlotte Whitton, 'Retrospects and Prospects: Canadian Council on Child and Family Welfare, 1922–1935,' 6

16 Bennett Papers, vol. 798, Charlotte Whitton to Bennett, 9 April 1932, 'Memo re the Distribution of Unemployment Relief'; Whitton to Bennett, 18 April 1932

17 PAC, Charlotte Whitton Papers, MG 30, E 256, vol. 19, 'The Faith of a Social Worker,' nd

18 Bennett Papers, vols. 779–80, 'Report *re* Unemployment and Relief in Western Canada, Summer 1932,' 478107–9

19 Ibid., vol. 706, Bennett to Whitton, 26 April 1932; Whitton to Bennett, 31 May 1932

20 Ibid., vols. 779–80, 'Report *re* Unemployment and Relief in Western Canada,' 478800–1, 478928–30

21 Ibid., 478093–9, 478105, 478823, 478858–9

22 Ibid., 478946–7, 478812

23 Ibid., vol. 706, Whitton to Bennett, 16 June 1932

24 Ibid., vols. 779–80, 'Report *re* Unemployment and Relief in Western Canada,' 478125–8, 478848

25 Ibid., 478848–55, 478812

26 Ibid., vol. 706, Bennett to J.T.M. Anderson, 4 June 1932

27 Ibid, vols. 779–80, 'Report *re* Unemployment and Relief in Western Canada,' 478110–13

28 House of Commons, *Debates*, 28 April 1932, 2452

29 Bennett Papers, vol. 780, Ralph Webb to Bennett, 9 July 1932

30 Ibid., vol. 706, Whitton to Bennett, 16 June 1932; vol. 794, Andrew Davison (Calgary's mayor) to Bennett, 19 July 1932; Robert Barrowman (Lethbridge's mayor) to Bennett, 20 July 1932; Bennett to Davison, 23 July 1932

31 Ibid., vol. 798, R.J. Manion to Bennett, 21 Oct. 1932, enclosing memo on 'Transient Laborers moving in Trains'

32 Ibid., vol. 780, R.C. Rathbone, 'Report on Unemployment Relief in Edmonton,' 19 July 1932; vol. 794, Andrew Davison to Bennett, 26 July 1932; vo. 793, Bennett to G.A. Sylte, 5 Oct. 1932

33 House of Commons, *Debates*, 10 Oct. 1932, 50

34 James Eayrs, *In Defence of Canada: from the Great War to the Great Depression* (Toronto 1964), 256, 260, 125–6

35 Bennett Papers, vol. 781, W.J. Black to W.A. Gordon, 21 Oct. 1932; W.J. Black to S.F. Tolmie, 21 Oct. 1932

36 Ibid., vol. 781, W.J. Black to Gordon, 29 Oct. 1932; W.J. Black to Gordon, 29 Oct. 1932 (private); vol. 791, Black to Tolmie, 21 Oct. 1932; PAC, Department of Labour Records, RG 27, vol. 213, file 617, memo on 'Dominion Unemployment Relief Since 1930,' Jan. 1940, 64–5. See also Harry Cassidy, 'Social Services for Transients,' in L. Richter, ed., *Canada's Unemployment Problem* (Toronto 1939), 181–2.

37 RDCUR, 31 March 1941, 37; *Census of Canada,* 1931, XIII, 'Monograph on Unemployment,' 274

38 Bennett Papers, vol. 790, 'Unemployment Relief in a Metropolitan Community,' Bureau of Municipal Research, Toronto, 30 May 1934

39 John Taylor, '"Relief from Relief": the Cities' Answer to Depression Dependency,' *Journal of Canadian Studies,* XIV, 1, 1979, 19

40 Bennett Papers, vol. 793, George Cooper to R.B. Bennett, 18 Dec. 1933

41 Ibid.

42 Ibid., vol. 794, Bennett to Andrew Davison, 5 Aug. 1932

43 *Canadian Annual Review,* 1933, 71

44 House of Commons, *Debates,* 22 Nov. 1932, 1452

45 Bennett Papers, vol. 781, 'Memorandum *re* Heaps Motion,' 16 Nov. 1932

46 House of Commons, *Debates,* 22 Nov. 1932, 1452–6

47 Bennett Papers, vol. 813, memo from R.K. Finlayson to Bennett, nd (c Dec. 1932)

48 *Who's Who in Canada,* 1936–7, 1302; J.L. Granatstein, *The Ottawa Men: the Civil Service Mandarins 1935–1957* (Toronto 1982), 44–9

49 Bennett Papers, vol. 791, W.C. Clark to R.K. Finlayson, 7 Jan. 1933

50 Ibid., vol. 810, W.C. Clark to Bennett, 18 Jan. 1933

51 Ibid., vol. 813, memo from R.K. Finlayson to Bennett, nd (c Dec. 1932)

52 Ibid., vol. 813, memo from G.D. Finlayson to Bennett, 12 Dec. 1932

53 Ibid., vol. 813, memo from R.K. Finlayson to Bennett, nd (c Dec. 1932)

54 Alvin Finkel, *Business and Social Reform in the Thirties* (Toronto 1979), chap. 6

55 Carl J. Cuneo, 'State Mediation of Class Contradictions in Canadian Unemployment Insurance, 1930–1935,' *Studies in Political Economy,* 3, 1980, 44–6

56 Bennett Papers, vol. 810, Ross McMaster to Bennett, 29 Oct. 1932. See also vol. 811, J.E. Walsh (general manager of the CMA) to Bennett, 10 Jan. 1933; Chas. Roland (Employers Association, Manitoba) to Bennett, 12 Jan. 1933

57 Ibid., vol. 810, Vancouver Board of Trade to Bennett, 19 Nov. 1932; Thomas Bradshaw to Bennett, 2 Nov. 1932; A.O. Dawson to Sir George Perley, 21 Dec. 1932. See also vol. 811, W. McL. Clarke (secretary, Canadian Chamber of Commerce) to Bennett, 13 Jan. 1933.

58 Ibid., vol. 791, E.A. Macpherson to Bennett, 7 Jan. 1933
59 Ibid., vol. 791, W.C. Clark to R.K. Finlayson, 7 Jan. 1933
60 Ibid., vol. 561, 'Minutes of the Dominion-Provincial Conference,' 17–19 Jan. 1933, 346894–955
61 Ibid., 346910–17
62 PAC, J.W. Dafoe Papers, MG 30, D 17, vol. 7, Grant Dexter to Dafoe, 25 Jan. 1933
63 RDCUR, 1 March 1932, vi-vii; 31 March 1933, 25; 31 March 1934, 49
64 Bennett Papers, vol. 566, Bennett to the four western premiers, 9 March 1933
65 House of Commons, Debates, 24 Feb. 1933, 2450
66 Ibid., 24 Feb. 1933, 2464; 2 March 1933, 2657
67 Bennett Papers, vol. 562, Watson Sellar to the minister of the Treasury Board, 20 April 1933
68 Ibid., vol. 566, R.K. Finlayson to Bennett, 23 May 1933; E.A. Macpherson to Bennett, 27 May 1933; Ralph Webb to T.G. Murphy, 9 May 1933; 'Minutes of interview between John Bracken and acting premier Sir George Perley,' 12 June 1933
69 Ibid., vol. 566, W.C. Clark to Perley, 12 June 1933; memo from Andrew Maclean to Perley re: 'Premier of Manitoba,' 17 June 1933; 'Minutes of interview between Bracken and Perley,' 12 June 1933
70 Winning Free Press, 22 June 1933
71 Bennett Papers, vol. 794, W.M. Dickson to A.E. Millar, 29 May 1933; vol. 566, 'Minutes of interview between Bracken and Perley,' 12 June 1933
72 H. Blair Neatby, William Lyon Mackenzie King, III: 1932–1939: the Prism of Unity (Toronto 1976), 34–5; House of Commons, Debates, 24 Feb. 1933, 2466–9; 27 Feb. 1933, 2502–11, 2515
73 Neatby, The Prism of Unity, 42
74 PAC, Andrew McNaughton Papers, MG 30, G 12, vol. 37, O.D. Skelton to McNaughton, 27 Sept. 1933. On the widespread public support for the camps see also vol. 37, memo by the Trades and Labour Congress on 'Unemployed Transients,' included in H.H. Ward to McNaughton, 31 Jan. 1933, and vol. 59, outline of CCC&FW conference, 4 May 1933, on relief administration for single homeless men. See also editorials in Ottawa Citizen, 30 May 1933; Kingston Whig-Standard, 27 May 1933; Winnipeg Tribune, 26 Sept. 1933; Vancouver News-Herald, 8 Aug. 1933.
75 PAC, DND Records, RG 24, vol. 3183, file HQ 1376-11-38, clipping from Winnipeg Tribune, 26 Sept. 1933
76 RDCUR, 31 March 1935, 39; House of Commons, Debates, 24 Feb. 1933, 2455–63
77 See Paul Conkin, The New Deal (New York 1975), 45, and William Leuchtenberg, Franklin Delano Roosevelt and the New Deal (New York 1963), 11, 52; McNaughton Papers, vol. 49, O.D. Skelton to McNaughton, 27 Sept. 1933
78 CCSD Papers, vol. 17, report on CCC&FW conference between public and private relief agencies on 'Problems in the Social and General Administration of Unemployment

Relief,' 1–4 May 1933, 12–13. See also McNaughton Papers, vol. 59, McNaughton to
H.H. Stevens, 26 June 1933; vol. 98, 'Final Report on the Unemployment Relief
Scheme for the Care of Single Homeless Men Administered by the Department of
National Defence, 1932–36,' nd.

79 Bennett Papers, vols. 779–80, 'Report *re* Unemployment and Relief in Western
Canada,' 478930–3, 478946–7; McNaughton Papers, vol. 37, W.A. Gordon to Tom
Moore, 12 July 1933

80 Bennett Papers, vol. 800, 'Policy and Instructions for Administration of Relief Camps,'
April 1933

81 McNaughton Papers, vol. 37, W.A. Gordon to F.J. McManus, 26 Sept. 1933; Bennett
Papers, vol. 783, memo by McNaughton on 'The Department of National Defence
Unemployment Relief Scheme with Some Observations Concerning the United States
Civilian Conservation Corps,' Oct. 1933

82 McNaughton Papers, vol. 37, memo on meeting between W.A. Gordon and
McNaughton. 3 Oct. 1933; Bennett Papers, vol. 799, memo from R.K. Finlayson to
Bennett's secretary, 6 Oct. 1933. For the Communist viewpoint see Ronald Liversedge,
Recollections of the On-to-Ottawa Trek, ed. Victor Hoar (Toronto 1973), 35.

83 DND Records, vol. 2965, memo on meeting between Harry Hereford, Andrew
McNaughton, and William Finlayson, 6 July 1933

84 Ibid., vol. 2954, 'Confidential Memorandum on 22 July 1935 *Ottawa Citizen* editorial
entitled "No Strikers in U.S. Labor Camps," '; *Winnipeg Free Press*, 28 Oct. 1933

85 Broadfoot, *Ten Lost Years*, 96

86 Bennett Papers, vol. 797, 'Why? – the Diary of a Camp Striker,' ed. Edmund Francis
(1935), 17–18

87 Ibid., vol. 44, McNaughton to William Dickson, 10 Nov. 1933

88 CCSD Papers, vol. 17, file 68 (a), T. Wattler to Whitton, 20 May 1933

89 McNaughton Papers, vol. 41, G.S. Pearson to W.A. Gordon, 11 Dec. 1933; DND
Records, vol. 2962, A.A. Mackenzie to DOC Military District 13, 30 Nov. 1933

90 DND Records, vol. 2969, 'Unemployment Relief Departmental Reports,' 29 Nov. 1935;
vol. 2962, memo from H.H. Matthews, DOC Military District no 13, Nov. 1933;
McNaughton Papers, vol. 41, G.S. Pearson to Gordon, 11 Dec. 1933

91 DND Records, vol. 2965, memo of meeting between McNaughton, George Pearson, and
E.W. Griffiths, 22 Jan. 1934; McNaughton Papers, vol. 41, file 314, memo by
McNaughton, 3 April 1933; memo from R.J. Orde to McNaughton, 27 April 1933;
draft order-in-council enclosed in Orde to McNaughton, 6 June 1933

92 McNaughton Papers, vol. 41, file 314, McNaughton to DOC Military District no 11, 21
Dec. 1933; memo by McNaughton, 7 June 1933; memo on 'Schedule of Arrangement
for Communication Between Persons Under Detention in the Second Stage,' nd; memo
by McNaughton, 3 April 1933; DND Records, vol. 2965, memo of meeting between
McNaughton, George Pearson, and E.W. Griffith, 22 Jan. 1934

93 McNaughton Papers, vol. 44, file 319, McNaughton to W.M. Dickson, 2 Dec. 1933; vol. 41 file 314, McNaughton to DOC Military District no 11, 21 Dec. 1933; W.A. Gordon to G.S. Pearson, 1 Dec. 1933

94 Ibid., vol. 41, file 314, G.S. Pearson to Gordon, 1 Dec. 1933; Gordon to Pearson, 9 Dec. 1933; McNaughton to General Ashton, 3 Jan. 1934

95 Ibid., vol. 37, memo of meeting between McNaughton and W.A. Gordon, 3 Oct. 1933

96 RDCUR, 31 March 1934, 16–24; *Census of Canada*, 1931, XIII, 274; RDCUR, 31 March 1936, 33; Bennett Papers, vol. 706, Whitton to Bennett, 27 Sept. 1933; Whitton to Bennett, 4 Oct. 1933

97 CCSD Papers, vol. 15, file 68, Whitton to A. McNamara, 17 Nov. 1933; Bennett Papers, vol. 706, Whitton to Bennett, 4 Oct. 1933

CHAPTER 4

1 PAC, Bennett Papers, MG 26 K, 433, R.K. Finlayson to Bennett, 12 Sept. 1933

2 Ibid., vol. 276, W.D. Herridge to Bennett, 16 Jan. 1934

3 Ibid., vol. 798, Bennett to F.D.L. Smith, 18 July 1933; PAC, King Diary, 8 Sept. 1933

4 Bennett Papers, vol. 790, Bennett to J.B. Carswell, 28 Nov. 1933; vol. 797, R.K. Finlayson to secretary, British Ministry of Labour, 24 Nov. 1933; assistant secretary, British Ministry of Labour to Finlayson, 14 Nov. 1933; vol. 812, Arthur Steel-Maitland to Bennett, 21 Nov. 1933; H.G. Nolan to Bennett, 24 Nov. 1933; Bennett to Maitland, 14 Dec. 1933

5 Ibid., vol. 811, Sir Charles Gordon to Bennett, 6 Jan. 1934

6 Harry Cassidy, 'Is Unemployment Relief Enough?' *Canadian Forum*, Jan. 1934

7 PAC, CCSD Papers, MG 28, I 10, vol. 15, file 68, Whitton to A.A. Mackenzie, 4 Jan. 1934; Bennett Papers, vol. 798, Whitton to R.K. Finlayson, 11 Jan. 1934

8 Cassidy, 'Is Unemployment Relief Enough?'

9 Bennett Papers, vol. 782, transcript of interview of Bennett and his cabinet with delegation representing unemployed Ontario and Quebec workers, 22 June 1935

10 Ibid., vol. 804, Charlotte Whitton, 'The Challenge for Relief Control,' March 1934; CCSD Papers, vol. 16, file 68, H. MacNamara to Whitton, 5 Feb. 1934

11 Whitton, 'The Challenge for Relief Control'

12 Bennett Papers, vol. 798, Whitton, 'Memorandum Setting Forth Tentative Suggestions *Re* the Provision of Direct Unemployment Relief, 1 April 1934–31 March 1935,' nd

13 Ibid., vol. 798, Whitton, 'The Essentials of a Relief Programme for Canada 1934–35,' 19 Jan. 1934; CCSD Papers, vol. 16, file 68, Whitton to Dr Frank Sanderson, 21 March 1934

14 Whitton, 'The Essentials of a Relief Programme for Canada 1934–35'

15 CCSD Papers, vol. 16, file 68, Tom Moore to Whitton, 1 Feb. 1934

16 Ibid., vol. 16, file 68, Harry Cassidy to Whitton, 26 Jan. 1934; Leonard Marsh to Whitton, 13 Feb. 1934

17 Bennett, Papers, vol. 804, Whitton, 'The Essentials of a Relief Control Programme for Canada,' March 1934 (revised version)
18 Ibid., vol. 561, R.K. Finlayson to R.H. Coats, 4 Jan. 1934
19 Ibid., vol. 181, 'Minutes of the Dominion-Provincial Conference, 17 Jan. 1934
20 RDCUR, 31 March 1934, 28, Appendix H; 31 March 1933, 25, Appendix G
21 PAC, Dafoe Papers, MG 30, D 17, vol. 7, Grant Dexter to J.W. Dafoe, 17 Jan. 1934
22 Bennett Papers, vol. 566, Bennett to J. Anderson, nd. (draft letter)
23 Ibid.,vol. 181, 'Minutes of Dominion-Provincial Conference, 17 Jan. 1934'; see also PAC, McNaughton Papers, MG 30, G 12, vol. 63, memo on 'Dominion-Provincial Conference on Unemployment Relief,'; 20 Jan. 1934
24 Margaret Ormsby, 'T. Dufferin Pattullo and the Little New Deal,' in Ramsay Cook, ed., *The Politics of Discontent* (Toronto 1967), 30–5
25 Bennett Papers, vol. 570, Edgar Rhodes to Bennett, 12 Dec. 1933
26 Ibid., vol. 799, Pattullo to Bennett, 1 March 1934; vol. 569, H.H. Stevens to Bennett, 3 March 1934; Bennett to Stevens, 7 March 1934
27 Ibid., vol. 799, Bennett to Pattullo, 2 March 1934; vol. 569, Bennett to Pattullo, 24 March 1934; Edgar Rhodes to John Hart, 24 March 1934; Pattullo to Bennett, 28 March 1934; Pattullo to Bennett, 29 March 1934
28 Ibid., vol. 569, Bennett to Pattullo, 30 March 1934; T.P. Mackenzie to Bennett, 30 March 1934
29 Ibid., vol. 570, S.H. Logan to Pattullo, 4 April 1934; S.H. Logan to Bennett, 4 April 1934
30 Ibid., vol. 569, Rhodes to Bennett, 2 May 1934; Bennett to Pattullo, 2 May 1934; Pattullo to Sir George Perley, 7 May 1934; vol. 805, Pattullo to Bennett, 11 June 1934
31 Ibid., vol. 569, John Hart to Rhodes, 1 June 1934; vol. 805, Rhodes to Hart, 11 June 1934; Pattullo to Bennett, 11 June 1934; vol. 570, Bennett to Pattullo, 5 July 1934; Bennett to Pattullo, 6 June 1934; Pattullo to Bennett, 6 July 1934
32 Ibid., vol. 790, Montreal Chamber of Commerce to Bennett, 31 May 1934; CCSD Papers, vol. 15, file 68, Kathleen Snowden to Charles Morse, 27 July 1934
33 CCSD Papers, vol. 15, file 68, Joseph Piggott to W.H. Lovering, 26 July 1934; Bennett Papers, vol. 790, G.C. Wilson to Bennett, 10 April 1934
34 Bennett Papers, vol. 792, E. Browne-Wilkinson to R.K. Finlayson, 17 Aug. 1934; Finlayson to E. Browne-Wilkinson, 21 Aug. 1934
35 Ibid., vol. 182, A. McNaughton and R.K. Finlayson to Bennett, 28 July 1934; vol. 782, S.A. Cudmore, 'Report on Unemployment,' 4 Jan. 1934; Census of Canada, 1931, XIII, 'Monograph on Unemployment,' 274; RDCUR, 31 March 1935, 52; Bennett Papers, vol. 790, Bennett to W.J. McCully, 6 Aug. 1934
36 Bennett Papers, vol. 797, A.W. Merriam to Mrs Martin Welch, 20 Aug. 1934
37 Ibid., vol. 797, Pattullo to Bennett, 1 June 1934; vol. 792, Taschereau to Gordon, 1 June 1934; vol. 785, Angus Macdonald to Gordon, 7 June 1934; vol. 792, J. Bracken to

Gordon, 27 June 1934; vol. 795, J.E. Brownlee to Bennett, 9 May 1934; vol. 795, DOC RCMP Edmonton, 5 June 1934; vol. 792, Jimmy Stitt to Bennett, 5 June 1934

38 Ibid., vol. 790, W.A. Gordon to all provincial premiers, 12 June 1934; vol. 182, George Perley to Bennett, 12 July 1934; Bennett to Perley, 12 July 1934

39 Ibid., vol. 182, 'Minutes of the Dominion-Provincial Conference on Relief Policy,' 31 July 1934

40 Ibid., vol. 182, memo from Finlayson and McNaughton to Bennett, 28 July 1934; 'Minutes of the Dominion-Provincial Conference on Relief Policy,' 31 July 1934

41 Ibid., vol. 182, Bennett to Jimmy Stitt, 30 July 1934; CCSD Papers, vol. 15, file 68, Whitton to W.H. Lovering, 1 Aug. 1934

42 Bennett Papers, vol. 182, 'Minutes of the Dominion-Provincial Conference on Relief Policy,' 31 July 1934

43 RDCUR, 30 March 1935, 5–6, 34; 31 March 1936, 36. From 1 April until 31 July 1934 the total relief load per month averaged approximately 1,241,250 individuals. From 1 August until 31 March 1935 it averaged 1,239,375. Federal support on a monthly average for the two periods dropped from $2,240,338 to $1,753,000 or 22 per cent from the point at which direct relief on a percentage basis was replaced by fixed grants-in-aid. On a province by province basis the figures are as follows (all calculations are averaged on a monthly basis):

	April–July	August–March	
New Brunswick	$ 13,826	$ 25,000	(up 78%)
Nova Scotia	37,875	40,875	(up 7.8%)
PEI	1,596	2,125	(up 33%)
Quebec	556,501	500,000	(down 11%)
Ontario	942,812	600,000	(down 37%)
Manitoba	138,690	135,000	(down 2.6%)
Saskatchewan	220,760	200,000	(down 11%)
Alberta	102,787	100,000	(down 2.8%)
BC	225,459	150,000	(down 34%)

44 Neil McKenty, *Mitch Hepburn* (Toronto 1967), 51–65

45 Christopher Armstrong, 'The Politics of Federalism: Ontario's Relations with the Federal Government, 1896-1941' (PHD dissertation, University of Toronto, 1972), 509–10; Bennett Papers, vol. 798, editorial from *Edmonton Journal*, 16 Aug. 1934

46 PAC, DND Records, RG 24, vol. 2969, memo on 'Employment and Relief 1934' by Andrew McNaughton, 12 Jan. 1934

47 House of Commons, *Debates*, 18 April 1934, 2267

48 Bennett Papers, vol. 798, Bennett to F.A. Sherman, 3 Jan. 1934

49 *Statutes of Canada*, 24–25 Geo. V, chap. 59, 1349; House of Commons, *Debates*, 26 June 1934, 4299. For the limited economic impact of the bill see A.E. Safarian, *The Canadian Economy in the Great Depression* (Toronto 1972), 156

50 Bennett Papers, vol. 813, R.H. Coats to R.K. Finlayson, 2 Feb. 1934; vol. 812, Bennett to Arthur Steel-Maitland, 14 Dec. 1933; House of Commons, *Debates*, 13 Feb. 1934, 522

51 Bennett Papers, vol. 812, R.K. Finlayson to Bennett, 25 May 1934

52 Ibid., vol. 812, Bennett to Sir Thomas White, 30 Aug. 1934

53 Ibid., vol. 812, R.K., Finlayson to Bennett, 25 May 1934

54 Ibid., vol. 813, R.H. Coats to R.K. Finlayson, 2 Feb. 1934

55 Ibid., vol. 797, R.K. Finlayson to secretary, British Ministry of Labour, 24 Nov. 1933; assistant secretary British Ministry of Labour to Finlayson, 14 Nov. 1933

56 Ibid., vol. 813, R.H. Coats to R.K. Finlayson, 2 Feb. 1934; vol. 812, memo by F.G. Price on 'Notes on a Possible Unemployment Insurance Scheme for Canada,' enclosed in Arthur Steel-Maitland to Bennett, 30 April 1934; PAC, Department of Insurance Records, RG 40 3, vol. 1, 'Summary of Intercensal Data Compiled by the Bureau of Statistics,' nd reproduced in House of Commons, *Debates*, 18 Feb. 1935, 934

57 Department of Insurance Records, vol. 1, A.D. Watson to R.K. Finlayson, 11 April 1934; G.D. Finlayson to A.D. Watson, 'Memo on Coverage, Exclusions and Exemptions, Eligibility Conditions, etc.' 6 April 1934

58 Price, 'Notes on a Possible Unemployment Insurance Scheme for Canada'; Bennett Papers, vol. 780, 'Report on Unemployment Relief in Edmonton,' 10 June 1932

59 Ibid., 'Unemployment Insurance: Memorandum on Rates of Benefits,' nd (April 1934)

60 CCSD Papers, vol. 100, file 191, 'The Cost of Living,' 1939

61 Department of Insurance Records, vol. 1, A.D. Watson, 'Actuarial Report on the Contributions Required to Provide the Unemployment Insurance Benefits Within the Scheme of the Draft of An Act entitled "The Employment And Social Insurance Act," ' 14 June 1934; H.H. Wolfenden, 'Memo on "The Drafting of the Revision of the Employment and Social Insurance Act," ' 5 Jan. 1935; A.D. Watson to R.K. Finlayson, 3 April 1934

62 Ibid., A.D. Watson, 'Notes on the Main Provisions of the Employment and Social Insurance Bill,' 15 Jan. 1935; 'Unemployment Insurance: Memorandum on Rates of Benefit,' nd; A.D. Watson to H.H. Wolfenden, 12 Jan. 1935

63 Ibid., vol. 1, A.D. Watson, 'Actuarial Report,' 14 June 1934

64 Ibid., vol. 1, H.H. Wolfenden, 'Actuarial Report,' 1 Feb. 1935

65 Bennett Papers, vol. 812, R.K. Finlayson to Bennett, 25 May 1934; vol. 813, R.K. Finlayson to Leonard Marsh, 9 May 1934. For details of the bill see *Statutes of Canada*, 25–26 Geo. v, 208

66 A similar pattern was followed with Bennett's Bank of Canada legislation which left monetary policy in the hands of private bank shareholders, not the government. As H. Blair Neatby notes, the bank bill indicated Bennett's belief that 'governments presumably could not be trusted to resist inflationary pressures; monetary policy was too important to be left to politicians,' *William Lyon Mackenzie King*, III: *1932–1939: the Prism of Unity* (Toronto 1976), 53. One might add that the insurance bill indicated

Bennett's belief that unemployment policy was also too important to be left to politicians.

67 Richard Wilbur, 'R.B. Bennett as a Reformer,' Canadian Historical Association, Historical Papers, 1969, 106; House of Commons, Debates, 11 April 1934, 2045–7

68 House of Commons, Debates, 13 April 1934, 2162–3

69 Bennett Papers, vol. 812, R.K. Finlayson to Bennett, 25 May 1934. See also Finlayson's memoir cited in Wilbur, 'R.B. Bennett as a Reformer,' 106

70 Bennett Papers, vol. 182, draft letter from Bennett to all provincial premiers, 31 Aug. 1934. (The letter was sent on 12 September 1934.)

71 Ibid., vol. 813, Bennett to Perley, 8 Sept. 1934; R.K. Finlayson to Richard Baker, 12 Sept. 1934; Finlayson to Perley, 12 Sept. 1934; Richard Baker to Bennett, 30 Aug. 1934

72 Donald Forster and Colin Read, 'The Politics of Opportunism: the New Deal Radio Broadcasts,' Canadian Historical Review, LX, 3, 1979, 326–30

73 Ibid., 333–4

74 Bennett Papers, vol. 713, Bennett to J.H. Woods, 3 Jan. 1935

75 Ibid., vol. 276, W.D. Herridge to Bennett, 12 April 1934

76 Ibid., vol. 276, Herridge to Bennett, 20 Nov. 1934

77 House of Commons, Debates, 29 Jan. 1935, 280; Bennett Papers, vol. 713, Bennett to T.A. Moore, 7 Jan. 1935

78 PAC, Department of Labour Records, RG 27, vol. 162, copy of Privy Council appeal no 101 of 1936, 'Attorney-General of Canada vs. Attorney-General of Ontario and others in the matter of the Employment and Social Insurance Act 1935'; Bennett Papers, vol. 433, R.K. Finlayson to Sir George Perley, 21 March 1935

79 Forster and Read, 'The Politics of Opportunism, 347

80 House of Commons, Debates, 12 March 1935, 1638–9

81 Dafoe Papers, Dexter to Dafoe, 4 Jan. 1935

82 Armstrong, 'The Politics of Federalism,' 520–1

83 Bennett Papers, vol. 276, W.D. Herridge to Bennett, 12 April 1934; Herridge to Bennett, 20 Oct. 1934

84 Ibid., vol. 812, E.J. Harker to Bennett, 4 Feb. 1935

85 Ibid., vol. 792, M. Peterson (city clerk) of Winnipeg to Bennett, 29 Sept. 1934; W.R. Clubb to W.A. Gordon, 11 Feb. 1935; vol. 801, statement released by Sir George Perley, 26 April 1935; vol. 782, Bennett to F.A. Reinhardt, 8 July 1935; vol. 807, Bennett to Perley, 8 April 1935

86 House of Commons, Debates, 12 Feb. 1935, 774; 29 Jan. 1935, 283–5

87 CCSD Papers, vol. 15, 'The Relief Outlook in Canada,' Dec. 1934

88 Bennett Papers, vol. 812, letter and memo from Wendall Clarke, Canadian Chamber of Commerce, to all members of Parliament, 13 April 1935. (It should be noted that Clarke was a member of the CCC & FW governing board and had maintained a continuing

correspondence with Whitton over relief policy.) See also vol. 790, Resolution forwarded to Bennett by the Ontario Associated Boards of Trade and Chambers of Commerce, 14 Jan. 1935

89 John Taylor, 'Urban Social Organization and Urban Discontent: the 1930's,' in David Bercuson, ed., *Western Perspectives 1* (Toronto 1974), 33

90 Bennett Papers, vol. 784, J.E. Brownlee to W.A. Gordon, 2 Dec. 1933

91 *Toronto Daily Star*, 17, 24 April 1935 (I am indebted to Desmond Glynn for this reference); Patricia V. Schulz, *The East York Workers' Association: a Response to the Great Depression* (Toronto 1975), 27–33

92 See, for example, Ronald Liversedge, *Recollections of the On-to-Ottawa Trek*, ed. Victor Hoar (Toronto 1973), an excellent blend of documents, memoir, and narrative.

93 See the *Report of the Macdonald Commission* reprinted in Liversedge, *Recollections of the On-to-Ottawa Trek*, 139. See also the *Report* of the Vancouver Council of Social Agencies on the camps, 9 March 1934, in DND Records, vol. 2973.

94 Evan's comment to the Regina Riot Inquiry Commission is reported in Liversedge, *Recollections of the On-to-Ottawa Trek*, 125.

95 DND Records, vol. 3184, clippings from *Vancouver Sun*, 20, 22, 23 Feb. 1934

96 Liversedge, *Recollections of the On-to-Ottawa Trek*, 133; DND Records, vol. 2972, 'Unemployment Relief: Draft Reports and Administrative Reports,' nd

97 McNaughton Papers, vol. 38, McNaughton to Bennett, 25 May 1934

98 Bennett Papers, vol. 797, 'Why? the Diary of a Relief Camp Striker,' 3–4

99 Bennett Papers, vol. 802, Sir George Perley to Gerry McGeer, 15 May 1935 (this letter was drafted by McNaughton)

100 Ibid., vol. 782, memo from McNaughton to W.L. Dickson, 21 March 1934

101 DND Records, vol. 3185, clipping from *Winnipeg Free Press*, 24 Oct. 1934

102 Bennett Papers, vol. 801, memo by McNaughton, 16 Oct. 1934. American New Deal relief administrators also faced a similar problem with regard to their works program which quickly resulted in the scrapping of the Civil Works Administration and the phasing out of the Works Progress Administration after 1936. See William W. Bremer, 'Along the "American Way": the New Deal's Work Relief Programs for the Unemployed.' *Journal of American History*, LXII, 3, Dec. 1975, and Frances Fox Piven and Richard Cloward, *Regulating the Poor: the Functions of Public Welfare* (New York 1971), 112–13.

103 See, for example, the premiers' unanimous praise for the federal relief camps at the 31 July 1934 dominion-provincial conference in Bennett Papers, vol. 182.

104 Bennett Papers, vol. 801, McNaughton to Bennett, Dec. 1934; Bennett to Pattullo, 28 Dec. 1934

105 Ibid., vol. 801, Pattullo to Bennett, 3 Jan. 1935; vol. 802, R.G. Reid to Bennett, 4 June 1935; John Bracken to Bennett, 10 June 1935; J.G. Gardiner to Bennett, 12 June 1935

106 RDCUR, 31 March 1936, 32

107 Bennett Papers, vol. 802, memo from the BC Conservative Association to C.A. Stewart, 15 May 1935
108 Ibid., vol. 276, W.D. Herridge to Bennett, 14 May 1935
109 PAC, Whitton Papers, MG 30, E, 256, vol. 4, Bennett to Whitton, 15 Feb. 1939

CHAPTER 5

1 PAC, King Diary, 26 June 1935
2 RDCUR, 31 March 1936, 32
3 H. Blair Neatby, *William Lyon Mackenzie King*, III: *1932–1939: the Prism of Unity* (Toronto 1976), 148
4 Ibid., 153; PAC, Floyd Chalmers Papers, Chalmers to Colonel Maclean, 12 Feb. 1934. As Chalmers noted after an interview with King, 'His economic and political views seem to have been influenced in a rather interesting and unique way by the depression. While most statesmen and politicians have swung sharply to the left as a result of their contact with social problems, King has come back much more to the middle of the road, almost to the right.' (I am grateful to H. Blair Neatby for giving me access to his notes on the Chalmers Papers.) For King's thoughts on conflict see *Industry and Humanity* (Toronto 1973), 21–2; for his ideas on unemployment see House of Commons, *Debates*, 27 Feb. 1933, 2502; for his response to Roosevelt's New Deal see King Diary, 17 Jan., 8 Feb. 1934.
5 Neatby, *The Prism of Unity*, 153; see also King Diary, 14 March, 30 April 1936.
6 Chalmers Papers, R.B. Borden to L.A. Taschereau, 17 Oct. 1935
7 Christopher Armstrong, 'The Politics of Federalism: Ontario's Relations with the Federal Government, 1896–1941' (PHD dissertation, University of Toronto, 1972), 531
8 Ibid.
9 PAC, RG 47, vol. 60, 'Minutes of the Dominion-Provincial Conference,' 13 Dec. 1935. There is some dispute over the size of the increase. Neatby, *The Prism of Unity*, 157, puts it at 15 per cent; Armstrong, 'Politics of Federalism,' 533–4 at 75 per cent. Armstrong is correct. See PAC Department of Labour Records, RG 27, vol. 213, file 617, memo on 'Dominion Unemployment Relief: Relief Since 1930,' Jan. 1940, 25.
10 King Diary, 13 Dec. 1935, For King's regret at an increase he found 'too generous' see entries for 18 and 19 Dec. 1935.
11 The phrase was used by King in his major campaign speech on unemployment: 'The Liberal Unemployment Programme,' Queen's University Archives, Norman Rogers Papers, nd (c Oct. 1935). For King's conviction that the NEC would save 'many millions of dollars' see King Diary, 8 April 1936; Neatby, *The Prism of Unity*, 151.
12 Neatby, *The Prism of Unity*, 32–3
13 Rogers Papers, box 2, Rogers to James Craig, 27 March 1935
14 Ibid.
15 Ibid., Rogers to Harry Cassidy, 1 Aug. 1935; Rogers to Norman Senior, 7 May 1935

16 *Statutes of Canada*, I Ed. VIII, chap. 7, 47–50; House of Commons, *Debates*, 6 April 1936, 1850; 24 March 1936, 1391

17 Toronto *Globe and Mail*, 16 May 1936

18 Rogers Papers, Rogers to Harry Cassidy, I Aug. 1935

19 *Globe and Mail*, 16 May 1936

20 Ibid., *Who's Who in Canada*, 1936–7, 117

21 Donald Forster and Colin Read, 'The Politics of Opportunism: the New Deal Radio Broadcasts,' *Canadian Historical Review*, LX, 3, 1979, 328–30; *Globe and Mail*, 16 May 1936

22 King Diary, 8 April 1936; 7 April 1936; House of Commons, *Debates*, 3 April 1936, 1786. The phrase 'effective co-operation' is from the National Employment Commission Act.

23 House of Commons, *Debates*, 10 Feb. 1936, 41–2; 2 April 1936, 1751; 3 April 1936, 1764

24 *Canadian Forum*, May 1936

25 PAC, King Papers, MG 26, J 4, vol. 197, 137466-7, speech by King on the National Employment Commission during the 1935 campaign

26 PAC, DND Records, RG 24, vol. 3032, *Report of the Rigg Commission*, 11 Jan. 1936

27 King Diary, 24 Jan. 1936; House of Commons, *Debates*, 25 Feb. 1936, 542; 17 Feb. 1936, 244–5

28 DND Records, vol. 3062, Ashton to Norman Rogers, 27 Jan. 1936; vol. 3034, J.M. Varey to O.C. White, 18 April 1936; House of Commons, *Debates*, 20 June 1936, 3996

29 DND Records, vol. 3034, E.M. Johnston to T. Magladery, 18 April 1936; T. Magladery to all district superintendents, nd (c March 1936)

30 House of Commons, *Debates*, 20 June 1936, 3996; 20 April 1936, 1971; 4 May 1936, 2489–92. To make matters worse, the railway workers who had been laid off since 1930 would remain unemployed, for the government made no stipulation that they be hired along with the men from the relief camps. Instead, Ottawa would only subsidize the wages of ex-relief-camp workers. See House of Commons, *Debates*, 4 May 1936, 2479, 2488–9.

31 House of Commons, *Debates*, 23 March 1936, 1368

32 Ibid., 17 Feb. 1936, 242; 30 March 1936, 1592–3; 7 April 1936, 1873

33 Ibid., 24 March 1936, 1400; 30 March 1936, 1599, 1581

34 King Diary, 28 and 27 March, 30 April 1936. The cut was vigorously opposed by Rogers and to mollify the labour minister it was staggered over four months, see ibid., 30, 31 March 1936; on provincial protest see House of Commons, *Debates*, 6 April 1936, 1808

35 King Diary, 28 March 1936

36 *Toronto Daily Star*, 10, 8, and 7 July 1936 (I am indebted to Desmond Glynn for these references.)

37 *Social Worker*, V, 2, Nov. 1936

38 PAC, CCSD Papers, MG 28, I 10, 155, memo from Jean Walker, 22 Oct. 1936, containing extracts from *Ottawa Citizen*, 18 Aug., 12 Sept. 1936; vol. 120, clipping from *Ottawa Journal*, 1 Sept. 1936

39 *Social Worker*, Nov. 1936

40 CCSD Papers. vol. 120, file 1905, Bessie Touzel to Mary Jennison, 13 Nov. 1936; *Social Worker*, Nov. 1936

41 *Social Worker*, V, 3, Dec. 1936

42 CCSD Papers, vol. 120, file 1905, Marjorie Bradford to D.L. Morrell, 20 May 1936

43 Ibid., Muriel Tucker to Frank Clarke, 17 June 1936

44 Ibid., 21, 22 April 1936; Department of Labour Records, vol. 213, file 617, memo on 'Dominion Unemployment Relief: Relief Since 1930,' Jan. 1940, 34

45 Neatby, *The Prism of Unity*, 157–60. See Douglas Library, Queen's University, Norman Lambert Diary, 9 Dec. 1933, for early reference by Dunning to idea of a loan council. (I am grateful to H. Blair Neatby for this reference.)

46 H. Blair Neatby, *The Politics of Chaos: Canada in the Thirties* (Toronto 1972), 143–61

47 Neatby, *The Prism of Unity*, 157–60

48 Floyd Chalmers Papers, Chalmers to Colonel Maclean, 14 Dec. 1935. See King's statement to the premiers on this point at the 1935 conference, cited in Armstrong, 'The Politics of Federalism,' 536.

49 Armstrong, 'The Politics of Federalism,' 540; King Diary, 15 May 1936

50 Neatby, *The Prism of Unity*, 161

51 King Diary, 14 May, 5 Aug. 1936

52 Department of Labour Records, NEC files, vol. 63, minutes of NEC meeting, 26 Aug. 1936: vol. 66, Whitton to Harry Baldwin, 22 July 1936.

53 J.L. Granatstein, *The Ottawa Men: the Civil Service Mandarins* (Toronto 1982), 153–6

54 Ibid.; Department of Labour Records, NEC files, vol. 74, memo by W.A. Mackintosh on 'The Economic Fundamentals of Recovery,' 29 July 1936

55 Department of Labour Records, NEC files, vol. 64, minutes of NEC meeting, 30 July 1936

56 Ibid., vol. 76, memo by Mackintosh on 'Housing Renovation and Construction as a Source of Employment,' 31 Aug. 1936; vol. 75, memo on 'An Estimate of the Housing "Backlog"' Dec. 1936; vol. 78, Purvis to Rogers, 2 Sept. 1936

57 Rogers Papers, Alan Chambers to Rogers, 11 Sept. 1936, including the Interim Report of the Youth Employment Committee of the National Employment Commission, 25 Aug. 1936; Department of Labour Records, NEC files, vol. 64, 'Report of the Youth Employment Committee,' 9 Oct. 1936

58 See, for example, King's comments on Young's 'indefensible laissez-faire attitude,' King Diary, 20 June 1935.

59 Department of Labour Records, NEC files, vol. 72, Report of the Committee on Land Settlement, 14 Nov. 1936; vol. 74, minutes of NEC meeting, 29 July 1936

60 King Diary, 3 Sept. 1936

61 Department of Labour Records, NEC files, vol. 63, memo on 'Single Homeless Adults,' enclosed in Purvis to Rogers, 26 Aug. 1936

62 Ibid., vol. 60, Harry Baldwin to Purvis, 23 July 1936; vol. 63, Purvis to Rogers, 26 Aug. 1936; vol. 82, Baldwin to Harry Cassidy, 1 Aug. 1936

63 Ibid., vol. 60, Baldwin to Purvis, 23 July 1936

64 'Strikers' Nights,' letter to the *Vancouver Sun*, May 1935, cited in Michiel Horn, ed., *The Dirty Thirties: Canadians in the Great Depression* (Toronto 1972), 339–40

65 Department of Labour Records, NEC files, vol. 60, Arthur Purvis to Norman Rogers, 26 Aug. 1936

66 Ibid., vol. 60, Baldwin to Purvis, 23 July 1936

67 Ibid., vol. 63, Purvis to Rogers, 26 Aug. 1936; vol. 66, memo by Harry Hereford and W.M. Jones to Rogers, 19 Oct. 1936; vol. 72, R.A. Rigg to W.M. Dickson, 23 Oct. 1936; vol. 66, memo by Tom Moore, 22 Aug. 1936

68 Ibid., vol. 67, minutes of meeting of Farm Placement Committee, 7 Aug. 1936; vol. 61, memo from Purvis to Mackenzie King, 16 Jan. 1937

69 Ibid., vol. 66, H. Spencer Relph to Humphrey Mitchell, 16 Sept. 1936, outlining telephone instructions from Purvis

70 Ibid., vol. 63, minutes of NEC meeting, 30 July 1936; vol. 63, Purvis to Rogers, 26 Aug. 1936; vol. 59, telegram from Rogers to all provincial ministers of labour, 10 Sept. 1936; vol. 63, report by Humphrey Mitchell, 13 Oct. 1936; also vol. 62, A MacNamara to Humphrey Mitchell, 25 Aug. 1936

71 King Diary, 10 Sept. 1936; see also entry for 21 April 1936 on King's preference for 'back to the land.' Because of his $477,000 increase in funding for relief settlement, the number of families placed on the land rose from 134 to 1085 between 1936 and 1937 and doubled to 1919 in the following year.

72 Department of Labour Records, NEC files, vol. 63, report by Humphrey Mitchell, 13 Oct. 1936; vol. 70, George Pearson to James Gardiner, 26 Oct. 1936; Gardiner to Pearson, 29 Oct. 1936; Rogers Papers, W.M. Dickson to Rogers, 9 Oct. 1936; Department of Labour Records, NEC files, vol. 66, George Pearson to Purvis, 6 Oct. 1936; vol. 66, memo by Humphrey Mitchell, 20 Jan. 1937

73 Department of Labour Records, NEC files, vol. 72, R.A. Rigg to W.M. Dickson, 21 Oct. 1936; Rigg to Dickson, 23 Oct. 1936; vol. 72, A.A. Mackenzie to Purvis, 24 Oct. 1936; vol. 70, telegram from Calgary City Council to Rogers, 14 Oct. 1936

74 Ibid., vol. 61, memo from Purvis to King, 16 Jan. 1937; vol. 66, memo by Humphrey Mitchell, 20 Jan. 1937

75 King Diary, 18 Dec. 1936; 28 Jan. 1937

76 Neatby, *The Prism of Unity*, 162. The formula demanded unanimous consent in sensitive areas such as educational guarantees for religious minorities, but in the area of social legislation proposed the consent of only two-thirds of the provinces which together represented 55 per cent of the Canadian population.

77 King Diary, 17 Aug. 1936. A point made by Donald Forster in his memo on

'Dominion-Provincial Financial Relations: 1935–39.' I am indebted to H. Blair Neatby for giving me access to this and other memos prepared for the King biography.

78 King Papers, J 1, vol. 215, memo on the 'Meetings of the National Finance Committee held on December 9–11 1936,' 186211–12

79 King Diary, 8 Jan., 16 Feb. 1937; also Neatby, *The Prism of Unity*, 197–200

80 Hepburn's quote is from Armstrong, 'The Politics of Federalism,' 545.

81 House of Commons, *Debates*, 25 Feb. 1937, 1214

82 King Diary, 4 Jan. 1937

83 Department of Labour Records, NEC files, vol. 71, memo on 'Rural Relief in Ontario,' 4 Jan. 1937. The NEC estimated that 15 to 20 per cent of rural relief fell into this category.

84 Ibid., vol. 61, memo from Purvis to Rogers, 18 Feb. 1937; House of Commons, *Debates*, 25 Feb. 1937, 1216–17

85 Ibid., vol. 63, memo from Purvis to Rogers, 9 Feb. 1937

86 Ibid., vol. 61, memo from Purvis to Rogers, 18 Feb. 1937; vol. 75, report of 'Meeting on Low-Rental Housing,' 6 Jan. 1937. House of Commons, *Debates*, 25 Feb. 1937, 1216; King Papers, J-1, vol. 241, statement issued by Rogers, on *Interim Report* of the NEC, 18 Aug. 1937

87 Ibid., vol. 78, Purvis to Rogers, 29 Jan. 1937

88 King Diary, 22 Feb. 1937

89 Ibid., 8 Jan. 1937; Department of Labour Records, NEC files, vol. 61, Purvis to Rogers, 18 Feb. 1937; vol. 74, memo by Mackintosh on the 'Economic Fundamentals of Recovery,' 29 July 1936; King Papers, J 1, vol. 241, statement by Rogers, 18 Aug. 1937

90 Norman Lambert Diary, 4 May 1937. (I am grateful to H. Blair Neatby for this reference.)

91 King Diary, 30 June 1936, 8 Jan., 25 Feb. 1937. See also King's complaint that his ministers had 'lost all sense of responsibility to the taxpayer' and had 'gotten into the habit of yielding to pressure and particularly with unemployment, doing the thing that is likely to help some Province,' 23 Feb. 1937.

92 Charlotte Whitton, 'The Relief Outlook in Canada,' *Child and Family Welfare*, XII, 5, 1937, 26; Frieda Held, 'The Way Back for the Unemployment Relief Case,' Canadian Conference on Social Work *Proceedings* 6th Bienniel Conference 1938, 155

93 Department of Labour Records, NEC files, vol. 86, Purvis to G. Bateman, 4 June 1937

94 *Globe and Mail*, 16 May 1936; Department of Labour Records, NEC files, vol. 62, memo from Mary Sutherland to Norman Rogers, 19 Aug. 1936; vol. 63, Final Report of the Women's Employment Committee, 10 Dec. 1937

95 King Papers, J 1, vol. 229, King to Mary Sutherland, 11 April 1936; vol. 220, Ian Mackenzie to King, 20 April 1936; King to Ian Mackenzie, 5 May 1936; King Diary, 20 Dec. 1937

96 Department of Labour Records, NEC files, vol. 62, Sutherland to Norman Rogers, 22 Feb. 1937

97 Department of Labour Records, Lacelle files, vol. 213, memo on 'Dominion Unemployment Relief since 1930,' Jan. 1940, 26, 28; House of Commons, *Debates*, 2 March 1937, 1426

98 RDCUR, 31 March 1941, 36–8. During the life of the 1936 Relief Act (1 April 1936–31 March 1937) the average monthly total of those on relief was 1,105,542. The comparable figure for the 1937 act was 925,010.

99 Cited in Armstrong, 'The Politics of Federalism,' 556. Hepburn's outrage was justified. In March 1937 the federal government made the decision to restrict the total spending on grants-in-aid for the 1937–8 fiscal year to $19.5 million. In fact, Ottawa spent somewhat less than this ($19,272,150) despite the fact that by the fall of 1937 the economy once more plunged into recession, and relief rolls climbed steadily upward throughout the winter of 1937–8. See Department of Labour Records, NEC files, vol. 78, Purvis to Rogers, 20 March 1937; Lacelle files, vol. 213, file 617, 'Dominion Unemployment Relief: Relief Since 1930,' Jan. 1940, 28. For the effect of the relief cut in moving Hepburn into an alliance with Duplessis against Ottawa in the summer of 1937 see King Papers, J 1, vol. 237, Ian Mackenzie to King, 28 July 1937. Hepburn's comment was ironic for, at the same time, King complained that the 'Province, municipality each wish to throw entire [relief] burden on Dominion,' King Diary, 14 July 1937.

100 *Toronto Daily Star*, 24 Nov. 1937. (I am indebted to Desmond Glynn for this reference.)

101 Department of Labour Records, NEC files, vol. 61, Purvis to Rogers, 21 July 1937; Canada, *Interim Report of the National Employment Commission* (Ottawa 1937), 13–14, 19

102 NEC *Interim Report*, 11–13, 18; *Child and Family Welfare*, XIII, 3, Sept. 1937, text of speech by Purvis on 'The Obligations of Government Towards Social Security'; Department of Labour Records, NEC files, vol. 74, text of speech by Purvis, 29 Nov. 1937

103 Department of Labour Records, NEC files, vol. 66, Whitton to Tom Moore, 24 July 1937; see also her article 'The Relief of Unemployment,' in *Child and Family Welfare* May 1936, XII, 1

104 NEC *Interim Report*, 15–16. Whitton made her opposition to a national relief system explicit in her later criticisms of the Rowell-Sirois report. 'I am ... appalled,' she wrote to Harry Cassidy, 'to find that plans apparently contemplate the actual setting up of staff and budgets and the actual administration of aid in cash or in kind – I presume the former – right across Canada in city, rural, mining and widely differing areas ... [A] Dominion power will not be able to pay $27.00 in Saint John, $13.00 in a nearby town, $40.00 in Calgary and $45.00 in Winnipeg ... these differentials must be left to local authority'; CCSD Papers, vol. 99, file 179, Whitton to Cassidy, 16 Dec. 1940

105 Department of Labour, Records, NEC files, vol. 75, memo by Whitton on 'The Organization of Aid to Persons in Distress,' March 1937. See also her article on 'The Relief of Unemployment.'

106 NEC *Interim Report*, 18
107 King Papers, J 1, vol. 241, statement issued by Rogers on the *Interim Report* of the NEC, 18 Aug. 1937
108 Department of Labour Records, NEC files, vol. 78, Purvis to Rogers, 13 Sept. 1937
109 Purvis, 'The Obligations of Government towards Social Security'
110 King Papers, J 1, vol. 234, King to Duplessis (and all other premiers), 5 Nov. 1937; King Diary, 14 Sept., 12 Nov. 1937
111 King Diary, 12 Nov. 1937
112 R.F. Thompson, 'Local Administration of Public Welfare,' Canadian Conference on Social Work *Proceedings* 5th Bienniel Conference 1937; *Toronto Daily Star*, 25 June 1937 (I am indebted to Desmond Glynn for this reference.)

CHAPTER 6

1 PAC, King Diary, 22 and 23 Dec. 1937
2 PAC, Department of Labour Records, RG 27, Lacelle files, vol. 166, memo by Dr Christie Tait on 'Insurance Bill in Canada,' 23 Oct. 1937
3 Canada, *Final Report of the National Employment Commission* (Ottawa 1938), 29–30; Department of Labour Records, NEC files, vol. 66, Purvis to Mary Sutherland, 8 Jan. 1938
4 King Diary, 21 Dec. 1937; W.A. Mackintosh, 'Canadian Economic Policy from 1945 to 1957 – Origins and Influences,' in Hugh Aitken and John Deutsch, eds., *The American Impact on Canada* (Toronto 1958), 53; NEC *Final Report*, 27–8
5 This was certainly King's conclusion. See King Diary, 18 March, 25 Jan. 1938.
6 Ibid., 20 Dec. 1937
7 Ibid., 21 Dec. 1937
8 Ibid., 21, 23 Dec. 1937, 23 Jan. 1938
9 Department of Labour Records, NEC files, vol. 66, Purvis to Neil McLean, 22 and 30 Dec. 1937; Purvis to E.J. Young, 19 Jan. 1938; vol. 78, memo of telephone conversation between Purvis and Rogers, 19 Jan. 1938; vol. 66, deletions in final report of NEC submitted to Rogers on 22 Dec. 1937; NEC *Final Report*, 32
10 King Diary, 23 Jan. 1938
11 Ibid.
12 PAC, King Papers, MG 26, J 1, vol. 243, Sutherland to King, 29 Dec. 1937 enclosing first draft of her minority report
13 King Diary, 22 and 11 Jan., 11 March 1938
14 Ibid., 11 Jan. 1938
15 NEC *Final Report*, 30
16 Canada, *Report of the Royal Commission on Dominion-Provincial Relations*, Book II (Ottawa 1940), 18; PAC, CCSD Papers, MG 28, I 10, vol. 99, file 178, Purvis to Whitton, 14 June 1938

17 King Diary, 21 Dec. 1937, 25 Jan. 1938
18 Ibid., 25 Jan. 1938
19 King Papers, J 4, vol. 197, Ian Mackenzie to King, 25 Jan. 1938; King Diary, 25 Jan. 1938
20 King Diary, 25 Jan. 1938
21 See, for example, H. Blair Neatby, 'The Liberal Way: Fiscal and Monetary Policy in the 1930's,' in Victor Hoar, ed., *The Great Depression* (Toronto 1969), 107–9; Neatby, *The Politics of Chaos: Canada in the Thirties* (Toronto 1972), 83–5.
22 NEC *Final Report*, 34–5, 25
23 Ibid., 25–6
24 Ibid., 36; review of the NEC *Final Report* by Leonard Marsh in the *Canadian Journal of Economics and Political Science*, V, 1939, 80–5. For a lucid discussion of Keynes' attitude toward government spending see John A. Garraty, *Unemployment in History, Economic Thought and Public Policy* (New York 1978), 219–21.
25 King Diary, 11 and 18 March 1938
26 House of Commons, *Debates*, 4 April 1938, 2001; 6 April 1938, 2091
27 King Papers, J 4, vol. 197, précis of press comment on NEC *Final Report*, 19 April 1938; House of Commons, *Debates*, 6 April 1938, 2085–91; 7 April 1938, 2114–15; 28 April 1938, 2350–3. For a different interpretation of the whole NEC *Final Report* episode see Neatby, *William Lyon Mackenzie King*, III: *1932–1939: the Prism of Unity* (Toronto 1976), 247–8, 254–5.
28 King Papers, J 4, vol. 222, memo by J. Pickersgill, nd (c 1939), on 'Summary of Correspondence with the Premiers of the Provinces re Unemployment Insurance, 1937–38'
29 Neatby, *The Prism of Unity*, 226–7
30 King Papers, J 1, vol. 245, Aberhart to King, 3 Feb. 1938
31 Conrad Black, *Duplessis* (Toronto 1977), 159–92
32 Neatby, *The Prism of Unity*, 242–3; Reginald Whitaker, *The Government Party: Organizing and Financing the Liberal Party of Canada 1930–1958* (Toronto 1977), 307–40
33 Hepburn to Duplessis, 24 Jan., 14 Feb. 1938, cited in Christopher Armstrong, 'The Politics of Federalism: Ontario's Relations with the Federal Government, 1896–1941' (PhD dissertation, University of Toronto, 1972), 554
34 Neatby, *The Politics of Chaos*, 119; King Papers, J 1, vol. 234, Duplessis to King, 30 Dec. 1937
35 King Papers, J 4, vol. 221, memo by E.A. Pickering on 'The Problems Involved in Replying to the Acknowledgments of the Premiers,' 24 Feb. 1938
36 King Diary, 20 Jan., 25 Feb. 1938
37 Ibid., 2 Nov. 1937; 20 Jan., 25 Feb. 1938. King's strategy re the amendment can be found in the King Papers, J 4, vol. 221, in a memo by him 'Re Unemployment Insurance,' 23 Jan. 1938. By this point King had already determined to wait at least

until the Rowell Commission submitted its report and he even argued that 'it may be necessary to secure this agreement in a general election.'

38 King Diary, 22 Jan. 1938. The reference to 'coercion' is contained in the memo cited above.

39 King Papers, memo from E.A. Pickering to King, 19 Jan. 1938, cited in D.E. Forster, 'Dominion-Provincial Relations, 1935–39: the Unemployment Insurance Amendment, 1937–39,' 22–3 (I am grateful to H. Blair Neatby for giving me access to this memo); King Diary, 25 March, 3 May 1938

40 House of Commons, *Debates*, 6 June 1938, 3561–2; King Diary, 20 Dec. 1938

41 King Diary, 11 Jan. 1938; King Papers, J 1, vol. 257, Rogers to King, 19 Jan. 1938

42 RDCUR, 31 March 1941, 38; Department of Labour Records, Lacelle files, vol. 213, file 617, memo on 'Dominion Unemployment Relief Since 1930,' Jan. 1940, 27–8

43 Toronto *Globe and Mail*, 16 March 1938. Both the Hepburn and Duplessis administrations' reactions are cited in D. Forster, 'Unemployment and Relief Policy, 1935–39.' Pattullo's warning is in King Papers, J 1, vol. 256, Pattullo to King, 9 May 1938.

44 Queen's University Archives, Norman Rogers Papers, statement released by Rogers, 12 March 1938

45 Ibid.; House of Commons, *Debates*, 28 April 1938, 2379

46 King Diary, 1 April 1938

47 Ibid., 30 March, 1 April, 5 May 1938; Neatby, *The Prism of Unity*, 253

48 King Diary, 5, 9, 13, 16 May 1938; House of Commons, *Debates*, 20 May 1938, 3094. Note this figure is at variance with the fifty million dollar total given by Neatby, *The Prism of Unity*, 256.

49 Neatby, *The Prism of Unity*, 257; King Diary, 1 April 1938; House of Commons, *Debates*, 16 June 1938, 3924, 3899

50 House of Commons, *Debates*, 20 May 1938, 3094

51 Ibid., 31 May 1938, 3385–7, 3394

52 Ibid., 8 June 1938, 3651–61. 'Economic rental' was defined as a rental which gave a return of 9½ per cent on the cost of construction plus the annual municipal taxes.

53 King Diary, 1 April 1938

54 Department of Labour Records, Lacelle files, vol. 211, memo by Humphrey Mitchell on single homeless men in the West, 25 March 1938

55 Department of Labour Records, NEC files, vol. 70, telegram from George Pearson to James Gardiner, 26 Oct. 1936

56 Ibid., Lacelle files, memo by Mitchell on single homeless men in the West, 25 March 1938

57 Ibid.

58 Department of Labour, Lacelle files, vol. 211, copy of *Sitdowners' Gazette*, nd; Mitchell to Rogers, 31 May 1938; Mitchell to Rogers, 15 June 1938; King Papers,

Pattullo to Ian Mackenzie, 23 June 1938, cited in Forster, 'Unemployment and Relief Policy,' 85

59 Department of Labour Records, Lacelle files, vol. 211, Mitchell to Rogers, 17 June 1938, reporting statement of Pearson in *Vancouver Province*, 17 June 1938; Mitchell to Rogers, 23 June 1938, reporting statement of Pattullo in *Vancouver Sun*, 23 June 1938

60 Ibid., Mitchell to Rogers, 15 June 1938, reporting statement of Pattullo in *Vancouver Province*, 15 June 1938. King Papers, Pattullo to Mackenzie, 22 June 1938, cited in Forster, 'Unemployment and Relief Policy,' 85–6

61 King Papers, Pattullo to King, 23 June 1938, cited in Forster, 'Unemployment and Relief Policy,' 87; Pattullo to King 24 June 1938, cited in ibid., 88

62 Department of Labour Records, Lacelle files, vol. 211, Mitchell to Rogers, 25 May 1938. King Papers, King to Pattullo, 25 June 1938, cited in Forster, 'Unemployment and Relief Policy,' King Diary, 6 July 1938; House of Commons, *Debates*, 6 June 1938, 3588–9

63 King Papers, Pattullo to King, 5 July 1938, cited in Forster, 'Unemployment and Relief Policy,' 95

64 Ibid., King to Pattullo, 6 July 1938, cited in Forster, 'Unemployment and Relief Policy,' 96; Department of Labour Records, Lacelle files, vol. 211, Mitchell to Rogers, 8 July 1938; Mitchell to Rogers, 9 July 1938. For an excellent fictional account of the entire episode see Irene Baird's *Waste Heritage* (Toronto 1939).

65 King reached a different conclusion. To him the whole episode confirmed the folly of the NEC's recommendation that Ottawa take over relief. As he noted in his diary for 25 June 1938, 'It is a singular irony that this thing which (Rogers) has been responsible for having the Employment Commission recommend, has turned out ... to being [sic] the most difficult of all problems with which as Minister he has been faced, even to the point of making clear that it may involve the use of force at the instance of the Federal Government whereas under arrangements as they are at present, force can only be employed at the instance of municipal or provincial authorities.' Bennett reached an identical conclusion much earlier in the Depression. See House of Commons, *Debates*, 1 July 1931, 3249.

66 PAC, Department of Finance Records, RG 19, vol. 3990, memo by J. Pickersgill on 'The Case for Federal Administration of Unemployment Relief,' Oct. 1938

67 Ibid., vol. 3990, memo by W.C. Clark to Pickersgill, 1 Nov. 1938

68 The decision was taken in a cabinet meeting on 22 December 1938; see King Diary for that date. For relief totals see RDCUR, 31 March 1941, 36–8. At the time the decision was made, the number on relief was down 7.7 per cent compared to the same point one year earlier.

69 House of Commons, *Debates*, 25 April 1939, 3150, 3146

70 King Papers, J 1, vol. 273, Norman McLarty to King, 29 Dec. 1939; King Diary, 16 Jan. 1940

71 King Papers, J 1, vol. 291, King to McLarty, 5 Jan. 1940; King Diary, 5 and 16 Jan. 1940

72 King Diary, 16 Jan. 1940

73 King Papers, J 1, vol. 283, King to Aberhart, 16 Jan. 1940; Aberhart to King, 14 and 22 May 1940. Quebec premier Godbout still expressed a lingering preference for concurrent legislation rather than constitutional amendment, but federal officials told him this was 'impossible' as it might pit the provinces in competition with one another for industry through provisions in their insurance schemes; vol. 291, McLarty to Godbout, 1 March 1940

74 Department of Finance Records, vol. 3989, memo from W.A. Mackintosh to W.C. Clark on 'The Draft Unemployment Insurance Bill,' 20 Jan. 1940

75 Department of Labour Records, Lacelle files, vol. 166, memo by Christie Tait on 'The Insurance Bill in Canada,' 23 Oct. 1937, 3–4; House of Commons, *Debates*, 12 Feb. 1935, 727–8: House of Commons, 1940, *Special Committee on Bill No. 98 respecting Unemployment Insurance, Minutes of Proceedings and Evidence*, 22 July 1940, 3–4. Other details of the 1940 Act are from Department of Labour Records, Lacelle files, vol. 166, 'Outline of the Unemployment Insurance Bill, 1940,' nd (c Jan. 1940) and memo on 'Contrast between the Unemployment Insurance Bill 1940 and the Employment and Social Insurance Act, 1935,' nd. Coverage under the act actually reached only 44–52% of the labourforce between 1942 and 1950, well below government estimates, owing to rapid changes in the workforce. See Carl J. Cuneo, 'State, Class and Reserve Labour: the Case of the 1941 Canadian Unemployment Insurance Act,' in Paul Grayson, ed., *State, Class, Ideology and Change: Marxist Perspectives on Canada* (Toronto 1980), 147; and Leslie A. Pal, 'Revision and Retreat: Canadian Unemployment Insurance, 1971–1981,' paper presented to the First Conference on Provincial Social Welfare Policy, Calgary, 5–7 May 1982.

76 Tait's memo, 'The Insurance Bill in Canada,' 42–3, gives a good summary of the advantages of the flat-rate principle; see also *Special Committee on Bill No. 98*, 26–8; Department of Labour Records, Lacelle files, vol. 166, memo on 'Dependency and Unemployment Insurance,' nd (c 1940).

77 Cuneo, 'State, Class and Reserve Labour,' 138; Leonard Marsh, *Report on Social Security for Canada 1943* (Toronto 1975), 99; *Special Committee on Bill No. 98*, 9, 27; Tait, 'The Insurance Bill in Canada'

78 King's diary comment when the bill became law is worth noting: 'The Senate today passed the Unemployment Insurance Bill ... This is really a great achievement for the Liberal Party ... For all time to come that will remain to the credit of the Liberal Party under my leadership. It was when I was nominated leader that the party for the first time committed itself to this particular reform.' That it had taken over twenty years to effect it passed unnoticed by King; King Diary, 1 Aug. 1940.

79 *Special Committee on Bill No. 98*, 5, 8

80 Queen's University Archives, W.A. Mackintosh Papers, box. 6, file 151, memo by Alex Skelton on the 'Sirois Report and the War,' 24 July 1940

81 Department of Labour Records, Lacelle files, vol. 614, memo by Eric Stangroom on 'Federal Responsibility,' 30 Oct. 1944; also 'Report of the Committee on Unemployment Assistance,' 20 April 1946

82 Canada, Report of the Royal Commission on Dominion-Provincial Relations, Book II (Ottawa 1940), 22

83 Ibid., 23–4, 27

84 Ibid., 23

85 Ibid., 109, 81–5

86 Ibid., 21, 27, 81

87 Mackintosh Papers, box 6, file 151, memo by Alex Skelton on the 'Sirois Report and the War,' 24 July 1940; King Papers, Graham Towers to King, 15 Aug. 1940

88 House of Commons, Debates, 29 April 1941, 2345; King Diary, 26 March 1941; for the political circumstances surrounding the calling of the 1941 Dominion-Provincial conference and the decision to force the provinces out of their tax fields see J.L. Granatstein, Canada's War: the Politics of the Mackenzie King Government, 1939–1945, (Toronto 1975) 159–74

CONCLUSION

1 RDCUR, 31 March 1941, 40; Canada, Report of the Royal Commission on Dominion-Provincial Relations, Book II (Ottawa 1940), 20

2 W.L. Morton, The Kingdom of Canada (Toronto 1969), 463, 467; Royal Commission on Dominion-Provincial Relations, Book II, chap. 1, 'The Social Services'; J.M.S. Careless, Canada: a Story of Challenge (Toronto 1963), 366, 370; Kenneth McNaught, 'The 1930's,' in R.C. Brown and J.M.S. Careless, eds., The Canadians (Toronto 1968), 250, 259; H. Blair Neatby, 'The Liberal Way: Fiscal and Monetary Policy in the 1930's.' in Victor Hoar, ed., The Great Depression (Toronto 1969), 107

3 PAC, King Diary, 11 March 1938

4 PAC, King Papers, MG 26, J 1, vol. 291, King to Norman McLarty, 5 Jan. 1940

5 Linda Grayson and Michael Bliss, eds., The Wretched of Canada (Toronto 1971), x

6 Michiel Horn, The League for Social Reconstruction: Intellectual Origins of the Democratic Left in Canada, 1930–1942 (Toronto 1980), 5–7

7 Frances Fox Piven and Richard Cloward, Regulating the Poor: the Functions of Public Welfare (New York 1971), 3

8 Report of the Royal Commission on Dominion-Provincial Relations, Book II, 18

9 Dennis Guest, The Emergence of Social Security in Canada (Vancouver 1980), 142

10 Ibid, 166; the qualifying period was lowered to eight weeks, coverage was widened to include an additional 2.3 million workers, benefits were raised to two-thirds of the

contributor's wage and were extended to those unemployed owing to sickness, disability, or pregnancy.

11 Clarence Barber and John McCallum, *Unemployment and Inflation: the Canadian Experience* (Toronto 1980), 1–4; for a critique of 'insurance-induced' unemployment see C. Green and J.M. Cousineau, *Unemployment in Canada: the Impact of Unemployment Insurance* (Ottawa 1976); Herbert G. Grubel, Dennis Maki, and Shelley Sax, 'Real and Insurance-Induced Unemployment in Canada,' *Canadian Journal of Political Science*, VIII, 2, 1975; for an analysis of the recent cutbacks in unemployment insurance see Leslie A. Pal, 'Revision and Retreat: Canadian Unemployment Insurance, 1971–1981,' paper presented to the First Conference on Provincial Social Welfare Policy, Calgary, 5–7 May 1982; for Prime Minister Trudeau's comment that the unemployed have become 'too fussy about what jobs they'll take' see *Toronto Star*, 17 Aug. 1978. The last comment is by Metropolitan Toronto chairman Paul Godfrey as reported in *Star*, 2 Sept. 1978.

Index